50 FAMOUS BRITISH LOCOMOTIVES

D&C

David and Charles

50
FAMOUS BRITISH LOCOMOTIVES

Peter Herring

A DAVID & CHARLES BOOK
Copyright © David & Charles Limited 2009

David & Charles is an F+W Media, Inc. company
4700 East Galbraith Road
Cincinnati, OH 45236

First published in the UK in 2009

Text copyright © Peter Herring 2009
Photographs copyright © see page 183

Some of the text and images contained in this edition were first published as *Yesterday's Railways*

ISBN-13: 978-0-7153-3343-3 hardback
ISBN-10: 0-7153-3343-7 hardback

Printed in the UK by Butler Tanner & Dennis Ltd, Frome, Somerset
for David & Charles
Brunel House, Newton Abbot, Devon

Director of Editorial and Design: Alison Myer
Commissioning Editor: Jane Trollope
Editorial Manager: Emily Pitcher
Editor: Tim Hall
Assistant Editor: James Brooks
Art Editor: Martin Smith
Production Controller: Bev Richardson
Indexer: Cherry Ekins

Visit our website at www.davidandcharles.co.uk

David & Charles books are available from all good bookshops;
alternatively you can contact our Orderline on 0870 9908222 or write
to us at FREEPOST EX2 110, D&C Direct, Newton Abbot, TQ12 4ZZ
(no stamp required UK only); US customers call 800-289-0963 and
Canadian customers call 800-840-5220.

Contents

Introduction

Here are fifty British locomotive designs, steam and diesel, built across seven decades, whose celebrity didn't come solely from being revolutionary, super-powerful or breaking records. For some, fame came from battling against adverse conditions as much as adverse gradients.

Four Pacifics line up at Steamtown Carnforth in the early 1990s (never to be repeated). BR Standard 4-6-2s No70000 *Britannia* and No71000 *Duke of Gloucester* share the roads with LMSR Stanier Pacifics No56201 *Princess Elizabeth* and No46203 *Princess Margaret Rose.*

Being famous – if ever a term has been devalued, that has to be it. Which means careful consideration is needed when drawing up a list of – for want of a better term – famous railway locomotives. None starts out by being famous: they are there to do a job. Which is why suburban tank engines, shunters and hard-working freighters share the limelight here with the elite green, blue and red prima donnas of the express passenger domain.

Our starting point is 1900 when the need for bigger, more powerful locomotives was met by engineers such as the Great Northern Railway's Henry Ivatt, whose 4-4-2 Atlantics come first in our 50. However, the outstanding locomotive engineer of the period was George Churchward, who equipped the GWR with a fleet of locomotives significantly in advance of those on any other British railway. Churchward's ideas, from boiler design to the standardisation of components, influenced all subsequent locomotive development in Britain.

Then there were four

The 1923 'Grouping' had a significant effect on locomotive development. With Midland Railway people and policy dominating the largest of the 'big four', the London, Midland & Scottish, a decade of near stagnation resulted. It took an ex-GWR man, William Stanier, to update and restock the LMSR fleet. Before then, with Nigel Gresley at the helm, the London & North Eastern Railway was building Britain's first production series of Pacifics. Gresley's design was the first of a new breed of high-power, fast-running and – by British standards – 'big engines'.

With the outbreak of war in 1939 emphasis shifted towards simplicity of construction, flexibility of use and ease of maintenance. There were exceptions. On the Southern Railway, Oliver Bulleid designed two classes of Pacific that incorporated all manner of advanced ideas. Significantly, the first of the BR Standard designs, the 'Britannia' Pacific of 1951, did not copy them. Eleven more Standard classes followed, of which the finest was the 9F 2-10-0 freight engine.

Driven by diesels

By the time the last of the 9Fs was built in 1960, British Railways was taking delivery of the first of what, in the subsequent rush to eliminate steam, would become a deluge of diesel-locomotive classes. By 1962, it was operating 19 classes of main-line diesel. Most were underpowered and some hopelessly unreliable. Nevertheless, several proved their worth, notably the 'Brush 4' that is still in service to this day. Some even earned the affection of dyed-in-the-wool steam enthusiasts.

Throughout the upheavals of the grouping, nationalisation, modernisation and two wars, Britain's railways continued serving their customers and, overall, serve them well, a tribute to an often unfairly maligned workforce. This selection of locomotives from 1900 to 1965 is necessarily personal but, I believe, representative.

Lining up at Didcot Railway Centre's '40-75' Celebration: 'City' class 4-4-0 No3440 *City of Truro*; 'Hall' 4-6-0 No5900 *Hinderton Hall*; 'Modified Hall' No6998 *Burton Agnes Hall*; 5101 class 2-6-2T No4144.

Gresley A4 Pacifics make a return to Doncaster, July 2003 – No4468 *Mallard* (left) and No60009 *Union of South Africa*.

Front-rank express diesel power on parade at Eastleigh, 24 May 2009. L-R: Western Region's Class 52 'Western' NoD1015 *Western Champion*; London Midland Region's Class 45 'Peak' No45.060 *Sherwood Forester*; Eastern/North Eastern/Scottish Regions' Class 55 'Deltic' No55.022 *Royal Scots Grey*.

On classifications

Where appropriate, locomotives have been categorised by the classification system employed by British Railways, itself derived from LMSR practice. In this system, locomotives were classified according to their principal role (P for passenger, F for freight and MT for mixed traffic – locomotives equally suitable for passenger or freight duties). Additionally, to indicate the available power of the locomotive, these letters were preceded by a numerical index. In January 1951, this was expanded to eight ratings for passenger engines (0P to 8P) and nine for freight (0F to 9F), each beginning with the least powerful. Mixed-traffic classes ranged from 2MT to 7MT. Aside from their primary use, many locomotives were given a secondary rating for other work. The LNER A4 Pacifics, for example, were rated as 6F for freight duties, although their intended role was express passenger, hence their principal rating of 8P. This applied equally to classes primarily built for goods work; another Gresley design, the J39 0-6-0 was classified as 5F but additionally rated as 4P for passenger trains. Since 'P' always preceded 'F' in the BR system, it was described as 4P5F.

On specifications

It has been said that no two steam locomotive were alike, that there were always minor differences within even the smallest class. When sources, especially for older designs, also disagree, it can be appreciated that the technical details given for each of the classes here are a guide, albeit as accurate as researches have permitted. As to the ever-contentious question of using tractive effort as an indication of pulling power, it has always been quoted with the normal qualification in published tables.

Put simply, tractive effort is the effort which a locomotive can exert in moving a train from a state of rest (or, more specifically, the energy it exerts at the point of the driving-wheel treads). Power – the rate at which work is performed – includes a time factor and, consequently, a locomotive hauling a train of any given weight on a given gradient will produce a tractive power that varies with speed. Tractive effort is a theoretical figure expressed in pounds (lb) force and is usually calculated on the basis of 85 per cent of a locomotive's boiler pressure being applied to the pistons. The reduction takes into account the loss of pressure between the boiler and the cylinders. Drawbar tractive effort is the force exerted at the coupling between the locomotive and the train. Here we quoted cylinder tractive effort.

On preservation

It is extraordinary that of the 50 locomotives discussed here only two cannot be illustrated with preserved examples. One is Sir Nigel Gresley's P2 2-8-2 for the London & North Eastern Railway; the other is another LNER design, Arthur Peppercorn's A1 Pacific (now represented by the newly built No60163 *Tornado*).

There are 381 standard-gauge main-line steam locomotives preserved in Britain, a number that would have been some two-thirds less were it not for the 'miracle' of Woodham Brothers' scrapyard in Barry, South Wales. A commercial decision to cut up redundant wagons rather than more time-consuming steam locomotives led to the sale of more than 200 engines for preservation.

Back in 1968, the buyers of Fowler 4F No43924 were able to have it back in working order within two years. Some later restorations have taken the best part of two decades. Remarkably, however, more than 100 of these scrapyard survivors have steamed again, many returning to the main line.

The British Railways of the 1970s and later was happier to sell surplus locomotives than the bureaucracy of the 1960s. Thus the quantity of preserved diesels – 347 at the last count – now approaches that of steam locomotives.

When Atlantics Made Waves

A logical development of the internationally ubiquitous 4-4-0, the 4-4-2, or 'Atlantic', type made its debut in the United States in 1888. Its additional trailing truck not only supported a larger firebox but improved the locomotive's riding. Ten years later, the Great Northern Railway's Henry Ivatt introduced the Atlantic to Britain.

The smokebox headboard commemorating 150 years of Doncaster Works ('The Plant'), No990 poses outside the paint shop at its birthplace on a works open day, 27 July 2003.

Appointed head of the Great Northern's locomotive department in 1896, Henry Ivatt was entrusted with replacing the venerable Patrick Stirling. His predecessor was revered not only for the performance of his locomotives, but their looks. "Artistry in metal" was one summation of Stirling's work. However, by the turn of the century, his single-wheelers (engines with a single pair of large-diameter driving wheels) were being stretched by increasing train loadings on the King's Cross to Doncaster run. Seeking the greater power these loadings demanded, Ivatt looked to America where the 4-4-2 wheel arrangement had been in use since 1888. He was not alone: his counterpart on the Lancashire & Yorkshire Railway, John Aspinall, was working on a similar design. Both were breaking with tradition: Britain's railways seldom built 'big' since larger engines cost a company more to produce, maintain and operate.

Whether or not it was to register a British 'first', the GNR gave high priority to the construction of the first of the Ivatt Atlantics. Numbered 990 and named *Henry Oakley* (after the incumbent General Manager of the Great Northern Railway) it rolled out of Doncaster works in May 1898, beating Aspinall's prototype by a few months.

Ivatt placed great emphasis on boiler design and on No990 opted for a large-capacity vessel. It was this extra steam-raising capacity that would give the Atlantics their edge. While the diameter – 4 feet 8

inches – mirrored that of Ivatt's 4-4-0s, the barrel was much longer, 13 feet as against 10 feet 1 inch. The increase in heating surface was considerable: from 1,123 to 1,439 square feet. Doubtless Ivatt appreciated that it was not simply a matter of using the largest vessel the loading gauge would permit. Boiler size should be proportionate to the cylinders and the steam circuit. Given this, at 18.75 inches diameter with a stroke of 24 inches, the cylinders were comparatively small.

Into production

In March 1900 No990 was joined by the first of the production series, No949, and by the end of the year ten C2s were in service. Eleven further examples were delivered up to June 1903, when No254 became the 1,000th locomotive to be built at Doncaster. They proved fast, lively runners – so lively that Ivatt had to instruct drivers to rein in their steeds. There remained stretches of less-than-even track between London and Doncaster where, on the footplate, the jerking and swaying became unnerving. This was hardly surprising since there was only frictional damping of the side-to-side movement of the trailing axleboxes, with no springs to centre the axle on straight track. Had they been invited to express an opinion, the enginemen would have also informed Ivatt that the relatively small cylinders had proved inadequate for the boiler. These first Atlantics had to be worked at undesirable and uneconomic rates to achieve the

expected performance – in other words, the locomotives had to be thrashed to be effective.

Considering this, surprise was expressed when, in December 1902, Ivatt unveiled his 'Large Atlantic'. It had a boiler of – for its time – astonishing proportions: 5 feet 6 inches in diameter and 16 feet 4 inches long, adding up to a 65 per cent increase in heating surface over its predecessor. A wide firebox spanned the frame and extended to almost the full width of the locomotive. The grate area came out at 30.9 square feet, an increase of 15 per cent over No990 and a figure that would not be exceeded in Britain until the arrival of the first Great Northern Pacific two decades later. Yet the steam generated by this huge firebox and massive boiler fed cylinders of similar size to those of No990. That this imbalance

worked at all spoke volumes for the efficiency of the cylinders in using steam, aided by ample steam passages and an excellent blastpipe and chimney arrangement.

Improving the Ivatts

The 'Large Atlantic' would prove Henry Ivatt's most significant contribution to locomotive development. On entering traffic in January 1903, to the travelling public the prototype No251 must have appeared gigantic. Like No990 it underwent lengthy trials and series production did not begin until May 1904. Thereafter, the class was steadily enlarged up to 1910 by which time 94 examples of the original design were in traffic.

The appearance of the new engines coincided with the high-point in the careers of their predecessors. In the summer

One of Henry Ivatt's 'Large Atlantics', No291, speeds through Hadley Wood at the head of the 1.40pm service from King's Cross to Harrogate. When this photograph was taken, in 1909, the locomotive was just five years old, having been outshopped from Doncaster Works in June 1904. In total, 91 'Large Atlantics', classified LU by the Great Northern Railway and C1 by the LNER, were built between 1902 and 1911. No291 remained in traffic until April 1945.

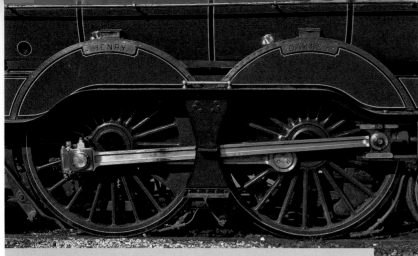

His name divided between the two wheel splashers, Henry Oakley was general manager of the Great Northern Railway at the time of the Atlantics' construction. The apple-green livery extended to the 6 feet 7.5 inches diameter driving wheels.

the opportunity to reduce the boiler pressure to 150 lb/psi and fit 20 inches diameter cylinders with 8 inch diameter piston valves.

Nigel Gresley, who took over from Henry Ivatt in 1911, admired the Atlantics and knew they would remain the GNR's premier express engines for the foreseeable future. He was also aware of the engines' deficiencies and made significant modifications, such as fitting some with 24-element superheaters.

The resulting improvements not only had an immediate effect on performance but brought unexpected rewards in later years. During the 1920s, when teething troubles sidelined Gresley's Pacifics, the Atlantics frequently came to the rescue. Striving to maintain the Pacifics' accelerated East Coast schedules resulted in some remarkable runs.

Foolproof flyers

Gresley's refurbishment programme ensured that, from 1927 there were sufficient numbers of superheated Atlantics to cover the classes' principal duties. Now the full potential of the superheated 'Large Atlantics' was realised as Gresley progressively increased the superheating surface. In one instance during 1936,

1902 timetable ten trains each day were scheduled to average 55 miles per hour between London and Grantham. The following year, one of the 1898 engines covered those 105 miles in just 104 minutes, a run that included a top speed of 69.8mph through Huntingdon.

By this stage in locomotive development the benefits of superheating were being acknowledged. The question of cylinder lubrication, however, made engineers cautious. Conventional low-temperature saturated steam had a built-in lubricating effect on valves and pistons; not so the searingly high temperatures of superheated steam. Once doubts about lubrication had been resolved through the development of oils and lubricators, superheating was welcomed as a means of increasing efficiency.

In 1909 Ivatt equipped one of the C2 class with an 18-element superheater that had been designed by German inventor, Wilhelm Schmidt. New cylinders, 20 inches diameter by 24 inches stroke, were fitted, piston valves replaced slide valves and the working pressure was lowered to 160 lb/psi. No988 was the Great Northern's first superheated engine and its 21 classmates were subsequently fitted with the device. Ivatt was sufficiently impressed to order ten superheated examples to the larger C1 design, taking

America's lead

Although US railroads had employed the 4-4-2 arrangement since 1888 it was not until 1895 that W.P. Henszey, a partner in the Baldwin Locomotive Company of Philadelphia, Pennsylvania, produced a landmark Atlantic design for the Philadelphia & Reading RR. The following year these Baldwin engines were powering what was then the fastest service in the world, that between Camden and Atlantic City, New Jersey. The Atlantic had evolved from the ubiquitous 4-4-0. Its extended frames and additional axle accommodated larger boilers and fireboxes and, theoretically, the trailing wheelset improved the riding. Generally a 4-4-2 delivered no significant increase in tractive effort over an equivalent 4-4-0 but its bigger boiler maintained that output for longer.

IN PRESERVATION

No251

Upon withdrawal in July 1947, the LNER's aim was as far as possible to restore this first of 'Large Atlantics' to its original condition. Simultaneously, classmate No2868 arrived at Doncaster for scrapping. Since this example retained its original cylinders and slide valves, it is believed the entire cylinder and frame assembly of No2868 was transferred to No251. Additionally, the boiler was substituted for one of the original type. How much of the original No251 remains on the locomotive now on display at the National Railway Museum, York?

No4404 took over from an ailing Pacific at Grantham. With a load of no less than 585 tons it then sprinted the 82.75 miles to York in 87.5 minutes. No4404 had not only kept to the Pacific schedule but beaten it by two-and-a-half minutes. Sixty miles were covered at an average of 64 miles per hour. Not to be outshone No4452 – deputising for a failed A4 Pacific on the up 'Silver Jubilee' from Newcastle – covered the 156 miles from Doncaster to King's Cross in 139 minutes, an average of 67.3 miles per hour. The fastest recorded speed by a 'Large Atlantic' was 93 miles per hour. One engineman had a succinct opinion of the design:

'So long as you kept pushing the coal into her she was Britain's finest foolproof flyer.'

With large numbers of newer Gresley engines now available and deliveries of Thompson B1 4-6-0s gaining pace, after World War II the Atlantics' usefulness declined. Scrapping of the older C2s had begun with No2982 in November 1935 and the last of the class, No3252, was retired in July 1945. Sixteen 'Large Atlantics' made it into Eastern Region stock but, by the end of 1950, all had gone. A final run from King's Cross to Doncaster took place on 23 November 1950 and, at its end, the last working Ivatt Atlantic, No294 (BR No62822) went for scrap. By then, the two prototypes, Class C1 No251 and C2 No990, had been preserved and, in 1953 and 1954, briefly returned to work specials. These would be the last main-line appearances of locomotives that, while falling just short of greatness, had few rivals when it came to glamour.

No990 *Henry Oakley*

This first of the Ivatt Atlantics, Doncaster Works number 789, was retired in October 1937 and preserved by the LNER. After appearing with No251 on the Doncaster centenary trains and other specials, No990 then had to wait over twenty years for another outing. Its next appearance was in 1975, at Shildon, County Durham, one of a host of famous locomotives in the cavalcade marking 125 years of the Stockton & Darlington Railway. Part of the National Collection, *Henry Oakley* then spent 1977-78 working on the Keighley & Worth Valley Railway before going on loan to the Bressingham Steam Museum, in Norfolk. More recently, in July 2003 both Ivatt Atlantics were reunited at Doncaster Works for open days celebrating 150 years of their birthplace. After the event, No990 returned to Bressingham.

IN DETAIL *(as built)*

	Class C1	Class C2
Built:	Doncaster 1902-03	Doncaster 1898-1910
Designer:	Henry Ivatt	Henry Ivatt
Number built:	22	94
Purpose:	Express passenger	Express passenger
Wheel arrangement:	4-4-2	4-4-2
Cylinders (x 2):	19 in* x 24	18.75 in* x 24 in
(Diameter x Stroke)		
Motion:	Stephenson link motion	
Valves:	Slide valves #	Slide valves #
Wheels: Coupled:	6 ft 8 in	6 ft 7.5 in
Leading:	3 ft 7.5 in	3 ft 7.5 in
Trailing:	3 ft 7.5 in	3 ft 7.5 in
Tender:	4 ft 2 in	4 ft 2 in
Boiler diagram:	Doncaster No3/LNER No1	Doncaster No2/LNER No4
Boiler: Max. Dia.	5 ft 6 in	4 ft 8 in
Pressure:	175 lb/psi	175 lb/psi
Heating surface:	2,500 sq ft	1.439 sq ft
Firebox:	141 sq ft	137 sq ft
Tubes and flues:	2,359 sq ft	1,302 sq ft
Superheater:	§	§
Grate area:	30.9 sq ft	24.5 sq ft
Tractive effort:	15,650 lb*	15,650 lb*
(@ 85% boiler pressure)		
Engine wheelbase:	26 ft 4 in	26 ft 4 in
Engine weight:	69 tons 8 cwt	58 tons 0 cwt
Coal capacity:	6 tons 10 cwt	5 tons 0 cwt
Water capacity:	3,500 gallons	3,670 gallons
Max. axleloading:	18 tons 0 cwt	16 tons 0 cwt
BR power class:	2P	n/a

* *Cylinders later enlarged to 20 inches diameter with superheating, resulting in an increase in tractive effort to 17,340 lb.*

\# *Later fitted with 8-inches diameter piston valves.*

§ *Both classes subsequently fitted with superheaters.*

Midland Railway
**Samuel Johnson/
Richard Deeley**

**4P 3-cylinder
compound
4-4-0** (1901)

The Crimson Ramblers

Compounding – a means of obtaining more work from each charge of steam entering a locomotive's cylinders – had several devotees among British engineers. The efforts of the Midland Railway's Samuel Johnson were among the most successful, and certainly the longest-lived.

In 1898 the Locomotive Superintendent of the Midland Railway, Samuel Johnson, had told a gathering of the Institute of Mechanical Engineers that he remained unconvinced of the benefits of compounding:

"The results of the working of compound locomotives, which I have studied somewhat closely, have not been such as in my opinion would up to the present time have warranted my adopting the compound system."

It represented quite a turnaround, therefore, when in 1901 two compound engines, Nos2631 and 2632, were added to the Midland fleet. That year had seen the final Johnson 'Singles' enter service, together with the last of his small-boilered

Its main-line adventures curtailed, Midland Compound No1000 stands on one of the turntable roads at the National Railway Museum, York. The smokebox shedplate ('1') indicates a Derby-based engine.

4-4-0s. Well before this the Midland's need for more powerful locomotives had been apparent, but the stimulus for building the compounds came from outside: the North Eastern Railway, and specifically Walter McKersie Smith, chief draughtsman at the NER's Gateshead Works. As an ex-Derby man, Smith knew Samuel Johnson well, although it was Richard Deeley, Johnson's works manager at Derby, who first enthused about the Smith system. Importantly, the NER was happy to let the Midland benefit from its draughtsman's idea.

The layout advocated by Smith (and employed by Johnson) consisted of two outside low-pressure cylinders fed by a single high-pressure cylinder situated between the frames, where it had to compete for space – not always successfully – with three sets of valve gear. A key feature of the arrangement was in starting the locomotive, always the trickiest aspect of compound working. Smith's was an ingenious solution. A smokebox valve allowed steam to be first supplied to a high-pressure inside cylinder and then diverted into two low-pressure outside ones. Therefore the locomotive could be started as a 3-cylinder 'simple' engine but, by the use of this non-return valve, the cylinders could be placed into compound mode, with steam from the high-pressure cylinder being used again in the low-pressure ones as intended.

The first Midland Compound 4-4-0, No2631, was built at Derby and entered service on 26 November 1901, with No2632 joining it before the end of the year. Both, however, were officially dated 'Derby January 1902'. In these engines, separate sets of valve gear operated each cylinder, with a piston valve for the inside and slide valves for the outside cylinders. It was efficient, but also made for a tight fit between the frames. With their large boilers, Belpaire fireboxes and seven feet diameter coupled wheels, these were big engines, at least by Midland standards. They were harnessed to double bogie tenders that held five tons of coal and 4,500 gallons of water.

Outshopped in 1903, Nos2633-35 differed from their predecessors in having only one set of gear to operate the valves of all three cylinders. While this relieved the crowding between the frames it theoretically made the locomotives less efficient. It was just one of the compromises that nurtured the equivocal response to compounding in Britain. The first five Midland Compounds, however, were an indisputable success both for haulage ability and economy. Nos2631 and 2632 went to work on the Leeds-Settle-Carlisle line while the others were allocated to operations out of London.

Compound changes

Richard Mountford Deeley replaced Samuel Johnson as head of locomotive matters on the Midland in 1903 but there was no dramatic change of policy (not that the Midland board would have allowed one). Deeley perpetuated the compound design, with both external and internal modifications. Along with the addition of superheaters, the most radical change was in operation. Deeley dispensed with the smokebox valve, which crews had proved less than adept at mastering, and simplified matters by arranging for the compounding to be worked from the regulator. Now it was this that, upon being partially opened on starting, automatically admitted high-pressure steam to all three cylinders. Upon opening the regulator further, an auxiliary valve closed, high-pressure steam was cut off from the outside cylinders and the engine began proper compound working. The Deeley engines also had a larger firebox and an increased working pressure of 220 lb/psi which led the boilers to be reclassified as G9AS.

Like their Johnson predecessors, the Deeley compounds did excellent work. They were ideal for the comparatively light, but tightly scheduled trainloads that characterised Midland passenger services. A batch was sent to the London area where they were used on expresses to Nottingham, Derby and Manchester and employed on Anglo-Scottish services. Their success led to a further 20 compounds being built in 1906. A final order was placed in 1908 and completed by March 1909. The combination of a deep-maroon livery, and their widespread use across the sprawling Midland network, earned the compounds the nickname of 'Crimson Ramblers'. When Deeley resigned that year, 45 compounds were in service. Over time, all the Johnson engines were rebuilt (visually and mechanically) to Deeley's style, although some years after the latter's departure.

It might have been thought that, as the Midland's premier express locomotives, the compounds were prime candidates for superheating. Not so: it took until 1913 for the first to be fitted with a superheater, under Henry Fowler's direction. The whole conversion process was painfully slow, the last not being superheated until 1928. In the early years, this could probably be attributed to the Midland's prevailing complacency. Even in their 'saturated' (i.e. non-superheated form) the compounds outclassed superheated 'simples' (non-compound engines) so why enter into the extra expense of superheating? The fact that superheating would substantially improve this already-fine machine was overlooked.

The engine of choice

Interestingly, in 1907, Deeley had produced a design for a 4-cylinder 4-6-0 compound – essentially a scaled-up 4-4-0 – which, had it been built would have revolutionised Midland locomotive policy. As it was, when the Midland ceased to

IN PRESERVATION

While the LMSR-built compounds survived in British Railways service until 1961, the Midland locomotives had all been withdrawn by 1953. By then, the doyen of the class, BR No41000, was in safe keeping, having been retired in October 1951, one month short of 50 years' service. There followed two spells working main-line specials until, in 1984, No1000 took up residence at the National Railway Museum, York. Since 2008 it has been on display in the Severn Valley Railway's new Engine House at Highley.

be in 1922, it had just 55 express passenger engines in what might be called the 'large' category: ten '990' class simple expansion 4-4-0s and 45 compounds.

Although acknowledged as successful within their limitations, the decision by the London Midland & Scottish Railway – which absorbed the Midland Railway in 1923 – to adopt the 'Midland Compound' as its standard express passenger locomotive astonished many observers.

Under first George Hughes and, from 1925, his successor as LMSR locomotive chief, the aforementioned Henry Fowler, construction of the compounds continued apace. The 195 LMSR-built compounds entered service between February 1924 and September 1932, the final four appearing with the reluctant approval of Fowler's successor, William Stanier. By this time, the LMSR had 240 compound 4-4-0s on its books. Most were built at Derby Works, but the ex-Lancashire & Yorkshire works at Horwich, near Bolton, constructed a quantity, as did outside contractors, the North British Locomotive Company of Glasgow and the Vulcan Foundry at Newton-le-Willows.

However, for all their good service, the compounds came to symbolise a limited ambition and lack of vision on the part of the Midland Railway and, through its later influence, early LMSR locomotive policy. The compounds' inability to cope with heavier trainloadings greatly contributed to the uneconomic double-heading that characterised many operations (and remained commonplace in the British Railways era). They were at their best and most economical on long-distance non-stop expresses. They were also relatively trouble-free: steam leakage past the piston valve, which accelerated as mileage between overhauls increased, was the chief cause for concern.

Although responsive locomotives the compounds needed sympathetic driving and firing. As a result, when operating outside traditional Midland territory, they frequently suffered at the hands of inexperienced crews. The technique for starting, for example, was far from easy to master. Ultimately, however, the Achilles heel of these engines was not their complexity, but simply increasing train lengths. Despite their limitations, LMSR-built examples remained at work until 1961, No41168 being the last in traffic.

Compound interest

Compound systems were devised to make more efficient use of the expansive properties of steam and experiments were conducted as early as 1850. When a locomotive exhausts its spent steam from the cylinders, the steam is still at a very considerable pressure above that of the atmosphere. This is wasteful: the steam clearly has more work left in it. Compound working was first used in stationary engines, ones not constrained by the confined area and mechanical complexity of the steam locomotive. Compounding was pioneered in Continental Europe and North America and, in 1876, the first successful compound locomotive entered service in France.

Unlike 'simple' locomotives, compounds are equipped with both high- and low-pressure cylinders. The former receive the normal charge of high-pressure steam from the boiler, but do not exhaust it in the usual way. Instead, that steam – now at reduced pressure – is used again in a low-pressure cylinder (or cylinders). Inevitably the mechanism needed to achieve this 'second use' of steam is more complex. The final exhaust pressure will be lower, too, which can pose problems elsewhere: the engine depends on the power of its exhaust to draw the fire and create a draught. However, these concerns can be offset by greater efficiency. Cylinder sizes on compounds have to be carefully calculated and the restrictive British loading gauge was an impediment.

The performance of compound locomotives varied widely. They were notably successful in France, where compounding reached its final form in André Chapelon's 242A1 4-8-4, but in Britain results were uneven. Francis Webb's

4-4-0 and 0-8-0 compounds for the London & North Western Railway were irredeemably flawed, but the Worsdell brothers – Thomas and Wilson – did better with their much simpler designs for the North Eastern Railway.

IN DETAIL *(Johnson-designed No2631/No1000, as built; changes through rebuilding in brackets.)*

Class '4'

Built:	Derby and Horwich works; North British Locomotive Company, Glasgow; Vulcan Foundry, Newton-le-Willows, Lancashire 1901-32
Designer:	Samuel Johnson/Richard Deeley
Number built:	240
Purpose:	Express passenger
Wheel arrangement:	4-4-0
Cylinders (x 3):	High pressure (1) 19 in diameter x 26 in stroke
	Low pressure (2) 21 in diameter x 26 in stroke
Motion:	Stephenson link motion
Valves:	8 in diameter (inside high-pressure cylinder only; slide valves on outside cylinders)
Wheels: Coupled:	7 ft 0 in (later reduced to 6 ft 9 in)
Leading:	3 ft 6.5 in
Tender:	3 ft 6 in (8-wheel double bogie tender)/ 4 ft 3 in (6-wheel tender)
Boiler diagram:	G8½ (rebuilt with superheated G9AS boiler)
Boiler: Max. diameter:	4 ft 9.125 in
Pressure:	195 lb/psi (220 lb/psi with G9AS boiler) §
Heating surface:	1,598 sq ft (1,681 sq ft when superheated)
Firebox:	150 sq ft (151 sq ft)
Tubes and flues:	1,448 sq ft (1,170 sq ft)
Superheater:	360 sq ft
Grate area:	26 sq ft
Tractive effort:	23,205lb (@ 85% boiler pressure)
Engine wheelbase:	24 ft 3 in
Total wheelbase:	47 ft 1.5 in
Coal capacity:	5 tons ¶/7 tons #
Water capacity:	4,500 gallons ¶/3,500 gallons #
Engine weight:	59 tons 10 cwt 1 qr (61 tons 14 cwt)
Max. axleloading:	20 tons 12 cwt 3 qr
BR power class:	4P

§ No1000 received a superheated G9AS boiler in November 1914. The pressure was reduced to 190 lb/psi in June 1916 but increased to 200 lb/psi in November 1922. ¶ Double-bogie tender. # Six-wheel tender.

The Century-maker

Great Western
Railway

**George Jackson
Churchward**

**3700 'City' class
4-4-0** (1903)

It's a date and place enshrined in railway folklore: 9 May 1904, Wellington, Somerset. But on that day was the Great Western's *City of Truro* the first thing on earth to reach a speed of 100 miles per hour? Whatever, the timings remain remarkable and appear to indicate a machine in the vanguard of locomotive engineering. Paradoxically, the 'Cities' were something of an anachronism.

Largely a rebuilding exercise, the 'City' class originated in 1902. That September, George Churchward rebuilt 'Atbara' class 4-4-0 No3405 *Mauritius* – then only one year old – with his new Standard No4 boiler. Exactly why he did this remains uncertain. Was it to assess the new steam-raiser, or had he concluded the existing 'Atbara' boiler was inadequate? Whatever the reason, it was a move that influenced all subsequent Great Western locomotive design and much elsewhere. *Mauritius* was the first Great Western engine to carry a taper boiler and, apart from Churchward's prototype 4-6-0 No100, became the most powerful engine in the fleet.

Following trials with *Mauritius*, an order was placed with Swindon works for ten similar locomotives, all for delivery during 1903. Though powerful by Great Western standards, the newcomers were lightweights compared with contemporary designs such as the Great Northern's Ivatt Atlantics and the North Eastern Railway's 4-4-0s. Aside from the advanced boiler design, they were more the summation of the four-coupled, double-framed format long pursued by Churchward's predecessor, William Dean. Where they scored was in their mechanical excellence. While their double frames were inevitably heavier and more expensive to construct than the single variety (and, by the early 1900s, been

On 8 May 2004 *City of Truro* was in steam to commemorate its record-breaking run of a century earlier, hauling a special from Bristol to Kingswear. Showing no sign of its 101 years, the Great Western 4-4-0 dashes along the seawall at Dawlish, south Devon.

rejected by most locomotive engineers) they allowed a significant increase in bearing surfaces. This much reduced the chance of axleboxes overheating at speed. Combining this mechanical reliability and robustness with a potent steam-raiser such as the Churchward boiler was always likely to result in a 'flier'.

After trials with *Mauritius,* an order was placed for ten engines, Nos3433-3442, to be built at Swindon in 1903. This batch was augmented by the rebuilding of nine 'Atbaras' between 1907 and 1909 and, over a two-year period from June 1910 to June 1912, all twenty engines received superheaters.

First with the post

Behind *City of Truro*'s record-breaking was the Great Western's desire to be first with the post. It competed with the London & South Western Railway for mail traffic offloaded from trans-Atlantic liners docking at Plymouth. Given that the L&SWR route to London's Waterloo was 15 miles shorter, Paddington had to rely on speed. On 9 May 1904, it was actively seeking to publicise its new service between Plymouth and the capital. The 'Ocean Mails Express' normally carried no passengers but when the GWR made a point of inviting on board the railway commentator, Charles Rous-Marten, it was clear something special was planned.

At 8.00am the Norddeutscher Lloyd liner *Kronprinz Wilhelm* dropped anchor

In the late 1950s, *City of Truro* was returned to working order for enthusiast specials. Waiting to leave Southampton on 23 May 1957, it has appropriate company in the shape of ex-L&SWR T9 4-4-0 No30285. The L&SWR's Plymouth services competing with those of the GWR were entrusted to T9s.

Career highlights

The 'Cities' put in startling performances from the outset. On 14 July 1903 *City of Bath* was in charge of a train that included two coaches conveying the Prince and Princess of Wales to Cornwall. The train was to run non-stop between Paddington and Plymouth and the 106.9 miles to Bath took just 92 minutes. Arrival at Plymouth was 37 minutes early, the engine having averaged 63.2mph for the 240 miles.

The 'Cities' were first regularly employed on the newly accelerated services between Paddington and Bristol and on the recently introduced 'Cornish Riviera Express'. In 1905, they began appearing on London–Birmingham trains, then still routed through Oxford. However, their time on the GWR's front rank duties was brief. They were superseded by Churchward's more powerful Atlantics and 4-6-0s and, by August 1913, just one was based west of Exeter: *City of Truro*, at Newton Abbot.

The class now found employment between Birmingham and Bristol and on the north-and-west route linking Chester, Shrewsbury, Hereford and Newport. Their final long-distance workings were from Paddington to Worcester, after which they found work on secondary routes.

in Plymouth Sound on her way from New York to northern Germany. Her UK-bound cargo was offloaded into five postal vans, adding up to a train weight of around 148 tons. Included in the load was a particularly valuable consignment: a large quantity of gold bullion. This was a payment made by the United States to the French government in connection with the construction of the Panama Canal. Evidently, there were good financial reasons for getting the gold to London as quickly as possible.

The lightning run

At the head of the train was an Exeter-based engine, 'City' class 4-4-0 No3440 *City of Truro.* Given that a high-speed run had been projected, it was a surprising choice: classmates Nos3433 *City of Bath* and 3442 *City of Exeter* were reputed to be faster machines. It was soon apparent this opinion was not shared by driver

Moses Clements. At 9.23am he received the 'right-away' from Millbrook Dock crossing and the historic run began. At times reaching speeds in the upper seventies, *City of Truro* took the south Devon banks in its stride and swept through Newton Abbot, 31 miles from Plymouth, in just under 37 minutes. Exeter St David's was passed in 55 minutes 55 seconds, an average speed of 55.8mph.

There now followed 30 miles of uninterrupted high-speed running, culminating in the five mile descent from Whiteball tunnel through Wellington and on to Taunton. On the climb from Exeter to Whiteball sidings, the engine averaged 60mph and then flew down Wellington bank in what Rous-Marten described as the 'hurricane descent' of 'the lightning special'. It was here that his stopwatch recorded a time of eight-and-four-fifths seconds for one quarter mile, corresponding to a speed of 102.3mph. The 10.8 miles from Whiteball summit to Taunton were covered in just 8 minutes 20 seconds, which contributed to an average speed from Plymouth of 59.3mph.

A matter of record

With 44 miles of almost level track between Taunton and Bristol, driver Clements was able to maintain the furious pace and over this stretch Rous-Marten recorded an average of 72.7mph. The train halted at Pyle Hill, half-a-mile outside Temple Meads, for one of its vans containing mail for the Midlands and the north to be detached. There was also an engine change. With coal running low, *City of Truro* was replaced by 4-2-2 No3065 *Duke of Connaught*, one of five standby locomotives stationed along the route of the 'Ocean Mails Express'.

Between Bristol and Paddington, No3065 also showed what it was capable of, with speeds in the upper eighties at times. *Duke of Connaught* reached London in 99 minutes 46 seconds; the entire journey from Plymouth had taken 3 hours 46 minutes and 48 seconds. This part of Rous-Marten's account remains undisputed; substantiating his precise calculation of 102.3mph is much tougher. Though accounts of the run promptly appeared in *The Railway Magazine* and *The Engineer*, neither quoted the claimed maximum speed of 102.3mph. Surprisingly, this was at the request of the Great Western. It was not so much that it questioned the figure, more that it did not want to alarm its passengers, the majority of whom would have viewed the prospect of travelling at over 100 miles an hour with terror! While keen to publicise its high-speed services in the broad sense, the GWR was not so enthusiastic about revealing the specifics. Though alluded to in subsequent magazine articles, the full details of *City of Truro*'s run were withheld from public scrutiny for 18 years.

Exact science?

The competence and integrity of Charles Rous-Marten has never been questioned, but doubts have been voiced about the observations that informed his calculations, and the precision of his stopwatch. Nevertheless, there is every chance that the combination of a fine engine and favourable conditions would have led to speeds around 100mph. Gravity would have made a significant contribution on the descending gradient from Whiteball tunnel and nothing exceptional would have been required from *City of Truro* in terms of power output. What did make a difference was the sound mechanical operation of the locomotive and its excellent riding qualities that, combined, gave the footplate crew the confidence to let the 4-4-0 have its head. Additionally, they knew the condition of the track was good and would not fail them.

Thirty years passed before another locomotive claimed a speed of 100mph, and the achievement of the LNER's *Flying Scotsman* was fully authenticated. By then, *City of Truro* had been withdrawn from service and was on display not, as might have been expected, at Swindon, Bristol or Paddington, but at York.

IN PRESERVATION

On 12 March 1931, *City of Truro* (by now renumbered 3717) was retired from Shrewsbury depot having run 1,000,483 miles during its 28-year career—a fair return on its £1,957 construction cost. The General Manager of the GWR, James Milne, had declared that he "did not consider the engine of outstanding importance". However, to his enduring credit, Chief Mechanical Engineer, Charles Collett, disagreed, as did the London & North Eastern Railway, which offered to display *City of Truro* in its York museum. Negotiations between Paddington and King's Cross began in August 1930 and, in the early hours of 20 March 1931, the engine left Swindon on its journey north. It would be a quarter of

a century before it returned to its birthplace.

Reginald Hanks, chairman of British Railways' Western Region, did much to restore the GW image during the 1950s. For example, he reintroduced long-defunct named expresses and had the rolling stock repainted in traditional chocolate-and-cream. Hanks also brought *City of Truro* back to Swindon, where it was put back into working order.

On 30 March 1957, the 4-4-0 worked the first of several specials, conveying members of the Ffestiniog Railway Society from Paddington to Ruabon. The following month, heading a return excursion from Swindon to Pontypridd, the engine touched 80mph. Evidently, even at the age of 54, *City of Truro* could still fairly be called a flier.

That September, the locomotive crossed the River Tamar for the first time, on a tour from Plymouth to Penzance that took it through Truro itself. However, No3440 was not limited to special workings. Remarkably, it was rostered for commuter trains between Reading and Paddington and became a regular choice for the 5.32pm Swindon-Bristol. Passengers must have believed they had entered a time warp!

City of Truro bowed out of service on 9 February 1961 but was subsequently overhauled, returning to celebrate the 150th anniversary of the Great Western Railway in 1985. It returned once again in 2004, following a spell in the National Railway Museum in York, to mark the centenary of its epic run from Plymouth, and remains in service to this day.

The third coming – and a fourth!

Celebrations marking the 150th anniversary of the Great Western Railway in 1985 would not have been complete without the appearance of *City of Truro*. However, inspection revealed that both the boiler and firebox required a daunting amount of work. Some 700 stays had to be renewed, along with all 276 boiler tubes and all 14 superheater elements and flues. The corrosion within the tender was such that all the bottom platework was replaced. Mercifully for those undertaking the overhaul at the Severn Valley Railway's workshops in Bridgnorth, the motion was in good condition: only the piston rings had to be changed.

On 3 September 1985, *Truro* entered service for a third time and began an intensive period of both main-line work and visits to preserved railways and steam centres. It even went to Utrecht to take part in an international cavalcade of locomotives marking 150 years of Netherlands railways. A last railtour, on 3 May 1992, preceded the expiry of No3440's main-line 'ticket' and, after a spell on the West Somerset Railway, the 90-year-old was recalled to the National Railway Museum in York.

The question now was whether *City of Truro* would steam again to celebrate the centenary of its epic run from Plymouth in May 2004. The high regard for this historic locomotive ensured that an appeal to finance the overhaul rapidly met its target and on 2 May it successfully undertook a test run from Birmingham to Stratford-upon-Avon. Six days later, *City of Truro* was at the head of the 'Ocean Mail 100' centenary special from Bristol to Kingswear, in Devon, and putting in a performance that belied its 101 years. The return run, two days later, was equally impressive, reaching Bristol eight minutes early. There was no record-breaking on Wellington bank, however, as the newly installed speedometer revealed.

City of Truro remains in service and has visited several preserved railways in the past five years. Much of the time has been spent on the Gloucestershire Warwickshire Railway but No3440 has broken new ground, travelling to Scotland to work on the Strathspey Railway and, in the autumn of 2007, memorably double-heading with the other surviving Great Western 4-4-0, No3217 *Earl of Berkeley*, on the Bluebell Railway.

A visit to the Bluebell Railway in October 2006 united the two surviving Great Western 4-4-0s for the first time in over twenty years. *City of Truro* simmers under the lamps at Sheffield Park with 'Dukedog' No9017 *Earl of Berkeley* on the adjacent road.

IN DETAIL
3700 'City'

Built:	Swindon Works, 1903-09
Designer:	George Jackson Churchward
Number built:	20
Purpose	Express passenger
Wheel arrangement:	4-4-0
Cylinders (x 2):	18 in x 26 in
Valves:	Slide valves originally employed; later replaced (1915-25) by piston valves on all but two of class (No3440 received piston valves in 1911)
Wheels: Coupled:	6 ft 8.5 in
Leading:	3 ft 8 in
Tender:	4 ft 1.5 in
Motion:	Stephenson link motion.
Boiler diagram:	Swindon Standard No4
Boiler max. diameter:	5 ft 6 in
Pressure:	200lb/psi
Heating surface:	1,670.15 sq ft
Firebox:	128.72 sq ft
Tubes and flues:	1,349.64 sq ft
Superheater: *	191.79 sq ft
Grate Area:	20.56 sq ft
Tender:	4 ft 1.5 in
Tractive effort:	17,790lb (@ 85% boiler pressure)
Engine wheelbase:	22 ft 6 in
Total wheelbase:	46 ft 9.25 in
Engine weight:	55 tons 12 cwt
Coal capacity:	6 tons
Water capacity:	3,500 gallons
Max. axleloading:	18 tons 10 cwt

* Engine No3440 City of Truro fitted with superheater.

A First for Freight

Great Western
Railway

**George Jackson
Churchward/
Charles Collett**

**2800/2884
class 8F 2-8-0**

(1903/1938)

Transitional would be the broad assessment of Churchward's first designs. Then, in 1903, he broke new ground with a prototype that was to become the forerunner of a new breed of British freight locomotive, one that met the needs of a new century and would come to number thousands.

I t was those – usually illicit – weekend visits to locomotive depots serving the industrial heartlands that brought home the scale of freight working, especially coal. Rows of Stanier 8Fs at Toton, 'Austerities' at Wakefield and LNER 04s at Mexborough simmered and slumbered under a sulphuric haze and waited to resume duties come Monday morning. It was a similar picture on Teesside and Tyneside, in West Yorkshire and eastern Scotland, in Cheshire and Derbyshire, and in South Wales where – in the early 1900s – the story of these 2-8-0 freight classes began.

At that time most of the goods traffic on Britain's railways remained entrusted to moderately powerful six-coupled locomotives. Remarkably among the major industrial nations, Britain was the only one where express passenger machines were invariably more powerful than their freight counterparts. A few more progressive concerns, however, had made the step up to eight-wheeled designs. Both the London & North Western and Lancashire & Yorkshire had built quantities of inside-cylinder 0-8-0s and were to be followed by the Caledonian, Great Central, North Eastern and Great Northern Railways. In Wales, the Vale of Neath Railway was the first to use eight-coupled tank engines.

In 1896 the Barry Railway followed the VoNR's example and invested in seven outside-cylindered 0-8-2 tanks. They were built by Sharp Stewart of Glasgow who then constructed three similar engines in 1901 for the Port Talbot Railway. Since both companies' operations in South Wales were intertwined with those of the Great Western, reports on the performance of these eight-coupled engines most likely filtered back to Swindon. There, George Churchward was scheming a range of standard designs that would include a heavy freight engine.

Although smaller companies such as the Barry Railway served the pits and ports of South Wales, the Great Western was the prime mover of coal out of what was then one of the largest mining areas in Britain. The coastal stretch between Newport and Port Talbot was also home to a growing steel industry and, again, the GWR had the task of bringing in raw materials – principally iron ore from the quarries of Oxfordshire and Northamptonshire – and transporting the finished products. Growth in both industries had brought heavier train loadings and a pressing need for more modern and powerful engines. Churchward answered that need with Britain's first 2-8-0, albeit 37 years after the type had made its debut in the United States. Since 1866, the Lehigh Valley Railroad of Pennsylvania – like the GWR, a major coal carrier – had used 2-8-0s to haul 300 ton trains on grades as steep as 1 in 40. With its leading pony truck, or guiding wheels, the 2-8-0 offered greater stability and better weight distribution than an 0-8-0 and the space for a larger boiler. Churchward had concluded that what suited Pennsylvania would work in Pontypool and, in June 1903, No97 was outshopped from Swindon to begin two years of operational trials.

To illustrate advances in railway freight vehicles, on 10 September 1985 No2857 visited Newport, in South Wales, to make the contrast with Class 56 Co-Co No56.037 hauling a rake of modern, purpose-built wagons. No2857 returned to the Severn Valley Railway with its haul, the first steam-hauled goods working on British Railways since 1968. Twenty-four years on, the 56s have disappeared from Britain's main lines while No2857 is being overhauled for a further ten years' service on the SVR.

Recalling the atmosphere of shed yards in the 1950s and 1960s – ash, oil, grease and cinders, all liberally doused with rain – two 2884 class 2-8-0s, resident No3850 and visiting No3802 from the Llangollen Railway, are prepared for service at Minehead, West Somerset Railway, on 16 March 2008. This was the first occasion since 1993 that two of the class had appeared together. Following GWR practice, 'LA' inscribed on the frame indicates a Plymouth Laira-based engine.

Some refinements

Along with its companion prototype, the 2-cylinder 4-6-0 No98, the newcomer was fitted with the Belpaire firebox and tapered boiler that would characterise most subsequent Great Western designs. Initially, pressure was set at 200 lb/psi, with 18 inches diameter cylinders. Tractive effort started out at 29,775 pounds but showed a modest increase in the production series. This followed the lifting of the steam pressure to 225 lb/psi and the substitution of the eight-and-a-half inch diameter piston valves by ones of ten inches. The most visible difference between No97 (later renumbered No2800 and, as a consequence, giving the class its identity) and the first of the 1905 production batch was the higher pitch of the boiler (8 feet 2 inches as opposed to 7 feet 8.5 inches).

The Swindon No3 superheater was incorporated into the class from 1909, with No2808 the first of the existing examples to be retrospectively fitted. Simultaneously, the cylinder diameter was enlarged to 18.5 inches. Other modifications centred on improving the weight distribution, varying the length of the smokebox and fitting larger diameter chimneys. With its swing-link pony truck, sharp curves were generally no bar to the 2-8-0s but the long, rigid wheelbase gave the Civil Engineer concern. To counter this the second and third pairs of coupled wheels had thinner flanges and the front pair of coupling rods were fitted with spherical joints that gave a limited amount of sideplay. In the GWR's classification, the 2-8-0s merited power class 'E' and the 'blue' route restriction code that permitted an axleloading up to 17 tons 12 cwt.

Following his usual practice, Churchward fitted Stephenson link motion between the frames with rocking shafts conveying the motion to the valves, which were positioned above the outside cylinders. Although the prototype, No2800, appeared harnessed to a 4,000 gallon tender, with a few exceptions the 2-8-0s were paired with a 3,500 gallon variety, weighing 40 tons and holding six tons of coal.

Freight engines they may have been, but the GWR did not want the 2800s looking drab. The prototype was turned out in black with red lining but the preferred livery for the production series was fully lined-out dark green. Wartime economies saw this become plain green after 1914 and lining was never reinstated. The 84 2-8-0s built during Churchward's reign remained the Great Western's principal long-haul freight locomotives throughout the 1920s and 1930s, supplemented for short-distance work by a tank engine version, the 4200/5205 class. The only cause for concern centred on the sealing of the internal steampipes. When replacement cylinder castings were fitted, most of the class had them replaced with the external variety.

Although 35 years had elapsed since the appearance of No97, little updating was needed when Churchward's successor, Charles Collett, added to the class. His principal modification was to adopt side window cabs. The safety valve bonnet was shortened, a whistle shield added, a housing placed on the left-side running plate to hold fireirons and some improvements made to the framing. Given the earlier problems, outside steampipes were employed from the outset. Minor they may have been, but the alterations nevertheless merited a fresh classification and, in March 1938, the 2884 class was born. By 1942, the total had almost doubled to 165 engines, all of which would become Western Region stock in 1948 (but not

IN PRESERVATION

No2807 Outshopped from Swindon in October 1905, No2807 is the oldest surviving Churchward 2800 and is being restored by Cotswold Steam Preservation Ltd, at Toddington, on the Gloucestershire Warwickshire Railway. It is on course for test steaming during 2009.

No2818 Delivered from Swindon in December 1905 and withdrawn in October 1963, No2818 represents this influential class in the National Collection and is presently on display at the National Railway Museum, York.

No2857 The last 2800 class 2-8-0 to work on the main line, when it hauled a demonstration goods train as part of the GW150 celebrations in 1985, No2857 is currently undergoing overhaul on the Severn Valley Railway.

No2859 Based on the Llangollen Railway in North Wales, No2859 is unrestored at the moment.

No2861 Withdrawn in March 1963, No2861 awaits restoration on Barry Island's Vale of Glamorgan Railway.

No2873 Its chassis sold to the South Devon Railway, what remains of No2873 has become a source of spares at Tyseley Locomotive Works in Birmingham.

No2874 After languishing in scrapyard condition on the Pontypool & Blaenavon Railway for 27 years, No 2874 has been

before twenty had been converted to take part in the government's ill-conceived oil-burning experiment of 1945-47).

On trial

Churchward's specification for the 2800 envisaged loads of up to 60 wagons. To test this, No2806 was coupled up to the Swindon dynamometer car, which measured on-the-road performance, and attached to a 54-wagon train. When this was handled with ease, the load was progressively increased until it reached 100 wagons. Since this still gave the 2-8-0 no difficulty, it became the optimum loading for the class. To demonstrate further the class's capabilities, during 1906 No2808 hauled a train of 107 loaded coal wagons weighing 2,012 tons between Swindon and Acton, in west London. Remarkably, this British record for haulage by a single steam locomotive stood until the mid-1980s when, at a Somerset quarry, a British Railways Standard 9F 2-10-0 (the preserved No92203) managed over 2,200 tons. It was fitting that the 2800 was eclipsed by the only heavy freight design that could be considered its superior.

The 2800 was also included in the post-nationalisation 'interchange trials' of 1948. How much was gleaned from these remains open to debate. One of the Collett-built engines, No3803 (now preserved on the South Devon Railway), was put up against its younger cousins, the LMSR's Stanier 2-8-0 and the Riddles/WD 2-8-0 and 2-10-0, and a class of comparable vintage, the ex-Great Central Robinson 04 2-8-0 of 1911. That No3803 emerged well in the tests, both for

Normally confined to the demonstration lines at Didcot Railway Centre, 1940-built 2884 class 2-8-0 No3822 has occasionally ventured further afield and been able to show its power. Here it sprints away from Cheltenham Racecourse with a morning Gloucestershire Warwickshire Railway service for Toddington on 9 May 2004.

bought by the West Somerset Railway. Its future is to be decided.

No2885 Part of the Birmingham Locomotive Works collection, cosmetically restored No2885 is on display at the city's Moor Street Station.

No3802 Owned by Great Western 3802 Ltd, restoration was completed at Llangollen, North Wales, in 2005.

No3803 A 23-year refit was completed in 2006 when No3803 entered service on the South Devon Railway, between Buckfastleigh and Totnes.

No3814 After 22 years at Woodhams', on 22 July 1986 No3814 moved to Grosmont

on the North Yorkshire Moors Railway where it remains a long-term project.

No3822 Bought by the Great Western Society, the restoration of No3822 was completed at Didcot Railway Centre in 1985, and it remains part of the working fleet at Didcot.

No3845 On 9 November 1989, No3845 became the 212th and penultimate locomotive to leave Woodhams' yard at Barry. It now awaits restoration on the Swindon & Cricklade Railway.

No3850 Withdrawn in August 1965 and secured for preservation by the West Somerset Railway in February 1984, No3850 finally entered traffic in 2006.

No3855 Located on the Pontypool & Blaenavon Railway, No3855 is still awaiting restoration.

No3862 Numerically the last survivor from among the 165 Churchward/Collett 2-8-0s, No3862 has been bought by a consortium of railwaymen and moved to the Chapel Brampton site of the Northampton & Lamport Railway with plans for restoration.

power and fuel consumption, was no surprise. Equally unsurprisingly there was little to choose between the classes involved: Stanier's 8F was derived from the Churchward design and the WD 2-8-0 was essentially a simplified version of the 8F. However, if a WR engineman was offered either in exchange for his 2800, the response would probably have been unprintable.

Despite the influx of 9F 2-10-0s after 1954, there was work for the 2800s up to the end of steam on the Western Region in 1965. They were now entrusted with duties ranging from pickup goods to mixed freights and parcels. On occasion examples were rostered for passenger turns, mainly West Country holiday reliefs. Six decades of service testified to the excellence of Churchward's original conception, and in 1953 this was reinforced by statistics produced by BR. These showed that between periodical repairs the 2-8-0s – some of which were over 40 years old – ran an average of 86,981 miles. Among other 2-8-0 classes, the Riddles/WD – surprisingly in view of its 'austerity' construction – achieved 62,624, while the London Midland's 8F managed only 50,361. Naturally, factors other than build quality have to be taken into account here, not least the nature of the work done and the differing standards of maintenance that were meted out to freight engines.

The Churchward/Collett 2-8-0s remained intact until April 1958 when the prototype, No2800, became the first to be withdrawn. The last to be retired was No3836 in November 1965. Sixteen have survived and, to date, five have been returned to working order. Four of those are currently operational, three having entered service over the past four years., and a fifth was on course to join them during 2009.

Fuel for thought

Between 1945 and 1947, post-war coal shortages saw 20 of the 2800s – along with many locomotives from the other railway companies – converted to oil-burning. The experiment was eagerly backed by the government, but enthusiasm waned once extra maintenance costs, such as the installation of oil storage facilities, were calculated and the bill arrived for the imported oil. The scheme was abandoned in 1948, the year that saw one of the 2-8-0s, No3803, emerge remarkably successfully from trials against more modern freight engines, including the LMSR 8F 2-8-0 and the WD 2-8-0 and 2-10-0. Such was their suitability for the task that it took the appearance in 1954 of the British Railways 9F 2-10-0 to displace the Great Western 2-8-0s from their main role of heavy mineral haulage. Even then, there was still work for the class up to the end of steam on the Western Region in 1965.

On home territory at Didcot, No3822 does the job it was built for – hauling freight. The canvas cover over the footplate was fitted to many locomotives during World War II to hide the glare from the fire, which could attract the attention of night-time bombing raids.

IN DETAIL *(as built)*	
Class	**2800/2884**
Built:	Swindon Works, 1903-1942
Designer:	George Churchward/Charles Collett
Number built:	165
Purpose:	Heavy freight
Wheel arrangement:	2-8-0
Cylinders (x 2):	18 in diameter x 30 in stroke
Motion:	Stephenson link
Valves:	10 in piston valves
Wheels: Coupled:	4 ft 7.5 in
Leading:	3 ft 2 in
Tender:	4 ft 1.5 in
Boiler diagram:	Swindon Standard No 1
Boiler: Max. diameter:	5 ft 6 in
Pressure:	225 lb/psi
Heating surface:	2,104 sq ft
Firebox:	154.78 sq ft
Tubes and flues:	1,686.6 sq ft
Superheater:	262.62 sq ft
Grate area:	27.07 sq ft
Tractive effort:	35,380 lb (@ 85% boiler pressure)
Engine wheelbase:	25 ft 7 in
Total wheelbase:	53 ft 7.75 in
Engine weight:	75 tons 10 cwt (76 tons 5 cwt for 2884 class)
Coal capacity:	6 tons
Water capacity:	3.500 gallons
Max. axleloading:	17 tons 5 cwt
BR power class:	8F

Those Classic Westerns

Great Western
Railway

**George Jackson
Churchward**

Charles Collett

**4500/4575/5101
classes**

2-6-2T (1906/1929)

Registering another 'first' for Britain's main-line railways, George Churchward included six-coupled tank engines with both guiding and trailing wheels in his range of standard locomotive designs for the Great Western. They proved both successful and influential.

The inspiration, as with the 2800 class 2-8-0, came from across the Atlantic. American railroads, with their often lightly laid tracks, had long recognised the benefits of both leading and trailing axles. Churchward saw the 2-6-2 arrangement as ideal for the twists and turns of the GWR's rural branches and secondary routes. He was so enamoured with the format that schemes were produced for what became known as the 'Small' and 'Large' Prairie tanks, with the latter one of the designs chosen to launch his re-equipping of the GWR's locomotive fleet. As was his custom, Churchward began with a prototype: No99, which rolled out of Swindon Works in 1903, would be the precursor not only of a series of mixed traffic 2-6-2 tanks but also three lighter and smaller classes for branch lines and similar secondary duties. No99 was allowed ample time to prove itself and production did not get underway until 1905.

As built, the prototype sported a short-cone taper boiler (not yet superheated), with a slender cast-iron chimney and short, straight sidetanks containing 1,380 gallons of water. Cylinders of 18 inches diameter and 30 inches stroke were contained in a pair of iron castings bolted back-to-back on the centre line of the engine. Piston valves, with – this being a Churchward engine – long travel and inside admission, were positioned above the cylinders and actuated through rocking shafts from Stephenson link motion located between the frames. The coupled wheels were 5 feet 8 inches diameter and the working pressure was set at 195 lb/psi. These all combined to deliver a tractive effort of 23,690 lb.

Experience with No99 led to Churchward making a number of modifications, notably increasing the water capacity and restyling the tanks. Now holding 2,000 gallons, they tapered gently from the centre point so as not to obstruct the line-of-sight from the cab. This became a characteristic of Swindon-built tank locomotives (apart from the pannier classes) and was copied by others including Stanier on

5101 class 2-6-2T No5158 pilots 'Castle' class 4-6-0 No5024 *Carew Castle* over Dainton bank, west of Newton Abbot, with the down 'Cornishman' on 3 September 1958.

More please

Churchward had assembled an outstanding team of engineers under him at Swindon and fully expected his designs to be improved and developed by those who followed him. However, his successor, Charles Collett, saw little that needed changing when the running department called for more locomotives. This was especially true of the 'Large Prairies'. Collett, who took over as Chief Mechanical Engineer in 1922, adapted the basic design for both fast suburban passenger traffic and heavy duty banking work. In all, a total of 306 'Large Prairies' of six classifications were built up to 1949.

Collett first decided that Churchward's 3100 series would become the 5100 class, with the prototype (the erstwhile No99) taking No5100. The original production engines, Nos3111-49, were renumbered Nos5111-49. Collett's new engines, however, displayed sufficient minor changes to warrant a new classification, the 5101 class. This became the most numerous of the 'Large Prairie' classes.

Not the yard of a Welsh shed in the 1950s but that of Barrow Hill Roundhouse in Derbyshire plays host to work-stained 4575 class 2-6-2T No5553 (sporting a Machynlleth – 89C – shedplate) on 12 July 2003. It has one of the larger GW tanks, 5205 class No5224 of 84G (Pontypool Road) for company.

his LMSR designs. The production series also received long-cone boilers, with the barrel length extended to 11 feet 2 inches.

Given added weight

Forty 'Large Prairies', or 3100 class, had been delivered when, in 1906, Churchward experimented further. No3150 was outshopped with a Swindon No4 boiler and an increased cylinder diameter of 18.5 inches, which produced a small gain in tractive effort. There was a greater increase with the ensuing production series. Introduced after a year's trial with No3150, Nos3151 to 3190 mustered a tractive effort of 25,670 lb. All the while the weight of the locomotives had steadily increased from the 72 tons 3 cwt of No99 to 75 tons 10 cwt (Nos3111-49) and then 78 tons 16 cwt.

In all other respects the 3150 series was identical to its predecessors but the additional power made the locomotives especially suitable for banking duties. They became a familiar sight on Severn Tunnel pilot duties; Sapperton bank, between Gloucester and Swindon, was another of their haunts. However, banking heavy trains incurred a cost. It put undue strain upon the frames, leading to buckling and – at worst – fractures. Churchward's solution was introduce the support struts that became a fixture on all Great Western engines using a leading pony truck.

The building of the last of the 3150 series, No3190 of 1908, also marked the completion of the class, at least as far as Churchward was concerned. He

nevertheless continued to modify the design. Engines were progressively fitted with larger diameter chimneys, top feed and superheating so that, by 1919, boiler pressure and tractive effort could be standardised at 200 lb/psi and 24,300 lb respectively. That year, Churchward instigated a plan to increase the Prairies' coal capacity with an extension to their bunkers. At first the added eighteen hundredweights brought weight distribution problems but fortunately these were quickly resolved.

Just capital

As the 5101 class grew through the 1930s, to the extent that 100 were in traffic by the outbreak of World War II in 1939, they became a familiar sight over most of the GWR system (apart from rural branch lines where they were excluded by their axleloading). An exception was the London region, where Collett had other ideas. Here, Churchward's 4-4-2 'County' tanks, which shared many components including cylinders and boiler, with the prototype Prairie, No99, were dominant. By 1930, however, it was evident that something more powerful was needed for the newly accelerated Paddington suburban duties. Collett's response was to increase the boiler pressure of the 5101 to 225 lb/psi to obtain a higher tractive effort of 27,340 lb. The outcome was the 6100 class, a series of 70 locomotives outshopped from Swindon between 1931 and 1935.

They proved ideal for the work, possessing both rapid acceleration and the ability to sustain high speeds. Handsome and impressive, the 6100s were the masters of the Slough, Reading and High Wycombe locals until the late 1950s, when diesel multiple units forced them to find work elsewhere. The doyen of the class, No6100, was the first to be retired in 1958 but nine saw out the last months of Western Region steam in 1965.

Collett also made modifications to examples of the 3100 and 3150 classes. A number of 3100s, including – yet again – the original No99, were rebuilt, becoming the new 8100 class. However, the outbreak of war in 1939 limited the conversions to just ten rather than the 40 envisaged. The 8100s enjoyed the higher boiler pressure (225 lb/psi) of the 6100 class, but with 5 feet 6 inches coupled wheels, and delivered a healthy tractive effort of 28,165 lb. They were very much Midlands and South Wales engines; in 1962-63, allocation lists reveal the survivors based at Tyseley (Birmingham), Worcester, Llanelli, Neath and Llantrisant. Those based at Carmarthen were called upon to handle the 'Pembroke Coast Express' for part of its journey.

Simultaneously with the 8100 series, Swindon produced a small series of specialist banking engines out of members of the 3150 class. Again the scheme was curtailed by wartime economies with just five engines being rebuilt. As with the 8100, the frames were reused with new cylinders and boilers (pressed to 225 lb/psi). Allied to 5 feet 3 inches driving wheels, the result was an impressive tractive effort of 31,170 lb that made this quintet ideal for its principal role.

Creative accounting

The rebuilding of the Prairie tanks (and other Churchward engines for that matter) produced something of a financial poser for Collett as he wrestled with the finer points of what constituted a new locomotive and what did not. While new locomotives were financed from a fixed renewal fund, repairs were paid for out of operating revenue. Did a cylinder exchange qualify as a repair? If those cylinders were of a different specification, and therefore made a change to the locomotive's performance, did that make it a 'new' engine? To avoid depleting his renewal fund Collett seized upon any accounting ruses open to him.

Whichever account they were debited to, though, the 'Large Prairies' gave good value. The first members of the original 3100 series to be withdrawn were Nos5127 and 5146 (ex-3127 and 3146). Last to be retired was No5148 (3148) in 1959. Scrapping of the 3150 category (discounting the five engines rebuilt as Nos3100-04 in 1938-39) began a year earlier, in 1947. The last of this 41-strong class, No3170, bowed out in 1958 while the ten 8100 class engines were scrapped between 1962 and 1965.

The 5101 class sustained its first retirement just seven years after the last was built, No5159 being cut up in 1956. However, the usefulness of the Prairies ensured large numbers – mostly of the later 41XX series and increasingly concentrated around the West Midlands, Worcester and South Wales – soldiered on into the 1960s. Their external appearance was now very different from what began as glossy black or lined green but, even in run-down condition, there was

no mistaking the robust, purposeful look of the Churchward design. At one time British Railways' Western Region could call upon over 300 of the 'Large Prairies' but, by the end of 1965, this had been reduced to just two: Nos4113 and No4161. A third example, No4176, although withdrawn in October 1965, survived as a stationary boiler until May 1967.

On reflection it was curious that not a single example of this historically important class was set aside for preservation as part of the National Collection. They were, though, despatched in numbers to Woodham Brothers' scrapyard at Barry, South Wales, and it was from there that ten of the 5101 class were saved. The sole survivor of the 6100 class, No6106, was bought from British Railways – in working order – by a member of the Great Western Society in November 1967.

The compact version

Churchward's 'Small Prairie' design has been described as the ideal branch line locomotive. Certainly, in terms of power-for-weight, there was little to touch the 4500 class 2-6-2T and it was the clear inspiration for later LMSR and British Railways Standard designs. Built at Swindon in 1905, the prototype, No115, was allowed less than a year to prove itself before the class went into production. Ten were then constructed at the workshops in Wolverhampton and numbered in the 44XX sequence.

The 4400s were well suited to their role, with the small coupled wheels supplying lively acceleration. Nevertheless, modifications were soon introduced. The straight-backed bunker acquired a lipped extension to increase coal capacity and other changes were gradually incorporated, the most significant of which was the fitting of superheated boilers, pressed to 180lb/psi.

Despite these changes, the 4400s displayed one serious drawback. While their 4 ft 1.5 in driving wheels could deliver acceleration, they also imposed an upper limit on speed, so compromising the class's usefulness. No further examples were built and the 4400 was superseded in 1906 by the 4500 class. This retained the best features of its predecessor but enlarged the scope of the 'Small Prairies', principally through the fitting of 4 ft 7.5 in diameter driving wheels. Although these took the working weight to 57 tons, no additional limitations on route availability were

One of the final members of the 5101 class (Swindon 1946), Didcot-based No4144 heads away from Watford (Metropolitan Line) and over the Grand Union Canal with a 'Steam on the Met' service for Harrow.

incurred. Other lessons learned from experience with the 4400s were incorporated, but Churchward remained unconvinced of the value of superheating in small tank engines. It would be a further eight years before superheaters were fitted from new (with Nos4540-54 of 1914-15). The retrospective addition of superheaters to existing locomotives began in 1913.

Wolverhampton was also given the job of building the 4500 class but the order for Nos4500-19 was the last placed there. The following twenty examples were Swindon-built, and were notable for an increase in boiler pressure, to 200lb/psi, and consequent raising of the tractive effort from 19,120lb to 21,250lb. Starting with the now-preserved No4555 of 1924, new locomotives were fitted with outside steampipes as standard, improved superheaters and enlarged bunkers that took the coal capacity to 3 tons 14 cwt. Nos4555-74 were last of the small Prairies

to be built to the original Churchward specification.

When the operating department requested more of the same, Charles Collett took the opportunity to increase the water capacity substantially. Larger side tanks, holding 1,300 gallons, were fitted and the extended range that this offered was judged to be worth the extra three tons on the locomotive weight. The modification, it was decided, warranted a new description, the 4575 class. One hundred locomotives were delivered between 1926 and 1929, and were assigned Nos4575-99 and 5500-74.

Both the 4500 and 4575 classes were good servants of the GWR and BR's Western Region. The West Country, with its many picturesque branch lines, was their regular haunt but examples were employed in South Wales and the West Midlands, and around Bristol, Gloucester, Machynlleth, Shrewsbury, Taunton

IN PRESERVATION

Ten of the 5101 class Prairies live on but only one of the 6100 class. It and five of the surviving 5101s have worked in preservation. Four 'Large Prairies' are presently active, while a fifth has been the subject of a bold, if controversial, rebuild.

No4110 Flagship locomotive of the Great Western Railway Preservation Group and under restoration in the GWRPG's workshops at Southall, west London.

No4115 Unrestored and in the care of the Vale of Glamorgan Railway, Barry, South Wales, No4115 has been earmarked to provide parts to recreate two long-lost Churchward

locomotives: a 4-4-2 'County' tank and a 4700 class 2-8-0.

No4121 Bought privately from Woodham Brothers' scrapyard, Barry, and stored at a site in Wiltshire. Condition unknown.

No4141 Presently in service on the Great Central Railway, Leicestershire, but was due to be withdrawn for overhaul during 2009.

No4144 Part of the Great Western Society's collection at Didcot Railway Centre, Oxfordshire, No4144 was restored during the 1990s but now awaits a ten-year overhaul.

No4150 Stored on the Severn Valley Railway awaiting restoration.

No4160 Returned to steam on the West Somerset in the early 1990s, a further overhaul has ensured that No4160 remains a reliable and useful member of the WSR fleet.

No5164 A ten-year overhaul was completed in 2003 and the engine is at work on the Severn Valley Railway.

No5193 Controversially converted into a tender engine—essentially a Churchward 4300 class 2-6-0—and renumbered a fictitious GWR No9351. In service on the West Somerset Railway.

No5199 In traffic on the Llangollen Railway, North Wales.

No6106 Out of service; static exhibit at Didcot Railway Centre, Oxfordshire, and part of the Great Western Society collection. In preservation, the 4500 class is represented by three examples, the 4575 class by eleven. Just three of these fourteen survivors have yet to be restored to working order.

No4555 After many years working on the South Devon Railway No4555 has moved to the Paignton & Dartmouth Railway where it is undergoing overhaul.

No4561 Withdrawn from Plymouth Laira in May 1962 with a mileage of 997,635, No4561 came to the West Somerset Railway in 1975 where restoration was completed in 1989. After several years on display at Bishops Lydeard, a second overhaul has begun.

No4566 Withdrawn in April 1962, after eight years at Barry No4566 came to the Severn Valley Railway where restoration was completed in 1975. No4566 remains part of the SVR's working fleet.

No4588 Rolled out of Swindon in 1927, No4588 was retired in 1962 and, after being restored at Swindon, went into service on the Paignton & Dartmouth Railway. Now requiring overhaul, the P&DR has put No4588 up for sale.

No5521 The restoration of No5521 was notable for the fitting of air-braking equipment (and a prominent smokebox-mounted air pump) to allow the engine to work on the main line, which it has—in Hungary and Poland! The GWR Prairie was a striking addition to a steam festival at Wolsztyn in April 2007. No5521 is usually based on the Dean Forest Railway in Gloucestershire.

No5526 Saved by the 'Project 5526 Group', restoration was part-undertaken at Swindon and completed at Buckfastleigh, on the South Devon Railway, where No5526 – wearing BR

and Worcester. A handful even reached the London area, working empty stock into and out of Paddington and freights on the Brentford branch. They possessed excellent acceleration and were capable of speeds up to 60 miles per hour.

Withdrawals began in 1950, with No4531, but the 'small Prairies' did not disappear entirely from BR metals for another fourteen years. The last to be retired from service were Nos5508, 5531, 5564 and 5569.

Prairie story

As might be deduced from the name, the 'Prairie' wheel arrangement – one leading axle (or pony truck), three coupled axles and a trailing axle – originated in the United States of America. However, the first examples, built by the Baldwin Locomotive Works in Philadelphia, went for export to what had been a traditionally British customer: New Zealand.

The type made its debut in Britain with six outside-cylinder tank engines constructed by Beyer, Peacock of Manchester for the Mersey Railway. Later still, 2-6-2 tank engines were built in considerable numbers beginning with the Great Western Churchward classes and ending with British Railways' Standard 3MT and 2MT classes of 1952-53. In Britain, Prairie tender engines were limited to Sir Nigel Gresley's V2 and V4 classes for the London & North Eastern Railway.

lined black livery – is in service.

No5532 After twenty years at Barry No5532 was moved to the Dean Forest Railway. Here it has donated its frames and other components to the restoration of No5538 (below). With wheelsets and boilers routinely exchanged, it is traditionally the frames which dictate a locomotive's number and No5538 has therefore been redesignated No5532! The 'old' No5532 looks set to be a source of spares.

No5538 Restoration of 1928-built No5538 (as No5532 – see above) is set to get underway on the Dean Forest Railway.

No5539 Another 1928 Swindon product, No5539 awaits restoration on the Llangollen Railway.

No5541 In 1972 No5541 made its way from Barry scrapyard to the Dean Forest Railway and was back in steam in 1975. It last worked in 2004 and is undergoing a further overhaul estimated at £100,000.

No5542 Acquired by the West Somerset Railway Association in 1976, No5542 was then sold to the Taunton-based '5542 Fund' who completed the restoration. It is now shared mainly between the WSR and the Gloucestershire Warwickshire Railway.

No5552 Rescued by Cornwall's Bodmin & Wenford Railway, restoration of No5552 was completed in 2003 and it remains a working member of the Bodmin-based fleet.

No5553 Undoubtedly No5553's greatest claim to fame is being the 213th and final locomotive to be rescued from Woodham's yard. In January 1990, it was bought by the Waterman Trust (founded by music producer, Pete Waterman) and restored to working order. The engine is normally based on the West Somerset Railway.

No5572 Retired in April 1962, No5572 was bought by the embryo Great Western Society in August 1971. Restoration was completed at the Didcot Railway Centre and No5572 was a regular performer throughout the 1980s. It is now stored at Didcot awaiting overhaul.

IN DETAIL *(as built)*

Classes	5101, 6100	4500/4575
Built:	Swindon Works 1929-49 (5101) 1927-30 (6100)	Wolverhampton and Swindon Works, 1906-29
Designer:	George Churchward/ Charles Collett	George Churchward/ Charles Collett
Number built:	140 (5101) 70 (6100)	175
Purpose:	Mixed traffic	Mixed traffic (chiefly secondary and branch passenger)
Wheel arrangement:	2-6-2	2-6-2
Cylinders (x2):	18 inches diameter x 30 inches stroke	17 in diameter x 24 in stroke
Motion:	Stephenson link	Stephenson link
Valves:	10 in piston valves	Piston valves
Wheels: Coupled:	5 ft 8 in	4 ft 7.5 in
Leading:	3 ft 2 in	3 ft 2 in
Trailing:	3 ft 8 in	3 ft 2 in
Boiler diagram:	Swindon Standard No2	Swindon Standard No5
Boiler: Max. diameter:	5 ft 0in	4 ft 9.5 in
Pressure:	200 lb/psi [5101] 225 lb/psi [6100]	200 lb/psi
Heating surface:	1,349 sq ft	1,215.52 sq ft
Firebox:	122 sq ft	94.12 sq ft
Tubes and flues:	1,145 sq ft	1,019.69 sq ft
Superheater:	82 sq ft	101.71 sq ft
Grate area:	20.3 sq ft	16.83 sq ft
Tractive effort:	24.300 lb [510] 27,340 lb [6100] (@ 85% boiler pressure)	21,250 lb (@ 85% boiler pressure)
Engine wheelbase:	14 ft 8 in	11 ft 6 in
Total wheelbase:	31 ft 8 in	26 ft 10 in
Engine weight:	78 tons 9 cwt	57 tons 18 cwt (4500) 61 tons 0 cwt (4575)
Coal capacity:	4 tons	3 tons 14 cwt
Water capacity:	2,000 gallons	1,000 gallons (4500) 1,300 gallons (4575)
Max. axleloading:	17 tons 5 cwt	15 tons 11 cwt
BR power class:	4MT (5101) 5MT (6100)	4MT

Great Central
Railway
John Robinson
8K class
(LNER 04) 8F
2-8-0 (1911)

A Great Servant to Many

The story of John Robinson's heavy freight 2-8-0 for the Great Central Railway is an extraordinary one. It encompasses at least nine countries, five engine builders, eight main–line railway companies, five rebuildings and two world wars. From workhorses to war-horses, they ended their days as far away as Australia and China.

Not that such a colourful history was anticipated when, in 1910, the still-youthful Great Central Railway decided it needed a more powerful class of freight engine. The impetus was the impending opening of its vast new docks complex at Immingham on Humberside. The GCR correctly anticipated a huge increase in coal traffic through the port (over 2.25 million tons were shipped during 1913) and needed the engines to handle it. The job of designing these machines went to its Chief Mechanical Engineer, the Newcastle-born John George Robinson.

Schemes were produced for a 2-10-0, a 2-8-2 and for two versions of 2-8-0, one with inside cylinders, the other outside. It was this last that got the vote. As was his custom, Robinson took an existing design as his starting point: the 8A class 0-8-0 of 1902. The boiler, shared with that of his Class 8 4-6-0 of 1902 and similar in outline to that of his celebrated Atlantics, was equipped with a superheater (both of Robinson's design and, for comparison, that of the German engineer, Wilhelm Schmidt). The cylinder diameter was enlarged from that of the 8A and, following the example of his one-time Great Western colleague, George Churchward, Robinson incorporated a leading pony truck. Aside from the fact that this gave a smoother ride, this supported the front end increased weight (an inevitable consequence of adding a superheater).

The first of the 2-8-0s, classified 8K and numbered 966, was outshopped from Gorton Works in Manchester in September 1911. Since it was unusual for the GCR to assemble large classes of engines (to date, Robinson's most numerous by far had been the 174-strong 9J 0-6-0) Gorton lacked the capacity quickly to meet the demand. The GCR invited tenders from outside and Kitson's of Leeds should have been the first beneficiaries with an order for twenty. However, they failed to meet the delivery date,

An open day on 6 August 2000 brought the last of the 04s, No63601, to ex-Great Western territory of Old Oak Common depot in London. It was not such an unusual event as might appear as the GWR bought over 40 surplus examples from the government during the 1920s.

opening the way for the North British Locomotive Company of Glasgow.

NBL put a tempting offer to the GCR: order 50 engines and pay for them in instalments! The agreed price was £4,500 (£50 less than Kitson's) and delivery was completed by the end of 1912. As a consequence, by June 1914 126 2-8-0s were in traffic. Robust and uncomplicated, the 8K steamed well and proved outstandingly reliable, qualities that would soon endear it to the wartime Ministry of Munitions.

By 1916, two years into World War I, the Ministry had requisitioned some 600 locomotives from Britain's railway companies. With no end to the conflict in sight, it now decided to build rather than borrow. Not only was the Robinson 2-8-0 a proven design, it enjoyed powerful backing: the Great Central's General Manager, Sir Sam Fay, had become the government's Director of War Transport. Orders were placed for over 300 engines for the military, specifically the Railway Operating Division (ROD) of the Royal Engineers. Deliveries began in August 1917 and, by February 1919, 305 had been despatched to France. They differed from the GCR engines in having air braking and carriage heating, allowing them to haul troop and ambulance trains. The major change, however, was under the boiler clothing: cheaper steel fireboxes replaced copper.

Surplus stock

Gorton works built only a handful of the ROD engines, the majority coming from four outside builders: Kitson's, North British, Nasmyth Wilson of Patricroft, Manchester, and Robert Stephenson & Company of Darlington. Anxious to avoid a post-war rise in unemployment as military work ended, the government extended construction until 1920, two years after the signing of the armistice. As a result, 521 government surplus ROD 2-8-0s languished in dumps around Britain. They were advertised for sale but just 53 found buyers, which was hardly

With the familiar clocktower in the background, O4/1 class 2-8-0 No 63605 runs tender-first through Wakefield Westgate with coal empties from Wrenthorpe yard bound for the Barnsley area. Spared any modifications, the engine remains as built by the Great Central at its Gorton (Manchester) works in June 1913 and lasted in traffic until August 1962. Its 4,000 gallon tender appears filled to its six tons coal capacity.

surprising as the government was asking up to £12,000 each for engines that had cost between £6,000 and £8,000 to build. Britain's war-battered railway companies were in no mood to line the Treasury coffers so an alternative was proposed: the remaining 468 locomotives could be hired.

It was an offer that a host of companies from Scotland's Caledonian Railway

IN PRESERVATION

No102/63601

This last of the British-based Robinson 2-8-0s had been for many years a Doncaster-based engine. After withdrawal in June 1963 from Frodingham depot in Scunthorpe it was stored at several locations including Doncaster Works and Stratford (London) before in 1976 finding a home, appropriately, in the ex-Great Central running shed at Dinting Railway Centre near Manchester. When the site closed, the engine was recalled by the National Railway Museum. However, an appeal to restore it to working order promoted by an enthusiasts' magazine proved successful. Sponsorship and support came from a number of organisations, but public donations – £55,000 out of a total cost of £75,000 – were the key factor in seeing No63601

steamed for the first time in over 36 years on 24 January 2000. The five-year overhaul was undertaken by today's Great Central Railway in its Loughborough workshops and No63601 remains there on loan from the National Railway Museum. It has made visits to gala events and open days, including Old Oak Common, London, in August 2000, and Doncaster Works in July 2003. Sadly, 2009 marked the final year of service for No63601 as its ten-year boiler 'ticket' expired. Three of the ex-ROD 2-8-0s sold to the Australian mining company of J&A Brown are preserved in New South Wales: two at Dorrigo, in the north of the state, the third at Richmond Vale Steam Centre, Kurri-Kurri.

to the Great Eastern, Lancashire & Yorkshire, London & South Western and South Eastern & Chatham grabbed at – possibly too eagerly as, in 1921, the hire agreements were summarily terminated and most locomotives recalled. Only the Great Western retained some of its quota. If it was a ploy to force companies into buying the engines, it failed, and they returned to the dumps. Queensferry, near Chester, was the largest repository with 198; up to 150 were stored at Tattenham Corner, near Epsom, in Surrey.

By 1923, with the engines deteriorating (especially their steel fireboxes) and devaluing, the government settled for whatever it could obtain – anything from £2,050 in 1925 to just £340 two years later. The last were disposed of in 1927, with the majority being bought by the Great Western, London & North Eastern and London Midland & Scottish Railways. Some, however, found more exotic homes. A batch was sold for use on both public and colliery railways in China, and thirteen were acquired by a mining company in New South Wales, J&A Brown. They arrived in Australia between 1926 and 1927 and the last was still at work in 1973, outliving its British counterparts by seven years. It had kept the same boiler for 47 years! The 131 ex-Great Central and 271 ROD 8K 2-8-0s that came into LNER ownership enjoyed similarly long careers.

Along LNER lines

Under Robinson, the 8K had undergone little modification, but the LNER went for rebuilding in a big way. There were superheater experiments, and – to counter the post-war shortage of good locomotive coal – trials using new types of fuel. Through a sequence of modifications and boiler changes, by 1944 eight sub-classes of the O4 class, as the 8K had become, had been created.

The changes centred mainly on replacing the Belpaire boilers (which Doncaster men, including Sir Nigel Gresley, seemingly loathed), with the LNER round-top variety, altering the cab design, and cutting down the boiler mountings to bring them within the LNER loading gauge (particularly for use in Scotland). The tall Robinson chimneys (which were prone to cracking) were eventually all replaced. The most dramatic changes, however, were implemented by Gresley's successor, Edward Thompson, who had included a 2-8-0 in his 'standard' locomotive scheme. Since wartime restrictions precluded the construction of a new design, Thompson got his 2-8-0 by rebuilding the O4. He fitted 58 engines with Type 100A boilers (as used on his B1 4-6-0), new cylinders with outside Walschaerts valve gear and B1-style cabs. They became the O1 class.

All points east

In 1941, a second world war brought a second call on the Robinson 2-8-0 from the military. This time, however, matters were not so straightforward. The LNER's tinkerings had deprived the class of a vital asset: uniformity. It was displaced in the Army's affections by the LMSR's Stanier 8F but not before a number were sent overseas. A total of 92, made up of 31 ex-Great Central and 61 ex-ROD examples, set out and all but two made it to Egypt, Palestine, Syria and Iraq. Some

ventured further, opening up the important supply line through Persia (Iran) and reaching the Soviet Union. None returned to Britain and, in 1947 – on the eve of nationalisation – the LNER finally received £524,000 in compensation.

Remarkably, the Robinson 2-8-0 saw service in at least nine countries and with eight British main line railway companies.

British Railways took 278 O4s and 51 of Thompson's O1 rebuilds into stock in January 1948. It also inherited 45 surviving ex-ROD engines from the Great Western. Most ended their days as they had begun them: hauling Yorkshire and Nottinghamshire coal. Withdrawals began in 1958, with the last O4 (amazingly some had escaped all the LNER's rebuildings) being retired in February 1966. It had outlasted the Thompson O1s by six months! That April saw the end for the remaining four O4/8 rebuilds, leaving only a dilapidated, but nonetheless preserved, No63601 (GCR No102) languishing at Doncaster.

IN DETAIL *(as built)*	
Class:	**8K (LNER O4)**
Built:	1911-20
Designer:	John Robinson
Number built:	666 (521 to government orders)
Purpose:	Heavy freight, especially mineral traffic
Wheel arrangement:	2-8-0
Cylinders (x 2):	21 in diameter x 26 in stroke
Motion:	Stephenson link motion
Valves:	10 in diameter piston valves
Wheels: Coupled:	4 ft 8 in
Leading:	3 ft 6 in
Tender:	4 ft 4 in
Boiler diagram:	No6 Standard
Boiler: Max. diameter:	5 ft 0 in
Pressure:	180 lb/psi
Heating surface:	1,745 sq ft
Firebox:	154 sq ft
Tubes and flues:	1,349 sq ft
Superheater:	242 sq ft
Grate area:	26.24 sq ft
Tractive effort:	31,326 lb (@ 85% boiler pressure)
Engine wheelbase:	25 ft 5 in
Total wheelbase:	51 ft 2.5 in
Engine weight :	73 tons 4 cwt
Coal capacity:	6 tons
Water capacity:	4,000 gallons
Max. Axleloading:	17 tons 1 cwt
BR power class:	8F

(Weights and dimensions refer to 8K class as first built.)

Mixing it

Churchward's 'standard' types included a mixed-traffic 2-6-0, distinguished from others of the breed by its swing-link bogie – a further example of North American influence at work at Swindon. The 4300s served the Great Western for fifty years and became the blueprint for a host of similar designs.

Great Western
Railway

George Jackson Churchward/Harold Holcroft

4300 class

4MT 2-6-0 (1911)

The first application of a pair of leading, or 'guide' wheels in conjunction with a six-wheeled locomotive appears to have been in France in 1841. Around the same time, a British concern, Eastwick and Harrison, who had set up a manufacturing facility in Russia, built a small number of 2-6-0s there. However, it was in North America, on twisting, turning and often unevenly laid tracks that the type came into its own. With the extra adhesion and greater power obtainable from six coupled wheels, it presented strong competition to that American standard, the 4-4-0.

At first, the leading two-wheel truck was fixed but, during the 1850s, a degree of flexibility was introduced, culminating in the work of a New Yorker called Levi Bissel. By adding sideways movement to the basic swivelling motion, his scheme for a leading truck gave unrivalled control and guidance into curves. Bissel patented his design in 1858 and by 1910 some 11,000 2-6-0s were in service on American railroads.

The 2-6-0 made its British debut in 1878, on a railway not known for innovation, the Great Eastern. Locomotive Superintendent William Adams built a class of fifteen but they failed to do justice to the advantages of the 2-6-0 and lasted in service less than a decade. There was no attempt at a revival until 1895 when two were built for the Midland & South Western Junction Railway. So far, Britain's railways had been underwhelmed by the 2-6-0. The importing of 80 of the type (in kit form) from Baldwin's of Philadelphia in 1899 did little to change opinion. They were bought by three companies – the Great Central, Great Northern and Midland – to counter a shortage of locomotive building capacity at home. When they failed to live up to expectation, the 2-6-0 format itself was unfairly dismissed as a "damned Yankee design".

Youthful inspiration

Some engineers saw beyond these initial failures. One was the Great Western's William Dean and, in 1900, he introduced the 2-6-0 to Swindon. The 'Aberdare' was a goods engine with coupled wheels of 4 feet 7.5 inches diameter and a swing-link pony truck. It proved a sound design and the inherent advantages of the

2-6-0 arrangement were now evident, not only to Dean's heir-apparent, George Churchward, but by an up-and-coming Swindon junior, Harold Holcroft.

One of a party of British engineers that toured the railroads of the eastern United States and Canada during 1909, Holcroft had noted the extensive use of outside-cylinder 2-6-0s for both passenger and freight work. However, these had relatively small coupled wheels and were restricted to a maximum speed of around 45 miles per hour. Holcroft reasoned that, with an increase in wheel diameter, the top speed could be raised to 55 or even 60 miles per hour.

Holcroft's idea reached Churchward and received rapid approval:

"Get me out a 2-6-0 with 5 feet 8 inches wheels, outside cylinders, the number four boiler and bring in all the standard details you can."

Framed by the semaphore signals, British Railways-liveried 4300 class 2-6-0 No7325 enters Bridgnorth station with a Severn Valley Railway service from Kidderminster. No7325 presently awaits overhaul.

4300 class 2-6-0 No7309 of Shrewsbury shed (84G) heads away from Aberystwyth with the up 'Cambrian Coast Express' one day in July 1957. Note the 'Conflat' wagon behind the tender.

December 1927 four engines were fitted with the casting and, to distinguish them from the rest of the class, were renumbered: Nos4351/85/86/95 became 8300/34/35/44. Although, after trials, this quartet reverted to the standard front-end arrangement (and their original numbers), between January and March 1928 65 of the 5300 series were equipped with the casting and had 3,000 added to their numbers to bring them into the 83XX series.

Unfortunately, this remedy came at a price. The GWR used colour coding to identify which of its classes could operate where (usually a question of how great an axleloading bridges could bear). The additional two tons of the 4300's front-end casting took the modified engines out of the 'blue' category into the much more restricted 'red'. This might not have mattered had there been enough 'blue' route locomotives of other classes, but after World War II, the scrapping of life-expired engines had left the GWR with a shortage in this area. So some 50 of the class were returned to their original 'blue' status by having their front-end casting removed.

However, this was small beer compared to the treatment of many of the class during the 1930s. The

With that, Britain's first truly mixed traffic locomotive was initiated, primarily as a replacement for ageing 4-4-0s on secondary services. Within a few days, the relatively inexperienced Holcroft – he was 29 – had completed the outline draft. Using standard parts meant that most of the drawings existed and only layout diagrams had to be freshly drafted. With much of the design based on the 3150 class 2-6-2 tank of 1906, Churchward saw no need for the usual prototype stage. An order for twenty was placed, with the first being completed in 1911.

A further twenty emerged in 1913 and construction continued into the era of Churchward's successor, Charles Collett, with the last delivered in 1932. A 1921 order for 35 engines was significant as it was placed, not at Swindon, but with Robert Stephenson's of Darlington. Stephenson's then supplied parts for a further 15 for assembly at Swindon. The 4300 class eventually numbered 342, second only to the 5700 class pannier tank (863 built) on the Great Western stock list.

Weighing up the options

Among the Collett-built examples Nos9300-19 were distinguished by a heavy front-end casting ahead of the running plate. This had been added after excessive flange wear had been revealed on the leading coupled wheels, particularly on engines operating over the sinuous curves of the Cornish lines. The intention was for this casting to transfer weight to the front end. In that way the pony truck applied greater sidethrust to the mainframes. These in turn absorbed more of the force exerted, deflecting it from the wheels. Between November and

IN PRESERVATION

No5322

Inevitably some of the Churchward Moguls ended up at Woodhams' yard at Barry, in South Wales, and eight were cut up there. Two, however, were spared the torch. No5322 was built at Swindon in 1917 and promptly requisitioned by the Railway Operating Department for war service. It was one of eleven 4300s, Nos5319-26/28-30, that went to France, repainted in ROD khaki livery but retaining their GWR numbers. No5322 was one of the last to return and by 1922 was based at Chester. Other allocations included Bristol, Cardiff and Weymouth and, finally, Pontypool Road from where No5322 was retired in April 1964. For long a static exhibit at Didcot Railway Centre, an overhaul was completed in late 2008, No5322 reappearing in the khaki livery it wore on war service.

No7325 (9303)

Fifteen years elapsed before Swindon outshopped the other preserved Churchward Mogul, originally as No9303. It went new to Penzance but within twelve months, had migrated to the other extreme of the GW system, Old Oak Common. By 1947 No9303 was a Reading engine. However, it was as No7325 that the 2-6-0 was finally

4300s remained intact as a class for just four years. Between 1936 and 1939, 100 were 'cannibalised' to provide parts – principally wheels and motion components – for Collett's 'Manor' and 'Grange' 4-6-0s. He had planned to 'recycle' the entire class but the constraints of wartime put an end to the scheme.

Green influence

The liveries carried by the Churchward Moguls varied little. In GWR days they wore unlined green, which became unlined black under British Railways. However, on 8 May 1956, the royal train was worked from Taunton to Barnstaple by Nos6372 and 6385 which were repainted lined green for the occasion. That autumn, unlined green was deemed the official livery for the class, but by the following February, Swindon was applying full lining. The class lasted in WR service until November 1964, when the four survivors were retired at Didcot (Nos6367 and 7327) and at Stourbridge Junction (Nos6364 and 6395).

The influence of Churchward's (and Holcroft's) 4300 was immense. It was swiftly followed by Gresley's K1 and K2 2-6-0s for the LNER., and by locomotive designers Richard Maunsell of the South Eastern & Chatham Railway and Lawson Billinton of the London, Brighton & South Coast Railway. With these designs the Mogul was finally established as a 'standard' type alongside the 4-4-0, 4-6-0 and 0-6-0. George Hughes introduced the type to the LMSR with his 'Horwich Mogul' (or 'Crab') of 1925 and these were augmented by Stanier and Ivatt. Gresley and Peppercorn added to the ranks of LNER 2-6-0s and, finally, after nationalisation three 2-6-0 classes were incorporated into the range of British Railways' Standard designs.

withdrawn from Pontypool Road in April 1964.
Moved to the Severn Valley Railway in 1975, restoration was completed at its Bridgnorth workshops in the autumn of 1992. The Mogul went on to make a number of main-line appearances but, now in the queue for overhaul, has become an exhibit in the Severn Valley's Engine Hall at Highley.

Why 'Moguls'?

The first of William Adams' Great Eastern 2-6-0s – No527 – appeared with the name *Mogul* painted on the sandboxes above the centre wheel splashers. The reason has never been certain – a tribute to the Mogul rulers of the Indian sub-continent or, more probably, following an American precedent? As early as 1866, a 2-6-0 of the Central Railroad of New Jersey appeared as *Mogul*, probably to indicate its power rather than suggest any oriental connection. It finally acquired generic status after use in a Master Mechanics' Association Report and in a Baldwin Locomotive Company advertisement, taking its recognised place alongside Atlantic, Consolidation, Pacific, Prairie and such like in the nomenclature of wheel arrangements.

IN DETAIL *(as built)*

Class	4300
Built:	Swindon Works; Robert Stephenson & Company, Darlington, 1911-32
Designer:	George Churchward/Harold Holcroft
Number built:	342
Purpose:	Mixed traffic
Wheel arrangement:	2-6-0
Cylinders (x 2):	18.5 in diameter x 30 in stroke
Motion:	Stephenson link
Valves:	9 in diameter piston valves
Wheels: Coupled:	5 ft 8 in
Leading:	3 ft 2 in
Tender:	4 ft 1.5 in
Boiler diagram:	Swindon No4
Boiler: Max. Diameter:	5 ft 6 in
Pressure:	200 lb/psi
Heating surface:	1,566 sq ft
Firebox:	122.92 sq ft
Tubes and flues:	1,228 sq ft
Superheater:	215.8 sq ft
Grate area:	20.56 sq ft
Tractive effort:	25,670 lb (@ 85% boiler pressure)
Engine wheelbase:	23 ft 9 in
Total wheelbase:	48 ft 6.75 in
Engine weight:	63 tons 17 cwt *
Coal capacity:	6 tons
Water capacity:	3,500 gallons
Max. axleloading:	19 tons 9 cwt
BR power class:	4MT

* Locomotives with modified front ends weighed an additional two tons.

Great Eastern
Railway/London &
North Eastern Railway

**Stephen
Holden/Nigel Gresley**

**'1500'/
B12 class 4P3F**

4-6-0 (1911/1928)

The Lead at Stratford

It may not have compared with the epic runs to Perth or Penzance, but the Great Eastern's main line to Norwich had its challenges. The GER's solitary class of 4-6-0 not only had to take on those challenges but cope with the compromises the route placed on its design. Its success earned it a leading role in Scotland as well as at Stratford.

Those challenges began on leaving Liverpool Street with the 1 in 70 climb through the Bishopsgate tunnels. A second, steady climb started shortly after Stratford and culminated in the 1 in 103 to 1 in 85 of Brentwood bank. There were further, lesser climbs east of Colchester, with a 1 in 131 ascent to Haughley. After 1900, James Holden's 4-4-0 designs, notably the 'Claud Hamiltons', had mastered the Norwich services but faced increasing train loadings.

Having succeeded his father as Locomotive Superintendent of the Great Eastern Railway in 1908, Stephen Dewar Holden was generally content to perpetuate existing designs. However, he did acknowledge this need for more powerful express passenger engines and the outcome was one of only two new classes to be credited to him (even if the design was largely the work of his Chief

Draughtsman, Frederick Russell). The '1500' (or S69 as it was classified by its batch number) would be the Great Eastern's largest express passenger engine and its solitary class of 4-6-0s.

Although firmly a product of the 20th century – the first was outshopped in 1911 – the '1500' was a transitional design. Nineteenth-century features, including ornate styling, a copper-capped chimney and extensive use of brass beading were partnered by the relatively new process of superheating. In 1908, when the first sketches were made, superheating was still on trial. However, by the time orders were placed, Stephen Holden had become a convert and German-made Schmidt superheaters were incorporated. Later, superheaters designed by the one-time motive-power chief of the Great Central Railway, John Robinson, were fitted.

In original condition, with Belpaire boiler, S69 (B12) class 4-6-0 No1510 starts a lengthy up goods out of the loop at Trumpington level crossing, Cambridge on 18 October 1924. Built at Stratford in April 1913, at this time No1510 was a Norwich engine. It was withdrawn in June 1949.

As all Great Eastern locomotive chiefs, Stephen Holden's ambition was curbed by both weight and length constraints. These had been successfully accommodated when Frederick Russell schemed the predecessor to Holden's 4-6-0, the celebrated 'Claud Hamilton' 4-4-0. However, when it came to a six-coupled engine, it proved impossible to produce a locomotive as large as those of other railways' contemporary express types. Nonetheless, GER engines had to work as hard as any on the main line from Liverpool Street to Ipswich and Norwich. stops.

Perhaps the most distinctive feature of the design was its large, enclosed cab, with its side windows and extended roof. It afforded about the most substantial protection for the crew as could be conceived at the time. The effect was emphasised by the comparatively short tender, dictated by the short turntables employed on the GER: none was more than 50 feet in diameter.

Construction by the GER was spread over ten years, with 51 built at the company's Stratford Works between June 1911 and April 1921. A further 20 came from William Beardmore of Glasgow, the first locomotives built for the GER by an outside firm since 1884.

Initially, the principal duties of the '1500' class 4-6-0s were expresses to Norwich and boat trains to Harwich (Parkeston Quay). The enlargement of the class during 1920-21 saw its use on the Cambridge line and on services to Yarmouth and other east coast ports. A snapshot of allocations before the 1923 grouping would have found nineteen examples at Ipswich, nine at Cambridge, seven at Norwich, five at Parkeston and two at Yarmouth (South Town). The largest contingent, however, was reserved for Stratford, with twenty-eight.

Flanked by one of the diesel multiple units that displaced the B12s from secondary duties, No61572 makes a spirited start from Sheringham with a North Norfolk Railway service on 8 September 2002. The exhaust to the rear belongs to another of the NNR's Great Eastern survivors, J15 0-6-0 No65462.

IN PRESERVATION

The sole surviving inside-cylinder 4-6-0 in Britain entered traffic on 24 August 1928. Numbered 8572, it spent eleven years based at Stratford, in London, before in March 1939 being transferred to Parkeston. Apart from a six-week stay at Grantham during 1953, the remainder of its working life was spent in Great Eastern territory, based at Colchester and Ipswich as well as Stratford. Its final move came in October 1959 to Norwich, where fortunately it came under the care of shedmaster, Bill Harvey.

It was Bill Harvey who effectively 'hid' this last of the B12s from official eyes and succeeded in putting off her departure to the scrapyard. His efforts were rewarded when the fledgling Midland & Great Northern Joint Railway Society acquired the locomotive, appropriately given the class's GER classification, for £1,500. Following this No61572 was stored at various locations before arriving at the North Norfolk Railway's base at Sheringham in 1967. Restoration did not begin in earnest until 1983, with the now-retired Bill Harvey bringing his expertise to the project.

After eight years in the workshop at Weybourne, the M&GNJRS took the momentous decision to ship the locomotive to the MoLoWa works in Germany for completion of its rebuilding. A twelve-year project reached fruition on 3 March 1995 when the B12 was

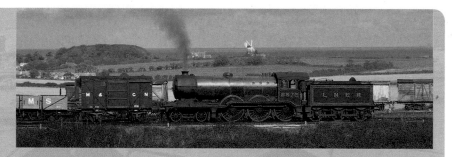

recommissioned, sadly not by Bill Harvey, who had died the previous year, but by another legendary ex-LNER engineman, R.H.N. (Dick) Hardy. Bill Harvey's contribution was recognised by the headboard carried on the inaugural run from Sheringham to Holt.

The B12 went on to serve the North Norfolk Railway well and, wearing its BR guise of No61572 and repainted lined black, gained approval for main-line running. This resulted in a memorable appearance at London Underground's 'Steam on the Met' event. After appearing at the North Norfolk Railway's autumn 2007 gala, where it formed a remarkable trio of Great Eastern survivors alongside N7 tank No69621 and J15 0-6-0 No65462, the B12 was withdrawn for overhaul.

Storming the final stretch of the 1 in 269 climb into Rickmansworth, No61572 is at the head of an Amersham-bound 'Steam on the Met' service during May 2000. The Norwich (32A) shedplate is appropriate: it was here that shedmaster, Bill Harvey, 'hid' the engine until its preservation had been secured.

reverted to their old Great Eastern sequence of 1500 to 1580. One B12 did not survive long enough to be renumbered and, by nationalisation in January 1948, a further seven had been condemned. The B12s now put in increasing appearances on the ex-Midland & Great Northern Joint line linking Peterborough and March with King's Lynn and the Norfolk coast ports. They worked the principal passenger trains until the arrival of newer Class 2 and Class 4 2-6-0s. A couple of B12s lingered on until the line closed in 1959.

Gresley's guinea-pig

The Great Eastern had been an air-braked railway, and one of the first modifications made by the LNER, therefore, was to fit vacuum ejectors to the B12s so that they could work with the vacuum-braked stock of the other constituent companies, specifically that used on the cross-country boat trains to Harwich. Then, purely experimentally, in 1926 Nigel Gresley replaced the Stephenson link motion of No8516 with Lentz oscillating cam poppet valve gear (apparently with some success as No8525 was similarly fitted).

The B12 also became a guinea-pig for Gresley's forays into feedwater heating. During 1926, No8509 was equipped with a Worthington-Simpson feedpump, the trial lasting three years. However, a French system enjoyed much longer use. The ACFI equipment (named after the Association des Chemins de Fer Industrielles that developed it) was fitted to no fewer than 53 of the class between 1927 and 1933. There were meaningful savings in coal and water were but the cost of maintaining the equipment began to outweigh the benefits and it fell out of use.

Scottish solution

From the late 1920s track improvements had allowed the B12s on the Essex coast branches. However, the traffic department saw the B12 as the solution to its motive power needs on the ex-Great North of Scotland Railway routes, lines with as many restrictions as the old Great Eastern. Using No8526, bridge stress tests had been conducted in the area as early as 1926 but it took a further five years for B12s to be transferred to Scotland in any quantity. Five made the journey north that year and, by 1942, twenty had arrived to replace ageing, underpowered 4-4-0s. By the time they reached Scotland, permanent way upgrading and the consequent lifting of weight restrictions allowed a larger boiler to be fitted to the B12s. The process had begun in 1932, with the new vessel a Doncaster-built Gresley design.

Whether by chance of not, under the LNER's post-war renumbering the B12s

IN DETAIL

Class	'1500' (B12)
Built:	1911-28
Designer:	Stephen Dewar Holden/Nigel Gresley
Number built:	81
Purpose:	Express passenger
Wheel arrangement:	4-6-0
Cylinders (x 2):	20 in diameter x 28 in stroke
Motion:	Stephenson link *
Valves:	10 in piston valves (reduced to 9.5 inches with rebuilding after 1932)
Wheels: Coupled:	6 ft 6 in
Leading:	3 ft 3 in
Tender:	4 ft 1 in
Boiler diagrams:	Diagram 25 (99) ¶/25A/99A §
Boiler: Max. diameter:	5 ft 1.625 in ¶/5 ft 6 in §
Pressure:	180 lb/psi
Heating surface:	1,834 sq ft §/1,919 sq ft ¶
Firebox:	143.5 sq ft
Tubes and flues:	1,489.1 sq ft
Superheater:	201 sq ft §/286.4 sq ft ¶
Grate area:	26.5 sq ft §/31 sq ft ¶
Tractive effort:	21,969 lb (@ 85% boiler pressure)
Engine wheelbase:	28 ft 6 in
Total wheelbase:	48 ft 3 in
Engine weight:	63 tons 0 cwt (B12/1)/65 tons 19 cwt (B12/2)/69 tons 10 cwt (B12/3)/64 tons 19 cwt (B12/4)
Coal capacity:	4 tons
Water capacity:	3,700 gallons
Max. axleloading:	15 tons 13 cwt
BR power class:	4P3F

Some locomotives experimentally fitted with Lentz oscillating cam poppet valve gear, later removed (see text).

¶ LNER Doncaster-type boilers introduced from May 1932. Diagram 99A boilers were fitted to Class B12/3 engines; Diagram 25A boilers were paired with Scottish-base B12/4s.

§ Original Great Eastern Belpaire boilers. Diagram 99 boilers, fitted to Class B12/2 locomotives, were included in the 25A classification from 1938.

The Derby Favourites

Midland Railway/
London Midland &
Scottish Railway

Henry Fowler

4F 0-6-0 (1911)/
3F 0-6-0T (1924)

If two locomotive types could be said to typify the Midland Railway, and the philosophy of its Derby-based engineers, they would be the six-coupled goods and shunting engines. The Midland began using 0-6-0s in the 1840s and the LMSR only stopped building them in 1941 by which time a flawed, if hard-working, design was thoroughly outdated.

Fowler 4F 0-6-0 No 43944 awaits departure from Shipley with a cross-country service from Paignton to Bradford. This was one of batch of 50 4Fs that the Midland contracted out to Armstrong Whitworth of Scotswood-on-Tyne. As MR No3944, it was delivered in 1921. Although primarily freight locomotives, the 4Fs were no strangers to passenger work.

In 1845, the Midland Railway absorbed one of the earliest railway companies, the Leicester & Swannington, and took possession of what are generally regarded as Britiain's first inside-cylinder six-coupled engines. The MR's Locomotive Superintendent, Mattherw Kirtley, evidently approved of the newcomers and adopted the type as his standard goods engine. In 1875, two years after replacing Kirtley, Samuel Johnson instigated the mass production of Midland 0-6-0s. From that date until 1902, seven classes totalling 865 engines were delivered from four outside contractors. All had 17 inches by 26 inches cylinders and 4 feet 10 inches coupled wheels and the working pressure was universally set at 140 lb/psi. It was not until 1880 that Derby Works turned out its first locomotive of this type: No1452, which cost precisely £1,990 9s 6d!

Towards the end of his time at Derby, Johnson did look to faster, if not necessarily larger 0-6-0s mainly for what were known as the 'Bradford Wool Trains' that worked between West Yorkshire and London. They were, though, essentially a development of what had gone before, this at a time when others were opting for eight rather than six wheels for the heaviest goods work. When Johnson retired in 1903 the Midland's approach to locomotive design had changed little over six decades.

Richard Deeley, the new Locomotive Superintendent, almost certainly recognised the flaws in the policy but his six years in charge appear to have been insufficient to effect a change. He did what his predecessors had done: rebuild elderly 0-6-0s (more than 100 by the end of 1904) and build new ones, fulfilling orders placed by Johnson. Construction continued up to 1908. At least the Deeley engines were larger and more powerful, with boilers pressed to 175 lb/psi.

The next generation

Henry Fowler, who took over from Deeley in 1909, settled for an updated version of the established Midland 0-6-0. He did, though, concede that increased power was desirable and the new design merited a '4' in the classification system devised by Deeley compared to the '3' of the final Johnson design. The two prototype 4F 0-6-0s, Nos3835 and 3836, that emerged from Derby Works in autumn 1911 did sport one innovation: superheaters. The former was fitted with the type developed by the German inventor, Wilhelm Schmidt, while the latter incorporated a version of the double-pass superheater developed by the Great Western at Swindon. Both were incorporated into a new boiler, Type G7S, which had a working pressure of 160lb/psi and incorporated a Belpaire firebox.

Midland practice obliged the use of inside cylinders, but slide valves were now replaced by eight-inch inside-admission piston valves. These operated the Stephenson link motion through rocking shafts. For comparison, No3835 had cylinders of 20 inches diameter and 26 inches stroke while those of No3836 had a reduced diameter of 19 inches. The greater efficiency of both valves and cylinders had the benefit of bringing an increase in tractive effort of around sixteen per cent over the earlier 3F designs.

A coupled wheel diameter of 5 feet 3 inches was selected, with the wheelsets spaced to what had become the Derby standard of 8 feet and 8 feet 6 inches. All wheels had underhung laminated springs. A novelty was the addition of a vacuum brake that would prove its worth over the years as 4Fs were called upon to work passenger, parcels and empty stock trains – invariably a lively experience as speeds exceeded the 45 miles per hour mark! Paired with 2,950 gallon tenders retrieved from a pair of 4-4-0s, the prototype 4Fs were allocated to Saltley shed in Birmingham and used on both passenger and goods work.

During the summer of 1912, comparative tests were undertaken with two saturated (i.e., non-superheated) Deeley 0-6-0s to compare fuel consumption. The route chosen was the regular 'test track' between Toton, the main concentration point for East Midlands coal traffic, and Brent yard in north-west London, a run of 126 miles. Southbound, the locomotives were attached to loaded trains of around 600 tons and, on the return, hauled rakes of 50 or 100 empty wagons. Problems immediately occurred with the joints between the superheater elements and superheater headers on both engines. In addition, after only two runs, No3836 had to be fitted with new valves and liners. Nevertheless, results showed the locomotive with the Schmidt superheater, No3835, to be the most economical, with worthwhile savings in both coal and water.

Despite this success, five years passed before the 4F 0-6-0 went into production. Doubtless the delay was due in part to the outbreak of war in 1914, and to the fact that the company already had a stock of no fewer than 1,495 0-6-0 tender engines, amounting to around 50 per cent of its fleet (and 21 per cent of the national total of six-coupled goods engines). The second largest contingent – belonging to the North Eastern Railway – was around half that size.

In May 1917, and with the working pressure raised to 175 lb/psi, the first of the production batch of Fowler 4Fs, No3837, was outshopped from Derby and was followed into traffic by 14 further examples. By 1922, the running numbers had reached No4026 with all bar 50 being Derby products. The exceptions, Nos3937-86, came from Armstrong Whitworth on Tyneside, who also supplied five engines specifically for the Somerset & Dorset route (S&DJR Nos57-61). The earlier examples were paired with second-hand tenders but, from No3877, the new 3,500 gallon straight-sided design, holding four tons of coal and weighing 41 tons 4 cwt, was attached. Construction continued steadily up to the grouping in 1923, when 197 4Fs were in traffic.

Repeat orders

The prevailing Midland influence within the newly formed LMSR – personified by Fowler's motive-power chief, James Anderson – ensured that, with only minor modifications such as exchanging right-hand for left-hand drive (from No4207 onwards), the 4F was adopted as its standard freight locomotive. More were built every year up to 1928. Bafflingly, throughout this period, little attempt appears to have been made to correct fundamental deficiencies, although the fitting of mechanical axlebox lubricators from 1919 onwards was a wise move.

With the introduction of the 8F 2-8-0 in 1935, it would have been reasonable to assume that the LMSR's reliance on the 4F 0-6-0 would end. Instead, the operating department persuaded William Stanier to authorise the construction of a further 45 examples. These last engines, Nos4562-4606, took the number of 4Fs

Rekindling the abiding image of 4Fs in BR days, visiting the Great Central Railway, No44422 plods through Swithland Sidings on 24 June 1995 with a lengthy mixed goods bound for Loughborough.

built by the LMSR between 1924 and 1941 to 575 and the class total to 772. All entered British Railways service in 1948, becoming Nos43835-44606. Only two BR classes were greater in number: the Great Western 5700 pannier tanks (863) and the LMSR Stanier 5MT 4-6-0, which eventually totalled 842.

Derby's other dynasty

Almost as commonplace as its 0-6-0s, was the Derby-designed six-coupled shunter. As early as 1874 the Midland Railway began taking delivery of such engines to a design by its Locomotive Superintendent, Samuel Johnson. Though successful, not even Johnson could have imagined that, along with becoming the Midland's standard shunting engine, his work would form the basis of a locomotive that was still in service 90 years later.

This '1102' class would become just the first of four 0-6-0 tank designs introduced by Johnson so that, by 1902, the number of six-coupled shunters on the Midland stood at 350. Enlarged versions were then produced including the '2441' that, rebuilt with Belpaire fireboxes and an improved cab design, became the basis for the LMSR's 3F 0-6-0 tank of 1924, known to all enthusiasts as the 'Jinty'.

All members of the '2441' classes became LMSR property and, though it may have taken 23 years, from August 1919 to October 1942, all were deemed worthy of rebuilding with G51/2 Belpaire boilers. Classified 3F, all entered BR

The 3F tanks were frequently called upon to work local and branch passenger trains. With a GWR 'Siphon C' van attached, the Severn Valley Railway's No47383 accelerates away from Bewdley with a train for Kidderminster. Withdrawn from Westhouses shed, Nottinghamshire, No47383 was bought directly from British Railways.

IN PRESERVATION

Midland Railway/LMSR 4F 0-6-0
No43924 The only survivor from among the 192 Midland-built 4Fs, No43924 is still undergoing a lengthy overhaul in the Haworth workshops of the Keighley & Worth Valley Railway.

No4027 The first of the LMSR-built 4Fs, outshopped form Derby in 1924, the National Collection's No4027 is currently being overhauled at York.

No44123 Built at Crewe in 1925, No44123 is in the early stages of restoration at Bitton, on the Avon Valley Railway.

No44422 Derby-built in 1927 and currently the sole working 4F 0-6-0, No44422 is nominally based on Staffordshire's Churnet Valley Railway but regularly visits other heritage railways.

Midland Railway/LMSR 3F 0-6-0T
No47279 A Vulcan Foundry product (1924) No47279 was first steamed on the Keighley & Worth Valley Railway in 1988.

No7298 Built by Hunslet's of Leeds in November 1924 No7298 arrived at its present home of the Llangollen Railway, in North Wales, during 1983.

No47324 The restoration of this 1926-built tank was completed on the East Lancashire Railway in April 2005.

No47327 Numerically the first of a quartet of 'Jinties' bases at the Midland Railway at Butterley, in Derbyshire, No47327 arrived there in 1970. With priority given to restoring classmate No47357, it did not steam until January 1992.

No47357 Second of the Butterley-based 3F tanks, No47357 moved there in 1975 and, when the centre's operating line opened in August 1981, hauled the first train.

No47383 October 1926 saw LMSR No16466 leave the Vulcan Foundry works to join the substantial stud of 3F tanks at Devons Road in London. Bought directly from British Railways, No47383 was moved to the Severn Valley Railway and first steamed in September 1973. It is currently on display in the SVR's Engine Hall at Highley.

No47406 During sixteen years at Barry, No47406 was reduced to little more than a boiler, wheels and frames. However, preservationists were undeterred and restoration is progressing on the Great Central Railway.

No47445 Third of the Butterley-based 'Jinties', No47445 has yet to be restored following preservation in June 1970.

No47493 Built by Vulcan Foundry, LMSR No16576 entered traffic at Devons Road in February 1928, remaining there for 26 years. Withdrawn from traffic in December 1966, the 'Jinty' spent five years at Barry before being rescued for the embryo East Somerset Railway. It hauled the first public train over the ESR in April 1980. No47493 is now the principal locomotive attraction on Kent's Spa Valley Railway.

No47564 Fourth of the Midland Railway Butterley's 'Jinties', only the wheels and frames of No47564 remain but it may become the basis of a 'new-build' project.

service in 1948, as Nos47200-59. In 1914, no fewer than 42 of the class had been based at the London depot of Kentish Town. Though this was reduced to 12 by 1920, Cricklewood shed, three-and-a-half miles to the north, now mustered 29. It retained the largest allocation until wholesale scrapping began in the late 1950s. The first retirements did not come until 1954 and the last example, No47250, remained on BR's books up to June 1965.

A straightforward choice

It is easy to see why the LMSR settled on the Midland design as its standard, all-purpose shunting engine. It was proven, simple in construction and straightforward to maintain and operate. Few modifications were deemed necessary and the non-superheated Belpaire boiler was retained, with an increase of one inch in cylinder diameter. The smokebox was lengthened and the top half of the coal bunker extended, enlarging capacity from 2 tons 2 cwt to 2 tons 5 cwt.

The most prominent feature of the 3F tank, however, was its large steam dome. This housed a vertical regulator valve and incorporated two pilot slots that opened in advance of the two main ports, so reducing pressure on the main valve. Vertical pipes within the dome supplied steam to the injectors, blower valve, vacuum ejectors, steam brake and sanding gear.

From a driver's viewpoint the boiler of the 3F tank steamed as well as that of any larger locomotive and they were comfortable engines – important during a long stint of shunting. The driver had a tip-up wooden seat with ample leg room and the consensus seems to be that the 3F tank was a pleasure to drive and fire. Additional floor space was gained from having the sidetanks jutting out well beyond the top half of the cab – useful armrests when looking along the train on empty-stock manoeuvres. Most of all, however, crews appreciated the smart response of the controls, especially during complex engine movements.

Under Henry Fowler, who became Chief Mechanical Engineer of the LMSR in 1925, the total of 3F tanks was increased to 422, with orders shared between five private builders. Initially 222 engines were based on the LMSR's Western Division, and 133 at Midland Division depots. Of the remainder, 40 went to the Northern Division and 20 were assigned to the Central area,

In 1935, 16 were on the books of Camden shed in London but, to the east, the ex-North London depot at Devons Road, Bow, was home to a remarkable 61 examples. Crewe South was next with 26, some of which gained a measure of celebrity as Crewe Works pilots. When just a few weeks old, No16675 (BR No47592) was sent to Crewe Works and, remarkably, remained based there for 38 years until March 1966.

It took another six-coupled design to displace the 'Jinties', BR's ubiquitous 350 horsepower diesel shunter, later Class 08. Type 1 and 2 diesels then took over their local freight workings but, despite this, the first withdrawal – apart from engines lost in wartime France – came as late as 1959 with No47331. However, by 1964, half the class had been scrapped and 1966 saw no fewer than 76 go to the breakers. The final five clung on into 1967, with the last on BR's books being No47629. Surprisingly, just one example, No47445, was bought for industrial use.

IN DETAIL

Class	4F 0-6-0	3F
Built:	1911-41; Crewe, Derby, Horwich, St Rollox Works; Andrew Barclay. Kilmarnock; Armstrong Whitworth, Scotswood-on-Tyne; North British Locomotive Company, Glasgow; Kerr Stuart, Stoke-on-Trent	1924-30; Beardmore & Co, Glasgow; W.G. Bagnall & Co, Stafford; Hunslet Engine Company, Leeds; North British Locomotive Co, Glasgow; Vulcan Foundry, Newton-le-Willows, Lancashire; Horwich Works
Designer:	Henry Fowler	Henry Fowler
Number built:	772	422
Purpose:	General goods	Shunting, empty stock, pickup goods
Wheel arrangement:	0-6-0	0-6-0T
Cylinders (x2):	20 in diamater x 26 in stroke	18 in diameter x 26 in stroke
Motion:	Stephenson link	Stephenson link
Valves:	8 in diameter piston valves	Slide valves
Wheels: Coupled:	5 ft 3 in	4 ft 7 in diameter
Tender:	4 ft 3 in	-
Boiler diagram:	G7S	G51/2
Boiler: Max. diameter:	4 ft 8 in	4 ft 2 in
Pressure:	175 lb/psi	160 lb/psi
Heating surface:	1,410 or 1,470 sq ft	1,064 sq ft/1,171 sq ft
Firebox:	123 sq ft	97 sq ft
Tubes and Flues:	1,034 sq ft	967 sq ft/1,074 sq ft
Superheater:	253 sq ft or 313 sq ft	-
Grate area:	21.1 sq ft	16 sq ft
Tractive effort:	24,555 lb/psi (@ 85% boiler pressure)	18,400/ 20,835 lb (@ 85% boiler pressure; variations according to boiler type.)
Engine wheelbase:	16 ft 6 in	16 ft 6in
Total wheelbase:	38 ft 9.25 in	-
Engine weight:	48 tons 15 cwt	49 tons 10 cwt ¶
Coal capacity:	4 tons	2 tons 5 cwt
Water capacity:	3,500 gallons	1,200 gallons
Max. axleloading:	18 tons 0 cwt	17 tons 14 cwt
BR power class:	4F	3F

¶ *Some locomotives weighed 50 tons 10 cwt.*

London's Extension Leads

Sporting their rich green-and-maroon livery, John Robinson's 'Director' 4-4-0s were among the most handsome engines, with a performance to match.

The man often described as an artist among locomotive engineers – John Robinson – produced two unqualified masterpieces: the 8K 2-8-0 of 1911, and the 11E/11F 'Director' class 4-4-0s of 1913/1919. Robinson's first class of 4-4-0s, the 11B, appeared in 1901, just a year after he had joined the Great Central Railway as Locomotive Superintendent. He followed this with other types of express passenger engine, all intended for the Manchester-Sheffield-Marylebone service inaugurated with the opening of GCR's 'London Extension' in March 1899. The most celebrated of the newcomers were the Atlantics of 1903; the most problematic his designs for 4-6-0s.

Nevertheless, having graduated to six-coupled engines, to revert to a four-coupled format might seem a backward step. The tried-and-trusted 4-4-0, however, supplied the basis for a surprisingly modern and efficient machine, one that – by some margin – would outlive all other GCR express classes.

The 'London Extension' was a well-engineered stretch of railway. Nothing less could fulfil the dream of the Great Central's Sir Edward Watkin. Undaunted by the challenge of tunnelling beneath the English Channel, he saw it as the first stage of a route that would link the cities of northern England with Continental Europe. That would take a further ninety years, and Great Central trains came no nearer to France than the London terminus at Marylebone.

Robinson took up his post with the Great Central on 1 July 1900, succeeding Harry Pollitt whose 4-4-0 designs had been the mainstay of express passenger services over the 'London Extension'. In general, though, Pollitt had bequeathed Robinson a troubled legacy. The works at Gorton urgently needed investment in new plant and machinery, something the GCR board was reluctant to sanction. The consequence was that, at one time, no fewer than 322 engines out of a fleet of 965 were either under or awaiting repair.

Chairman's privilege

The first of the 'Directors', No429, was outshopped by the Great Central's Gorton works in 1913 and initiated the process of naming the 4-4-0s after GCR board members. No429 became *Sir Alexander Henderson* (it almost goes without saying that Henderson was the company chairman!). A further nine engines followed that year with all but one but based to Neasden shed in north-west London. The exception was No438 *Worsley-Taylor* which remained at Gorton (there

was a locomotive depot close by the works) for almost a year before joining its classmates. Their impact was immediate – and wide: an article in the August 1916 edition of the eminent American technical journal, *Railway Mechanical Engineer,* was lavish in its praise of this 'eight-wheel English locomotive'.

The Americans were right: the 11E was a winner. It could match, or better the 4-6-0s on most trainloadings and did so using significantly less fuel. The class came to dominate the Manchester to Marylebone expresses, with particularly impressive performances over the stretch between Leicester and London. With

Repainted in BR livery for its last weekend in service, No62660 *Butler Henderson* forms a classic 4-4-0 duo with 'Schools' No30926 *Repton* at Loughborough on 22 February 1992.

A successful revival

The GCR's General Manager, Sir Sam Fay, wanted timings on the London Extension that would compete with the Midland and L&NWR's London to Manchester schedules. That meant speed but, with trains becoming heavier, that had to be partnered with greater power. Acknowledging that existing engines were not up to the task, and despite having to deal with the broader problems of his department, within a year Robinson had his 11B 4-4-0 in traffic. When, a decade later, his 4-6-0s failed to meet expectation, Robinson looked again at the proven 11B. One innovation, of which Robinson was one of the strongest advocates, had brought a fresh lease of life to the four-coupled express engine. That was the superheater. The outcome, in the opinion of many, would be the finest inside-cylindered 4-4-0s produced in Britain, the Great Central's 11E and 11F, known to all enthusiasts as the 'Directors'.

Loadings over the Marylebone-Manchester route had levelled off and there was no longer a requirement for ever greater reserves of power. What was needed now was efficiency and reliability and the new 4-4-0 offered both. It had a superlative boiler design, with ample heating surfaces and steam capacity. While the firebox dimensions and grate area mirrored those of Robinson's 4-6-0s, a shorter boiler made for a much better steam-raising capability.

the timetable calling for 56.6 miles per hour averages here, near mile-a-minute runs on 300-ton trains became commonplace. The combination of superheated steam in large cylinders, with improved steam distribution from a first-class boiler had significantly extended – at least in Britain – both the scope and the lifespan of the 4-4-0.

With the wartime emphasis on delivering freight locomotives, the GCR built no more 4-4-0s until 1919 by which time the 11E had evolved into the 11F, or 'Improved Director'. Most of the details of the 11E were retained, but the cabs were substantially improved with double windows instead of the simpler curved sidesheets. Changes to the heating surfaces resulted in even better performances under steam.

The new engines, all of which were initially based at Neasden, could manage 70 miles per hour with ease, at times reaching 90mph. On one trip, with a load of 295 tons, No5504 *Jutland* covered the 103 miles from Leicester to Marylebone in just under 105 minutes. In doing so it touched 82 miles per hour at Stoke Mandeville and 84 at Braunston. Performances of that calibre ensured the 'Improved Directors' were not displaced from the principal expresses until newer Gresley-designed engines arrived during the late 1930s.

Scotland and the Somme

With the 'Improved Director' came a change in naming policy, a direct consequence of the war that had ended in November 1918. Although Nos506 and 507 emerged from Gorton Works in 1919 and 1920 saluting two new GCR directors, Butler Henderson and Gerard Powys-Dewhurst respectively, and a further three honoured members of the royal family, the final five proudly wore perhaps the most solemn and poignant names ever carried by British locomotives. They venerated rivers and cities of France and Belgium that had given their names to some of the bloodiest encounters: the Somme, the Marne, Mons, Ypres, and Zeebrugge. A sixth engine, Jutland, commemorated the greatest naval battle.

In December 1922, No511 *Marne* became the final locomotive built under Great Central auspices before the company was absorbed into the newly created London & North Eastern Railway. Surprisingly, though, it was not to be the last of the 'Directors'. The LNER's Chief Mechanical Engineer, Nigel Gresley, faced a little difficulty in Scotland. With the 1923 'grouping' imminent, the directors of the North British Railway halted spending on new locomotives and left the LNER to solve the resulting motive-power shortage. Gresley

Profile of *Butler Henderson* at Rothley, on today's Great Central Railway. It sports the full green-and burgundy livery of the original GCR. The cab was remarkably spacious for its time.

IN PRESERVATION

Midland Railway/LMSR 4F 0-6-0

Although its builder's plate gives a date of 1920, No506 *Butler Henderson* was completed at Gorton ahead of schedule in December 1919. It was promptly sent to Marylebone for inspection by the Great Central hierarchy, which included her namesake, a recent appointment to the board. Renumbered No5506 by the LNER, for almost twenty years it worked regularly over the 'London Extension'. However, between 1927 and 1932, *Butler Henderson* had spells on the ex-Great Northern lines and occasionally worked the 'Queen of Scots'. One run, on 1 July 1930, was particularly memorable: No5506 hauled its 290-ton train of seven Pullman cars over the 76.5 miles from King's Cross to Peterborough in 74 minutes, an average of 62 miles per hour. The maximum attained was 88.5 miles per hour. During 1938, No5506 was reallocated to Sheffield Darnall and spent two decades on duties over the ex-Manchester, Sheffield & Lincolnshire Railway metals. Renumbered 2660 by the LNER in October 1946, it subsequently became British Railways (Eastern Region) No62660 and was withdrawn from Darnall on 28 October 1960.

Saved for the British Transport Museum collection, *Butler Henderson* was cosmetically restored to its 1919 condition at its birthplace of Gorton, reappearing in GCR livery on 10 January 1961. Following the formation of the Main Line Steam Trust, the charitable

needed a quick fix that bypassed the process of designing something afresh.

Evidently an admirer of Robinson's work and, changing little more than the boiler mountings to suit the more restricted Scottish loading gauge, Gresley placed orders for a further 24 'Improved Directors'. Delivered between July and November 1924, they were dispersed among five sheds: Haymarket and St Margaret's in Edinburgh received six and five respectively, Glasgow's Eastfield became home to six, Dundee to five and Perth two.

Dignity in demise

After being reallocated from Neasden and Gorton to depots such as Annesley, Lincoln and Mexborough, by the spring of 1958 all but one of the English-based 'Improved Directors' had congregated at Darnall shed in Sheffield. The exception was No62663 *Prince Albert*, which was cared for at Staveley, in Derbyshire. Shedmasters at Darnall still had no hesitation in rostering the 4-4-0s for quite heavy cross-country trains although with each sighting they became ever more dilapidated. However, even at their begrimed worst, with flaking paintwork, there was still something imposing and dignified about the 'Directors'.

The Scottish examples had seen in the British Railways era based at either Eastfield or Haymarket but spent long periods in store. In 1957, some were transferred to Thornton Junction in Fife and reappeared on trains to Edinburgh, Glasgow and Dundee. It was a short reprieve, however, and withdrawals began in September 1958.

First of the English 'Improved Directors' to be torched was No62665 *Mons*, which was taken out of store at Staveley in May 1959 and despatched to the

organisation set up to support the resurrected Great Central Railway in Leicestershire, the NRM placed *Butler Henderson* in the Trust's care and it arrived at Loughborough on 15 March 1975. Six years later the MLST was given the go-ahead to put the 4-4-0 back in working order. Reclaimed by the NRM, *Butler Henderson* is now on display at Barrow Hill Roundhouse, Staveley, in Derbyshire. The chances of a second return to steam are slim as the locomotive requires major firebox surgery.

Ten successful years running on today's GCR, which included hauling a special train on the day of the reopening between Rothley and Leicester North, concluded on 24 February 1992. For her final few days, the 4-4-0 was repainted British Railways lined black as No62660 but was then returned to an 'exhibition finish' Great Central green-and-burgundy.

breakers. By December 1960, all but one of its ten classmates had joined *Mons* on the scrapline, with Darnall's No62666 *Zeebrugge* officially the last in traffic.

Locomotive to remember

One of Robinson's last express passenger engines for the GCR – a 9P 4-6-0 of 1917 – was selected as a memorial to the company's employees killed in World War I. The nameplate of No1165 *Valour* was inscribed: "To the memory of GCR employees who gave their lives for their country 1914-1918." On every Armistice Day up to 1938, it was customary for *Valour* – always turned out in immaculate condition – to work a special between Marylebone and Sheffield for a remembrance service. Regrettably, *Valour* went for scrap and just one of its nameplates survives, on display in the National Railway Museum.

IN DETAIL

Class	11E/11F (D10/D11)
Built:	1913-24, Gorton Works; Kitson & Co, Leeds; Armstrong Whitworth, Scotswood-on-Tyne
Designer:	John Robinson
Number built:	45
Purpose:	Express passenger
Wheel arrangement:	4-4-0
Cylinders (x2):	20 in diameter x 26 in stroke
Motion:	Stephenson link
Valves:	10 in piston valves
Wheels: Coupled:	6 ft 9 in
Leading:	3 ft 6 in
Tender:	4 ft 4 in
Boiler diagram:	GCR No5 Standard/LNER No14
Boiler: Max. diameter:	5 ft 3 in
Pressure:	180 lb/psi
Heating surface:	1,963 sq ft (11E/D10); 1,752 sq ft (11F/D11)
Firebox:	157 sq ft (11E/D10); 155 sq ft (11F/D11)
Tubes and flues:	1,502 sq ft (11E/D10); 1,388 sq ft (11F/D11)
Superheater:	304 sq ft (11E/D10); 209 sq ft (11F/D11)
Grate area:	26.6 sq ft
Tractive effort:	19,645 lb (@ 85% boiler pressure)
Engine wheelbase:	25 ft 3 in
Total wheelbase:	48 ft 8.5 in
Engine weight:	61 tons 0 cwt (11E/D10); 61 tons 3 cwt (11F/D11)
Coal capacity:	6 tons
Water capacity:	4,000 gallons
Max. axleloading:	19 tons 16 cwt (11E/D10); 19 tons 18 cwt (11F/D11)
BR power class:	3P2F

The Glory of the 'Glens'

If one locomotive type represented the 'Scottish school' of design, it was the 4-4-0. Among the most celebrated were the 'Glens' of the North British Railway. They served Scotland for five decades.

The smoke is deceptive: No 256 *Glen Douglas* had not steamed for three decades when captured at Bo'ness on 24 October 1993. It had gone there for overhaul but is now to return to Glasgow still a static exhibit in 2011.

Speedy, sturdy and flexible enough to cope with their severe gradients and sharp curves, all five principal Scottish railways put their trust in the 4-4-0 as a 'maid-of-all-work' passenger engine. First used by the Great North of Scotland Railway in 1862, by 1921 there were 826 in service north of the border. The largest stock (213) belonged to the North British Railway and, of those, William Paton Reid was responsible for 99, divided among five classes.

The largest Scottish company, serving both the east and west of the country and linking Edinburgh with the city of Carlisle and the border town of Berwick-upon-Tweed, the NBR was also the busiest. This was more by accident than design since the company's management was anything but enterprising. Ruled by its Chairman, George Wieland, a man to whom spending was anathema, the NBR's policy was to patch up even the most run-down engines to keep them working. New construction was authorised only reluctantly.

A further consequence of Wieland's (and others') penny-pinching was a rapid turn-over in locomotive superintendents. From its earliest days to the 1923 Grouping, the NBR employed nine, more than other company bar the Great Eastern. The inevitable outcome was little continuity of design but there was one exception: Matthew Holmes, who ruled for 21 years from 1882 until 1903. Illness forced Holmes' retirement in 1903 and he was replaced by William Reid.

Holmes had many qualities as an engineer but imagination and innovation were not among them. Reid was different and immediately after taking office – and inspired by David Jones' famous goods 4-6-0 for the Highland Railway – proposed a similar machine for the NBR's taxing 'Waverley Route' between Edinburgh and Carlisle. His superiors were unconvinced and Reid, too, was compelled to question the suitability of a 4-6-0 on such a twisting and turning line. Instead he settled on a 4-4-2, or Atlantic type. Notwithstanding some early concerns, and a prodigious appetite for coal, it was an outstanding design and acknowledged as a classic.

However, in common with the majority of British railways, the NBR saw the 4-4-0 as the main answer to its requirement for passenger tender engines (it deployed more than 200 between 1871 and 1921). Beginning in 1906 and drawing on the work of his predecessors, Drummond and Holmes, Reid met the need with

Hugging the northern shore of the Firth of Forth, between Culross and Kincardine, preserved 'Glen' No256 *Glen Douglas* heads a railtour along the ex-NBR line linking Dunfermline and Alloa.

a series of designs. They were larger than their forebears but retained inside frames and cylinders, a type of construction introduced into Britain by the NBR.

The era of large-boilered, four-coupled bogie express locomotives had been initiated in 1896 by John Mcintosh's 'Dunalastair' 4-4-0s for the Caledonian Railway. The North British had lagged behind but, in William Reid, had someone well able to close the gap. Between July and September 1909, the North British Locomotive Company (a separate concern from the North British Railway), delivered six 4-4-0s, with 6 feet 6 inches coupled wheels, to Reid's design. Numbered 895-900, they would be the first of the legendary 'Scotts', so called because they were named after characters created by Scotland's greatest novelist, Sir Walter Scott.

Enter the 'Glens'

The culmination of Reid's development of the 4-4-0 emerged from Cowlairs in September 1913 – officially the 'K' class, but destined to become revered by railway enthusiasts as the 'Glens'. Essentially, the 'Glens' were a superheated version of one of Reid's earlier designs and were built specifically to work the taxing West Highland line between Glasgow, Crianlarich, Fort William and Mallaig. Initially, only nine were ordered, but construction resumed in 1917 and continued off-and-on until September 1920, by which time the class numbered 32. They demonstrated to the NBR's board the fuel economies resulting from superheating, which was music to their ears given the ravenous appetites of the Reid Atlantics.

The first four 'Glens' were equipped with 24-element superheaters of the type patented by the Locomotive Superintendent of the Great Central Railway, John Robinson, and sold through the Superheater Company. Three further examples then came out of Cowlairs with a rival apparatus, the work of the German designer Wilhelm Schmidt. The NBR was by no means the only railway to conduct such a comparison and, as generally elsewhere, the Robinson version won the day with the Schmidt devices being replaced, possibly as much a consequence of their Teutonic origin as anything.

The free-steaming, free-running qualities of the 'Glens' made them popular with footplatemen, while their versatility endeared them to the operating department. Though designed for passenger work, they proved equally adept at handling fast goods trains and it is a tribute to the soundness of Reid's design that, apart from inevitable reboilering, the 'Glens', like the 'Scotts', were never rebuilt under LNER ownership (the North British became part of the LNER at the 1923 grouping). They were handicapped, however, by being limited to 190-ton loads over the West Highland that required regular double-heading. Curiously, the tightwads of the NBR tolerated the practice, which was not eliminated until Gresley's K4 class Moguls arrived in the 1930s.

Although employed throughout the NBR system, the largest contingent of 'Glens' was based at Eastfield for West Highland duties. Twenty-four started their working lives there with a handful out-stationed at Fort William and Mallaig. At the 1923 grouping, nineteen remained on Eastfield's books with eight at St Margarets (Edinburgh), four at Thornton Junction (Fife) and a solitary example at the Dundee depot.

Doubtless for economy, North British custom was to paint locomotive names on the wheel splashers rather than attach plates. The Cowlairs worksplate, indicating a build date of 1913, is bolted into place below.

Half the class remained Eastfield-based up to nationalisation in 1948 with the rest divided between St Margaret's and Thornton. During 1953, British Railways' Scottish Region transferred eight 'Glens' to the ex-Great North of Scotland Railway territory to replace life-expired GNoSR 4-4-0s. This was about as far as they ventured away from NBR metals although there was at least one sighting south of Berwick. On New Year's Day 1940, bleary-eyed locospotters at York were treated to the remarkable and unexplained appearance of No2495 *Glen Luss*.

Nationalised service

The LNER made few modifications to the class, although in the mid-1930s all the Reid-designed 4-4-0s exchanged their dual-fitted Westinghouse brakes for Gresham & Craven steam brakes. Repainted in the LNER's passenger livery of lined apple-green (although swapping this for lined black during World War II), all 99 Reid 4-4-0s came through the conflict unscathed. Increasingly, however, they began to lose work to the LNER's new mixed traffic design, Edward Thompson's B1 4-6-0.

Withdrawals of the 'Glens' had begun in 1946 but only two of the 32-strong class were scrapped by the LNER (Nos2486 and 2491). The rest entered British Railways stock as Nos62467-85/87-90/92-98 (although several never lasted long enough to carry their BR numbers). Three more of the class had been despatched by 1950 but the remaining 27 survived until September 1958. By this time the 'Glens' were mainly to be found at Hawick, Kittybrewster (near Aberdeen) and Keith and invariably employed on goods traffic.

Along with No62484 *Glen Lyon*, No62496 *Glen Loy* became the last of the 'Glens' to be retired, from Eastfield in November 1961. After ten months in storage at Bo'ness, *Glen Loy* was cut up by Connell's of Calder in September 1962. Thankfully, three years earlier, following withdrawal from Keith shed, No62469 *Glen Douglas* had been set aside for preservation and was proudly returned to North British condition, with its distinctive lined olive-green livery, at its birthplace of Cowlairs Works.

IN PRESERVATION

In August 1959 the sole survivor from 99 Reid-designed North British 4-4-0s, No256 *Glen Douglas*, along with three other famous Scottish veterans, was returned to running order to work specials. She joined Caledonian 'Single' No123, the Highland Railway 'Jones Goods' 4-6-0 No103 and Great North of Scotland Railway 4-4-0 No49 *Gordon Highlander* in a quartet that undertook railtours throughout Scotland. Although officially withdrawn in December 1962, *Glen Douglas* remained available for specials until 1965 when all four engines were installed at the Glasgow Museum of Transport. She made her last outing on 28 August that year, hauling the Railway Correspondence and Travel Society's 'Fife Coast Railtour'.

However, while her partners have been museum pieces for the past 50 years, in 1992 *Glen Douglas* was taken to the Bo'ness & Kinneil Railway on the southern shore of the Firth of Forth. Here the locomotive was inspected with the hope that she could be steamed to mark the centenary of the West Highland line in 1994. Sadly, an overhaul never came about and *Glen Douglas* remains in the care of the Scottish Railway Preservation Society at Bo'ness. She should return to Glasgow in 2011 to take up a place in the new Museum of Transport.

IN DETAIL

Class:	'K' (D34)
Built:	1913-20, Cowlairs Works, Glasgow
Designer:	William Paton Reid
Number built:	32
Purpose:	Express passenger
Wheel arrangement:	4-4-0
Cylinders (x2):	20 in x 26 in (diameter x stroke)
Motion:	Stephenson link
Valves:	10 in piston valves
Wheels: Coupled:	6 ft 0 in
Leading:	3 ft 6 in
Tender:	4 ft 0 in
Boiler: Max. diameter:	5 ft 0 in
Pressure:	165 lb/psi
Heating surface:	1,346.06 sq ft
Firebox:	139.7 sq ft
Tubes and flues:	1,153.14 sq ft
Superheater:	192.92 sq ft
Grate area:	21.13 sq ft
Tractive effort:	20,260 lb* (@ 85% boiler pressure)
Engine wheelbase:	23 ft 7 in
Total wheelbase:	46 ft 8.5 in
Engine weight:	57 tons 4 cwt
Coal capacity:	7 tons
Water capacity:	4,235 gallons
Max. axleloading:	19 tons 2 cwt
BR power class:	3P

Some sources quote a tractive effort of 22,100 lb.

A Horse for a Course

Midland Railway /
Somerset & Dorset
Joint Railway

**Henry Fowler/
James Clayton**

7F 2-8-0 (1914/1925)

The 'course' was the Somerset & Dorset Joint Railway, whose route between Bath and Bournemouth crossed the Mendip Hills. The 'horse' was a rugged 2-8-0 that took those hills in its stride. Instructed to devise something single-handedly capable of taking heavy mineral trains over these stiff gradients, the Midland's design team – led by the gifted James Clayton – broke the mould to produce one of its finest locomotives.

Evening sunlight catches 7F 2-8-0 No88 as it rumbles over the level crossing at Blue Anchor with the 5.30pm Minehead–Bishops Lydeard service on 24 Match 2007. Owned by the Somerset & Dorset Railway Trust, No88 returned to service on the West Somerset Railway in 2005.

Its finances in poor shape, in 1876 the Somerset & Dorset Railway had agreed to joint administration by the Midland and London & South Western Railways. Given its role in linking the Midlands with south coast ports, both companies wanted to keep the S&D in business. The joint leasing agreement placed the L&SWR in charge of the permanent way and gave the Midland responsibility for locomotives and rolling stock. Unfortunately nothing in its motive-power fleet suited the line's long, and often severe gradients, especially when it came to goods and mineral traffic.

It now seems improbable but Somerset once boasted a large coalfield. Centred on Radstock, mining began in the mid-1600s but it took until the 1870s for rail links to be established. In July 1874 the Somerset & Dorset extended its route from Poole to Evercreech as far as Bath. Here it established a connection with the Midland Railway, bringing the North Somerset coalfield to within fifteen miles of a potentially lucrative rail link with Bristol, Gloucester, Birmingham and beyond. By the turn of the century, Somerset's collieries were generating one-and-a-quarter million tons of coal.

The best the Midland could use to carry this coal were medium-power 0-6-0s. Loads were restricted and invariably required either double-heading or banking assistance from a second engine. This added appreciably to operating costs and did nothing for the S&D's fragile finances. At root lay the Midland's 'small engine' policy' that entrusted almost all its goods traffic to 0-6-0s.

The Locomotive Superintendent of the Somerset & Dorset Joint Railway (as the combined enterprise became titled), M.H. Ryan, had long argued for more powerful locomotives. In 1907, two designs for 0-8-0s were submitted but rejected on weight grounds. It took until 1914 for his wish to be granted and for the Midland to produce a powerful eight-coupled machine tailored to the demands of the S&D – the 7F 2-8-0. With the solitary exceptions of the ten-coupled Lickey banker and an experimental 2-6-2, it would be the largest locomotive ever built by the Midland. It could – and should – have been the precursor of a new generation of Midland freight engines, equivalent to the eight-coupled designs of the Great Central, Great Northern and Great Western. Sadly, that was not to be: the 7F pointedly remained a horse for its course.

Local difficulties

For the most part, the tracks of the Somerset & Dorset proved robust enough for the 7F 2-8-0s. The weight limit of every bridge on the line had been checked before the engines' maximum axleweight was decided. Two minor ones, however, were overlooked but – embarrassingly – they were sited on the line leading into Bath Green Park locomotive depot! Strengthening was needed before the 7Fs could be stabled there. While they were denied access to Bath depot, it was decided to service the 7Fs at Radstock. Again, there were complications: the engines' chimney cap, dome and cab roof ventilator fouled the shed roof and had to be altered to fit.

Additionally, the engines were too long for the S&D's turntables and required to do a great deal of tender-first running until the installation of a longer turntable at Bath in 1934. Briefly, tender cabs were fitted to make this more agreeable but proved so draughty that crews preferred the protection offered by the traditional tarpaulin tender sheet against the Mendip weather.

Commemorating the closure of the Somerset & Dorset route 30 years earlier, in 1996 the West Somerset Railway transformed itself into the S&D for a weekend. 7F No53808 enters Evercreech Junction (Williton) with the first down service of the day, passing 4F 0-6-0 No44422 on a freight, on 9 March 1996.

Somerset & Dorset Joint Railway No85 was the sixth of the first batch of 7F 2-8-0s, emerging from Derby in August 1914. Here, in 1918 it underwent trials on the Midland main line between Toton and Brent but failed to impress. The tender cab, prominent here, had been discarded by 1925.

Clayton's chance

The Chief Mechanical Engineer of the Midland, Henry Fowler, asked his senior draughtsman at Derby, James Clayton, to come up with a design that could take heavy coal trains over the Mendips unaided. Clayton was given a more-or-less free hand and seized this rare opportunity to break with established Midland practice. The use of outside cylinders on a Derby-designed freight locomotive, for example, was unprecedented. However, Clayton did not require his colleagues to come up with anything radically innovative and most of the components were sourced from existing stock.

Boosted by a 21-element Schmidt superheater, the Type G9AS boiler used on the Midland's compound 4-4-0s was fitted and married to a Belpaire firebox and circular smokebox. Outside-admission, short-travel piston valves were operated by Walschaerts valve gear, with the cylinders inclined at an angle of 1 in 12 to avoid

fouling platform faces. By including a leading pony truck, Clayton redistributed the weight and overcame the objections that had ruled out the earlier 0-8-0 proposals. The guiding truck was also an advantage when negotiating the twists and turns of the route.

Mindful of the loads behind the locomotives as they descended steep gradients, great importance was placed on braking. There were three steam-brake cylinders on the engine and another on the tender. All the wheels, including those of the pony truck, were braked. In addition, Ferodo brake blocks with their better wearing properties (and consequently longer life) were fitted in preference to cast-iron ones. Eventually, vacuum-brake gear was fitted to all 11 7Fs, allowing them to work passenger trains.

Paired with a six-wheel, 3,500 gallon tender holding five-and-a-half tons of coal, the first of the S&DJR 2-8-0s, No80, entered traffic in March 1914. By

August, Derby had completed order 4209 with a further five examples (Nos81-85) and they quickly proved their worth. Despite an adhesion weight of only 56 tons the eight-coupled wheelbase made for a sure-footed machine and the power on offer was of a different order from the resident 0-6-0s – a tractive effort of 35,932lb compared to 24,555lb.

The success of the 2-8-0s prompted thoughts that their numbers and sphere of operations could be extended. A prime candidate was the procession of coal trains that ran day-in, day-out between the East Midlands and London. In 1918, No85 was tried on this traffic but failed to impress. Pitted against pairs of elderly London & North Western 0-8-0s and considerably less powerful Midland 0-6-0s, No88 enjoyed no greater success during 1926-27.

During the early 1930s, No9676 (the ex-S&DJR No86) was among the 7Fs that spent time on the books of Toton depot in Nottinghamshire. Again they were strangely unable to replicate their performances over the Mendip Hills. One downside was a sudden and prodigious appetite for coal – around 87lb per mile – and, as on the S&D, the engines did not respond well if fired on inferior fuel.

IN PRESERVATION

No88 (53808)

The last member of the class to receive a general overhaul, No53808 was withdrawn in March 1964 and sent for scrap to Woodham Brothers' yard at Barry, South Wales. It languished there until rescued by the Somerset & Dorset Railway Trust in 1970. It first went to the Trust's original home, Radstock on the now-closed S&D route. In 1976, No53808 was taken to the Trust's new base at Washford, on the West Somerset Railway, where it was restored to working order and entered traffic in 1987. Following its most recent overhaul, the 7F re-entered service in its original guise of S&DJR No88 and wearing the company's Prussian-blue livery.

Morning sunshine illuminates the footplate controls No88, including the double-handed regulator, as it awaits its first duty of the day at Minehead. 4P5G on the cabside indicates the Midland's first rating for the class (4 passenger, 5 goods).

Runaway train

The narrow-bore tunnels on the Somerset & Dorset route were the unpleasant side of working on this otherwise agreeable railway. Clearance with some of the larger locomotive classes – the 7Fs, for example, stood 13 feet 3 inches above rail level – was as little as one foot. When the tunnel was on a gradient, requiring the engine to work hard, conditions could be hellish and, on 20 November 1929, they proved fatal.

Combe Down tunnel, near Bath, was on a rising gradient of 1 in 100 and, moreover, was unventilated. That day, 7F 2-8-0 No89 was pounding away at the head of a 37-wagon up goods and, such was the choking atmosphere, the crew passed out. With its unconscious driver and fireman slumped on the footplate, the out-of-control locomotive and train breasted the summit of the climb and then hurtled downhill, derailing at the entrance to Bath goods yard. The driver was killed, as were two other employees, but amazingly the fireman escaped with his life. As it was relatively new, No89 was not written off but repairs amounted practically to a rebuild.

Somerset sunset

Summer weekends saw every available engine appropriated for holiday traffic over the Somerset & Dorset and their vacuum brakes allowed the 7Fs to work their share. They were permitted to take ten coaches unassisted over Masbury summit near Shepton Mallet – two more than either the British Railways Standard or LMSR Class 5MT 4-6-0s, or the Southern Railway 'West Country' Pacifics.

At speed, however, the 7Fs' lubrication left something to be desired but they came into their own on goods work, handling everything that was asked of them and averaging 22,500 miles a year. For five decades the 7F 2-8-0s remained synonymous with the Somerset & Dorset, but by the late 1950s they were being supplanted by LMSR and BR Standard types, not least the 9F 2-10-0s. Withdrawals of the 1914-built examples began with the doyen of the class, No53800, in 1959 and by 1961 only seven of the eleven remained. They were chiefly rostered on southbound freights to Evercreech Junction and Templecombe and worked northwards on similar turns to Westerleigh yard, north of Mangotsfield, and Avonmouth.

Summer 1962 saw the 7Fs' last use on express passenger services and the final 1914-built engine was retired that year. The 1925 examples survived until 1963-64, with No53807, the last in service, being withdrawn in October 1964.

Following its transfer from Southern to Western Region control, the Somerset & Dorset was effectively killed off, and the final services were withdrawn in March 1966. Rail links to the two remaining collieries were maintained using other lines, and limited extraction using road transport continued into the 1980s, but the last trainload of Somerset coal ran on 16 November 1973.

No53809

This second of the surviving 7Fs also had to be rescued from Woodhams' scrapyard. In this instance the buyer was an individual, the late Frank Beaumont. No53809 was moved to Kirk Smeaton, near Doncaster, in 1975 for its restoration to begin. Subsequently relocated to the Midland Railway Centre its restoration was completed there in time for the engine to appear at the Rainhill cavalcade of 1980, marking the 150th anniversary of the Liverpool and Manchester Railway. During the 1980s No53809 undertook a number of railtours, including a recreation of the most famous of S&D services, the 'Pines Express', only between York and Sheffield rather than Bath and Bournemouth.

During 1987 No53809 ventured close to one-time Somerset & Dorset territory, working on the L&SWR main line between Andover and Yeovil. Like its classmate, No53809 returned to traffic after overhaul in 2006 and was able to join No88 at the West Somerset Railway's gala that March – the first time two 7F 2-8-0s had been seen in action together since 1964. No53809 has since visited the North Yorkshire Moors Railway and, in autumn 2008, the Bluebell Railway.

IN DETAIL *(as built)*

Built:	Derby Works. 1914; Robert Stephenson & Hawthorn, Darlingfton, 1925
Designer:	Henry Fowlerf/James Clayton
Number built:	11
Purpose:	Heavy freight
Wheel arrangment:	2-8-0
Cylinders (x 2):	21 inches diameter x 28 inches stroke
Motion:	Walschaerts
Valves:	10 inches diameter piston valves
Wheels: Coupled:	Wheels: Coupled: 4 ft 7.5 in **
Leading:	3 ft 3.5 in **
Tender:	4 ft 3 in
Boiler diagram:	G9AS *
Boiler: Max. Diameter:	4 ft 9.125 in *
Pressure:	190 lb/psi
Heating surface:	1,618 sq ft
Firebox:	147.25 sq ft
Tubes and flues:	1,180 sq ft
Superheater:	290.75 sq ft §
Grate area:	28.4 sq ft
Tractive effort:	35,932 lb ** (@ 85% boiler pressure)
Engine wheelbase:	25 ft 9 in
Total wheelbase:	48 ft 11.25 in
Engine weight:	64 tons 15 cwt (with G9AS boiler) ¶
Coal capacity:	5tons 10 cwt
Water capacity:	3,500 gallons
Max. axleloading:	15 tons 16 cwt
BR power class:	7F

** *Subsequently increased to 4 feet 8.5 and 3 feet 4.5 inches respectively with the fitting of new wheel tyres, reducing tractive effort to 35,926 lb.*

* *The final five engines were at first fitted with the larger G9BS boiler with a diameter of 5 feet 3 inches, a tube heating area of 1,323 square feet, 148 square feet of firebox and a superheater area of 374 square feet.*

§ *Later enlarged to 360 square feet.*

¶ *68 tons 11 cwt with GB9S boiler.*

North Eastern
Railway

**Sir Vincent
Raven**

**Classes
T2, T3 (LNER
Q6, Q7) 6F/8F
0-8-0** (1913/1919)

Doing the Heavy Work

Slowly but steadily ascending from the coast to the high hills, a thousand tons of iron ore in tow, and with full regulator and rocketing exhaust, such a scene summed up the North Eastern Railway's 0-8-0s. Strong and dependable, they were at one time our most powerful heavy haulers. They went on to be among the last pre-grouping locomotives to serve Britain's railways.

North Eastern Railway territory lay between Doncaster and the Scottish border. To the west, it served the West Riding of Yorkshire and the northern Pennines. To the east flowed the four great rivers that generated so much of the company's freight business: Humber, Tees, Tyne and Wear. Industry, as well as seaborne trade, had grown up around these waterways: steel, shipbuilding and a broad range of engineering. All depended on the NER to deliver the raw materials – ore, coal, coke, limestone, oil – and take out the finished products. Iron ore had to reach blast furnaces high in the Durham fells while, in the opposite direction, vast quantities of coal went for shipment overseas or to southern England.

By the 1900s, freight accounted for more than 60 per cent of the NER's traffic and was growing. Like its counterparts serving other industrial heartlands of Lancashire, Cheshire and the Midlands, the NER had a huge fleet of six-coupled goods engines. However, its Locomotive Superintendents had not followed the

lead of, for example, the London & North Western or Lancashire & Yorkshire and introduced eight-coupled designs that generated greater power and adhesion.

That changed in August 1901 when the works at Gateshead outshopped the first of Wilson Worsdell's T class 0-8-0s, No2116. At 4 feet 7.5 inches diameter the wheels were typical for heavy-freight locomotives but the cylinders, at 20 inches diameter with a 26 inches stroke, were large.

Ten T class 0-8-0s emerged during 1901 and quickly proved their worth, handling 1,200 to 1,300 ton coal trains from Pelaw Colliery to Tyne Dock, near South Shields, and returning, undaunted by the 1 in 47 climb from the quayside, with up to 60 empties. During 1902, Worsdell ordered ten more 0-8-0s, classified T1. That summer both classes were put to work on the demanding trans-Pennine route over Stainmore summit, which linked Darlington with Tebay, on the LNWR's west coast line. Again, performances were impressive: trainloads of 40 loaded coke wagons and two brake vans were handled unassisted.

With a good head of steam, Q7 No901 heads past Esk Valley with a local service for Goathland on 7 October 1990. The Darlington-built (1919) 0-8-0 was making its North Yorkshire Moors Railway debut after overhaul by volunteers from the North Eastern Locomotive Preservation Group.

Under his successor, Vincent Raven, development of the Worsdell eight-coupled design continued and, in February 1913, the superheated, piston-valved T2 appeared (piston valves were now preferred over slide valves, especially for superheated engines). The prototype, No1247, sported a bigger boiler and the frames were lengthened by six inches to accommodate an extended firebox. Several superheater designs were tried but, by the time of grouping in 1923, all of the class had received the German Schmidt-type, with the original working pressure of 160 lb/psi raised to 180 lb/psi.

Since its principal role was to operate loose-coupled mineral and goods trains, the T2 had no train-braking system, just a single brake cylinder that linked the brakes on both engine and tender. If this failed, the crew was in trouble, and there were mishaps, mostly down to the failure of the metal link. The NER nevertheless persisted with the system. Braking aside, the T2 was a success. Here was an engine that could be driven all-out: full regulator and full forward gear, and developing 1,000 horsepower at the drawbar, for seemingly endless periods (albeit at slow, mineral-train speeds). The output was nearly two-and-a-half times greater than the best of the NER's 0-6-0s, the Worsdell P3.

Current comparison

In 1915 the NER completed the electrification of the arduous Newport–Shildon line. The opportunity was taken to compare the T2s with the new Bo-Bo electric locomotives, which had a nominal tractive effort of 28,000 lb. With loads of up to 700 tons the 0-8-0s held their own against the newcomers. Clearly there was no need to alter the design and no changes were made until 1938 when the boiler design was updated. This would be the only modification that either the LNER or British Railways felt these engines required. All 120 T2s (now classified Q6) entered BR stock and continued to serve the North Eastern Region for a further two decades. After World War II they began to venture out of NER territory on freights to Edinburgh, Peterborough and even as far as Woodford Halse in Oxfordshire. One Q6, No63372, was withdrawn following an accident in 1960 and another, N63457, was cut up in 1961. However, many of the remaining 118 served for several more years, withdrawals coming between 1963 and 1967.

The T2 (Q6) had shown itself more than capable of meeting the NER's expectations of a mineral engine so the decision to build a series of more powerful 3-cylinder machines was curious, even allowing for Chief Mechanical Engineer, Vincent Raven's, fondness for the arrangement. He contended that the smooth starting torque achievable with three cylinders would be ideally suited to the NER's heavy, slow-speed hauls of coal, ore and limestone. Additionally, three cylinder engines were less prone to wheelslip. Raven was still seconded to the military at the time and most likely supplied an outline brief to the Assistant Chief Mechanical Engineer, A.C. Stamer, who undertook the detail work.

The newcomer – designed to work 1,400 ton loads unassisted on gradients of 1 in 200 – would be considerably stronger than its predecessor. The cylinders required three castings: one each for the outside cylinders and a central block

Undertaking a typical duty for the class, T2 (LNER Q6) 8F 0-8-0 No63344 threads the junctions at Reilly Mill, south of Durham, with a rake of coal empties. All 120 of the class entered British Railways service and 17 lasted into 1967, based at Sunderland, Tyne Dock and West Hartlepool.

containing the inside cylinder and a common steam chest. Each piston valve was operated by a set of valve gear positioned between the frames, with all three cylinders driving on to the second axle. Though sharing the same diameter – 5 feet 6 inches – of the T2, at 16 feet 8.25 inches the boiler of the newcomer was considerably longer (12.625 inches to be exact). The price that enginemen had to pay for this was a very cramped cab.

Limited edition

An order for just five engines, classified T3, was placed on 15 May 1918. Evidently, the NER's traffic managers thought the need for such locomotives (with a tractive effort of 36,963 lb they were the most powerful freight engines in Britain) was limited. Moreover, there was a practical disadvantage, one that Gresley would encounter with his P1 2-8-2s for the LNER. The locomotives might be able to handle very long trains but many sidings and passing loops were too short to accommodate them. Size and weight were additional factors that restricted where they could work.

Harnessed to a 4,125 gallon tender, the first of the T3s, No901, was outshopped from Darlington in November 1919. A month later, the NER organised a test train over the Newcastle to Carlisle line. The make-up consisted of 60 loaded coal wagons, a brake van and the company's dynamometer car, making a total of 1,402 tons. No901 handled it with ease, generating both high power and steady acceleration. There were no problems starting on a 1 in 298 grade and, on the return, with a reduced load of 787 tons, the 0-8-0 was untroubled by gradients as severe as 1 in 107.

On another trial run, this time in Scotland, the third of the class, No903 took 755 tons up the 1 in 75 of Glenfarg bank between Perth and Edinburgh with full regulator and full forward gear. Such performances led the NER to allow the T3s loads twenty per cent greater than the maximum allowed earlier 0-8-0s.

Despite such prowess, no further T3s were built by the North Eastern Railway, probably to the relief of footplate crews who disliked having to lubricate and maintain the centre cylinder and valve gear, or 'middle engine' as they called it. Instead, the enlargement of the class came under London & North Eastern Railway auspices. Its Locomotive Committee authorised an additional ten T3s – Q7s in the LNER classification – on 4 October 1923 and these emerged from Darlington between March and May the following year.

At the same time the T3s began the duty that they will always be most associated with, the Tyne Dock to Consett iron-ore traffic. One of the toughest jobs on Britain's railways, this involved lifting 700 tons to the steelworks 1,000 feet above sea level. On the steepest sections, as severe as 1 in 35 and 1 in 42, one 0-8-0 pulled while another pushed.

IN PRESERVATION

No2238 (LNER No3395/BR No63395)

Class T2 0-8-0 No2238 was completed at Darlington on 3 November 1918, one of eight built that year. It was sent to Gateshead for running in and then allocated to Blaydon shed on Tyneside, remaining there for 25 years. During September 1965, No63395 became the final Q6 to be overhauled at Darlington and, together with Hartlepool's No63387, was the last of its class in service. Withdrawn on 9 September 1967, the engine was stored for several months at Tyne Dock before, on 1 April 1968, she became the property of the North Eastern Locomotive Preservation Group (NELPG). The Q6 came to its new home of the North Yorkshire Moors Railway on 25 June 1970, travelling from Thornaby to Grosmont under its own steam. Having covered an impressive 11,368 miles in NYMR service, in 1982 No2238 was withdrawn for overhaul. NELPG's other commitments meant that it would be eighteen years before work started and the most comprehensive refit undertaken by its volunteers was completed in 2008.

No901 (LNER No3460/BR No63460)

First based at Blaydon, in 1923 the prototype T3 (Q7) No901 was transferred to Hull (Dairycoates) and spent several years chiefly on coal traffic between South Yorkshire and Humberside. By 1929, it was back in the north-east, working out of Haverton Hill, on Teesside, then Stockton, West Hartlepool and Darlington before joining its classmates at Tyne Dock during World War II. Withdrawn on 3 December 1962 as BR No63460, No901 had been earmarked for preservation as part of the National Collection and went into storage at various locations before coming to York in 1978. In 1979 No901 went to the North Yorkshire Moors Railway in the care of NELPG, and after restoration from 1982 it entered traffic on the NYMR in 1990. Withdrawn in 1999 and stored at Grosmont it was reclaimed by the NRM in June 2004, to go on display at its new Locomotion museum at Shildon, County Durham.

By 1943 all fifteen 0-8-0s had congregated at Tyne Dock and were almost exclusively employed on ore trains. It was for these that, in 1951, new bogie hopper wagons of 56 tons capacity were delivered to the North Eastern Region. They had air-operated doors to more efficiently discharge their loads and five 0-8-0s were equipped with Westinghouse pumps to operate them. They were the mainstay of this duty until usurped by BR Standard 9F 2-10-0s in the late 1950s.

There was now little work for the Q7s. The NER had a substantial quota of 9Fs and an increasing number of English Electric Type 3s (Class 37), one of the more competent of early diesel designs. Being a class of just 15 was an added disadvantage and all were retired in November and December 1962.

IN DETAIL *(as built)*

Class	T2 (Q6) *	T3 (Q7) ¶
Built:	Darlington Works; Armstrong Whitworth,	Darlington Works Scotswood-on-Tyne (50)
Designer:	Sir Vincent Raven	
Number built:	120	15
Purpose:	Heavy mineral haulage	
Wheel arrangement:	0-8-0	0-8-0
Cylinders (x 2*/3¶):	20 in x 26 in * (Diameter x Stroke)	18.5 in x 26 in ¶
Motion:	Stephenson link	Stephenson link
Valves:	8.75 in piston valves	8.25 in piston valves
Wheels: Coupled:	4 ft 7.5 in	4 ft 7.25 in
Tender:	3 ft 8.25 in	3 ft 8.25 in
Boiler diagram	LNER No50 †	LNER No49
Boiler: Max. diameter:	5 ft 6 in	5 ft 6 in
Pressure:	180 lb/psi §	180 lb/psi
Heating surface:	1,730 sq ft	2,221 sq ft
Firebox:	140 sq ft	166 sq ft
Tubes and flues:	1,229 sq ft	1,663 sq ft
Superheater:	361 sq ft	392 sq ft
Grate area:	23 sq ft	27 sq ft
Tractive effort:	28,800 lb (@ 85% boiler pressure)	36,963 lb
Engine wheelbase:	17 ft 2 in	18 ft 6 in
Total wheelbase:	42 ft 7.75 in	44 ft 3.875 in
Engine weight:	65 tons 18 cwt	71 tons 12 cwt
Coal capacity:	5 tons 10 cwt	5 tons 10 cwt
Water capacity:	4,125 gallons	4,125 gallons
Max. axleloading:	17 tons 12 cwt	19 tons 0 cwt
BR power class:	6F	8F

† Diagram 50A from 1938 after changes to boiler design.
§ Originally 160 lb/psi.

They were Just Capital

Both the Great Eastern and Great Northern Railways conveyed commuters from north-east and east London, Hertfordshire and Essex to work in the capital. Both produced tank engines perfectly tailored to the task.

Great Eastern
Railway/Great
Northern Railway
London & North
Eastern Railway

**Alfred Hill/Sir
Nigel Gresley**

**L77 (N7)/N2
classes**

0-6-2T (1914/1920)

The Great Eastern Railway's suburban service was the most intensive in Britain. On an average weekday there were over 1,200 movements into and out of its London terminus of Liverpool Street, which was ideally situated for the growing numbers of city office workers. By 1919, the GER was handling 107.5 million journeys annually. The operation cried out for electrification but an estimate of £3 million for the Enfield line alone persuaded the GER to retain steam traction and improve where it could. A relatively modest £80,000 was spent on updating track and signalling and this, in tandem with operational improvements, allowed peak-hour train frequency from Liverpool Street's west-side platforms to be increased by 75 per cent. These enhanced services on commuter lines to Chingford, Enfield and Palace Gates were hailed by the *Railway Gazette* as 'the last word in steam-operated suburban train services'hinnor.

The extraordinary thing was that, for decades, these services were operated by a fleet of small, modestly powered locomotives. As loadings continued to increase, however, it became clear to the GER's Locomotive Superintendent, Alfred Hill, that something more powerful was needed. James Holden had schemed an 0-6-2 tank engine in 1907 and it is likely that Hill, who was Works Manager at Stratford at the time, took this as his starting point. Hill opted for small-diameter coupled wheels: at 4 feet 10 inches they were six inches smaller than those of the existing 2-4-2 tanks.

In contrast, the boiler, was large – 4 feet 9 inches in diameter – and fitted with a Belpaire firebox and, in a departure for the Great Eastern, where Stephenson motion was standard, inside Walschaerts valve gear was employed with piston valves. One standard GER fitting to be incorporated was the Westinghouse compressed-air brake. This had always been vital to the efficiency of its suburban operations, with the requirement for rapid acceleration away from the many, closely spaced station stops (fourteen in just 10.75 miles on the Enfield Town run).

Small beginnings

Hill had two prototypes for his 0-6-2 tank, Nos1000 and 1001, built at Stratford during December 1914 and February 1915 respectively. For comparison, No1000 was fitted with a saturated (i.e. non-superheated) boiler while that of No1001 contained a 12-element superheater, the first Great Eastern locomotive to receive such a device. Both engines proved ideal for their intended role but further construction was deferred until after the war, then entering its second year. It was not until June 1921 that the class was enlarged and then only with ten non-superheated examples, Nos1002-11. By the Grouping in January 1923, when the Great Eastern became part of the LNER, there were still only 12 N7s in traffic.

Although a further batch of ten, this time with 18-element superheaters, was outshopped from Stratford between December 1923 and March 1924, the numbers were insufficient to displace the veteran 0-6-0 and 0-4-4 tanks that continued to be the mainstay

Visiting one-time GWR territory of the Chinnor & Prince's Risborough Railway, N2 0-6-2T No69523 starts away from a manual crossing stop near the junction with the Thame branch. King's Cross (indicated by the 34A smokebox shedplate) was for a time home to no fewer than 60 of this class. No69523 is now the sole survivor.

of suburban services. The 1923-24 engines, Nos990E to 999E, were notable for not only marking the end of engine building at Stratford but for being the last steam locomotives built for any main-line railway in London.

The 'stop-start' building programme for the 0-6-2 tanks was now about to change dramatically. The LNER's Chief Mechanical Engineer, Nigel Gresley, evidently appreciated the qualities of the design and placed orders for a further 112 N7s, as the L77 had been reclassified by the LNER. Superheaters were now fitted as standard, and round-top fireboxes, as opposed to the Belpaire variety, began to be introduced. Earlier examples were equipped with superheaters as reboilering fell due, a process that took until 1931. By now the class had earned 'Group Standard' status and – in typical LNER fashion – Gresley's subsequent developments of Alfred Hill's original required four sub-classes. Construction of the N7 concluded with Doncaster-built No2631 on New Year's Eve 1928 – 14 years to the day since the first N7 had left Stratford.

Out of London
The N7s proved the ideal inner-suburban tank locomotive, able to maintain timings on the Enfield and Chingford runs that were not far off those of today's electric multiple units. Given their head on longer trips out to Hertford or Bishop's Stortford, 60 miles per hour along the flatland of the Lea Valley with 250 tons in tow was far from unusual.

Under Gresley, the N7s were not confined to the London area, or to Great Eastern territory. Nevertheless, from 1940 until just after nationalisation in 1948, 126 of the 134 N7s were based either at Stratford or one of the depot's sub-sheds of Chelmsford, Enfield Town, Ilford, Southend (Victoria) or Wood Street (Walthamstow). The first 12 Great Eastern-built N7s were Stratford engines all their working lives.

In 1949 11 N7s were push-pull fitted and departed GE territory to work a new service from Marylebone to South Ruislip. Two years on, they were transferred to King's Cross for the Finsbury Park–Alexandra Palace service. East Anglian byways also saw push-pull equipped N7s and, during the 1950s, Hatfield regained some to work the ex-Great Northern branches to St Alban's and Dunstable.

Three N7s spent time at Annesley in Nottinghamshire and in 1954 four of the push-pull equipped engines were posted to the West Riding of Yorkshire. The following year, N7s arrived on the ex-London Tilbury & Southend line replacing life-expired ex-Midland 0-4-4 tanks on the Romford–Upminster–Grays–Tilbury service. A handful went to Melton Constable, at the heart of Midland & Great Northern territory in Norfolk.

Others were employed on the ex-Great Central route between London Marylebone and Aylesbury and hauled LNER services over the Metropolitan Line to Watford. Push-pull examples worked the Chesham branch prior to its take-over by London Transport. On the Liverpool Street lines, a challenger appeared in the shape of the Thompson L1 2-6-4 tank and these began to take over some of the outer-suburban services to Cheshunt, Broxbourne and Hertford.

However, the N7s retained their dominance of the Chingford and Enfield Town services right up to electrification in 1960, when 69 remained in service.

On 20 November 1960, No69685 worked the final steam-hauled suburban passenger train from Liverpool Street to Hertford East. They had capably handled the heavily loaded and tightly timed Liverpool Street west-side suburban services for more than 30 years. N7s continued to work the Stratford to North Woolwich branch but, by the winter of 1961, only 25 remained in service. The last eight, all based at Stratford and including examples from all five builders, were retired in September 1962.

Scaling the heights
As elsewhere around the capital, suburban services out of King's Cross expanded as farms and fields gave way to houses. At first Barnet, Edgware, Finchley and Highgate were the destinations, then Hatfield, Hertford and Hitchin and the

IN PRESERVATION
Great Eastern Railway/London & North Eastern Railway L77/N7 class 3MT 0-6-2T No999E/7999/9621/69621
With perfect symmetry, the working life of the only N7 tank to be preserved began and ended at Stratford. On 19 March 1924, No999E left the works there, the final locomotive to be built at the Great Eastern Railway's plant. Thirty-eight years on, across the tracks at Stratford shed and as British Railways No69621, it was one of the last eight N7s in service. The locomotive had spent most of that time based in either London or East Anglia, first at Stratford but for six months of 1925 across the capital, at Neasden, specifically to work shuttles to the British Empire Exhibition at Wembley.

The ensuing 23 years were spent back at Stratford, during which time No7999 was rebuilt as a type N7/4 with round-top firebox and short travel valves. December 1948 brought a transfer to Parkeston and, for the next eleven years, the N7 led a relatively nomadic life. Spells at Stratford alternated with periods at Colwick, near Nottingham (twice), the ex-Great Central shed at Woodford Halse and Lowestoft. Its final three years, however, were spent wholly at the Stratford depot.

Upon withdrawal No69621 was bought by Dr Fred Youell, and spent many years stored in the roundhouse at Neville Hill depot, Leeds. It then found a home at the East Anglian Railway Museum, Chappel & Wakes Colne in Essex, arriving there on 9 September 1979. A cosmetic restoration was undertaken with the engine re-emerging in GER royal-blue livery. Then, in 1981, it was decided to return the N7 to main-line condition, a task that occupied eight years. In August 1989, as BR No69621, it appeared in steam as part of the Shenfield–Southend line centenary celebrations. The next summer was spent on the Swanage Railway in Dorset where the N7 ran 3,172 miles.

During 1991, the N7 brought steam back to the Mark's Tey to Sudbury line and, the following May, took part in London Underground's 'Steam on the Met' event. During the remainder of the decade it became a popular visitor to the Nene Valley, Severn Valley, East

'new towns' of Letchworth and Welwyn Garden City. The first twelve-and-a-half miles to Potter's Bar were covered at a steady climb, which earned this area its nickname – the 'Northern Heights'. Besides services out of King's Cross, Great Northern trains served Moorgate, in the City of London. Here platform space was so restricted that, while standing at the head of trains, engines were close to fouling the first set of points. Additionally, reaching Moorgate meant using the tracks of the Metropolitan Railway, which had severe weight and clearance limits.

Over six decades, Great Northern and LNER locomotive chiefs produced solutions to scaling the 'Heights'. Archibald Sturrock and Patrick Stirling put their faith in the 0-4-4 tank. In 1906 Stirling's successor, Henry Ivatt, produced the prototype for his N1 class 0-6-2 tank. No190 had 5 feet 8 inches coupled wheels (similar to the earlier 4-4-2Ts), cylinders of 18 inches diameter and 26 inches stroke, slide valves, a four ton coal capacity and side tanks holding 1,600 gallons of water. The fuel capacity was largely determined by the need to keep the axleloading

to 18 tons to suit the Metropolitan's limit. The N1 boiler had been proven on the D1 and D2 4-4-0s, as well as four classes of 0-6-0s, and was an excellent steam producer. It helped supply the acceleration needed by any frequent-stop service and allowed the N1 to maintain fast speeds on the climb out of King's Cross.

An initial batch of ten N1s was in service by 1909 and this was increased to 56 by 1912, all but four fitted with condensing apparatus. Instead of exhausting through the chimney, this device took used steam from the cylinders and returned it to the sidetanks where, as the name implies, it condensed into water. It was an ingenious way of reducing exhaust when the locomotives were working through the tunnels to Moorgate, where the blast hitting the low roof would have had very unpleasant consequences for crew and passengers.

Ivatt's N1 ruled the 'Heights' for some 13 years but, after World War I, loadings needed something more powerful. By now, motive-power matters were entrusted to Nigel Gresley, who asked the Doncaster drawing office for some proposals.

Lancashire and North Norfolk Railways. The most memorable outing, however, came on 26 March 1991 when No69621 returned to Stratford. It was named after its designer, A.J. Hill, in a ceremony that also marked the closure of the major repair facility there. What better representative to commemorate the end of 150 years of locomotive construction and overhaul in London E15?

In 2000, the N7 returned to the North Norfolk Railway, which had agreed to fund the

necessary ten-year boiler overhaul. It returned to traffic on 10 August 2005 and, despite requiring some firebox work and the manufacture of a new big end, has since performed regularly and reliably on the railway.

Great Northern Railway/London & North Eastern Railway N2 class 0-6-2T No4744/69523

One of the 50 N2s built by North British (works number 22600), GNR No1744 entered service in February 1921 at King's Cross and remained a 'Top Shed' locomotive until May 1962 when it was briefly reallocated to New England, Peterborough. During that period she was renumbered 4744 and then, in 1948, 9523 before finally becoming British Railways No69523, the guise worn in recent years. The last months at Peterborough were spent in storage and the locomotive was withdrawn, along with all the other surviving N2s, in September 1962.

Unlike its classmates, however, No69523 escaped the torch and was bought by the Gresley Society in October 1963. On 26 February 1964, and wearing LNER No4744, the N2 moved to the Keighley & Worth Valley Railway where it gained fame as 'The Scotch Flyer' in the original film version of *The Railway Children*.

A boiler tube failure then required considerable work and an offer to undertake it came from the Main Line Steam Trust, which was reinstating part of the ex-Great Central main line between Loughborough and Rothley, in Leicestershire. No4744 moved there on 21 November 1975. Boiler repairs occupied two-and-a-half years and the N2 steamed for the first time on the GCR on 16 April 1978. For several years, it was one of the mainstays of the line, registering over 20,000 miles by 1986 – then by far the highest mileage among the GCR's engines.

A further overhaul saw the engine appear as BR No69523, with the work undertaken to main-line standards. This allowed a return to London to take part in the highly successful 'Steam on the Met' events between Harrow-on-the-Hill, Watford and Amersham. No69523 also memorably took part in a North Norfolk Railway gala with No69621, the first time in over three decades that an N2 and N7 had been seen alongside each other. No69523 was set to return to traffic on the Great Central Railway after its latest overhaul at Easter 2009.

To the limit

Gresley was a proponent of three-cylinder propulsion and this was the layout that Doncaster incorporated into designs for both a 2-6-2 and a 2-6-4 tank to supplant the N1. Both were rejected by the Civil Engineer because they would be too long for the layout at Moorgate (even the N1 tank had a mere 18 inches clearance between its leading wheels and the points). Once aware of this limitation, Gresley realised he had little option but to stay roughly with the size of the N1 while updating it wherever feasible. The outcome was a locomotive that would command the 'Northern Heights' for some forty years.

Though superficially similar to the N1, the newcomer was technically superior, chiefly through the incorporation of Gresley's twin-tube superheater, larger cylinders and the use of piston valves. The GNR Diagram 6 boiler was dimensionally identical to that of the N1 but high-pitched to provide adequate clearance for the piston valves above the cylinders. This, added to the squat boiler mountings (dictated by loading-gauge constraints over the King's Cross to Moorgate section) lent the N2, as it was classified, an imposing profile. With four tons coal capacity and 2,000 gallons in the sidetanks, the design was schemed to the maximum height – 12 feet 7.5 inches – and weight allowable over the Metropolitan lines.

By the end of 1921 60 N2s were in traffic, all based at King's Cross (known to all as 'Top Shed'). Five were subsequently transferred to Hornsey and a further five to Hatfield. By January 1922, however, the King's Cross allocation had been restored to 60, working alongside 41 Ivatt N1s. There was no question that the N2 represented a considerable advance over the latter.

The 'Met' reputation

Whatever work they may have undertaken in Scotland, West Yorkshire and elsewhere, it was in the London area, and specifically on the King's Cross 'Met Link', that the N2s gained their reputation. The 'link' – or roster – consisted of some 45 N2s each of which was entrusted, as far as was practicable, to two of the 90 footplate crews in the 'Met Link'. Allocating crews their 'own' engine engendered pride in the N2s' appearance and performance. The suburban duties were also entrusted to ten crews from Hornsey and four from Hatfield, with one diagram requiring an N2 to cover 246 miles in about twenty hours. Between leaving the shed around 5.00am and returning at 1.02am the following morning, it would have appeared at King's Cross nine times.

The capabilities of the N2s were tested as they left King's Cross and blasted through Gasworks and Copenhagen tunnels before roaring up Holloway bank, all at a ruling gradient of 1 in 107. For crews working through from Moorgate, there was the added challenge of the intermediate stop at the old platform 16 at King's Cross. This was located on a 1 in 37 gradient and a curve of seven chains radius – the notorious 'Hotel Curve' after the adjacent Great Northern Hotel. Restarting a heavy train here was a true test of skill, especially as the N2 could have difficulty starting on a gradient.

All 107 N2s entered British Railways stock and, for a further ten years, remained an essential part of the King's Cross scene. The first withdrawal came in January 1956, with No69562, and the last examples were retired in 1962 but, thanks to the efforts of the Gresley Society, one of the final seven N2/2s has survived to represent this most famous of Sir Nigel's tank locomotive designs in the preserved ranks.

IN DETAIL

Class:	L77/N7	N2
Built:	Gorton and Stratford Works; Robert Stephenson & Company, Darlington; William Beardmore & Company, Glasgow, 1914-28	Doncaster Works; Beyer, Peacock, Manchester; Hawthorn, Leslie, Newcastle-upon-Tyne; North British Locomotive Company, Glasgow; Yorkshire Engine Company, Sheffield, 1920-29
Designer:	Alfred Hill	Sir Nigel Gresley
Number built:	134	107
Purpose:	Suburban and semi-fast passenger	Suburban and semi-fast passenger
Wheel arrangement:	0-6-2T	0-6-2T
Cylinders (x 2):	18 in diameter x 24 in stroke	19 in diameter x 26 in stroke
Motion: :	Walschaerts (inside)	Stephenson link
Valves:	9 in diameter piston valves	8 in diameter piston valves
Wheels: Coupled:	4 ft 10 in	5 ft 8 in
Trailing:	3 ft 6 in	3 ft 8 in
Boiler diagram: :	LNER Diagram 30/Diagram 98/Diagram 101*	GNR No6/LNER No7
Boiler: Max. diameter:	4 ft 9 in (4 ft 8 in*)	4 ft 8 in
Pressure:	180lb/psi	170 lb/psi
Heating surface:	1,394.2 sq ft (1,072.3 sq ft*)	1,205 sq ft
Firebox:		113 sq ft (107.3 sq ft*) 118 sq ft
Tubes and flues:	1,281.2 sq ft (830.8 sq ft*)	880 sq ft
Superheater: :	134.2 sq ft (Diagram 101 boilers)	207 sq ft
Grate area:		17.7 sq ft 19 sq ft
Tractive effort:	20,512 lb (@ 85% boiler pressure)	19.945 lb (@ 85% boiler pressure)
Engine wheelbase:	16 ft 3 in	16 ft 3 in
Total wheelbase:	23 ft 0 in	23 ft 9 in
Engine weight:	61 tons 16 cwt to 64 tons 17 cwt depending on boiler and firebox type	70 tons 5 cwt ¶
Coal capacity:	3 tons 10 cwt	4 tons
Water capacity:	1,600 gallons	2,000 gallons
Max. axleloading:	16 tons 3 cwt (18 tons 19 cwt*)	19 tons 11 cwt
BR power class:	3MT	3MT

Dimensions and areas marked with asterisks (*) relate to Diagram 101 boilers.
¶ Class N2/4 weighed 72 tons 10 cwt.

The 'Arthurs' of Legend

The names were heroic and often the performances, too.
Yet the origins of the Southern's 'King Arthurs'
are almost as curious as that of the mythical monarch.

London & South
Western Railway/
Southern Railway

**Robert Urie/ Richard
Maunsell**

**N15 'King
Arthur' class 5P
4-6-0** (1918/1925)

The idea originated with John Blumenfeld Elliott, the Southern Railway's Publicity Assistant. The company's trains served four counties – Cornwall, Hampshire, Somerset and Wiltshire – with links, some tenuous, to the Arthurian legends. An apt source of names, concluded Elliot (who clearly knew his Thomas Malory and Geoffrey of Monmouth) for the Southern's premier express locomotives. His chairman, Sir Herbert Walker, suggested getting the view of the Chief Mechanical Engineer, Richard Maunsell. The response was blunt:

"Tell Sir Herbert I have no objection, but I warn you it won't make any difference to the working of the engine!"

Maunsell, one imagines, had little time to compliment Elliot on his moment of inspiration. He was preoccupied with more basic concerns, such as how to update a fleet of 2,285 locomotives with an average age of 28 and divided among no fewer than 125 classes. Maunsell had included a new fast passenger design in his proposals to update the Southern's fleet but, such was the urgency, that starting from scratch was not practicable. That urgency had been fuelled by the Chief Operating Manger, E.C. Cox, who had stipulated that expresses of 500 tons should be capable of an average start-to-stop speed of 55 miles per hour. It was not an unreasonable expectation; it was just that the Southern had no engines that were capable of meeting it.

To meet Cox's demand, Maunsell would have to improve on an existing design and his attention turned to one developed in 1918 by Robert Urie for the London & South Western Railway, the N15. It had been the success of his first 4-6-0 for the L&SWR, the mixed traffic H15 of 1914, that had spurred Urie to develop it into an out-and-out express passenger engine. The diameter of their driving wheels was increased by seven inches over that of the H15, to 6 feet 7 inches, and the bore of the cylinders enlarged to 22 inches, which was an almost unprecedented size for the time. The cylinder stroke of the H15 was retained, along with its outside Walschaerts valve gear.

The first of the new engines was built at a cost at Eastleigh Works in August 1918 and cost £6,740. Numbered 736, by the end of the year it had been joined by two classmates, Nos737 and 738. On paper, this 2-cylinder 4-6-0 design appeared sound. Well-balanced coupled wheels and substantial motion parts contributed to the N15's smooth riding but there was a downside: the hammer-blow inflicted on the track was one of the highest of any British locomotive. Wear-and-tear on the rails, though, was the least of the N15's problems. Compared with the H15, the N15 boiler was smaller, with a slight taper on the front ring. Additional modifications included reduced superheater and firebox heating areas.

It was in theory a more efficient steam-raiser and, while the wartime speed limit of 60 miles per hour remained in force, appeared adequate for the task. When restrictions were removed, however, and schedules accelerated, concerns were raised. Irrespective of the crews' efforts, steam pressure dipped alarmingly when the N15 was worked hard during journeys of any length. Added to this, there was a propensity for hot axleboxes and the occasional frame fracture, all of which

The cost of repainting raised by a group of photographers, on 4 November 1994 the last of the 'King Arthurs' made its debut as British Railways No30777 *Sir Lamiel*. The venue was the one-time home to several of the class, Stewart's Lane in Battersea, south London, then still a diesel depot. The backdrop of Hampton's Depository is familiar from the many photographs taken in the shed yard.

explains why only seven further examples were built up to the end of 1919.

Three years elapsed before more N15s were built, ten being delivered between June 1922 and March 1923 and bridging the absorption of the London & South Western into the newly created Southern Railway. The price for each engine now varied between £7,116 and £8,257, depending on the cost of materials, and the newcomers were distributed between Nine Elms, Salisbury and Exmouth Junction (Exeter) sheds.

Maunsell's quest

Before resuming production of the N15 Maunsell's priority was to discover and cure the problems in the steam circuit. During 1924, the poorest of the class, No742, underwent trials to find the source of the problem. It did not disappoint, as boiler pressure slipped to 150 lb/psi and then to just 100 lb/psi. Output fell as low as 650 horsepower. Maunsell, however, retained his faith in the soundness of Urie's design and his modifications succeeded in transforming its performance. Outside steampipes, larger steam passages and longer valve travel tackled the steaming, while a larger blastpipe and chimney, similar to that of Urie's H15, sharpened the exhaust and enhanced the draughting. At the same time the working pressure was increased to 200 lb/psi.

Together, the changes brought about the kind of benefits Maunsell had hoped for. On test, a modified engine achieved a sustained output of 1,500 horsepower at a pressure of 190 lb/psi – quite an improvement on No742's dismal showing. However, Maunsell still only had a class of 20 and the process of modifying them all would take time (five years to be exact).

Fortunately, Maunsell discovered that approval to rebuild ten of the under-whelming G14 class 4-6-0s had not been implemented: the engines were still pottering around the south and west. To keep the accountants happy he announced that they were to be reincarnated as N15s and ten G14s were brought to Eastleigh. In truth, little was re-used – chiefly the bogies and some smaller fittings – and to all intents these were new engines. They did, however, retain their 'water cart' tenders and original running numbers: Nos448-457.

On their own the improved Urie engines and the 'rebuilt' G14s were

not going to cope with the demands of the revised timetable for summer 1925, especially on the West of England line to Exeter and Plymouth. With no spare capacity in its workshops, the Southern placed an order for twenty N15s – or 'King Arthurs' – to Maunsell's modified design with the North British Locomotive Company of Glasgow. The engines were delivered in just three months and all were in service by July 1925. A follow-up order for a further ten was completed in October that year.

It was quite an achievement by North British although, as the newcomers – dubbed 'Scotchmen' or 'Scotch Arthurs' – began to develop faults, suspicions were voiced that, in its haste, NBL had cut a few corners. This was never established but some locomotives did require extensive repairs, including the fitting of new boilers.

Once the problems with the North British engines had been resolved the 'King Arthurs' settled into their role as the mainstay of the Southern's express passenger services. Only one other major modification proved necessary, and it was a British first: the adoption of smoke deflectors. The problem of drifting smoke with the Maunsell engines was chiefly a consequence of its high-pitched boiler, short chimney and soft blast, particularly when working – as intended – at short cut-offs. However, the Southern's decision to reposition signals on the ex-L&SWR main line on gantries and directly over the running lines exacerbated matters.

Maunsell experimented with various devices, from large, square German-style

IN PRESERVATION

No777/30777 *Sir Lamiel*

Delivered in June 1925, No777 *Sir Lamiel* was one of the so-called 'Scotch Arthurs' (or 'Scotchmen') built in Glasgow by the North British Locomotive Company, works number 23223. It began working out of Nine Elms shed in London and from May 1934 spent some time at Stewarts Lane, working boat trains and Kent coast expresses. It then went to Bournemouth but was mainly a Nine Elms locomotive until 1947, working out of Waterloo on the Bournemouth and Exeter lines. In January of that year, it exchanged its wartime black livery for lined malachite green. There then followed three-and-half years on the books of Eastleigh depot.

In 1951, by now renumbered British Railways No30777, the engine was transferred to the Eastern Section, mainly working out of Dover shed. The Kent Coast electrification saw *Sir Lamiel* back on the Western Section in 1959 for a final two years service, initially at Feltham and then Basingstoke. It was withdrawn from Basingstoke shed in October 1961 with a final mileage of 1,257,638.

After storage at various locations around the country, including Fratton, near Portsmouth, and Stratford in east London, in June 1978 the National Railway Museum entrusted *Sir Lamiel* to the Humberside Locomotive Preservation Group. At Hull's Dairycoates depot, the HLPG returned *Sir Lamiel* to working order. It steamed for the first time in more than twenty years on 21 February 1982 and made its main-line debut on 27 March with a railtour over the Settle and Carlisle line. No777 subsequently visited other unfamiliar territory, working between York,

deflectors to small shields placed around the chimney. When, following wind tunnel tests, the final shape was decided upon, it was progressively fitted to the 'Arthurs' between August 1927 and November 1929. It went on to become the Southern 'standard', being fitted to the S15 4-6-0s, the 'Lord Nelsons', 'Schools' and Maunsell Moguls.

Externally, the differences between the original N15s and the Maunsell engines were minimal, chiefly the substitution of the high-arched cab of the Urie design for the narrower Maunsell design, which conformed to the Southern's composite loading gauge. This allowed the N15s to work over the Eastern Section where they proved an immediate success on Kent coast expresses and the Dover boat trains. Their introduction allowed the loadings to be increased from 300 to 425 tons.

Last knights

The Arthurian 'Round Table' was completed during 1926-27 with the construction, at Eastleigh this time, of 14 N15s (Nos793-806) specifically for the Southern's Central Section, essentially the London to Brighton line. These were distinguishable by the compact six-wheel tenders that permitted the engines to be turned on the shorter turntables in this area. In subsequent years the distinctions between the Urie, Maunsell and Central Section engines disappeared as locomotives exchanged tenders.

Marking the 50th anniversary of D-Day, on a rainy 6 June 1994 No777 *Sir Lamiel* hauled shuttles between Salisbury and Southampton. Here the 'King Arthur' heads coastwards through Eastleigh, home to one of the Southern Railway's principal locomotive works.

In combining the qualities of the Urie design with his advances, Richard Maunsell had created a classic. Following an indifferent beginning, the 'King Arthurs' had evolved to become one of the great British locomotive designs. They were popular with footplate crews and gained a reputation for reliability and consistently good performances.

However, this did not stop Maunsell's successor, Oliver Bulleid, from tinkering. In 1940, No755 *The Red Knight* was fitted with Bulleid-pattern cylinders of 21-inches diameter, the French Lemaître multiple blastpipe and a wide chimney. The improvement in performance was significant but wartime constraints meant that only four further examples were similarly treated.

In a rare excursion beyond Southern territory, during World War II ten N15s were loaned to the London & North Eastern Railway and sent to its depot at Heaton, on Tyneside, for goods duties. The 1950s, however, found all the 'Arthurs' at familiar locations. They served ex-L&SWR lines from Nine Elms, Feltham, Basingstoke, Eastleigh, Bournemouth and Salisbury depots, and covered the Kent coast from three London sheds: Stewarts Lane, Hither Green and Bricklayer's Arms, along with Ashford and Dover. They had, by now, been displaced from the Brighton line by electrification and replaced on the majority of West of England services by Bulleid Pacifics.

The majority of the 74 'King Arthurs' served southern England for more than three decades. The first withdrawal was one of the Urie engines, No30754 *The Green Knight*, in January 1953. It had suffered one of the banes of the Urie design, fractured frames. Four more Urie N15s were scrapped in 1955, although simultaneously five underwent major repairs. The last of the Urie locomotives, No30738 *Sir Pellinore*, was withdrawn from Basingstoke in March 1958. Their final mileages ranged from the 1,151,285 miles of No30754 to the 1,464,032 amassed by No30745 *Tintagel*, withdrawn in February 1956 after a 37-year career. The majority of the Maunsell engines saw in the 1960s, with the last, No30770 *Sir Prianius*, retired – as the final Urie example – from Basingstoke in November 1962. Many of the Arthurian names, however, lived on as they were transferred to the Southern Region's British Railways Standard Class 5 4-6-0s.

The 'King Arthurs' were perhaps best summed up by Harold Holcroft, one of

and Carlisle line. No777 subsequently visited other unfamiliar territory, working between York, Leeds and Scarborough, along the North Wales coast and between London Marylebone and Stratford-upon-Avon. However, these outings were followed by a nostalgic return to the ex-London & South Western main line to Salisbury and Exeter.

Withdrawn with a burst superheater tube in 1987, a second overhaul was completed in 1989 and, in 1994, the engine was repainted in British Railways lined green as No30777. Among *Sir Lamiel*'s later main-line runs, one stands out: a magnificent run between Portsmouth and London on 1 April 1995, double-heading with another Maunsell engine, S15 4-6-0 No828.

For several years, *Sir Lamiel* has been in the care of the Great Central Railway where its latest overhaul, in the GCR's Loughborough workshops, saw the 'Arthur' returned to main-line order and it has worked railtours both in the north and south of England.

Starting south from York, No777 *Sir Lamiel* begins the last leg of one of the British Railways-sponsored 'Scarborough Spa Expresses' on 12 July 1983. The curved smoke deflectors were peculiarly Southern, being fitted to Maunsell's 'Lord Nelsons', 'Schools', S15s and earlier 2-6-0 classes.

Maunsell's design assistants at Waterloo:

'They did the job they were designed for in a completely competent manner; they were economical in running, rode well and were easy to maintain…one could always measure up to a job.'

A difference of opinion

The 'Arthurs' put in outstanding work on the London–Salisbury–Exeter route. On one occasion, the now-preserved No777 *Sir Lamiel* covered the 83 miles from Waterloo to Salisbury in 73 minutes, 13 minutes inside schedule. Unfortunately, driver Fred Stickley's effort earned not praise from the Locomotive Running Superintendent, but a reprimand for recklessness. As the crestfallen Stickley departed, he was escorted into the Chief Mechanical Engineer's office and congratulated on showing what an 'Arthur' could achieve. It would seem Maunsell thought the timetable compilers underestimated his engines. and attained celebrity status in the early 1930s with a remarkable run from Salisbury to Waterloo with the up 'Atlantic Coast Express'. With a load of around 345 tons, the 83 miles were covered in 72 minutes 41 seconds at an average speed of 69.2 miles per hour. Arrival in London was 13 minutes ahead of schedule. The average over the 54.4 miles from Andover to Surbiton was 80.2 miles per hour with a maximum of 90 miles per hour at Byfleet.

This performance, which was believed to represent the limit of the N15's capabilities, probably contributed to *Sir Lamiel*'s selection some 30 years later for preservation as part of the National Collection.

Naming niceties

The allocation of names was not random. The North British and Central Section engines, together with the Drummond 'rebuilds' all honoured Knights of the Round Table, with the addition of Queen Guinevere and King Arthur himself. Beginning with No736 *Excalibur*, the Urie engines recalled a mix of characters and places. There was one late change: No767 was to have been named *Sir Mordred* until his traitorous role in the legend was pointed out. The more acceptable *Sir Valence* was substituted. One anomaly was missed, however: *Elaine* (No747) and *Maid of Astolat* (No744) were one and the same lady.

IN DETAIL (as built)

Class	N15 'King Arthur'	
	Urie engines	**Maunsell engines**
Built:	1918-27	
Designer:	Robert Urie	Richard Maunsell
Number built:	74	
Purpose:	Express passenger	
Wheel arrangement:	4-6-0	
Cylinders (x2):	22 in x 28 in	20.5 in x 28 in
	(Diameter x Stroke)	
Motion:	Walschaerts	
Valves:	11 in diameter piston valves	
Wheels: Coupled:	6 ft 7 in	
Leading:	3 ft 7 in	
Tender:	3 ft 7 in¶	
Boiler: Max. diameter:	5 ft 4.75 in	5 ft 5.75 in
Pressure:	180 lb/psi	200 lb/psi
Heating surface:	2,186 sq ft	2,215 sq ft
Firebox:	162 sq ft	162 sq ft
Tubes and flues:	1,1716 sq ft	1,716 sq ft
Superheater:	308 sq ft	337 sq ft
Grate area:	30.0 sq ft	30.0 sq ft
Tractive effort:	23,900 lb	26,200 lb
	(@ 85% boiler pressure)	
Engine wheelbase:	27 ft 6 in	
Total wheelbase:	58 ft 0 in	
Engine weight:	80 tons 19 cwt	77 tons 17 cwt
Coal capacity:	5 tons	
Water capacity:	5,000 gallons ¶	
Max. axleloading:	19 tons 17 cwt	20 tons 4 cwt
BR power class:	5P	

¶ *Central Section six-wheel tenders had wheels of 4 ft 0 in diameter and held 3,500 gallons.*

The 'Goods Arthurs'

London & South
Western Railway/
Southern Railway

**Robert Urie/
Richard Maunsell**

**S15 class 6F
4-6-0** (1920/1927)

As with the 'King Arthurs', the Southern's finest freight design evolved out of an earlier failure. The S15s would become the final 4-6-0s built at Eastleigh and served southern England almost to the end of steam.

Though primarily a passenger carrier, as might be expected of a railway serving the Channel ports and Medway towns, freight traffic was not unimportant to the Southern Railway. The dilemma for Chief Mechanical Engineer, Richard Maunsell, was that investment in electrification left little for new steam locomotive construction and priority had to be given to passenger engines such as the 'King Arthur'. Maunsell's most successful freight class, the S15, was both derived from an earlier design and adapted much from the 'Arthurs'. The S15s, the last 4-6-0s to be built for the Southern, never enjoyed the glamour of the 'Arthurs' or 'Lord Nelsons' but they would outlive both and be among the last of their type to serve in southern England. Only the British Railways Standard 4-6-0s would outlast them there.

The origins of the S15 went back to 1905 when the Locomotive Superintendent of the London & South Western Railway, Dugald Drummond, constructed five 4-cylinder 4-6-0s remarkable for their huge boilers. These F13

class engines were followed by the smaller G14s of 1907 and the T14 4-6-0s, which were outshopped between 1910 and 1916. All shared a fundamental flaw: they were too lightly constructed for their size.

The failings of these locomotives would have been familiar to Drummond's Works Manager at Eastleigh, Robert Urie. When, after 1912, it became his turn to produce new 4-6-0s for the L&SWR, Urie immediately simplified matters by dispensing with middle cylinders and reverting to a 2-cylinder format.

With its two large outside cylinders, six feet diameter coupled wheels, outside Walschaerts valve gear and high running plates, Urie's H15 4-6-0 represented a significant departure for the L&SWR. Recently recruited from the North British Locomotive Company, Urie's Chief Draughtsman, Thomas Finlayson, was well versed in devising big-cylindered 4-6-0s for export. In comparison to the Drummond designs, the H15 was built like a battleship. It had generous bearing surfaces and a front end (cylinders and exhaust arrangement) that was intended

One of the Maunsell S15 4-6-0s, No30838, approaches Battledown Flyover, west of Worting Junction, with a heavy goods for Southampton on 30 May 1964. It is here that the West of England route to Salisbury and Exeter parts company with the Southampton line. Eastleigh-built No30838 lasted to become one of the final five S15s, being retired in September 1965.

to make the most of the steam generated by the large boiler. Nevertheless, like several Urie classes, the H15s were unpredictable steamers and initially only eleven were built. A restricted steam flow at the front end meant they struggled to attain speeds much above 55 miles per hour.

Undeterred, and despite it being wartime, Urie decided to press ahead with two new 4-6-0 designs. Many components – chiefly the boiler, cylinders and valve gear – were shared. The main difference was in driving-wheel diameter: 6 feet 7 inches for the express passenger locomotives, the N15s (forerunner of Maunsell's 'King Arthurs'), and 5 feet 7 inches for the freight engines. Fitted with cylinders of 21 inches diameter by 28 inches stroke and with stepped running plates and stovepipe chimneys, the latter were classified S15.

Though ordered in 1917, post-war steel shortages meant that the first of the S15s did not enter traffic until February 1920. By the end of 1921 20 were in service, Nos496-515, all built at Eastleigh.

Enter the 'Goods Arthurs'

The Southern's comparatively modest need for freight engines made it difficult for Maunsell to justify drafting an entirely new design. He recognised the S15's failings, however, and before adding to the total, undertook a wholesale revision of the front-end layout, adopting the successful features of the 'King Arthurs'. The boiler pressure was increased from 180 lb to 200 lb/psi and the cylinder diameter reduced by half-an-inch to 20.5 inches. The valve travel was lengthened and larger outside steampipes fitted along with a bigger ashpan (which would effectively improve the air flow).

Crucially, the draughting was improved and a new type of superheater, to Maunsell's design, replaced the Eastleigh model. In all respects the boiler was a straight copy of that of the 'King Arthur', one of several components interchangeable between the two classes. Thus the S15s became known as the 'Goods Arthurs', the finest freight engines to see service on the Southern Railway.

IN PRESERVATION

No499 The oldest-surviving locomotive built at Eastleigh, completed in May 1920, No499 was condemned on 5 January 1964 after running 1,241,024 miles. Sold to Woodham's for £1,040, No499 spent sixteen years there before being bought by the Urie Locomotive Society. For many years it languished at Ropley, on the Mid-Hants Railway, before being moved to a workshop in Bury. Here, preliminary work has begun on a full restoration.

No30506 Withdrawn having completed 1,227,897 miles, No30506 made its way to Barry. The Urie Locomotive Society was able to complete its purchase in March 1973. Wearing Southern lined green livery No506 returned to steam in July 1987. She was later repainted in BR black as No30506 and served the MHR well until withdrawn in 2001. The Urie Locomotive Society has since reached an agreement with the MHR for No30506's overhaul and operation on the line until 2018.

No30825 Withdrawn from Salisbury in January 1964 No30825 was despatched to Woodham's where boiler and chassis parted company. The former was acquired by the Urie Locomotive Society for No30506 (above) and the latter made its way to the North Yorkshire Moors Railway, to be used as a source of spares for the NYMR's other S15, No30841 (below). However, the situation has been reversed.

Aware that the frames of No30841 were slightly out of true, the NYMR decided to fit its freshly overhauled boiler to the frames of No30825, a move that – according to established practice – meant the 'composite' locomotive must carry the latter number. No30841 has, therefore, effectively ceased to exist! No30825 has now been passed to work over the Esk Valley line to Whitby.

No828 Returned to its birthplace and the care of the Eastleigh Railway Preservation Society, the restoration of No828 was completed in July 1993, an achievement recognised by the Association of Railway Preservation Societies' highest award. No828 undertook railtour work throughout southern England, and then spent time on the Swanage Railway. It has since moved to the Mid-Hants Railway where ERPS members have begun an overhaul.

No30830 After 13 years stored on the Bluebell Railway, in September 2000 No30830 left for eventual restoration on the North Yorkshire Moors Railway.

No841 No841 was condemned in January 1964 after covering 838,964 miles and spent eight years at Barry before being bought by the Essex Locomotive Society. In 1977 the S15 was moved to the Nene Valley Railway and, the following year, the North Yorkshire Moors Railway.

No841 worked on the NYMR until 1981 and was then withdrawn for overhaul, returning in 1986 and remaining in traffic until 1994. It has now donated its boiler and other components to the rebuilding of classmate No30825 (above).

No847 This, the last 4-6-0 built for the Southern Railway, left Eastleigh in December 1936. It was retired in January 1964 with a mileage of 931,829 and later moved to the Bluebell Railway where restoration was completed in November 1992. It is currently undergoing overhaul.

Both the Urie and Maunsell S15s spent most of their time on the Southern's Western Division, shared between Exmouth Junction (Exeter), Feltham and Salisbury depots (eventually all the Urie engines were concentrated at Feltham and, with a few exceptions, remained there until withdrawal). Four locomotives – Nos828, 829, 831 and 832 – remained at Salisbury all their working lives, from 1927 up to withdrawal in 1963-64. Outside the Western Division, five S15s were for a time allocated to Hither Green, in south-east London, while Nos833-37 were originally based at Brighton.

War and after

World War II changed the nature of the Southern's operations. Freight traffic grew substantially, especially during the build-up to D-Day in 1944. The delivery of 40 Bulleid-designed Q1s in 1942 – the last and most powerful 0-6-0s to be built in Britain – allowed some S15 duties to be reassigned. However, the Q1 did not have the braking power of the S15, curbing its use on fast goods services. The bulk of the work in the south-west remained entrusted to the 45 S15s.

After the war, the installation of a new 70-feet diameter turntable at Okehampton allowed S15s over the north Devon line and Nos844-46 joined their classmates at Exmouth Junction in the autumn of 1946 (to be followed by Nos841-43 in 1948). These engines, together with those based at Salisbury, remained the principal freight locomotives over the West of England main line during the 1950s. Until supplanted by Bulleid's 'Light Pacifics' they also shared secondary passenger services with the 'King Arthurs'.

Unsurprisingly, the older Urie engines were the first S15s to be withdrawn. All 20 were axed between November 1962 and April 1964. The first Maunsell example to be retired was Salisbury's No30826 with an accumulated mileage of 1,364,577, representing an annual average of 38,352. (The highest final mileage recorded by a S15 was the 1,411,643 miles of No30823.)

The surviving S15s continued to find some work but by the beginning of 1965 just six remained, Nos30824, 30833, 30837, 30838, 30839 and 30842, the last steam locomotives at Feltham. No30833 was retired that May but the others lasted until September. They were stored at Feltham for several months before being towed to South Wales for scrap but, in some cases, unlikely salvation.

With the ruins of Corfe Castle as a backdrop, S15 No828 heads away from Corfe Station bound for Swanage with a typically Southern mixed rake in tow on 20 August 1998. No828 has since left the Swanage Railway for overhaul on the Mid-Hants.

IN DETAIL (as built)

Class	S15	
	Urie engines	**Maunsell engines**
Built:	1920-36	
Designer:	Robert Urie	Richard Maunsell
Number built:	45	
Purpose:	Heavy freight	
Wheel arrangement:	4-6-0	
Cylinders (x2):	21 in x 28 in	20.5 in x 28 in
	(Diameter x Stroke)	
Motion:	Walschaerts	
Valves:	11 in diameter piston valves	
Wheels: Coupled:	5 ft 7 in	
Leading:	3 ft 7 in	
Tender:	3 ft 7 in	
Boiler: Max. diameter:	5 ft 5.75 in	
Pressure:	180 lb/psi	200 lb/psi
Heating surface:	2,186 sq ft	2,215 sq ft
Firebox:	162 sq ft	162 sq ft
Tubes and flues:	1,716 sq ft	1,716 sq ft
Superheater:	308 sq ft	337 sq ft
Grate area:	30 sq ft	28 sq ft
Tractive effort:	28,198 lb	29,857 lb
	(@ 85% boiler pressure)	
Engine wheelbase:	26 ft 7.5 in	
Total wheelbase:	57 ft 1.5 in¶	
Engine weight:	79 tons 16 cwt	78 tons 5 cwt §
Coal capacity:	5 tons	
Water capacity:	5,000 gallons	3,500 gallons
	(8-wheel tenders)	(6-wheel tenders)
Max. axle loading:	20 tons 1 cwt	20 tons 0 cwt
BR power class:	5F	

¶ 54 ft 0.5 in when paired with shorter wheelbase tenders.
§ Maunsell engines Nos823-837 weighed 80 tons 14 cwt.

Great Northern
Railway / London
& North Eastern
Railway

Sir Nigel Gresley

**Class A1/
A3 7P6F**

4-6-2 (1922)

What Made *Scotsman* Fly?

Like the champion racehorses from which they took their names Nigel Gresley's A1/A3 Pacifics were thoroughbreds that stayed the course. Gresley's career reached its zenith during the 1920s and 1930s with some of the finest and most famous of British locomotive designs. They, and the expresses they hauled, excited world-wide attention and initiated an era of high-speed rail travel.

Gresley A3 Pacific No60039 *Sandwich*, seen striding through Welwyn North at the head of a London–Leeds express on 29 September 1960, began its working life at Gateshead depot. Much of its career, though, was spent at Grantham and King's Cross.

Gresley had been eager to produce a high-power passenger design for some years but it was not until after World War I that loadings on the East Coast route called for such a locomotive. With increased train lengths and heavier rolling stock, loadings of 400 tons-plus had become common. Gresley foresaw a time when 600 tons would be commonplace and resolved that future GNR locomotives would be a more than a match. It was preferable, he argued, to build engines with capacity to spare rather than smaller machines that were regularly pushed to their limits. Construction costs would be higher but would be offset by savings in operating and maintenance bills. The approach became known as the 'big engine' policy.

To support his argument he could point to North America and Continental Europe where, by 1920, the 4-6-2, or 'Pacific', had become the most popular express passenger type. In Britain, however, there had been no appetite for such big engines, as the Great Western had demonstrated. Its No111 *The Great Bear* of 1908 – then the solitary British Pacific – was little more than a publicity exercise. Weight restrictions precluded it from working anywhere other than between Paddington and Bristol! The Great Western, along with other major concerns such as the London & North Western and London & South Western, settled for developing the 4-6-0 format. Gresley could have followed but had become a convert to the wide fireboxes that had proved crucial in the success of the Great Northern's 4-4-2 Atlantics, the work of his predecessor, Henry Ivatt. That dictated the use of a supporting trailing truck and a 4-6-2 arrangement.

Gresley also favoured the balancing of the reciprocating forces in a locomotive and achieved this with the 3-cylinder layout of his Pacific. All three cylinders drove on to the centre coupled axle, with Walschaerts gear driving the valves of the outside cylinders. However, given the confined internal space, a form of 'derived' or 'conjugated' gear operated the valves of the middle cylinder. To minimise the potential for this inside gear to over-ride at high speed, short- rather than long-travel valves were stipulated. It was a rare instance of Gresley taking a wrong turn. Equally, his faith in a steam pressure of only 180lb/psi was misplaced.

Unwelcome comparisons

The order for two prototype Pacifics was issued in January 1921 and the first was completed the following March. Classified A1 and wearing No1470 *Great Northern*, the engine caused quite a stir. It not only impressed with its size – enormous by British standards – but its sleek lines. Based at Doncaster shed, No1470 entered service in April and was joined by the second prototype, No1471, on 10 July. That day, an order was approved for a further ten.

The locomotives were designed for 600 ton trains and, on a test run on 3 September, No1471 *Sir Frederick Banbury* was asked to tackle such a load. It took a 20-coach train from King's Cross to Grantham, averaging 70 mph on the level and reaching 45 mph on the ascent of Stoke bank. No1471 had been the last of the Pacifics to appear under Great Northern auspices. By the time the first

Non-stop to Scotland

Gresley's assistant, Tom Spencer, persuaded his chief to reconsider the valve gear arrangement of the Pacifics and, in 1927, A1 No2555 *Centenary* was equipped with redesigned long-travel gear. On test, a significantly reduced fuel consumption of over ten pounds per mile was achieved – equivalent to a saving of over a ton on the London to Newcastle run. Long-travel gear was adopted for new construction and existing engines altered as they entered the works for repair or overhaul. Gresley also acknowledged that a higher working pressure was needed and all new locomotives received boilers pressed to 220lb/psi and larger superheaters. The LNER decided that these modifications warranted a new designation, and introduced the A3 class (also known as the 'Super Pacifics'). The original A1s received A3 boilers as theirs fell due for renewal.

The Pacifics' improved coal consumption allowed the LNER to introduce non-stop running, first – in the summer of 1927 – between London and Newcastle-upon-Tyne and, the following year, Edinburgh. The 10.00am from King's Cross – the 'Flying Scotsman' – was inaugurated on 1 May 1928, hauled, appropriately, by the eponymous Pacific, by now renumbered 4472. Corridor tenders connected to the first coach of the train permitted crew changes during the journey. At 392.75 miles this became the longest non-stop journey in the world but it was hardly the fastest, with 8 hours 3 minutes allowed for the run – an average of just 47.5 miles per hour. Doubtless the LNER would have liked to cut the time but it was still hamstrung by an agreement made 30 years earlier between the east and west coast companies. Four years had to pass before the timings could be accelerated.

No4472 hit the headlines again on 30 November 1934 when it achieved the first fully-authenticated 100 miles per hour by a steam locomotive. The following year, classmate No2750 *Papyrus* touched 108 mph on a high-speed trial between London and Newcastle, still the world record for a non-streamlined locomotive. The LNER certainly got it right when it named the majority of A1/A3 Pacifics after champion racehorses.

IN PRESERVATION

No4472/60103 *Flying Scotsman*

Constructing No1472 set the LNER back £7,944 and it was the first engine to carry the company's glorious apple-green livery. It remained unnamed until February 1924 when, during repairs at Doncaster, it was renumbered 4472 and was fitted with the now world-famous *Flying Scotsman* nameplates.

On 15 January 1963, King's Cross shed rostered *Scotsman* for the 1.15 pm London to Leeds service, which it would take as far as Doncaster. Where better to retire it from service, and with a creditable 2,076,000 miles worked? And where better for local businessman, Alan Pegler, to announce that he had bought the engine for £3,000? In 1969 Pegler took *Scotsman* on a tour of the United States. It was a financial disaster. Sir William McAlpine, of construction company fame, stepped in to save the locomotive. Twenty years on, No4472 ventured further afield, to Australia, where it set a world record for a non-stop run by a steam locomotive of 422 miles.

In 1985, ownership changed again, to Dr Tony Marchington, owner of a pharmaceuticals' company but his Flying Scotsman plc foundered and the locomotive's fate was again uncertain. Thankfully, public affection for the 81-year-old proved undiminished. The Virgin Group's Richard Branson offered to match, pound-for-pound, the sum raised from a public appeal and, within five weeks, the total had passed £365,000. All told, the public raised £790,000, including a single donation of £50,000. Adding this to a grant from the National Heritage Memorial

Fund, the National Railway Museum was at last able to submit a total bid of £2.31 million to the auctioneers.

In April 2004, 41 years after withdrawal, *Flying Scotsman* was at last added to the list of historic locomotives owned by the nation. After repairs at York, it resumed main-line running under the NRM banner. Now, though, *Scotsman* is once again sidelined at the National Railway Museum and the subject of a public appeal for funds to complete an expensive boiler overhaul.

production Pacific, No1472, rolled out of Doncaster in February 1923, the Great Northern Railway had been absorbed into one of the post-Grouping 'Big Four' companies, the London & North Eastern. Who would have imagined that LNER No1472 was destined to become the most famous steam locomotive in the world – *Flying Scotsman*?

Before long reports were coming in that the Pacifics' coal consumption was worryingly high and that the valve settings required fresh thought. It is difficult to believe these did not concern Gresley but, uncharacteristically, he took no action and, during 1924 and 1925, Doncaster works and the North British Locomotive Company each produced 20 engines to the original specification. Then came the lesson of the exchange trials.

The British Empire Exhibition at Wembley, held during 1924, had brought together *Flying Scotsman* and one of the Great Western's 'Castle' class 4-6-0s. In a spirit of friendly competition, comparative trials were arranged and, to the dismay of Gresley and his staff, the smaller 'Castle' proved superior in almost every department. Not only did No4079 *Pendennis Castle* maintain the Pacific schedules, it consumed 10 per cent less coal in the process. Eventuall;y, at the urging of members of his staff, Gresley took the lessons on board and the Pacifics' performance was transformed.

After World War II, the 78-strong A1/A3 Pacifics remained a mainstay of east coast express passenger services, even if the prestige trains were now entrusted to the streamlined A4s. Gresley had died

in 1941 and his successor, Edward Thompson, elected to make his mark by rebuilding the first of the A1/A3s, No4470 *Great Northern*, as the prototype for one of his ill-starred Pacific designs. His action was seen as vindictive and roundly condemned.

During the late 1940s, the arrival of new A1 and A2 Pacifics designed by Arthur Peppercorn saw the A3s relegated to lesser duties. However, in 1957 – 20 years after A3 No2751 *Humorist* had demonstrated the benefits of the device – they were given a new lease of life with the fitting of Kylchap double blastpipes and chimneys. Equally belatedly, it took until 1958 for the problem of drifting smoke to be cured with the fitting of German-style 'trough' smoke deflectors. That year saw the first withdrawal of an A3, No60104 *Solario*, after accident damage. Most were retired between 1962 and 1964, with 56 examples being cut up in that period. The last, No60052 *Prince Palatine*, was condemned in January 1966. By then, the most famous member of the class, *Flying Scotsman*, was already three years into its new life in preservation.

The genius that was Gresley

Who can name of the designer of the Japanese Dangan Ressha (Bullet Train) or France's Train à Grand Vitesse (TGV)? And whose name is attached to those monsters, the Union Pacific Big Boy and Challenger? Exactly. The name of Herbert Nigel Gresley, on the other hand, is inseparable from the Pacific locomotives that, for four decades, commanded the crack east coast expresses.

However, Gresley's achievements were more far-reaching. Over a period of 30 years, he equipped the London & North Eastern Railway with a range of advanced locomotive types, from shunters to suburban tanks and fast freight engines. For some commentators the V2 2-6-2, arguably the finest heavy mixed traffic engine of any British railway, was the highpoint of his career.

In many ways, the forerunner of the Pacifics was Gresley's 3-cylinder 2-6-0 of 1920, the first British locomotive to carry a boiler six feet in diameter. The design was additionally significant as the first application of the refined version of Gresley's conjugated valve gear. In this, drive for the middle cylinder was taken from the outside motion, eliminating the need for a third set of Walschaerts gear. Based on a design by Harold Holcroft, this – along with the 3-cylinder layout – became the standard for almost all Gresley's later locomotives.

The building of these – by the standards of the time – giant engines was evidence of Gresley's engineering mastery and great vision. Not for the last time, he was entering uncharted territory but his ideas were often rooted in the pioneering work of others. He absorbed much from discussions with other engineers, notably France's André Chapelon, and avidly consulted technical papers.

Not all Gresley's experiments enjoyed success. The most spectacular failure was a revolutionary 4-cylinder compound built in 1929-30 and alternately known as the 'Hush Hush' or, less flatteringly, 'Galloping Sausage'. Much more impressive, both in looks and performance, were the P2 2-8-2s of 1934.

A significant feature of the P2 was the employment of the Kylchap double blastpipe and chimney, the work of the Finnish engineer, Kyîsti Kylala, and André Chapelon. Gresley was impressed by the device and began fitting it to the streamlined A4 Pacifics under construction at Doncaster. Testifying to its effect on performance, one engine so equipped was the record-breaking *Mallard*.

Of around 1,500 steam locomotives built to Gresley's designs only four were withdrawn before 1948. Now, though, several Gresley classes can be recollected solely through photographs and models and only 11 Gresley-designed engines have been preserved.

The low sun of a winter morning lights *Flying Scotsman* and its volcanic exhaust as its tackles the 1 in 285 climb out of London's Marylebone towards Lord's Tunnel with a 'Santa Steam Pullman' for High Wycombe.

IN DETAIL *(Changes through rebuilding in brackets)*

Class	A1/A3
Built:	1922-35; Doncaster Works; North British Locomotive Company, Glasgow
Designer:	Sir Nigel Gresley
Number built:	79
Purpose:	Express passenger
Wheel arrangement:	4-6-2
Cylinders (x3):	20 in x 26 in (A1); 19 in x 26 in (A3)
Motion:	Walschaerts; Gresley-Holcroft conjugated gear to inside cylinder
Valves:	8 in diameter piston valves
Wheels: Leading:	3 ft 2 in
Coupled:	6 ft 8 in
Trailing:	3 ft 8 in
Tender:	4 ft 2 in
Boiler diagrams:	94 (A1); 94HP (A3)
Boiler: Max. diameter:	6 ft 5 in
Pressure:	180 lb/psi (A1); 220lb/psi (A3)
Heating surface:	3,455 sq ft (A1); 3,443 sq ft (A3)
Firebox:	215 sq ft
Superheater:	525 sq ft (A1); 706 sq ft (A3)
Tubes and flues:	2,715 sq ft (A1); 2,522 sq ft (A3)
Grate area:	41.25 sq ft
Tractive effort:	29,835lb (A1); 32.909lb (A3) (@ 85 % boiler pressure)
Engine wheelbase:	35 ft 9 in
Total wheelbase:	60 ft 10.625 in
Engine weight:	92 tons 9 cwt (A1); 96 tons 5 cwt (A3)
Coal capacity:	5,000 gallons
Water capacity:	5 tons
Max. axleloading:	20 tons 0 cwt (A1); 22 tons 1 cwt (A3)
BR power class:	7P6F

The 'Castles' of the West

One of the undisputed classics among steam locomotives, and ever an enthusiasts' favourite, for 40 years the 'Castles' were the mainstay of the GWR and, after 1948, BR Western Region express passenger services.

The announcement by the Great Western was unequivocal. Its works at Swindon had completed 'the most powerful express passenger engine in Great Britain' and, on 23 August 1923, No4073 *Caerphilly Castle* went on display at Paddington Station. The Great Western's pride was understandable, even if the 'most powerful' label – based on a tractive effort of 31,625 lb – was a wholly nominal calculation. Other factors that might have resulted in an alternative assessment, such as drawbar horsepower, were downplayed. Paddington's public relations people went to work and were rewarded with results they could only have

dreamed about. For example, a book about the 'Castle' sold 40,000 copies in a month. However, even they could not have imagined that their greatest publicity coup would come courtesy of the London & North Eastern Railway.

There was nothing especially new about the design: it was, literally, a 'Super-Star', a logical development of Churchward's 4-cylinder 'Star' class 4-6-0 of 1907 and incorporating nothing that Churchward would not have recognised.

He had envisaged a bigger-boilered 4-6-0 but the scheme was thwarted by weight restrictions. Though it became the heaviest locomotive to be allowed over

The Great Western Society's No5051 was one of the 'Castles' that exchanged names during the 1930s for those of GWR directors, in this case, *Earl Bathurst*. Paired with a Hawksworth straight-sided tender, No5051 undertakes a Travelling Post Office (TPO) demonstration at Didcot Railway Centre.

A king and his 'Castle'

The tenth member of the 'Castle' class, No4082, was completed at Swindon in April 1924, just in time to undertake a special duty. A visit to the works by King George V and Queen Mary was scheduled for 28 April and the GWR's publicity department made the most of the event. Its newest locomotive was rostered to haul the royal train from Paddington and it was no surprise to find No4082 carrying the nameplates *Windsor Castle*. Later, the King drove the engine the short distance from the works to Swindon station. Thereafter, No4082 became the GWR's 'royal engine' and had the solemn honour of hauling George V's funeral train in 1936.

Windsor Castle was requested for a similar role in February 1952, this time to convey the coffin of King George VI from Paddington to Windsor. Unfortunately, it was undergoing repair but the simple expedient of switching names and numbers saved the day. No4082 exchanged identities with No7013 *Bristol Castle*, and the two engines never reverted to their original guises.

Laying down the challenge

It is thought the idea of 'exchange trials' between the 'Castle' and one of the LNER's new Gresley Pacifics came from the GWR's General Manager, Felix Pole.

It had been decided to display *Caerphilly Castle* at the 1924 British Empire Exhibition. To emphasise that this was a 'working' engine and not an exhibition piece, a point was made of having the 'Castle' work up from the West Country just 24 hours earlier. Cleaned and polished, No4073 took its place in the Palace of Engineering with the pride of the LNER, A1 4-6-2 No4472 *Flying Scotsman*. Though a considerably bigger engine, Great Western devotees pointed out that the tractive effort of the Gresley design was a comparatively modest 29,835 lb.

Pole wanted to prove the 'Castle's superiority in practice as well as theory. Along with power, there was a question of economy to be settled. Collett had claimed a coal consumption for the 'Castle' of 2.83 lb per drawbar-horsepower-hour. Since other engineers gave themselves a pat on the back if a figure of 4 lb per hour was achieved, the claim attracted scepticism. However, on the LNER, Nigel Gresley sounded against any comparative tests. It had already been suggested that there was room for improvement in his Pacific design and he did not want it underlined in such a high-profile way.

Nevertheless, the LNER management took up the challenge and comparative runs were arranged for the spring of 1925. The East Coast main line between King's Cross and Doncaster hosted 'Castle' No4079 *Pendennis Castle*, pairing it first with Pacific No4475 *Flying Fox* and then No2545 *Diamond Jubilee*. Similarly, in tandem with No4074 *Caldicot Castle*, No4474 *Victor Wild* ran between Paddington and Plymouth. While the LNER engines were not outclassed, no one, least of all Gresley, was left in any doubt about the GWR engines' superiority.

the West of England main line, the 'Castle', too, had to be tailored to the Civil Engineer's dictates.

Responsibility for the 'Castle' lay with Charles Collett, who had succeeded Churchward as the GWR's Chief Mechanical Engineer on 1 January 1922. Collett saw no immediate need to depart from Churchward's programme of standardisation among locomotive types. The principal express services remained entrusted to the highly capable 'Stars', now numbering over 70. However, increased train loadings, especially on the holiday routes to the West Country, were pushing the 'Stars' to their limit. Something more powerful was required – and quickly.

Collett set about producing the required design with characteristic pragmatism. If new engines were to be built within a short time, they had to employ as many standard components as possible. Continuing weight restrictions on the West of England main line between London and Plymouth limited Collett's options and the obvious course was to create a more powerful version of the 'Star'. A larger boiler and increased cylinder diameter gave him the extra output required, some ten per cent more than the 'Star'. The maximum axleloading was stretched to 19 tons 14 cwt but remained within the Civil Engineer's 20 tons limit. The newcomer was allowed to haul an additional 35 tons above the 'Star' limit of 420 tons between Paddington and Taunton, and 315 tons, compared to its predecessor's 288 tons, from Taunton to Plymouth.

On the Plymouth run, for example, while the Gresley Pacific kept time, *Caldicot Castle* was trimming fifteen minutes off the schedule. Moreover, Charles Collett was being vindicated: it was not solely the acceleration and sustained fast running of his 4-6-0 that impressed, or its haulage capability, but its economy. This was so remarkable that the findings were questioned. The LNER, and Nigel Gresley, were not slow to take the lessons on board. The eminent railway commentator, Cecil J. Allen, however, was left unmoved. He concluded:

'Publicity, indeed, seems to have gained more than science in the locomotive exchange of 1925.'

The exchange with the LNER was not the only occasion on which a 'Castle' starred on another of the 'big four' railways. In 1926, No5000 *Launceston Castle* was lent to the LMSR, which was in urgent need of a new express passenger design. First employed between Euston and Crewe and then between Crewe and Carlisle, the engine so impressed the LMSR board that it ventured to order 50 'Castles' from Swindon. The overture was rejected, as was an audacious follow-up request to borrow the drawings. Nevertheless, the 'Castle' unquestionably influenced the LMSR's 'Royal Scot' 4-6-0 of 1927.

Cheltenham racer

The performances of the 'Castles' soon became the stuff of legend. Several of the GWR's crack expresses were entrusted to them. These included the 'Bristolian' and the 'Cheltenham Flyer' which, during the 1920s and early 1930s, was the fastest scheduled service in the world. In the 1929 timetable, the 'Flyer' was allowed just 70 minutes for the 77.3 miles from Swindon to Paddington, an average speed of 66.2 miles per hour. Within three years, five minutes had been clipped off that timing, requiring an average of 71.4 mph.

Then, on 6 June 1932, No5006 *Tregenna Castle* delivered a world-record run. Hauling a six-coach load weighing 195 tons, it covered the distance in just 56 minutes 47 seconds, an average of 81.6 mph. The maximum speed was 92 mph, with a mean of 87.5 mph over 70 miles. It was undoubtedly prearranged: why otherwise that morning at Paddington, before working the down train, had an official photograph of driver Ruddock and fireman Thorpe been taken on the 'Castle' footplate?

While high-speed exploits helped forge the 'Castle' legend, the consistency of day-to-day running was of greater importance, as was reliability. This was further enhanced from 1934 when Nos5023-32 became the first locomotives in Britain to be built using optical instruments to line up the frames, axleboxes and cylinders. The Carl Zeiss equipment, which was already in use with German State Railways, allowed closer tolerances on machined parts and brought higher mileages between overhauls. For example, No5030 *Shirburn Castle* ran 420,000 miles before any repairs became necessary that required a boiler lift.

IN PRESERVATION

There are eight surviving 'Castles'. These include the prototype, No4073 *Caerphilly Castle* and the participant in the 1925 exchange, No4079 *Pendennis Castle*. Bought from British Railways in 1964, after over twenty years spent in Western Australia, the latter was repatriated to Britain in 2000. Four other 'Castles' have hauled railtours in recent years and two of those – No5029 *Nunney Castle* and No5043 *Earl of Mount Edgcumbe* – are currently passed for main-line running.

No4073 *Caerphilly Castle* Part of the National Collection, after decades in the Science Museum, No4073 is now exhibited at STEAM Swindon.

No4079 *Pendennis Castle* Under restoration by the Great Western Society at Didcot Railway Centre.

No5029 *Nunney Castle* First returned to steam in 1991 and certified for main-line running.

No5043 *Earl of Mount Edgcumbe* Restoration was completed at Tyseley Locomotive Works, Birmingham, in late 2008. Normally based at Tyseley for main-line running,

No5051 *Drysllwyn Castle / Earl Bathurst* Based at Didcot Railway Centre and stored awaiting a ten-year boiler overhaul.

No5080 *Defiant* Nominally a Tyseley engine, presently on display at Buckinghamshire Railway Centre, Quainton Road.

No7027 *Thornbury Castle* Undergoing restoration at Tyseley Locomotive Works, Birmingham.

No7029 *Clun Castle* BR's last working 'Castle', now stored at Tyseley awaiting its turn for overhaul.

On 12 June 1994, No5029 *Nunney Castle* supplied the motive power for a series of shuttles between Didcot and Oxford commemorating the 150th anniversary of railways reaching the university city. Didcot power station supplies the backcloth as the 'Castle' approaches Culham.

Two million miles and more

For over 40 years, the 'Castle' was the standard express engine of the GWR and British Railways' Western Region, a period unmatched by any equivalent class of locomotive. In all, including sixteen conversions from 'Star' 4-6-0s, 179 'Castles' were built over a period of 28 years, all at Swindon and with few changes to the original specification. The most significant modification was the fitting of 66 examples with double chimneys and improved superheaters. No4090 *Dorchester Castle* was the first to be fitted with the final development of the superheater, a four-row version that further reduced maintenance and extended boiler life, as well as reducing water consumption. Even in their twilight years, 'Castles' were registering high-speed runs: 100 miles per hour and above was attained more than once at the head of enthusiast specials. Fittingly, the last scheduled steam-hauled service from Paddington, the 4.15pm to Banbury on Friday, 11 June 1965, was entrusted to a 'Castle', the now-preserved No7029 *Clun Castle*.

Unsurprisingly, withdrawals began with those engines rebuilt from 'Stars'. Bizarrely, No100 *A1 Lloyds* was retired in March 1950, six months before the last of the class, No7037, was outshopped from Swindon. Scrapping of the 'Castles' proper got underway in January 1959 with No4091 *Dudley Castle* and the 'Castle' story officially ended in December 1965, with the withdrawal of *Clun Castle* from Gloucester shed. Records revealed that the highest mileage attained by a member of the class was by No4080 *Powderham Castle* which covered 1,974,461 miles during a 60-year-career beginning in March 1924. However, since mileage compilations ceased on 28 December 1963, No4080 may well have passed the two million mark by its retirement in August 1964. Rebuild No4037 *The South Wales Borderers* attained a higher mileage than any other GWR engine: 776,764 as a 'Star' and 1,652,958 as a 'Castle', adding up to 2,429,722 – an average of more than 57,800 miles a year.

IN DETAIL *(as built)*

Class	4073 'Castle'
Built:	1923-50
Designer:	Charles Collett
Number built:	179 (including rebuilds from 'Star' class engines)
Purpose:	Express passenger
Wheel arrangement:	4-6-0
Cylinders (x4):	16 in diameter x 26 in stroke
Motion:	Inside Walschaerts valve gear with rocking shafts to outside motion
Valves:	8 in piston valves
Wheels: Coupled:	6 ft 8.5 in
Leading:	3 ft 2 in
Tender:	4 ft 1.5 in
Boiler diagram:	Swindon Standard No8
Boiler: Max. diameter:	5 ft 9 in
Pressure:	225 lb/psi
Heating surface:	2,312 sq ft (2,213 sq ft*)
Firebox:	163.76 sq ft
Tubes and flues:	1,885.62 sq ft (1,669.24 sq ft*)
Superheater:	262.62 sq ft (380 sq ft*)
Grate area:	30.28 sq ft (29.4 sq ft*)
Tractive effort:	31,625 lb (@ 85% boiler pressure)
Engine wheelbase:	27 ft 3 in
Total wheelbase:	54 ft 6.25 in
Engine weight:	79 tons 17 cwt (80 tons 15 cwt*)
Coal capacity:	6 tons
Water capacity:	4,000 gallons
Max. axleloading:	19 tons 14 cwt (20 tons 0 cwt*)
BR power class:	7P

* Changes in locomotives with 4-row superheaters

London Midland &
Scottish Railway

**George Hughes/Henry
Fowler
Sir William Stanier**

**6P5F (5MT)
2-6-0 (1926)**

**5MT
2-6-0 (1933)**

Workhorses of the West Coast

With their large, steeply angled cylinders and boilers squatting between the frames, it is easy to see why the Horwich Moguls earned the nicknamed of 'Crabs'. Seven years on, it was Crewe's turn to produce a 2-6-0 and for William Stanier to make his debut.

Hughes/Fowler Mogul No42856 of Crewe South (5B) hammers along the West Coast Main Line at Acton Bridge, between Crewe and Warrington, with what appears to be an excursion working. The stock is of very mixed vintage. Outshopped from Crewe in March 1930, No42856 lasted in traffic until November 1964. At nationalisation, on 1 January 1948, it was one of five 'Crabs' on the books of Crewe South.

Prototype of the Hughes/Fowler Mogul, the National Collection's No2700, at Barrow Hill on 12 July 2003. With the large cylinders and high running plate, it is easy to see how the nickname 'Crab' was attached to the class.

When it evaluated its inheritance of over 400 classes of locomotive, the motive-power chiefs of the London Midland & Scottish Railway might reasonably have assumed that one would meet the need for a modern, reasonably powerful, general-purpose design. Not so. Inexplicably, not one of the major English constituents – the London & North Western, Midland or Lancashire & Yorkshire – had followed the lead of Churchward on the GWR and built a medium-sized, go-anywhere 2-6-0. Maunsell had produced them at Ashford, as had Gresley at Doncaster and Billinton at Brighton.

The advantages of a general-purpose design are many. The broader the range of a locomotive, the more use can be made of it. Consequently more efficient use is made of footplate crews, running-shed facilities and fuel and construction costs are repaid earlier. Naturally, there are roles outside its scope – high-speed passenger and heavy-haul freight for example – but the majority of tasks on Britain's railways came within the scope of the mixed-traffic 2-6-0 and 4-6-0.

A committee was set up by the LMSR hierarchy to examine its motive-power needs. Chaired by George Hughes, formerly of the Lancashire & Yorkshire, it consisted of the Chief Mechanical Engineers of all the constituent companies. A first-rate locomotive man, Hughes had been appointed the LMSR's first motive-power chief but even he failed to get agreement on the way forward, and could not persuade his colleagues to commit to a firm proposal. It was decided to call in Hughes' chief draughtsman, J.R. Billington.

It had emerged that, at its St Rollox works in Glasgow, the Caledonian Railway's design team had schemed a powerful 2-6-0. Twenty had even been authorised for construction. Unfortunately, what could be accommodated within the generous gauge and axleloading limits of the Caledonian would be too large and heavy for other parts of the LMSR, particularly the ex-Midland lines. Nevertheless, Billington handed the St Rollox drawings to his design team. After ten attempts the necessary compromise between size, power and route availability was met at last.

Under George Hughes' overall direction, the work was completed in his 'home' drawing office at the ex-Lancashire & Yorkshire works at Horwich, near Bolton. By 1924, blueprints for the 'Horwich Mogul' were ready for presentation to interested parties from the motive power and civil-engineering departments. What they saw probably took them aback, none more so than Hughes' ex-Midland colleagues accustomed to neat, modestly proportioned, inside-cylinder designs.

A look of surprise

Hughes had an aversion to high boiler pressures and insisted that the new design should operate at 180 pounds per square inch. If the required power output was to be delivered, this meant using large cylinders of 21 inches diameter with a 26 inches stroke. Positioning these conventionally, however, would take the overall height out-of-gauge. The compromise this demanded gave the newcomer its striking appearance. The front section of the running plate was raised over the cylinders, themselves steeply inclined at an angle of 1 in 9. Added to the squat smokebox, this gave the front end a hunched look that earned the engine its nickname of 'Crab'.

Similarly massive, the running gear was a match for the cylinders. Hughes chose Walschaerts valve gear, organised in a way that owed much to the K4 Pacifics of America's Pennsylvania Railroad. Long lap, long-travel piston valves were paired with generously sized steam ports and the 5 feet 6 inches diameter coupled wheelsets enjoyed the benefit of sturdy axleboxes. The plate frames were similarly robust.

Thought had been given to using an existing boiler, that fitted to the Midland's three-cylinder compound 4-4-0s. Billington and his team also ran the rule over the boiler of the London & North Western's *Prince of Wales* 4-6-0, and that used on Hughes' 4-6-4 Baltic tank locomotive for the L&YR. The outcome was a new parallel-boiler design with Belpaire firebox, the G9HS.

Progress on the 'Horwich Mogul' suffered a blow when, in March 1925, J.R. Billington died and was replaced as head of the design team by Derby's Herbert Chambers. Hughes had already elected to retire that year and was due to be replaced as CME by another ex-Midland man, Henry Fowler. Chambers' appointment was Fowler's cue to make his mark on the new design. G.M. Gass, Billington's assistant, was summoned to Derby to hear Fowler's proposed changes, which included substituting an existing Derby boiler for Hughes' design. Fowler thought the tooling costs for a new, non-standard boiler unjustifiable. George Hughes, however, had yet to retire and argued that, with a minimum of 100 2-6-0s to be ordered, numbers alone would ensure his boiler became a 'standard'.

Two varieties of LMSR class five power at Ramsbottom, on the East Lancashire Railway on 25 October 1997: Hughes/Fowler 2-6-0 No42765 pilots Stanier 5MT 4-6-0 NoM5337.

The basic format was therefore spared Fowler's tinkering but the use of a number of Midland fittings, such as the vacuum-controlled steam brake, clack valves and injectors, was conceded. Most significantly, Fowler dispensed with the proposed tender and replaced it with the 3,500 gallon Derby variety, although these were 18 inches narrower than the locomotives.

Steamed 'Crab'

The 'Horwich Mogul' was the first purely LMSR design to be constructed in quantity. It also had the distinction of being the only non-Derby inspired standard design produced under Henry Fowler's regime. A total of 245 entered service, with construction spanning six-and-a-half years – June 1926 to December 1932 – and shared between Crewe and Horwich works. With its ample boiler capacity, the 'Crab' ran freely at a fuel-efficient 60 miles per hour. Schedules could be maintained over steeply graded routes without over-taxing either engine or crew.

The LMSR finally had a locomotive equal to anything else in its power class and many judged the 'Crab' a stronger engine than the Stanier 'Black 5'. Apart from experiments with two German designs of poppet valve gear – the Lentz and the Reidinger – the 'Crabs' worked for some 40 years without modification.

Incorporating as they did many modern features, the 'Crabs' could only enhance the LMSR's ageing fleet. The first examples went to ex-Lancashire & Yorkshire sheds at Newton Heath (Manchester), Low Moor (Bradford), Accrington and Blackpool and were an immediate success. Soon they were seen throughout the LMSR system, from London to the Highland main line and the ex-Glasgow & South Western lines in Ayrshire, and on summer services to Yorkshire and Lincolnshire seaside resorts. The 2-6-0s handled freight with an ease that contrasted with the struggles of existing types, chiefly underpowered 0-6-0s and 0-8-0s. The important Water Orton (Birmingham) to Carlisle goods turns were entrusted to them, as well as fast freights from Birmingham to London and to York.

Some of their finest work was done over routes and with loads that made extreme demands on the boilers, such as the Midland route through the Peak District and the Settle–Carlisle line. On test during 1925 a 'Crab' took a 590 ton load over the 'long drag' between Settle and Ais Gill. Overall, they were remarkably strong machines and remained free from major

IN PRESERVATION

Hughes/Fowler 6P5F 2-6-0

No2700 Outshopped from Horwich on 19 June 1926, No2700 was based at the Manchester shed of Newton Heath for much of its working life. At nationalisation on 1 January 1948, it was one of 20 'Crabs' on the depot's books. Withdrawn on 19 March 1966, it was selected for preservation as part of the National Collection and is currently on display at Locomotion, the National Railway Museum's offshoot at Shildon, County Durham.

No42765 Completed at Crewe in August 1927 and wearing crimson-lake livery, No13065 entered service at the ex-Midland Railway shed at Kentish Town in north-west London. One of the last five 'Crabs' in service, it was withdrawn on 31 December 1966. Twelve years in Barry scrapyard culminated in the 'Crab' being bought privately and

it entered traffic on the East Lancashire Railway in 1994. A ten-year overhaul has begun in the ELR's Buckley Wells (Bury) workshops.

No42859 Withdrawn in December 1966, No42859 spent 19 years languishing at Woodham's, Barry. Potential buyers were deterred by the state of the firebox but the Humberside Locomotive Preservation Group were persuaded that the engine was worth saving and it left South Wales for Hull in December 1986. Restoration is now underway by Ace Locomotives at the one-time Royal Air Force base at Binbrook, in Lincolnshire.

Stanier 5MT 2-6-0

No42968 The sole survivor of this class of 40 began its career as LMSR No13268 at Willesden, London, in January 1934. Withdrawal came from Springs Branch (Wigan) in 1966. Bought by the Stanier Mogul Fund, No42968 was towed by rail from Barry to Bewdley, on the Severn Valley Railway, on 14 December 1973 but it would be a further eight years before the engine entered the SVR's works at Bridgnorth in Shropshire.

No42968 was first steamed in preservation on 12 November 1990 and entered traffic on the SVR the following spring. It remains part of the SVR's working fleet.

problems throughout their working lives. Both the LMSR's and BR's running departments would have been hard-pressed without their services. The first three of the 'Horwich Moguls' to be retired were Nos42864, 42893 and 42930 in July 1961 and most were scrapped between 1962 and 1964, with the last in 1967.

More please

William Stanier, the LMSR's new Chief Mechanical Engineer, met a demand for more 'Horwich Moguls' with a new 2-6-0 design, one that owed more to Swindon practice and specifically the GWR's 4300 class (Stanier had been mentored by Churchward) than Horwich.

Outline drawings were prepared at Euston but, as with the Hughes/Fowler Mogul, the detail design was done by the Horwich drawing office. The mandate was to produce a locomotive of equivalent power to the 'Crab' but employing the Churchward tenets of a domeless taper boiler with trapezoidal Belpaire firebox, long-travel piston valves, near-horizontal cylinders, streamlined steam exhaust passages and a jumper-top blastpipe. The boiler had a modest superheat temperature with a high working pressure (225 lb/psi), allowing a reduction in cylinder diameter from the 21 inches of the Hughes/Fowler Mogul to 18.

The first of the Stanier Moguls, No13245, rolled out of Crewe on 21 October 1933, attached to a six-wheel Fowler tender (Stanier's tender design had yet to be completed), and a further 39 2-6-0s were outshopped by March 1934. At first, the allocations of the 40 Stanier Moguls were tidily organised, with consecutively numbered batches going to each of the four divisions of the LMSR. Nos13245-54 were allocated to the Northern Division, Nos13255-66 to the ex-Midland lines, Nos13267-79 to the Western Division, and Nos13280-84 to the central area.

In later years the Stanier Moguls were concentrated on the west-coast lines with the largest contingents at Crewe South, Mold Junction (to the south-west of Chester) and Nuneaton. Additionally, Birkenhead, Crewe North, Speke Junction and Willesden had allocations. They were used principally as freight locomotives, but pressed into parcels and passenger service when required.

Withdrawals of the Stanier Moguls began with No42976 in July 1963 and No42984 that September. The last to be retired was No42963 in 1966. Only one was saved, No42968, by the Stanier Mogul Fund.

Sole survivor from among the 40 Stanier Moguls, No42968 starts away from Kidderminster with a Severn Valley Railway service for Bridgnorth on 20 September 2008.

IN DETAIL *(as built)*

Class	'4' (later 5P5F)	4F (later 5F)
Built:	Crewe, Horwich works 1926-32	Crewe Works 1933-34
Designer:	George Hughes/ Henry Fowler	William Stanier
Number built:	245	40
Purpose:	Mixed traffic	
Wheel arrangement:	2-6-0	
Cylinders (x 2):	21 in x 26 in (Diameter x Stroke)	18 in x 28 in
Motion:	Walschaerts §	
Valves:	11 in diameter (Piston valves)	10 in diameter
Wheels: Coupled:	5 ft 6 in	
Leading:	3 ft 6.5 in	
Tender:	4 ft 3 in	
Boiler diagram:	G9HS ¶	N/A
Boiler: Max. diameter:	5 ft 8.75 in	5 ft 8.375 in
Pressure:	180 lb/psi	225 lb/psi
Heating surface:	1,812 sq ft *	1,595 sq ft
Firebox:	160 sq ft	155 sq ft
Tubes and flues:	1,345 sq ft	1,216 sq ft
Superheater:	307 sq ft	224 sq ft
Grate area:	27.5 sq ft	27.8 sq ft
Tractive effort:	26,580 lb (@ 85% boiler pressure)	26,290 lb
Engine wheelbase:	25 ft 6 in	
Total wheelbase:	48 ft 11.125 in	49 ft 6 in
Engine weight:	66 tons 0 cwt	69 tons 2 cwt
Coal capacity:	5 tons	5 tons ⊠
Water capacity:	3,500 gallons	3,500 gallons ⊠
Max. axleloading:	19 tons 12 cwt	20 tons 3 cwt
BR power class:	6P5F	6P5F (later 5MT)

§ Certain locomotives built in 1931 equipped with Lentz rotary-cam poppet-valve gear and rebuilt in 1953 with Reidinger poppet-valve gear in 1952-53 – see text.

¶ Originally the boiler was designated Type SS by Horwich Works; it was reclassified G9HS when the Derby system was adopted in 1929.

* Reduced from the 1,828 square feet of the original batch of boilers.

⊠ Some locomotives later paired with Stanier 4,000 gallon tenders.

Great Western Railway

Charles Collett

Frederick Hawksworth

4900 'Hall' class
4-6-0 (1924)

6959 'Modified Hall' class
4-6-0 (1944)

Claim to Fame

The fame of the Great Western 'Hall' came from being Britain's first 4-6-0 mixed-traffic design, and the inspiration for more than 1,500 similar locomotives built up to 1957. Charles Collett brought it about by subtly modifying a Churchward classic and his successor, Frederick Hawksworth, later left his mark on the class.

Collett's 'Hall' class 4-6-0 No4930 *Hagley Hall* approaches Craven Arms with the Shrewsbury–Hereford leg of a 'Welsh Marches Pullman' on 26 February 1983. No4930 is currently sidelined awaiting overhaul.

A locomotive as adept at hauling fast freight as well as passenger trains remained a novelty in the 1900s. The 4-6-0 wheel arrangement was also relatively rare, having only made its British debut in 1894. No one – even the Great Western's far-thinking George Churchward – was convinced of the superiority of six coupled wheels over four. He arranged comparative trials between prototype 4-6-0s and 4-4-2s, even importing engines from France for the exercise. The vote finally went to the 4-6-0; among other factors its greater adhesive weight would be an advantage on the steep gradients of the West of England line.

One of the Churchward 4-6-0s that won the argument was No100, a two-cylinder machine built in February 1902. Named *William Dean* after Churchward's venerable predecessor as Locomotive Superintendent, it was notable for its two outside cylinders, their siting dictated by the exceptionally long piston stroke of 30 inches. Displaying significant changes from No100, the following March a further prototype appeared, No98. This was the first application of the trademark GWR taper boiler (that of No100 had been of the parallel type) and it introduced a standard cylinder casting that would be incorporated into all GWR two-cylinder locomotives built over the ensuing four decades.

Four years later, these two locomotives, but principally No98, supplied the blueprints for Churchward's 'Saint' and 'Lady' classes, two-cylinder

Looking immaculate, Tyseley-based 'Hall' No4965 *Rood Ashton Hall* brings the stock of a returning railtour for Birmingham into Kidderminster Station on 22 September 2001. No4965 is set for a rapid overhaul and return to the main line.

designs to complement the more powerful four-cylinder 'Star' class 4-6-0. With their 6 feet 8.5 inches diameter drivers, the 'Saint', 'Lady' and later 'Court' 4-6-0s were clearly intended for passenger work, as planned for in Churchward's range of 'standard' types.

A saint's conversion

Charles Collett replaced Churchward as Chief Mechanical Engineer in 1922 and at first was content to continue the great man's work. It was evident, though, that his one class of truly mixed-traffic engines, the 4300 2-6-0s. were being stretched by many duties. Something more powerful was needed but it had to keep within the axleloading limits that had put paid to Churchward's proposed general-purpose machine. There appears to have been no thought of scheming an entirely new locomotive; instead thoughts turned to adapting an existing design that had excellent features. One suggestion was to rebuild a quantity of 4300s as 4-6-0s but Collett instead chose to modify an earlier Churchward six-coupled locomotive, the two-cylinder 'Saint' dating from 1902.

The guinea-pig role went to No2925 *Saint Martin* but its appearance changed little. The principal modification was the substitution of its 6 feet 8.5 inches driving wheels for ones of 6 feet 0 inches diameter. Additionally, the cylinders were realigned so that their centre lines coincided with the centres of the driving axles. The frame was altered, the valves given longer travel and the spartan cab upgraded to the side-window type employed on the 'Castle'.

Renumbered 4900, the modified *Saint Martin* emerged from Swindon in 1924 to undertake three years of trials. Experience led Collett to introduce other modifications including altering the pitch of the taper boiler and fitting outside steampipes. The bogie-wheel diameter was reduced by two inches, from 3ft 2in to 3ft 0in and the valve setting amended to give an increased travel of 7.25 inches. There had been an increase in engine weight of 2.5 tons to 75 tons, but a tractive effort of 27,275lb compared favourably with the 24,935b of the 'Saint'.

Satisfied with No4900's performance, Collett placed an order for 80 engines.

At a cost of £4,375, the first of the production series, No4901, entered service in December 1928. To complement the 'Castles', the names were chosen from the baronial halls of England (together with a handful from Oxford University) and applied in alphabetical order beginning with *Adderley Hall* and ending with No4980 *Wrottesley Hall*.

In what amounted to a further extended trial, the first 14 were sent to prove themselves on the arduous Cornish main line. Success there was repeated on other demanding sections of the GWR system. Even before the first order had been completed, construction of a further 178 had been approved. By 1935, 150 were in service and the 259th and last 'Hall', No6958 *Oxburgh Hall*, (by now alphabetical order had been abandoned!) was delivered in April 1943.

While the 'Castles' and 'Kings' may have been the most celebrated of the Great Western 4-6-0s, the 'Halls' arguably made the more significant contribution to the wider development of British steam traction. They were the first high-power mixed-traffic locomotives, and as such precursors of the Stanier 'Black 5', Thompson B1 and BR Standard 5MT 4-6-0.

'Hall' change

Frederick Hawksworth succeeded Charles Collett as Chief Mechanical Engineer of the Great Western in 1941. He was fifty-seven. That it had taken such a talent so long to reach the top (Hawksworth had joined the GWR in 1898, aged 15) was in part due to Collett's reluctance to relinquish the post. However, it was also a reflection of a complacency that had set in on the Great Western. After being

Dappled sunlight picks out 'Hall' No5900 *Hinderton Hall* resting in the running shed at Didcot Railway Centre. One of the Centre's first arrivals, it is almost 30 years since No5900 last steamed.

IN PRESERVATION

No4920 *Dumbleton Hall* Restored from scrapyard condition by the Dumbleton Hall Society, No4920 ran 37,000 miles on heritage lines before falling due for its ten-year boiler overhaul in November 1999. It is stored at Buckfastleigh, on the South Devon Railway, awaiting work to begin.

No4930 *Hagley Hall* Bought from Woodham's, Barry, by Severn Valley (Holdings) Ltd in June 1972, *Hagley Hall* returned to steam in September 1979. Now on display in the SVR's Engine Hall at Highley, some cosmetic work has been done while the Friends of Locomotive 4930 *Hagley Hall* raise funds for a full overhaul.

No4936 *Kinlet Hall* Its restoration undertaken at several locations over a 19-year period, *Kinlet Hall* steamed for the first time in 36 years on 16 February 2000. That June, it was certified for main-line use and is presently based at Tyseley Locomotive Works in Birmingham.

No4942 *Maindy Hall* Saved from scrap by the Great Western Society, No4942 is being rebuilt at Didcot Railway Centre as a 'Saint' class 4-6-0, none of which was preserved. It will be renumbered No2999 and renamed *Lady of Legend*.

No4953 *Pitchford Hall* Owner, microbiologist Dr John Kennedy, estimates the restoration of *Pitchford Hall* to have

cost between £800,000 and £1 million – an extraordinary figure when compared with the £5,000 or so it cost to build in 1929. Following a debut at Crewe Works' open days in September 2005, *Pitchford Hall* has joined the list of main-line-certified locomotives and is one of three 'Halls' that are currently based at Tyseley, Birmingham.

No4965 *Rood Ashton Hall* For decades, as an ex-scrapyard hulk, this locomotive was believed to be classmate No4983 *Albert Hall*. However, close examination of its chief components revealed its true identity. Restored to main-line condition at Tyseley, No4965 remains based there. An appeal has been launched to 'fast-track' *Rood Ashton Hall*'s seven-year overhaul.

No4979 *Wootton Hall* Stored at a private site in Lancashire one day No4979 will provide welcome, if improbable, motive power for the Lakeside & Haverthwaite Railway in the Lake District.

No5900 *Hinderton Hall* After enjoying some main-line running during the 1970s and early 1980s, the Great Western Society's *Hinderton Hall* has been limited to static display at Didcot Railway Centre with refurbishment limited to a mid-1990s repaint.

No5952 *Cogan Hall* Owned by the Cambrian Railways Trust, *Cogan Hall* awaits restoration, and is kept at the Trust's headquarters of Llynclys South Station, south of Oswestry in Shropshire.

in the vanguard of locomotive development throughout the first three decades of the twentieth century, it had handed the initiative to Gresley on the LNER and Stanier on the LMSR, the latter a graduate of the Swindon school.

Other factors contributed: a downturn in traffic caused by the trade depression of the 1930s and a consequently deteriorating financial position forced frugality on the locomotive department. Collett had to create new locomotives out of old, by rebuilding redundant 4300 2-6-0s, for example, of reviving Victorian designs such as that for the 1400 class 0-4-2T.

Hawksworth, too, was constrained by circumstances. Several bold ideas were frustrated by wartime conditions and, after 1945, the growth of corporate responsibility for motive-power policy (in the shape of the government-appointed Railway Executive). He devised a 4-6-2 which, in theory, would have been the most powerful express passenger locomotive ever built in Britain. When its rejection coincided with the Southern's Oliver Bulleid gaining approval for his far more radical 'Merchant Navy' design, Hawksworth was understandably angered.

Throughout his eight years in charge on the GWR, Hawksworth generally had to settle for making his mark with the pragmatic rather than the prestigious and this included updating the 'Hall'. It would, though, mark the most radical change in Swindon practice since the Churchward era. Hawksworth's use of plate frames throughout the design was a daring break with the Churchward gospel. The cylinders were cast separately from the smokebox saddle and bolted to the frames on each side. A stiffening brace was inserted between the frames and extended to form the smokebox saddle. The exhaust pipes leading from the cylinders to the blastpipe were incorporated into this assembly.

Additionally, Churchward's bar-frame bogie, which had been adapted for the original 'Hall' in 1924, was replaced by a plate-frame structure with individual springing and lengthening the engine wheelbase by two inches. Throughout, the wider use of fabrications instead of castings reflected the wartime American practice that British engineers had been gradually adopting.

There were changes, too, above the running board. Hawksworth wanted to equip the design better to cope with the varying quality of coal available. One way was to increase the size and degree of superheating. A larger three-row superheater and header regulator were fitted into the Swindon No1 boiler. The cylinder steam passages were improved and a larger-diameter steampipe fitted between the cylinders and smokebox. (Subsequently the superheater elements were shortened, reducing the heating surface by some twenty square feet.)

Improvements were subsequently made to the draughting on some engines, while others were fitted with hopper ashpans. Many of the later examples were attached to Hawksworth's simplified design of a straight-sided tender that gave the crew greater protection from the elements.

The first of the 'Modified Halls' was outshopped from Swindon in March 1944. It carried plain black livery and was unnamed (it was to be another three years before all of the initial batch of twelve locomotives received names). When construction ceased in 1950, the class numbered 71 and carried the numbers 6959-99 and 7900-29. The 6959 class 4-6-0s proved popular with both footplate and maintenance staff. They ran freely, steamed well, and were capable of sustained high-speed running.

The now-preserved No7903 *Foremarke Hall*, which was deputising for a

No5967 *Bickmarsh Hall* Stored awaiting restoration on the Pontypool & Blaenavon Railway, South Wales.

No5972 *Olton Hall* Restored and operated by the West Coast Railway Company out of its Carnforth, Lancashire, base, *Olton Hall* has achieved world-wide recognition as the locomotive that hauls the 'Hogwarts Express' of Harry Potter fame. As such, it wears a decidedly non-GWR maroon livery!

No6960 *Raveningham Hall* First steamed in preservation in 1975, *Raveningham Hall* travelled widely before arriving at Williton, on the West Somerset Railway, in early 2009 for its latest overhaul to be completed.

No6984 *Owsden Hall* Seen as a long-term restoration at Toddington on the Gloucestershire Warwickshire Railway, although work on the chassis is underway.

No6989 *Wightwick Hall* Restoration is progressing well at the Buckinghamshire Railway Centre, Quainton Road, as was evident when No6989 was displayed at a BRC gala day in October 2008.

No6990 *Witherslack Hall* Ownership having passed from the *Witherslack Hall* Locomotive Society to the Great Central-based David Clarke Railway Trust, overhaul of No6990 is being undertaken in the GCR's Loughborough workshop.

No6998 *Burton Agnes Hall* This was the locomotive that had the melancholy distinction of hauling the Western Region's last timetabled steam-hauled service on New Year's Day 1966. By then, it had already been bought from British Railways by the Great Western Society, the group's first tender engine. A main-line performer during the 1970s and 1980s, No6998 was last steamed in May 1995. It is on display at Didcot Railway Centre, awaiting a full overhaul.

No7903 *Foremarke Hall* Its restoration completed five years ago *Foremarke Hall* moved to its current home of the Gloucestershire Warwickshire Railway in June 2004 and remains a mainstay of the working fleet.

No7927 *Willington Hall* One of several ex-scrapyard locomotives stored on the Barry Island Railway, the owner, the Vale of Glamorgan Council, has agreed to No7927 being 'cannibalised' to help two new engine projects. Its boiler will become part of Llangollen-based 'Grange' 4-6-0 No6880 *Betton Grange*, while its chassis components have been earmarked for a Great Western Society project that will eventually see the 'resurrection' of Hawksworth 'County' No1014 *County of Glamorgan*.

IN DETAIL *(as built)*

Class	4900 'Hall' ¶	6959 'Modified Hall'
Built:	Swindon Works	
	1928-43	1944-50
Designer:	Charles Collett	Frederick Hawksworth
Number built:	258	71
Purpose:	Mixed traffic	
Wheel arrangement:	4-6-0	
Cylinders (x 2):	18.5 in x 30 in (Diameter x Stroke)	
Motion:	Stephenson link	
Valves:	10 in diameter piston valves	
Wheels: Coupled:	6 ft 0 in	
Leading:	3 ft 0 in	
Tender:	4 ft 1.5 in	
Boiler diagram:	Swindon No1	
Boiler: Max. diameter:	5 ft 6 in	
Pressure:	225 lb/psi	
Heating surface:	2,103.98 sq ft	2,052.1 sq ft *
Firebox:	154.78 sq ft	154.9 sq ft
Tubes and flues:	1,686.6 sq ft	1,582.6 sq ft
Superheater:	262.6 sq ft	314.6 sq ft *
Grate area:	27.07 sq ft	
Tractive effort:	27,275 lb (@ 85% boiler pressure)	
Engine wheelbase:	27 ft 1 in	27 ft 3 in
Total wheelbase:	53 ft 4.5 in	53 ft 6.5 in
Engine weight:	75 tons 0 cwt	75 tons 16 cwt *
Coal capacity:	6 tons	
Water capacity:	4,000 gallons ⊠	
Max. axleloadng:	18 tons 19 cwt	19 tons 5 cwt *
BR power class:	5MT	

¶ Figures refer to production series, Nos4901 onwards.

* Later reduced to 295 sq ft and with consequent reductions in total heating surface to 2,032.5 sq ft, engine weight to 75 tons 7 cwt and maximum axleloading to 19 tons 2 cwt.

⊠ Especially early in their careers the Collett 'Halls' were frequently paired with Churchward 3,500 gallon tenders.

Fired by oil

Although immersed in the Swindon tradition, Hawksworth was not blinded by it. He displayed a readiness to examine any alternative to the coal-fired steam locomotive, especially in the aftermath of World War II when coal supplies became beset by problems of both quality and quantity. The GWR backed his plan to convert a substantial percentage of the fleet to oil firing. Initially, 172 locomotives were altered, including 'Castles', 'Halls' and heavy freight 2-8-0s. The scheme impressed the government, which asked Hawksworth to supply details to the other railway companies. Several millions were spent on setting up oil-firing countrywide before reality dawned: Britain was exporting its coal to import oil. While the figures might have added up for the GWR's limited experiment, this was never going to be replicated country-wide. The plan was abandoned with all the locomotives involved reverting to coal-firing, doubtless to the exasperation of Hawksworth and the GWR board.

'Castle', set a post-war record for a run from Paddington to Plymouth of under four hours. In a further outstanding run, on 9 September 1954 No7904 *Fountains Hall* – again replacing a 'Castle' – took over the up 'Bristolian' at Little Somerford. It covered the 89.7 miles to Paddington in just 72 minutes, seven less than the 'Castle' schedule. Consistently exceeding 80 miles per hour over the 47 miles between Wantage and West Drayton, No7904 registered 84 mph at Pangbourne and 83 mph at Twyford. After the unambitious designs of Collett's final years, the 'Modified Hall' had restored Swindon's reputation.

While the 'Castles' and 'Kings' were the most glamorous and celebrated of the Collett's 4-6-0s, his 'Halls' had a more enduring impact. They were the first true front-rank mixed-traffic locomotives, and as such precursors of the LMSR's Stanier 'Black 5', the LNER's Thompson B1 and British Railways' Standard 5MT and 4MT 4-6-0s.

The Southern's Sea-dogs

Southern Railway
Richard Maunsell
**LN 'Lord Nelson'
class 7P**
4-6-0 (1926)

The Southern Railway boasted 'Britain's Most Powerful Locomotive' once in its 25-year history, and then for only ten months. More than this brief pre-eminence, though, distinguished the 16 'sea-dogs' of the 'Lord Nelson' class. It wasn't all plain sailing for the Southern's sea-dogs.

A four-cylinder express passenger was envisaged in Chief Mechanical Engineer, Richard Maunsell's, plan to restock the Southern's ageing steam fleet. The requirement for new engines, though, was too pressing to await its development, hence the reworking in 1925 of the existing Urie two-cylinder N15 4-6-0. The success of the N15s – better known as the 'King Arthurs' – gave Maunsell time to refine his original idea. He had two key people to satisfy. The design had to meet the traffic manager's insistence on 55 miles per hour averages on 500-ton holiday expresses but had to comply with the civil engineer's maximum axleloading of 21 tons.

The detail design therefore became an ingenious exercise in weight saving, ranging from the use of high-tensile steels for the coupling and connecting rods to the machining of excess metal from moving parts. It was a masterly example of balancing power and weight. The newcomer came in at 83 tons 10 cwt, a slender seven hundredweights under the limit, yet the increase in tractive effort was dramatic: 33,150 lb compared to the 25,321 lb of the 'Arthurs'. It was this statistic that, in 1926, gained the first of the 'LN' class the tag of 'Britain's most powerful locomotive'.

Revolutionary idea

One of the intriguing features of the design was entirely down to Maunsell's assistant, Harold Holcroft. The search for a solution to the age-old

No850 *Lord Nelson* strides through Shorncliffe, between Folkestone and Ashford, in 1939 with a boat train for London Victoria.

Royal riders

No850 *Lord Nelson* rolled out of Eastleigh Works in August 1926 to a fanfare of publicity that befitted – in the words of the Southern Railway – 'The premier express locomotive in the British Isles'. Back then, the appearance of a new locomotive design, particularly an express type, aroused great interest and excitement. Maunsell and his colleagues were delighted when, during a visit to Ashford Works in Kent, the Duke and Duchess of York (later King George VI and Queen Elizabeth) took a ride on the footplate of No850. Appropriately, the visit took place on 21 October 1926 – Trafalgar Day.

Following its latest overhaul *Lord Nelson* went to the West Somerset Railway for 'running in' before taking up main-line duties (albeit briefly). With Minehead's North Hill in the background, No850 departs for Bishops Lydeard with the 10.10 service on 7 October 2006.

problem of balancing reciprocating masses led Holcroft to suggest setting the cranks on the 'Nelsons' at 135 degrees rather than the normal 180 degrees. He argued that this would lessen the stress on the axleboxes and motion and reduce hammerblow to the track. The arrangement was tried successfully on an existing 4-6-0 and Maunsell agreed to its adoption. The two cranks on one side of the locomotive were arranged at 135 degrees to each other and at 90 degrees to those on the opposite side, giving the characteristic eight unequally spaced exhaust beats per revolution.

There was speculation that Holcroft's crank settings would lead to difficulties starting heavy trains but it proved unfounded. Rather, the more even torque helped avoid wheelslip.

The prototype, No850, emerged from Eastleigh Works in August 1926 accompanied by publicity that befitted – in the Southern Railway's words – 'The premier express locomotive in the British Isles'. However, it was not until 12 October that *Lord Nelson* made its revenue-earning debut at the head of the 11.00am from Waterloo, the 'Atlantic Coast Express'. No850 took its 430 ton load as far as Salisbury and then returned to London on the up working.

There followed over two years of trials, chiefly on normal service trains and without the benefit of a dynamometer car to take measurements. Performance proved frustratingly inconsistent. At times, this free-running engine had no difficulty keeping time, frequently reaching speeds around 90 miles per hour. It did not take happily, however, to the hills west of Salisbury, as was shown during a run on 10 April 1927 when No850 struggled up Honiton bank with 521 tons in tow. This was the kind of load for which it had been designed but, in truth, 500 ton trains were a rarity on the Southern (only one platform at Waterloo could accommodate a coaching rake of such length).

Admirals all

Although doubts remained, by 1928 the performances of No850 were judged sufficiently satisfactory for production to go ahead at Eastleigh, although the original plan for 30 engines was halved. That May No851 joined the Southern's fleet, As with the 'Arthurs', the choice of names was inspired. With its trains serving the Royal Navy dockyards at Chatham, Plymouth and Portsmouth, the Southern decided the 4-6-0s should carry the names of famous British seafarers – Drake, Raleigh, Hood, Grenville, Anson, Collingwood, Rodney, Frobisher, Hawkins – and starting, of course, with Lord Nelson. The oblong nameplates of the 'Arthurs' were deemed too restrained. Instead large, curved gunmetal plates were fitted. Incongruously, given the emphasis on weight-saving, some of the longer ones – *Howard of Effingham*, for example – needed two men to lift them!

A drawback for any class of just 16 locomotives is that relatively few footplate crews will become thoroughly familiar with them. Consequently performances from the 'Nelsons' were not always as good as they might have been, added to which they were unlike any other Southern engines. They were the only class with a split-level grate, partly level and partly sloping. And what a grate it was: at 33 square feet in area and ten feet long, it was exceeded in size only by that of the 'Castle' and skilful firing was needed to ensure a proper spread of coal. The Operating Department became wary of letting inexperienced crews handle the

IN PRESERVATION

Following withdrawal in August 1962, No850 *Lord Nelson* was stored in the carriage sheds at Preston Park outside Brighton awaiting a move to a permanent home. However, it was 1976 before the locomotive made a move to the Steamtown workshops at Carnforth, Lancashire, where work began to return it to working order. The mechanical side was undertaken at Steamtown while the boiler was overhauled by Babcock Power Construction of Renfrew, in Scotland. Work was completed in May 1980, just in time for the 'Rocket 150' celebrations at Rainhill in Merseyside.

Wearing the later Bulleid malachite-green livery, No850 then undertook several years of railtour work. It registered only one minor failure and astounded sceptics with her performances over the Settle and Carlisle line. Boiler 'ticket' expired, *Lord Nelson* then went into store at Carnforth, although it did venture south, to Woking, in Surrey, in May 1988 to appear at an event marking the 150th anniversary of the London & South Western Railway.

During the 1990s, the National Railway Museum entrusted *Lord Nelson* to the Eastleigh Locomotive Society and a second overhaul in preservation got underway. No850 emerged from

'Nelsons' and the class became concentrated at just four running sheds: Nine Elms and Stewarts Lane in London, Eastleigh and Bournemouth.

Not so plain sailing

Although they remained 'top dog' on the Southern for power (unmatched for tractive effort even by Bulleid's 'Merchant Navy' Pacifics, albeit only by fifteen pounds) the 'Nelsons' were enigmatic machines that never quite earned the reputation or affection of the two-cylinder 'King Arthurs'. Several attempts were made to tackle the foibles of the 'Nelsons' and liven their performance but none produced noticeable improvements and none was extended to the whole class.

Following Maunsell's retirement in 1937, his successor, Oliver Bulleid, finally attained a level and uniformity of performance from the 'Nelsons' that met with the original expectations. He achieved this primarily by fitting the class with the French-designed Lemaître five-jet multiple blastpipe that improved the airflow through the firegrate. Unfortunately it required the fitting of a wider and comparatively crude-looking chimney. However, there was no denying the effectiveness of the Lemaître apparatus. Additionally, Bulleid redesigned the cylinders with larger and smoother steam passages and increased the diameter of the piston valves from eight inches to ten.

In their modified form, these 16 sea-dogs served for a further two decades. However, all made their final voyages between 1961 and 1962, with the last working Maunsell 'King Arthur' outliving the 'Nelsons' by one month.

During the early 1980s, *Lord Nelson* was based at Carnforth and saw regular use on railtours around north-west England. Note the slightly different livery and positioning of numbers from the opposite illustration as the 4-6-0 is turned on the Carnforth turntable on 25 August 1980.

its birthplace of Eastleigh Works during 2006 and went to the West Somerset Railway for running-in. Sadly, its return to main-line working has not been without problem. With the Eastleigh team now based on the Mid-Hants Railway, *Lord Nelson* will operate from the company's Ropley depot for the foreseeable future.

IN DETAIL *(as built)*

Class	LN 'Lord Nelson'
Built:	1926-29
Designer:	Richard Maunsell
Number built:	16
Purpose:	Express passenger
Wheel arrangement:	4-6-0
Cylinders (x4):	16.5 in diameter x 26 in stroke
Motion:	Walschaerts (separate set to each cylinder)
Valves:	8 in diameter piston valves (later 10 in)
Wheels: Coupled:	6 ft 7 in
Leading:	3 ft 1 in
Tender:	3 ft 7 in
Boiler: Max. diameter:	6 ft 2.5 in
Pressure:	220 lb/psi
Heating surface:	2,365 sq ft
Firebox:	194 sq ft
Tubes and flues:	1,795 sq ft
Superheater:	376 sq ft
Grate area:	33 sq ft
Coal capacity:	5 tons
Water capacity:	5,000 gallons
Tractive effort:	33,510 lb (@ 85% boiler pressure)
Engine wheelbase:	29 ft 6 in
Total wheelbase:	69 ft 9.75 in
Engine weight:	83 tons 10 cwt
Max. axleloading:	20 ton 13 cwt
BR power class:	7P

NB: Following the change of coupled wheels to ones of 6 ft 3 in diameter, the tractive effort of No859 Lord Hood increased to 35,500 lb. The fitting of a longer boiler to No860 Lord Hawke added 1 ton 6 cwt to the weight.

Great Western
Railway

Charles Collett

**6000 'King'
class 8P 4-6-0**

(1927)

The Throne of 'Kings'

Mighty and majestic as befitted their names, the 'King' class locomotives powered not only the GWR's prestige expresses but its publicity machine. To this day, these regal machines command a loyalty that would gladden the heart of any real-life monarch.

Wearing its train reporting number of '153' and sporting a single chimney (a double one was not fitted until March 1957), 'King' class 4-6-0 No5925 *King Henry III* climbs Dainton bank, between Newton Abbot and Totnes, with the 3.30pm Paddington–Penzance in August 1956.

The debate continues. Were the 'Kings' a bold solution to a genuine need for more powerful locomotives, or an excessive means of reclaiming lost prestige? By the mid-1920s, the design and performance of express passenger engines had attained fresh heights. The Great Western's 'Castles' were challenged by the LNER's Gresley Pacifics, the LMSR's 'Royal Scots' and, most surprisingly, a new design by Richard Maunsell of the Southern Railway. When it appeared in 1926, boasting a tractive effort of 33,500 lb, Maunsell's 'Lord Nelson' 4-6-0 could claim to be Britain's most powerful locomotive, taking the title from the 'Castle'.

The story goes that this so incensed the GWR's image-conscious General Manager, Sir Felix Pole, that he instructed the team at Swindon to build something to emphatically put the Southern in its place. This was to be irrespective of genuine need – prestige was at stake. Much of this may be apocryphal. Even for the GWR, commissioning a new locomotive design purely as a status symbol was unthinkable. Moreover, the idea of a 'Super-Castle' had been mooted before the 'Lord Nelsons' appeared. Nevertheless, Paddington's feathers had been ruffled.

Pole must have been pleased to learn from his Civil Engineer, J.C. Lloyd, that the potential barrier to such an engine – axleweight limits – had been overcome. With just four exceptions, the GWR's main-line overbridges could now withstand the 22.5 tons that the design would impose. The way was open for work to get underway and for Pole to stipulate that its tractive effort to exceed the previously unprecedented figure of 40,000 lb. The justification for such power, it was claimed, came from the traffic department, which wanted to run longer, and therefore heavier, trains particularly on the West of England main line. The anticipated loads would be beyond the capabilities of the 'Castles' and their predecessors, the 'Stars'.

If this was the case, say the doubters, and the need so pressing, why did the GWR wait three years before lengthening the platforms and remodelling the trackwork at Paddington to accommodate these longer trains?

The instruction went out to Chief Mechanical Engineer, Charles Collett, that the first of the new engines should be ready for the summer of 1927. That just left Collett and his team to find the formula that would generate the specified 40,000 lb of tractive effort, a process that began with the boiler. It was calculated that, with a steam pressure of 250lb per square inch (25 lb greater than that of the 'Castles') and cylinders of 16.25 inches diameter and 28 inches stroke, the nominal tractive effort would be 39,100 lb – not enough for Sir Felix. Collett then calculated that exchanging the 6 feet 8.5 inches diameter driving wheels of the 'Castle' for ones of 6 feet 6 inches would finally take the tractive effort over 40,000 lb, in fact to 40,300 lb to be exact.

Crowning moment

Despite using the 'Castle' as the basis of the design, the first drawings were not prepared until near the end of 1926, which put a summer debut out of the question. While the Traffic Department settled for an autumn introduction, Sir Felix Pole was angry. He had undertaken that the prototype would appear at the Fair of the Iron Horse, a celebration of the centenary of America's Baltimore & Ohio Railroad that was scheduled to open on 24 September.

While the staff at Swindon put in a good deal of round-the-clock working (completely new patterns, for example, had to be made for the driving wheels), the Paddington people gave thought to what names the newcomers should carry. With GWR engines already honouring abbeys, courts and castles, not to mention saints, a clear choice would have been cathedrals. However, it was decided something of greater prestige was merited and approval was

gained to use the names of English kings. The sequence would begin with the reigning monarch and so on 29 June 1927, No6000 *King George V* entered service, making its first public appearance at Paddington two days later. After running-in turns, on 20 July No6000 took charge of the 'Cornish Riviera Express' for the first time. The following month a further five engines rolled out of Swindon Works. They were named in reverse chronological order, beginning with *King Edward VII* and ending with *King George II*.

In traffic, the impact of the 'Kings' was immediate. They were the first engines able to take ten-coach trains over the Devon banks unaided and, to make the point, on 22 July 1927, No6001 *King Edward VII* powered up the grades at Rattery, Dainton and Hemerdon with 400 tons in tow. This permitted the GWR to rewrite the

Double tragedy

The most serious accident involving a 'King' class locomotive occurred during wartime, in the early hours of 4 November 1940. The 9.50 pm express from Paddington to Penzance, with No6028 *King George VI* at its head, left Taunton at 3.43am. It had been signalled on to the down relief line to allow a late-running newspaper train to pass on the parallel main line. Approaching Norton Fitzwarren, two miles west of Taunton, Driver Stacey made the error of misreading the signal for the main line, which was showing green, as his own. He had forgotten he was on the relief and overruled the warning siren in the cab. Stacey only realised his mistake when the newspaper train overtook him. There was no time to brake. Travelling at 45 mph, the Penzance express derailed on the trap points that protected the main line from the relief. Among the 27 fatalities, was No6028's fireman.

There was, though, much sympathy for Stacey when it later emerged he had suffered a double tragedy. The previous night his house had been bombed, yet despite this he had reported for work as normal.

Pausing on 'Welsh Marches Pullman' duty on 10 August 1983, the doyen of the 'Kings', No6000 *King George V* displays the unique bogie design that proved troublesome at the class's introduction. Also prominent, the bell presented by the Baltimore & Ohio Railroad in 1927.

schedule for the 'Cornish Riviera'. It was now allowed just four hours for the 225.5 miles from Paddington to Plymouth. Between London and Taunton the engines were allowed a maximum load of 500 tons and, although this was reduced to 360 tons unaided between Taunton and Plymouth, in both instances this represented an increase of 45 tons over the 'Castles'.

However, the introduction of the 'Kings' was not entirely problem-free. Reports of rough riding reached a potentially disastrous point on 10 August 1927 when No6003 *King George IV* was derailed at speed between Reading and Newbury. Fortunately, the train itself remained upright and there were no serious consequences. Given that the track was in good condition, the fault had to be with the locomotive. The finger pointed to the one truly innovative aspect of the design: the plate-frame front bogie with its four independently sprung wheels. The idea was sound enough: it simply had too little leeway to allow for axlebox wear or track imperfections. A cure was found by adding coil springs to the bogie.

Between February and July 1928, Swindon outshopped a further 14 'Kings', with No6019 *King Henry V* allocated to Wolverhampton depot and becoming the first of the class to be regularly employed on Paddington–Birmingham expresses. The class of 30 was completed between May and August 1930. There was no requirement to add to that total since the engines were still confined to the London–Plymouth (via both Bristol and Westbury), and London–Birmingham–Wolverhampton routes. It would be a further twenty years before they were allowed between Bristol and Shrewsbury and through the Severn Tunnel into South Wales. Consequently, the only depots regularly to have 'Kings' on their books were those at Old Oak Common (London), Bristol (Bath Road), Plymouth (Laira), Wolverhampton (Stafford Road) and, much later, from October 1960, Cardiff (Canton).

Alterations and achievements

Under GWR ownership the 'Kings' remained unaltered, apart from a laughable attempt to ape the 1930s vogue for streamlining. The bizarre embellishments to No6014 *King Henry VII* can only have been conceived with the intention of getting the idea dropped! What changes were made were dictated by outside circumstances. During and after World War II, the 'Kings' were denied their usual diet of high-grade Welsh coal and, as with other pedigree locomotives, performances suffered. With fuel quality remaining variable, it was vital to get the best from what was available. No 6022 *King Edward III* was fitted with a rebuilt boiler that had a high-degree superheater with a substantially greater heating surface (489 square feet compared to 313 square feet). Although the improvement was small, it was judged sufficient for all the engines to receive high-degree four-row superheaters when they fell due for reboiling.

A higher superheat temperature and better draughting were obvious first steps and, from 1955, all 30 were fitted with double chimneys and blastpipes and four-row superheaters.

Changes to the draughting, primarily the fitting of a smaller-diameter blastpipe, brought better results. Engine No6001 *King Edward VII* demonstrated the effectiveness of the new arrangement when, in July 1953, it hauled a 25-coach test train weighing no less than 800 tons between Stoke Gifford, Bristol, and Reading at an average speed of 60mph.

IN PRESERVATION

No6000 *King George V*

Upon its return from the United States in December 1929, No6000 took up normal duties, working out of Old Oak Common, although it became an obvious first choice for special trains. These included excursions from Paddington to Swindon Works to see other members of the 'King' class under construction. By the time it was chosen to inaugurate the new 'Royal Duchy' service between Paddington and Penzance on 28 January 1957, *KGV* had been equipped with a double chimney and blastpipe and it was to remain in this form until withdrawal in December 1962. That month *KGV* went into store at Swindon. Although its survival was assured, where and in what condition remained uncertain.

For much of the ensuing five years, *King George V* languished in the 'Stock Shed' at Swindon. Eventually, No6000 was offered a new role by an unlikely source: the Bulmer cider company of Hereford.

Bulmer's had bought a number of ex-BR Pullman cars with the intention of turning them into a visitor centre. The company's Managing Director, Peter Prior, thought the attraction would be enhanced by the addition of a steam locomotive and, upon learning of No6000's predicament, negotiated to lease the locomotive. After passing its steam test, No6000 moved to Hereford on 30 October 1968. For three years, the 'King' pottered up and down Bulmer's sidings – like a 'caged lion' according to one description – while those responsible for its upkeep formed themselves into the 6000 Locomotive Association to ensure its future.

The comeback 'King'

Since August 1968, only one steam locomotive – LNER Pacific *Flying Scotsman* – had been allowed on to Britain's main lines. Steam was not part of the modern 'Age of the Train' image. One person, however, was determined to fight the ban: Bulmer's Peter Prior. In the autumn of 1971, after a dogged battle with BR bureaucracy, he was victorious. On 15 September, No6000 undertook a supposedly 'secret' test run to Newport. Its success led to a railtour being approved for 2 October – the train that inaugurated the new era of main-line steam operation that continues to this day.

From 1990, and the expiry of its boiler 'ticket', until 2008 *King George V* was the main exhibit at STEAM, the Museum of the Great Western Railway at Swindon. It has since swapped places with another Swindon product, 9F 2-10-0 No92220 *Evening Star*, and gone on display at the National Railway Museum, York. Given that classmate No6024 *King Edward I* is available for main-line work, and that Didcot's No6023 *King Edward II* is likely to join it within the next two years, the chances of *KGV* being returned to working order are slim. However, given the affection felt for this great locomotive, the prospect cannot be entirely ruled out.

This was not the only remarkable run by the 'Kings' during the 1950s. At the head of the 'Bristolian', No6018 *King Henry VI* became the first of the class to top the 100mph mark, a feat repeated by No6015 *King Richard III*, which in 1956 attained 109 mph at the head of the 'Cornish Riviera Express'. The previous September, this engine had become the first of the class to be fitted with a double chimney; the rest of the class had been similarly equipped by early 1958.

One of British Railways' first actions had been to paint almost all the class in the proposed standard livery of ultramarine blue lined out in black and white. While this seemed to suit the LNER's Pacifics and even the Southern's 'Merchant Navies', it did little for Great Western 4-6-0s. Again, normality – in the guise of Brunswick green – was soon reapplied

In this condition, the 'Kings' remained on front-rank duties until early 1960, when diesels began taking over the West of England services. Although they enjoyed a memorable swansong on the Western Region's Birmingham and Wolverhampton services, which had been intensified during electrification of the London Midland Region's West Midlands route, by 1962 unfortunately nothing was left for them.

That February, No6006 *King George I* became the first to be withdrawn and by December all 30 had been retired. Ten of the class had come within 100,000 miles of attaining a working mileage of two million. With 1,950,462 miles on the clock, No6013 *King Henry VIII* came closest. The final salute came on 28 April 1963 when No6018 *King Henry VI* was brought out of storage to work a Stephenson Locomotive Society Special from Birmingham to Swindon and back, passing the 90mph mark on several occasions.

At the head of the 'Flying Dutchman' railtour from London Paddington to Newton Abbot, 'King' class 4-6-0 No6024 *King Edward I* makes a storming start from a stop at Slough on 9 November 1996.

No6023 *King Edward II*
No6024 *King Edward I*

Few would have disagreed with the downbeat assessment. 'We can't save this one,' was the verdict painted on No6023 *King Edward II* as the Great Western 4-6-0 rusted in the sea air. Or, by then more accurately 4-4-0, as the rear coupled wheels had been sliced in half with a cutting torch: the easiest means of re-railing following a shunting mishap. By the mid-1980s, restorers had achieved some minor miracles but casting a pair of 6 feet 6 inches diameter wheels had not been one of them. At least the other 'King' to end up in Woodham Brothers' scrapyard in South Wales, No6024 *King Edward I*, had a full set of wheels. Although its boiler was in a worse state, the conclusion was that repairing a

Swindon No12 presented less of a challenge than replacing a coupled wheelset. For that reason, 20 years is separating the 'restorations' of these two monarchs.

Disposal of No6023 *King Edward II* and No6024 *King Edward I* was delayed because the engines were used for bridge stress tests. They were earmarked for torching at the wonderfully named Slag Reduction Company of Briton Ferry, near Swansea. Fortuitously, someone noticed that the 'Kings' were barred from this stretch of line and the pair were diverted to Woodhams at Barry. No6023 would spend twenty years on the site, No6024 eleven.

After initial restoration work had been undertaken at Bristol, in 1989, the Great Western Society, already owners of 'Castle',

'Hall, 'Modified Hall' and 'Manor' 4-6-0s, negotiated to buy what remained of *KEII* for £15,000.

Wheel of fortune

The greatest task facing the restoration team was evident to all who visited Didcot Railway Centre. The mutilated wheelset was placed on display (with a collecting box attached) to show just what was needed. The popularity of the 'Kings' ensured that before long funds were there to pay for, first, a wooden pattern and then the casting itself. With due ceremony, *KEII* was united with its new wheelset on 1 July 1995, 65 years to the day since entering service.

By the end of 2006, No6023 stood in the workshop at Didcot looking virtually

a complete locomotive. One major task, however, remained – the refurbishment of the boiler. As with the majority of locomotive restorations this had been held back to ensure that *KEII* is working for as much as possible of the ten-year 'ticket' issued by the boiler insurers. Once steam is raised and the boiler passed by the inspector, time begins ticking away relentlessly.

Somewhat controversially, *KEII* will make its debut in the experimental blue, lined black-and-white, that British Railways applied to some express passenger classes between 1950 and 1952. Great Western purists have been assured, however, that *KEII* will eventually be repainted in the 1947 GWR green livery.

Continued on page 90

In retrospect, the 'Kings' embodied both the GWR's individuality and isolation. As the final development of the four-cylinder, six-coupled formula that began with Churchward's 'Stars' of 1906, they were magnificent locomotives. The price to pay for continuing that lineage was that newer and potentially fruitful ideas on improving performance went untried.

All aboard

The transatlantic journey of No6000 *King George V* began at Cardiff Docks on 2 August 1927, when the locomotive was loaded on to SS *Chicago City* of Bristol City Lines. The boiler and chassis had to be separated beforehand as none of the cranes was able to lift the complete engine on board. The ship docked at Baltimore on 21 August and No6000 was moved to the Mount Clare workshops of the Baltimore & Ohio Railroad. There, it was reassembled by the accompanying team from Swindon, led by Charles Collett's Principal Assistant, William Stanier.

On 24 September, *King George V* had the honour of leading the B&O centenary procession of modern locomotives around the exhibition grounds. Riding on the running plate up by the smokebox was a young woman dressed as Britannia, something she did every day until the show closed on 15 October. It must have been hot work!

The 'King' had impressed its hosts with its looks, but how would it perform? Two test runs were arranged over a 272-mile triangular route from Baltimore to Washington DC and on to Philadelphia, with a load of 543 tons. Despite indifferent-quality coal, No6000 performed superbly, as did the crew, Driver Young and Fireman Pearce of Old Oak Common depot in London. Speeds up to 74 mph were recorded and reaching 23 mph from a standing start on a 1 in 75 gradient showed the 'King' had muscle. To commemorate the visit, the Baltimore & Ohio struck gold medallions (alloy replicas of which were fitted to the cabsides) and the typically American brass bell that has since adorned No6000's front bufferbeam – apart of course from the couple of occasions when it has been stolen as a prank!

IN DETAIL *(as built)*

Class	6000 'King'
Built:	1927-30
Designer:	Charles Collett
Number built:	30
Purpose:	Express passenger
Wheel arrangement:	4-6-0
Cylinders (x4):	16.25 in diameter x 28 in stroke
Motion:	Inside Walschaerts valve gear with rocking shafts to outside cylinders
Valves:	9 in diameter piston valves
Wheels: Coupled:	6 ft 6 in
Leading:	3 ft 0 in
Tender:	4 ft 1.5 in
Boiler diagram:	Swindon Standard No12
Boiler: Max. diameter:	6ft 0in
Pressure:	250 lb/psi
Heating surface:	2,514 sq ft (2,502 sq ft*)
Firebox:	193.5 sq ft (195 sq ft*)
Tubes and flues:	2,007 sq ft (1,818 sq ft*)
Superheater:	313 sq ft (489 sq ft *)
Grate area:	34. 3 sq ft
Tractive effort:	40,300 lb (@ 85% boiler pressure)
Engine wheelbase:	29 ft 3 in
Total wheelbase:	57 ft 5.5 in
Engine weight:	89 tons 0 cwt
Coal capacity:	6 tons
Water capacity:	4,000 gallons
Max. axleloading:	22 tons 10 cwt
BR power class:	8P

* Alterations to heating surfaces following fitting of 4-row superheaters and double chimneys.

IN PRESERVATION cont.

What such purists tend to overlook is that of the restored *King Edward II* only the boiler, mainframes, bogie assembly, leading and centre wheelsets and axleboxes and a small part of the motion are original; all else is new. Moreover, given that the 'Kings' received new frames and cylinders as well as replacement boilers during the 1950s, it is conceivable that the bogie frame, along with the name and numberplates are the sole original items!

Crowning moments

The working career of No6024 *King Edward I* mirrored that of *KEII*. It entered service at Plymouth Laira in June 1930 and remained Devon-based, at either Laira or Newton Abbot, until transferred to Old Oak Common in 1954. It was a regular choice for the Birmingham and Wolverhampton expresses until, in 1961, being reallocated to Cardiff. As with No6023, *KEI* was retired in June 1962 and luckily ended up at Woodhams', where both 'Kings' were examined by members of what would become the 6024 Preservation Society.

As related above, renovating a boiler looked considerably more achievable than replacing a wheelset, and the saving hand was extended to No6024 *King Edward I*. The price – 'as seen' – was £4,000 with transport from the site extra. Finding a home for an engine as large as a 'King' was no easy matter. Eventually *KEI* moved to the fledgling Buckinghamshire Railway Centre, arriving at the ex-Great Central Railway station of Quainton Road in 1972. It would become its home for the next seventeen years.

An extension to the shed at Quainton Road meant that, during July 1986, No6024 finally had a proper roof over its head. This brought a welcome acceleration to the project and, in November 1987, the engine did its greatest mileage for 25 years when it was towed up and down the yard. Boiler and chassis were reunited on 28 March 1988 but there were a further eleven months' work before, on 2 February 1989, at around 1.30pm the regulator was opened and No6024 moved off shed.

It was the start of a new life in preservation that has seen No6024 become a mainstay of the main-line fleet and a favourite of many.

The Saga of the 'Scots'

The LMSR took a gamble with the 'Royal Scots', building a class of vitally needed engines straight off the drawing board. Turning good engines into great ones, though, had nothing to do with luck.

London Midland &
Scottish Railway

**Henry Fowler/James
Anderson/William
Stanier**

**'Royal Scot'
class 7P**
4-6-0 (1927)

Act in haste, repent at leisure goes the saying. That was the price the London Midland & Scottish Railway might have paid when, in some desperation, it ordered 50 of a new and untried design of express passenger locomotive. There was no prototype, no trials and, significantly, scant involvement by its Chief Mechanical Engineer, Sir Henry Fowler. There was though, a little help from an unexpected source.

By 1926, the superiority of Nigel Gresley's LNER Pacifics on prestigious Anglo-Scottish services was proving an embarrassment for its west-coast rival. The LMSR had nothing to match them. Moreover, there was little faith that its design team, outwardly under the guidance of Chief Mechanical Engineer Sir Henry Fowler, could produce something of equivalent stature. Apparently without reference to Fowler, his superiors sought assistance from the Great Western Railway. One of the GWR's highly successful 'Castle' class 4-6-0s, No5000 *Launceston Castle*, was borrowed for trials on the West Coast Main Line.

As No5000 *Launceston Castle* eclipsed the local competition in trials between Euston, Crewe and Carlisle, the LMSR became aware of what it was missing. Indeed, so impressed were the directors, they proposed buying 50 'Castles'. The GWR graciously declined the order, citing the difficulty of reworking the engine

Wearing the later LMSR livery of black lined out in maroon and straw, but in rebuilt condition with double chimney, taper boiler and Belpaire firebox, No6115 *Scots Guardsman* poses at the Birmingham Railway Museum (now Tyseley Locomotive Works) on 14 October 1989. It would be nineteen years before it steamed again, as BR No46115 at Carnforth.

American adventure

Between May and December 1933, a North American adventure confirmed the status of the 'Royal Scots'. The LMSR selected No6100 *Royal Scot* itself to fly the flag at the Century of Progress exhibition in Chicago. For its transatlantic tour, the engine was equipped with a new front bogie and axleboxes as part of a complete refurbishment at Derby Works. Especially for the visit, No6100 was harnessed to the eight-ton, six-wheel tender that would one day run behind the third of the Stanier Pacifics, the 'Turbomotive'.

On October 11, at the conclusion of the Chicago event, *Royal Scot* and its train of newly constructed luxury coaches set out on a tour of the United States and Canada visiting, among other cities, Denver, Montreal, San Francisco, St Louis, Winnipeg and Vancouver. The highlight was an unassisted climb of the Rocky Mountains, albeit with a modest load. In total, the train covered almost 11,900 miles without any mechanical failure, or the need to replace any parts – a considerable achievement. It was also visited by more than three million people (some of whom helped themselves to more than 500 light bulbs from the carriages!).

to meet the less-generous LMSR loading gauge – a polite get-out, if not an entirely convincing one.

This was bad news for the LMSR, which had publicly committed to accelerating its London to Scotland services from the summer of 1927. By-passing Fowler, the company's motive-power superintendent, James Anderson, took it upon himself to deliver the locomotives needed, which he judged to be three-cylinder, large-boilered 4-6-0s incorporating the features that had made other companies' latest designs so successful: high-degree superheat and long-travel valve gear, for example. Now he faced a race to get the engines built.

A helping hand

Anderson recognised that, in the time available, developing the design from scratch was out of the question. History has it that his request to

borrow a set of 'Castle' drawings from the GWR failed to elicit as much as a reply. By contrast, the Southern Railway was happy to assist the LMSR by supplying blueprints for its recently introduced 4-6-0, the 'Lord Nelson'. It fell to the chief draughtsman at Derby Works, Herbert Chambers, to adapt what he could of the 'Nelson' to the LMSR's requirements.

Designing the engine, however, was only half the task. Anderson had to find somewhere to build them, somewhere that excluded the LMSR's main works at Crewe and Derby. Neither could meet the stipulated timescale, but an outside contractor, the North British Locomotive Company, believed it could. In February 1927, the LMSR placed an order with the Glasgow builder, agreeing a price of £7,725 for each of 50 engines. Undertaking much of the detail design work itself, NBL was able to deliver the first of the 4-6-0s on 14 July and it completed the order on 15 November.

The LMSR soon capitalised on the performance of the newcomers. In July 1927, it bestowed the name 'Royal Scot' on the long-established 10.00am departure from Euston to Glasgow and Edinburgh. Soon after, it felt able to retime the 'Scot' to run non-stop over the 299 miles to Carlisle, and it inaugurated the new schedule on 26 September.

A call to arms

In October 1927, the LMSR decided its flagship express locomotives merited names. The doyen of the class, No6100, became *Royal Scot* while the remainder

The doyen of the class, No6100 *Royal Scot*, returned to public service on the West Somerset Railway during March 2009, subsequently appearing on the Llangollen Railway.

IN PRESERVATION

No6100 *Royal Scot*

Withdrawn in 1962, having covered 2,141,229 miles in a 35-year career, *Royal Scot* was bought by Butlin's for display at its holiday camp at Skegness (one of several engines acquired by the company). Subsequently, Butlin's placed *Royal Scot* in the care of Bressingham Steam Museum in Norfolk. Wearing the striking, if incorrect (the engine was rebuilt in 1950) livery of LMSR crimson lake, No6100 remained there for over 30 years, during which time Butlin's sold the engine to the museum.

Some five years ago, Bressingham released *Royal Scot* to the London Mainline Steam Group for a full overhaul. The task, which was undertaken in part of the one-time GWR steam shed at Southall, in west London, and at Crewe, was finally completed in March 2009.

either resurrected famous old L&NWR names (*Planet, Samson, Comet, Phoenix* and the like) or honoured British regiments. Eventually, with three exceptions (*The Boy Scout, The Girl Guide* and *The Royal Air Force*), the entire class adopted regimental names. So delighted was the LMSR with the performance of the 'Scots' that, in late 1929, it ordered a further 25 examples. This time, however, Derby Works had the capacity to build them and delivered the first, No6150, on schedule on 31 May 1930.

In their original form, the 'Royal Scots' fully repaid the LMSR's investment, even though they were displaced from the prestige west-coast expresses by Stanier's Pacifics, which began to appear in 1933. In terms of power, the latter were self-evidently in a different league. But when, in 1942, the 'Scots' were out-performed by a pair of nominally less powerful 'Jubilee' 5XP 4-6-0s, questions were asked. Along with other modifications, these engines had been fitted with the new Type 2A taper boiler. Would the 'Scots', whose boilers and smokeboxes were due for renewal anyway, benefit from a change?

In William Stanier's mind there was no argument and he initiated the rebuilding of the class, not only with new boilers and smokeboxes, but double blastpipes and chimneys, new bogies, new coupled wheel centres and – in some cases – new frames and cylinders. Rebuilding took from 1944 until 1955 and, in their new form, the 'Royal Scots' served both the LMSR and British Railways' London Midland Region well. All were withdrawn between 1962 and 1965.

No46115 *Scots Guardsman* heads a southbound parcels train on the West Coast Main Line, near Carstairs, on 16 April 1965. Built in 1928, No46115 starred in the famous documentary film 'Night Mail' and was the last 'Royal Scot' in service.

No46115 *Scots Guardsman*

Delivered in September 1927, No46115 became the final 'Scot' to be rebuilt by the LMSR before nationalisation, in August 1947. Most famously, though, No46115 'starred in *Night Mail*, the 1936 documentary that told the story of the legendary 'West Coast Postal'. After a number of 'false dawns' *Scots Guardsman* was bought for overhaul by the Carnforth-based West Coast Railway Company and, on 20 June 2008, took to the rails for a test run between Carnforth and Hellifield. It quickly gained main-line approval and undertook its first outing from Hellifield to Carlisle on 16 August. Its operational base remains at Carnforth.

IN DETAIL *(as built)*

Class	'Royal Scot'
Built:	1927-30, Derby Works; North British Locomotive Company, Glasgow
Designer:	Henry Fowler, James Anderson
Number built:	71
Purpose:	Express passenger
Wheel arrangement:	4-6-0
Cylinders (x3):	18 in diameter x 26 in stroke
Motion:	Walschaerts
Valves:	9 in diameter piston valves
Wheels: Coupled:	6 ft 9 in
Leading:	3 ft 3.5 in
Tender:	4 ft 3 in
Boiler diagram:	n/a (Type 2A)
Boiler Max. diameter:	5 ft 9 in (5 ft 10.5 in)
Boiler pressure:	250 lb/psi
Heating surface:	2,480 sq ft (2,219 sq ft)
Firebox:	189 sq ft (195 sq ft)
Tubes and flues:	1,892 sq ft (1,667 sq ft)
Superheater:	445 sq ft, later 399 sq ft (357 sq ft)
Grate area:	31.25 sq ft (31.2 sq ft)
Coal capacity:	5 tons 10 cwt (9 tons)
Water capacity:	3,500 gallons (4,000 gallons)
Tractive effort:	33,150 lb (@ 85 % boiler pressure)
Total wheelbase:	54 ft 9 in (54 ft 5.25 in)
Engine wheelbase:	27 ft 6 in
Engine weight:	84 tons 18 cwt (83 tons 0 cwt)
Max. axleloading:	22 tons 8 cwt (22 tons 0 cwt)

(Changes through rebuilding in brackets.)

Pannier Power

The GWR was alone among Britain's railways in using the six-coupled pannier tank as its principal shunting, empty-stock and light-goods locomotive. The oblong, side-mounted tanks became as characteristically Great Western as copper-capped chimneys.

Panniers paired: No5764 (visiting from the Severn Valley Railway) and No5786 (Llangollen Railway) arrive at Crowcombe Heathfield on the West Somerset Railway with the 2.05pm from Minehead on 30 March 2003.

It was another example of the Great Western doing things differently, but with justification. The reason for using oblong, side-mounted 'pannier' tanks was twofold. First, the introduction of square-topped Belpaire fireboxes on GW engines made saddletanks impractical. They could be shortened to cover just the boiler barrel but this considerably reduced the water space. Second, unlike the sidetank, which was mounted on the running board, the pannier allowed ready access to the inside valve gear and cylinders for inspection and maintenance.

The first, experimental introduction of pannier tanks came in 1898 when they were fitted to a solitary 4-4-0, No1490. Around 1903, the first six-coupled pannier tanks appeared and panniers went on to become the norm for new construction from about 1910.

IN PRESERVATION

No3650 Restoration completed at Didcot Railway Centre during 2008.

No3738 Another Didcot resident, currently undergoing overhaul.

No4612 Once 'written-off' for cannibalisation, No4612 was eventually restored and works on the Bodmin & Wenford Railway.

No5764 Once one of the London Transport panniers (L95), now a working member of the Severn Valley Railway fleet.

No5775 Another one-time London Transport engine (L89), No5775

awaits overhaul on the Keighley & Worth Valley Railway.

No5786 In traffic on the South Devon Railway, the erstwhile LT NoL92 was returned to working order at the now-defunct Bulmer Railway Centre in Hereford.

No7714 One of a trio of panniers based on the Severn Valley Railway, No7714 was first returned to working order during 1992 and continues in service.

No7715 One of the ex-LT panniers, No7715 has long resided in Metropolitan Railway territory at the Buckinghamshire Railway Centre. Recommissioned in April

5700 class 0-6-0PT No3632 takes the curve at Clink Road Junction, Frome, Somerset, and heads north-eastwards with a goods for Westbury on the 10 August 1962.

Significantly, no provision had been made by Churchward for a purpose-built shunting engine in his scheme for a series of new, standard locomotive classes. He had probably estimated that the GWR had sufficient small tank locomotives. Hundreds had been built during the 1890s and early 1900s and more were inherited when the GWR absorbed minor railways in South Wales. It was left to Churchward's successors, Charles Collett and Frederick Hawksworth, to produce the shunting engines for the new century, although there was much their Victorian forebears would have recognised.

By the late 1920s, many of the older shunting locomotives were approaching their expiry date, including the 2700 class of 1896, which still mustered a complete complement of 100. It was on this engine that Charles Collett based his design for the new, standard GW tank, the 5700.

Bulk orders

The main differences between the 5700 and its predecessor were an increase in boiler pressure from 180lb to 200lb/psi and the inclusion of a Belpaire firebox. A larger bunker was fitted, together with an enclosed cab, and the valve settings were improved. (like their predecessors, the 5700s employed slide valves and Stephenson link motion). None of these modifications, however, merited prototype testing and 100 were ordered off the drawing board with construction shared between Swindon and the North British Locomotive Company. As a contribution to a government scheme to create employment during the economic depression of the early 1930s, five other outside contractors then shared orders for a further 200 engines.

Deliveries from Swindon Works resumed in 1933 and continued uninterrupted for a further 17 years, by which time the 5700 panniers numbered 863. It was the second-most numerous class ever built in Britain exceeded only by the 900-plus 'DX' class 0-6-0s of the London & North Western Railway. The last to be delivered – appropriately from Swindon – was No6779 in 1950. Adding the subsequent variations on the 5700 – the lighter 1600 and 5400 series and Hawksworth's 1500 and 9400 classes – took the total of GWR-designed six-coupled pannier tanks to over 1,200. In all this time, the most significant change

1993, for a time it worked specials over London Underground tracks in its LT guise of L99. It is now undergoing overhaul on the Spa Valley Railway, Tunbridge Wells, Kent.

No7752 Much-travelled after restoration, it is now a resident at Tyseley Locomotive Works, Birmingham

No7754 Undergoing overhaul on the Llangollen Railway.

No7760 Restored to working order at the Birmingham Railway Museum (now Tyseley Locomotive Works) No7760 has also worn its London Transport identity of L90 and worked on the main line – including in tandem with NoL99 (above).

No9600 Another Tyseley-based pannier tank, No9600 has also been returned to main-line running condition. Carries – uniquely among surviving panniers – British Railways lined black livery.

No9629 Under restoration on Wales' Pontypool & Blaenavon Railway.

No9642 Its restoration completed, No9642 was located on the Gloucestershire Warwickshire Railway bur now requires further work before it can enter traffic.

No9681 A long-time resident and mainstay of services on the Dean Forest Railway in Gloucestershire.

No9682 Nominally part of the Southall Railway Centre stock, this 1949-built pannier has been returned to working order and presently works on the Chinnor & Prince's Risborough Railway in Buckinghamshire.

The tranquillity of the Grand Union Canal is broken as ex-London Transport panniers NoL90 (GWR 7760) and NoL99 (7715) sprint away from Watford with a 'Steam on the Met' shuttle for Harrow-on-the-Hill. Electric locomotive No12 *Sarah Siddons* supplies braking power.

in the 5700 was the fitting of eleven engines (Nos9700-9710) with condensing equipment and feedwater heaters. This allowed them to work eastwards from Paddington through the tunnels of London's Metropolitan Line.

The 5700s were versatile, free-running and surprisingly strong machines, attributes that frequently saw them entrusted with loads at odds with their size. The power generated at low speeds was remarkable, and they were equally at home on branch line or local goods, shunting and handling empty coaching stock. For two decades, its axleloading confined the 5700 to the 'blue' lines in the GWR's colour-coded system of determining route availability. Blue admitted an axleloading of between 16 and 18 tons. After 1950, however, the engines' negligible 'hammer-blow' on the track saw that relaxed to yellow (14 to 16 tons) which meant that there were few areas where the 5700 could not operate. In 1954, only five Western Region running sheds – Truro and the Welsh outposts of Abercynon, Treherbert, Aberystwyth and Machynlleth – did not have a 5700 on the books.

A handful of engines ventured away from the WR, undertaking banking work on the Southern's Folkestone Harbour branch, for example. They would do the hard work of propelling the heavy Pullman cars of the 'Golden Arrow' to the point where a Bulleid or 'Britannia' Pacific would take over for the run to London. They replaced veteran L&SWR tanks on pilot duties at London's Waterloo and five surplus 5700s were sold to the National Coal Board. In 1956, London Transport began acquiring them to replace life-expired ex-Metropolitan Railway locomotives on shunting work. They also hauled nocturnal engineers' trains and delivered loads to LT's waste disposal site, the 'Watford Tip'.

Up to 1963, a total of 14 pannier tanks saw service with London Transport and the final three – NosL90, L94 and L95 – remained at work until 1971, six years after the retirement of the last Western Region 5700. This trio now numbers among the 16 survivors, and the 5700 continues to prove its worth on preserved lines around the country.

IN DETAIL *(as built)*

Class	5700
Built:	1929-50; Swindon Works; Armstrong Whitworth, Scotswood-upon-Tyne; W.G. Bagnall, Stafford; Beyer, Peacock, Manchester; Kerr Stuart, Stoke-on-Trent; North British Locomotive Company, Glasgow; Yorkshire Engine Company, Sheffield.
Designer:	Charles Collett
Number built:	863
Purpose:	Light goods, shunting, empty stock, branch passenger
Wheel arrangement:	0-6-0PT
Cylinders (x 2):	17.5 in diameter x 24 in stroke
Motion:	Stephenson link
Valves:	Slide valves
Wheels: Coupled:	4 ft 7.5 in
Boiler diagram:	¶
Boiler: Max. diameter:	4 ft 5 in
Pressure:	200 lb/psi
Heating surface:	1,178.0 sq ft
Firebox:	102.3 sq ft
Tubes and flues:	1,075.7 sq ft
Grate area:	15.3 sq ft
Tractive effort:	22,515 lb (@ 85% boiler pressure)
Engine wheelbase:	15 ft 6 in
Engine weight:	47 tons 10 cwt*
Coal capacity:	3 tons 6 cwt
Water capacity:	1,200 gallons
Max. axleloading:	16 tons 15 cwt (17 tons 0 cwt on modified batches)
BR power class:	3F

¶ *The 5700 class used the boiler from the 2301('Dean Goods') class 0-6-0; it did not come within the Swindon Standard list.*
* *Locomotives with condensing apparatus weighed 50 tons 15 cwt; those with enlarged cabs 49 tons 0 cwt.*

The 'Schools' Run

The 'Schools' class was an inspired answer to some 'old bores' troubling the Southern Railway. In doing so it became the last of a long and distinguished line.

Southern Railway
Richard Maunsell
Class 'V' 'Schools'
5P 4-4-0 (1930)

Following repatriation from the United States, 'Schools' No30926 *Repton* has been an unlikely resident of the North Yorkshire Moors Railway. On a gala day, 7 October 1990, the BR-liveried 4-4-0 climbs past Darnholm on the final stretch of the 1 in 37 climb from Grosmont to Goathland. Evidently fearing the 6 feet 6 inches diameter coupled wheels might slip on the wet rails, the NYMR's running department has supplied banking assistance in the form of LNER Q7 0-8-0 No901.

Tunnels of unusually narrow-bore are a peculiar feature of the line between Tunbridge Wells, in Kent, and the seaside resort of Hastings, in East Sussex. Mountfield tunnel, near Battle, for example, has a width limit of just 8 feet 6.5 inches. Matters were not helped when the dimensions were further reduced by an additional lining, forced by the disintegration of the original tunnel walls. As if the tunnels were not problem enough, the line has many twists and turns. Together, they ruled out the larger, more powerful locomotives, which was acceptable as long as trainloadings on the route remained light. This allowed successive cash-strapped managements to avoid the cost of digging new tunnels or re-boring the existing ones.

By the late 1920s, however, the Southern Railway was becoming concerned by the line's limitations. Hastings was a popular seaside resort and commuter traffic was growing along the route. Improvements in the train service had to be made, ones that would demand more powerful motive power. Yet the gauge constraints remained. The task of reconciling the loadings with the limitations fell to the Southern's CME, Richard Maunsell, and he responded with what is generally agreed to be his most successful design, the Class 'V' 4-4-0. Some commentators judged these 40 engines the finest built by the Southern Railway in its 25-year existence. Outwardly, however, in reverting to the four-coupled format, they appeared a backward step.

Tailored to the task

The eccentricities of the Hastings line influenced many aspects of the design. The short frame length reduced the 'throw-over' on sharp curves and the rounded

Top marks

These last representatives of the four-coupled British passenger engine gave around 30 years' service on all three divisions of the Southern Railway (and BR's Southern Region). In that time they became a popular choice for royal-train haulage, particularly the annual Derby Day special from Victoria to Epsom Downs. On one occasion, as the train was about to depart, HRH Prince Philip was heard to remark jokingly to the SR's Superintendent of Operations, 'Do you really think your engine will get there?'

He replied: 'Sir, if Her Majesty's horse is half as good as our engine, it will come in first today!'

As one footplateman, Norman Harvey, commented:

'Most drivers seemed agreed that you could notch up a "Schools" to a very short cut-off indeed and they would run best with a mere cushion of steam in their cylinders.'

As to the original reason for the 'Schools' existence, when the narrow-bodied diesel units were life-expired and the line electrified, British Railways simply reorganised the signalling and reduced the double track to a single line down the middle of the tunnel!

profile fitted snugly within the width restrictions. To suit the line's loading gauge, the overall width of the locomotive was restricted to 8 feet 6.5 inches and cab height limited to 12 feet 10.75 inches. The maximum permissible distance between the centres of the outside cylinders was 6 feet 8 inches, insufficient to accommodate two cylinders of the required size. To generate a comparable power output, a three-cylinder layout was incorporated.

To this end, Maunsell and his drawing office first worked on a scaled-down, three-cylinder version of the 'Lord Nelson' 4-6-0, with three cylinders instead of four, but this proved unworkable. Almost certainly, Maunsell would have chosen to use the square-top Belpaire firebox employed on the 'Nelsons' rather than the round-top variety but, given the pronounced inward curve of the cab,

this would have overly restricted forward vision.

However, many components of the 'Lord Nelson', such as the cylinders and bogie, were incorporated in the 'V' and the cab design and layout were similar. All of which was a touch ironic. While the 'Nelsons' of 1926 did not quite live up to expectation, four years on, the 'V' was a success from the start.

An inevitable consequence of building such a compact but powerful machine was a high axleloading (21 tons) and this required the upgrading of the entire Tonbridge–Hastings route. Track renewals were still underway when, between March and July 1930, the first ten 'V's were outshopped from Eastleigh, straight off the drawing board: no trials were deemed necessary. Rather than stand idle, they were used on other main lines in Kent and Hampshire and promptly turned in some striking performances. As excellent steamers and responsive to drivers' dictates, they quickly earned the affection of engine crews. The only caveat was the need for careful starting to avoid the wheelslip that such a power-to-weight ratio invariably provoked. At 25,130lb, the tractive effort of the 'V' exceeded that of the 'King Arthur' 4-6-0s. More than that, it was the most powerful 4-4-0 in Europe.

As anticipated, when the Hastings line was ready for them, they became the masters of the 350 ton trains that ran between London and the East Sussex coast. No modifications were necessary, although smoke deflectors were fitted from 1931 onwards, as the engines entered the works for attention. Subsequently, Maunsell's successor, Oliver Bulleid, equipped around half the class with the Lemaître blastpipe and wide chimney arrangement, something that did nothing for their looks and made little difference to performance.

Given its favourable reception, Maunsell concluded that the 'V' could be used

IN PRESERVATION

Three 'Schools' live on. One, No925 *Cheltenham*, was selected for the National Collection, and two others were privately preserved: No30926 *Repton*, now based on the North Yorkshire Moors Railway, and No928 *Stowe*, which is on more familiar territory at the Bluebell Railway in East Sussex.

No925 *Cheltenham* Built at Eastleigh in April 1934, No925 *Cheltenham* first went to the Portsmouth and Bournemouth lines but spent most of its British Railways career on the Kent Coast line, being based at Dover in 1951 and Bricklayers Arms in 1958. It was among the last of the class to be withdrawn, from Basingstoke shed in December 1962.

Preserved as part of the National Collection, *Cheltenham* was moved to the National Railway Museum in 1977. It was steamed for the Rainhill cavalcade of 1980, which commemorated the 150th anniversary of the Liverpool & Manchester Railway, memorably running with another legendary 4-4-0 design, Midland Compound No1000. It is now a static exhibit at York.

No30926 *Repton* Outshopped from Eastleigh Works in May 1934, No926 *Repton* became one of a batch of ten 'Schools' (Nos924-933) allocated to Fratton shed, Portsmouth, for the Waterloo–Portsmouth 'direct' service. On the fastest trains they were allowed 90 minutes for the run with

an 11-coach load. When the Portsmouth line was electrified, the Fratton engines moved to Bournemouth. *Repton* remained at Bournemouth for some time, during which period it contributed to what many commentators consider the highpoint of the 'Schools' careers, hauling the Waterloo–Bournemouth expresses.

Following withdrawal from Basingstoke shed in December 1962, *Repton* entered Eastleigh Works at the end of 1964 for attention and repainting before being shipped from Liverpool to the United States. The locomotive had been bought by the founder of the Steamtown Museum at Bellows Falls, Vermont, and went on display there.

In 1989, *Repton* was repatriated and

promptly overhauled at the Grosmont workshops of the North Yorkshire Moors Railway, entering traffic on the NYMR in October 1990. In contrast to the other two preserved 'Schools', which carry Southern colours, *Repton* is in BR lined green as

more widely and extended construction beyond those required for the Hastings line. By 1935, the class had been enlarged to 40, the last of hundreds of four-coupled express passenger engines built for Britain's railways since the 1850s.

Star pupils

Following on the 'King Arthurs' and 'Lord Nelsons', the naming of the 'V' class was another masterstroke by Southern Railway's publicity department. A considerable number of private and public schools were located within the SR's boundaries, from Winchester to Lancing, Charterhouse, Dulwich, Sherborne, Westminster and King's Canterbury. Many a parent and pupil travelled to-and-from these seats of learning by train.

Wherever possible, each new engine was sent to the station nearest its school for a naming ceremony and for pupils to be photographed polishing the paintwork and the nameplate. These images were adorned with captions such as 'Keep the name bright!'. Each school was encouraged to 'adopt' its locomotive and the enlargement of the class saw schools outside southern England included: Cheltenham, Malvern, Marlborough, Rugby and Shrewsbury.

By 1947, all but three of the 'Schools' had returned to their alma mater of the Hastings route. The exceptions were Nos928-930 that were allocated to Brighton to work cross-country services as far as Salisbury. Following nationalisation, all were based on the Eastern Section until made redundant by electrification in 1959. Withdrawals began with Nos30919 and 30932 in January 1961 and concluded in December 1962, when all nineteen survivors were condemned.

Illustrating the period immediately following construction when the 'Schools' ran without smoke deflectors, No928 *Stowe*, runs off shed at Sheffield Park on the Bluebell Railway on 5 August 1990. A Bluebell Railway locomotive since 1980, *Stowe* presently awaits overhaul.

No30926. In recent years, *Repton* has ventured south to the Great Central, Mid-Hants and Severn Valley Railways. In 2003 it briefly assumed the guise of classmate No925 *Cheltenham* when visiting the Gloucestershire Warwickshire Railway to inaugurate the GWR's extension to Cheltenham Racecourse.

No928 *Stowe* Outshopped from Eastleigh in June 1934, *Stowe* was one of the batch of 'Schools' built for the Portsmouth line services. First allocated to Fratton, it moved to Bournemouth in 1937, becoming a notable performer on the Waterloo–Weymouth expresses. *Stowe* holds the record for the highest speed authenticated for the 'Schools': 98 miles per hour between

Dorchester and Wareham in 1938.

After spending most of its BR career at Bricklayers Arms, *Stowe* was withdrawn from Brighton in November 1962. Bought by Lord Montagu of Beaulieu, No928 went on display at the National Motor Museum until, in 1973, moving to Cranmore, home of the East Somerset Railway. *Stowe* remained a static exhibit there until July 1980 when it transferred to the Bluebell Railway. A rapid overhaul saw *Stowe* working on the Bluebell until 1992 when it was withdrawn for its compulsory ten-year overhaul. This work, which requires the construction of a new tender tank, will be undertaken by the engine's latest (since 2000) owners, the Maunsell Locomotive Society.

IN DETAIL *(as built)*	
Class	**'V' ('Schools')**
Built:	Eastleigh Works, 1930-35
Designer:	Richard Maunsell
Number built:	40
Purpose:	Express passenger
Wheel arrangement:	4-4-0
Cylinders (x3):	16.5 in diameter x 26 in stroke
Motion:	Walschaerts
Valves:	8 in diameter piston valves
Wheels: Coupled:	6 ft 7 in
Leading:	3 ft 1 in
Tender:	4 ft 0 in (6-wheel tender)
Boiler: Max. diameter:	5 ft 5.75 in
Pressure:	220lb/psi
Heating surface:	2,049 sq ft
Firebox:	162 sq ft
Tubes and flues:	1,604 sq ft
Superheater:	283 sq ft
Grate area:	28.3 sq ft
Tractive effort:	25,130 lb (@ 85% boiler pressure)
Engine wheelbase:	25 ft 6 in
Total wheelbase:	48 ft 7.25 in
Engine weight:	67 tons 2 cwt
Coal capacity:	5 tons
Water capacity:	4,000 gallons
Max. axleloading:	21 tons 0 cwt
BR power class:	5P

London Midland &
Scottish Railway

Sir William A. Stanier

**'Princess Royal'
class 7P**
4-6-2 (1933)

The Big Red Engines

The prototype 'Princess Royal' Pacifics were the first Stanier-designed locomotives to enter service on the London Midland & Scottish Railway. They marked the start of a momentous era, both for the LMSR and for high-speed running to the north-west and western Scotland..

Making a return to the West Coast Main Line, 'Princess Royal' Pacific No6201 *Princess Elizabeth* approaches Headstone Lane, 12 miles out of Euston, with a railtour for Liverpool on 6 June 2003. Following the introduction of the 'Coronation' Pacifics, the 'Princesses' did much of their best work on the Merseyside expresses.

B y West Coast standards, the first LMSR Pacific, No6200, was a giant. It must have been a breathtaking sight emerging from the Crewe paintshop on 27 June 1933, gleaming in its crimson-lake livery. For six years the 'Royal Scot' 4-6-0s had been putting in fine performances on the LMSR's West Coast expresses but they had their limitations. On the Euston–Glasgow run, loads were limited to 420 tons and engine changes were needed at Carlisle. Something that could comfortably handle 500 tons and cover the entire 401 miles unaided had become an operational priority. A request for just such a locomotive was awaiting William Stanier when he arrived at Euston on 1 January 1932. Within 18 months it had become a reality.

Even though he had grown up with Great Western 4-6-0s, like Gresley on the LNER, Stanier chose the 4-6-2 arrangement that allowed the use of a wide firebox and grate. Inevitably, though, Stanier drew on his Great Western background. Down to cylinder dimensions, valve events, boiler pressure and coupled-wheel diameter, the 4-cylinder 'King' became the basis for the new design but the massive taper boiler and firebox were in a different league. Stanier also broke with Swindon practice by using four independent sets of Walschaerts valve gear.

However, while No6200 looked impressive, its debut between London Euston and Glasgow on 22 September 1933 was less so. Certain Swindon principles imported by Stanier – low-degree superheat, for example – proved incompatible with a boiler of such proportions. This, combined with a restrictive steam circuit, left No6200 embarrassingly shy of steam. While work was underway to cure this problem, a second prototype entered traffic, No6201 emerging from Crewe on 3 November 1933. Its cost of £11,674 represented a substantial overspend of £2,465 on the projected price.

On 22 November No6201 was given charge of the down 'Royal Scot' and then, unannounced, worked a 502-ton test train from Euston to Glasgow, a run that demonstrated its potential. The climb to Shap summit, for example, took just 8 minutes 23 seconds, some two-and-a-half minutes under the scheduled time. Frustratingly for the LMSR, with just two Pacifics available, there was as yet no means of incorporating this kind of performance into the West Coast timetables.

Boiler performance remained a concern and Stanier continued with modifications, for example replacing the 16-element superheater with one of 32. Consequently further construction was delayed until the summer of 1935 when a further ten engines were ordered. By now royal approval had been obtained to name No6200 *The Princess Royal* and No6201 *Princess Elizabeth*, after the elder daughter of the Duke and Duchess of York, later Queen Elizabeth II. Beginning with her sister, Princess Margaret Rose, all the production engines recognised ladies of the aristocracy.

Record-breaking runs

It was not its illustrious name that secured No6201 its place among Britain's legendary locomotives. That was a result of the events of November 1936 when it demonstrated conclusively that any steaming deficiencies had been overcome. Test runs with No6201 from Euston to Glasgow and back were scheduled over two days. William Stanier was on government business in India at the time and

responsibility for the trials fell to a team that included Stanier's Principal Assistant, Robert Riddles. Despite having run 77,096 miles since its last general repair, the locomotive was in fine fettle.

With driver Tommy Clark of Crewe North on the regulator, and a seven-coach train of 225 tons, No6201 left Euston at 9.50am, ten minutes ahead of the down 'Royal Scot'. By Willesden Junction, it had accelerated to 66mph. Over 95mph was attained between Tring and Bletchley but the run was a far more complex matter than simply going hell-for-leather. Set six hours for the 401.4 miles to Glasgow, driver Clark would have to comply with some 50 speed restrictions.

However, the ultimate tests to face all West Coast locomotives were to come: the climbs of Grayrigg, Shap, and Beattock. The ascent from Carnforth to Shap was a record: 31.4 miles to an altitude of 916 feet at an average speed of 70mph. Between Tebay and Shap summit, the Pacific averaged an astonishing 64.5mph. It went 'over the top' at 57mph. Once out of the confines of Carlisle, No6201 again demonstrated its powers of acceleration, from 20mph to 85mph in the space of just six miles. It then maintained 70mph for the seven miles of 1 in 200 to the north of Floriston.

The distance from Beattock station to the summit of the bank is ten miles. That November day, No6201 swept up the 1 in 75 average gradient in 9 minutes 31 seconds. The minimum speed was 56mph and, at the summit, the Pacific touched 58mph. Glasgow Central was reached in 5 hours 53 minutes 38 seconds, representing an average speed of 68.1mph. The maximum speed was 95.7mph with, at one stage, 83mph sustained for 12 miles on practically level track.

Going a storm

That night, with the return run booked to set out the following lunchtime, an

At a location close to that opposite, and again heading for Liverpool, the imposing length of the boiler is evident as the first of the prototype Stanier Pacifics, No6200 *The Princess Royal*, strides through Hatch End with the 5.30pm express from Euston on 5 July 1941.

examination revealed part of the left-hand motion to have run hot. It had to be repaired before the engine could run again but there was no suggestion of cancellation. Robert Riddles, helped by a team of fitters, worked into the early hours to guarantee No6201 would make its date with history.

Daylight brought high winds and heavy rain to the western side of Britain. At 1.20pm the test train – now loaded to 255 tons thanks to an additional coach – left a storm-lashed Glasgow. Despite the conditions, Beattock and Shap were surmounted at 70mph. By Preston, the Pacific was five minutes ahead of schedule and, at Warrington, nine minutes up. The average speed between Winsford and Coppenhall Junction was 90mph, with a maximum of 95mph. At 11 minutes 3 seconds, the 15-mile climb through the Chiltern Hills in Buckinghamshire represented an average of 81.7mph. Overall, the southbound run was nine-and-a-half minutes faster than the northbound. Glasgow to Euston was completed 16 minutes inside the scheduled six hours at an average speed of exactly 70mph. In two days, No6201 had worked more than 800 miles at a mean of 69mph. It had demonstrated that on a difficult, complicated run the key to success lay in rapid acceleration and an approach to the formidable climbs based on high speeds up the gradients and controlled descents.

Its record-breaking over, locomotive No6201 returned to being just another member of the 'Princess Royal' class. The following year, the highly publicised introduction of the streamlined 'Princess Coronation' Pacifics took the spotlight away from the 'Princess Royals' and they relinquished the more prestigious Anglo-Scottish duties to the newcomers. At the outbreak of war in 1939, the 13-strong class, which included the experimental 'Turbomotive' (*see below*), was shared between Camden (London), Crewe North, Edge Hill (Liverpool), Carlisle (Kingmoor) and Upperby and Polmadie (Glasgow).

The 'Princess Royals' continued to serve the LMSR and BR's London Midland Region into the 1950s, becoming a familiar sight on the Euston–Liverpool

expresses, but the arrival of the English Electric Type 4 diesels saw them spending periods in store. With their high axleloading and sheer size such engines were unsuited to being relegated to secondary duties, though they did appear on parcels and fish trains in the north-west and Scotland. Additionally, summer motive-power shortages frequently saw them temporarily reinstated. The most unusual exploit of their final years came in 1956 when two of the class were temporarily allocated to the ex-Great Western depot at Old Oak Common, London. Here they provided emergency cover for 'King' class 4-6-0s withdrawn for modifications to their front bogies. The then 80-year-old Sir William Stanier must have allowed himself a smile at that development.

Apart from the ill-fated No46202 (*see page 103*), all were withdrawn between October 1961 and November 1962. There was, however, a glorious farewell for Carlisle Kingmoor trio of Nos46200, 46203 and 46201 *Princess Elizabeth* – which had surprisingly returned to traffic in January 1962 – on the Euston to Perth expresses. On 2 June 1962, the 'Aberdeen Flyer' railtour offered its passengers what appeared to be a final opportunity to ride behind Gresley and Stanier Pacifics on the routes where they had made their reputations. On the east coast, A4s Nos60004 *William Whitelaw* and 60022 *Mallard* shared the honours, while the return down the west coast was entrusted to Nos46200 and 46201.

The 'Turbomotive'

Unlike Nigel Gresley, his LNER counterpart, William Stanier was not fired by a desire to experiment – not that there was much scope for that on a railway where updating the entire locomotive fleet was paramount. However, the third of the planned prototypes used a new, and promising method of locomotive propulsion. Stanier was persuaded to visit Sweden's Grangesburg–Oxelosund Railway to see a new steam-turbine locomotive at work. Worthwhile savings in fuel and maintenance costs were attributed to the non-condensing Ljungstrom rotary

IN PRESERVATION

No6201 *Princess Elizabeth*

After covering 1,526,807 miles during its 29-year LMSR and BR career, *Princess Elizabeth* was withdrawn on 20 October 1962. At the time buying a locomotive from British Railways was virtually unknown. Captain Bill Smith had bought Great Northern saddletank No1247 and Alan Pegler had saved *Flying Scotsman* but the acquisition of *Princess Elizabeth* broke fresh ground. When the Locomotive 6201 Princess Elizabeth Society raised the asking price, it was the first time a group of enthusiasts had banded together to buy an engine of such size and complexity. The deal was signed in February 1963.

It would be thirteen years before No6201 returned to the main line, since when further and increasingly expensive refits have been necessary to keep it there. The last, completed in 2002, occupied nine years. The following year, railtours memorably took the Pacific back to Euston. When not on main-line duty, the Pacific is usually maintained at Bury, on the East Lancashire Railway.

No46203 *Princess Margaret Rose*

Arriving at the Midland Railway Centre in Derbyshire (now Midland Railway Butterley), from Butlin's, Pwllheli, in November 1975, No46203 made its return to the main line on 2 June 1990. The locomotive enjoyed an active career on the main line, covering 9,157 miles, until withdrawn in April 1996. Now in the care of the Princess Royal Class Locomotive Trust, *PMR*'s last public appearance was at Crewe Works open days in September 2005. An overhaul, expected to occupy two years, will see much of the estimated £100,000 cost spent on the boiler.

turbine employed in the 2-8-0 design. Stanier was sufficiently impressed for the third of the 'Princess Royal' Pacifics to adopt turbine drive.

The 'Turbomotive', as No6202 was swiftly nicknamed, was constructed at Crewe with turbines supplied by Metropolitan Vickers (who had prompted Stanier's original interest). Built at a cost of £15,210 (one-and-a-half times the price of a production series 'Princess Royal') it entered service in 1935 and, compared with most British locomotive experiments, was uncommonly successful. The performance figures told their story: 2,000 horsepower generated at over 70mph with a 500 ton load on a gradient of 1 in 300. However, the hoped-for economies in fuel consumption did not materialise. No6202 remained a 'one-off', with all the disadvantages that brings: long waits for spares, for example. During its 15-year career, it was employed mainly on the London–Liverpool run.

In March 1950, with the main turbine needing renewal, British Railways withdrew the 'Turbomotive'. It was decided to rebuild the locomotive as a more-or-less orthodox member of the 'Princess Royal' class, No46202 *Princess Anne*. The locomotive had been at work just eight weeks when was damaged beyond repair (although its boiler was reused) in the disastrous Harrow & Wealdstone collision of 8 October 1952.

Return to Crewe

The target date for the No6201's return from its second overhaul in preservation was the commemoration of the 150th anniversary of the opening of the Grand Junction Railway in 1837, timed to coincide with the inauguration of a Heritage Centre at Crewe. On 4 July 1987, No6201 was back at its birthplace ready to become acquainted with the other Princess Elizabeth, now Her Majesty the Queen.

After the royal appointment at Crewe, No6201 undertook a further six years of main-line running, adding the newly approved Crewe–Holyhead route to its roster. In June 1990, the other surviving 'Princess Royal' Pacific, No46203 *Princess Margaret Rose*, was approved for main-line running, so setting up the prospect of reunion that few would have predicted when the Stanier Pacifics were withdrawn. During 1991, the Settle–Carlisle line twice echoed to the sound of two 'Princess Royals' working over Ais Gill.

Withdrawn for overhaul in 1993, it was a full nine years before No6201 reappeared. However, the Pacific's incomparable main-line record (not a single failure since 1976) came to a – literally – shattering end on 3 April 2004. After a superb run over Shap, a dislodged core plug resulted in the locomotive's left-hand inside piston being smashed. In addition, the cylinder back cover was blown, a crosshead cracked and slide bars and a connecting rod bent. Repairs, estimated at £25,000, were completed in 2005 and 'Lizzie' retook its place on the main line.

IN DETAIL *(Prototypes as modified and production engines)*	
Class	**'Princess Royal'**
Built:	Crewe Works, 1933-36
Designer:	Sir William Stanier
Number built:	13
Purpose:	Express passenger
Wheel arrangement:	4-6-2
Cylinders (x4):	28 in x 16.25 in
Motion:	Walschaerts valve gear (4 sets, one for each cylinder)
Valves:	8 in diameter
Wheels: Coupled:	6 ft 6 in
Leading::	3 ft 0 in
Trailing:	3 ft 9 in
Tender:	4 ft 3 in
Boiler: Max. diameter:	6 ft 3 in
Pressure:	250 lb/psi
Heating surface:	3,114 sq ft
Firebox:	217 sq ft
Tubes and flues:	2,299 sq ft
Superheater:	598 sq ft
Grate area:	45 sq ft
Tractive effort:	40,285 lb (@ 85% boiler pressure)
Engine wheelbase:	37 ft 9 in
Total wheelbase:	63 ft 10 in
Engine weight:	104 tons 10 cwt
Coal capacity:	10 tons
Water capacity:	4,000 gallons
Max. axleloading:	22 tons 10 cwt
BR power class:	7P (subsequently uprated to 8P)

London Midland &
Scottish Railway

William Stanier

**Class 5P5F
(5MT) 4-6-0
(1934)**

The Beauty of a 'Black 5'

In a 34-year working life that saw it everywhere from the West Country to the Scottish Highlands, this most numerous of mixed-traffic 4-6-0s did everything asked of it. To its designer, William Stanier, the Class 5 was quite simply, 'a deuce of a good engine'.

Spurred by the success of the Great Western's 'Hall' 4-6-0s, William Stanier made a similar 'maid of all work' his highest priority on joining the LMSR from Swindon in 1932. With a route mileage of 7,909, broad variety of traffic and mixed bag of ageing pre-grouping classes, it was exactly the kind of 'standard' locomotive that the LMSR needed, Among the small number of new designs introduced since 1923, only one – the 'Horwich Mogul' of 1926 – came into that category and that had its limitations.

On the GWR, production of the 'Halls' had been preceded by three years of trials. Stanier lacked that luxury. Once drawings were prepared, orders for 50 engines were placed. Crewe Works was to construct 20 with the remainder coming from an outside contractor, Vulcan Foundry of Newton-le-Willows. By rights, the first to enter service should have been the doyen of the class, Crewe's No5000, but the Lancashire concern beat its Cheshire rival by some six months. It outshopped

No5020 in August 1934 and had completed not only the initial order for 30, but a further 20 engines by the time No5000 appeared in February 1935. For power the newcomers qualified for the LMSR's '5' rating with a livery of lined black. The enduring nickname of 'Black 5' was born.

Unlike the three-cylinder 'Jubilees', where hasty construction allowed serious design flaws to go unchecked, the two-cylinder Class 5 4-6-0 was largely a success from the start. On test, and with a load of 15 coaches, No5020 touched 77mph on a run from Euston to Crewe, prompting the *Locomotive Magazine*'s Cecil J. Allen to announce 'an excellent debut indeed for a moderately sized mixed-traffic loco'. On a further trial, with 60 vans behind the tender, No5020 had no difficulty in keeping to time. An LMSR report concluded: 'The two-cylinder 4-6-0 engine appears to be a very efficient and satisfactory mixed-traffic power unit.' The early impact of the 'Black 5' was felt most on the ex-Highland Railway lines where,

Stanier Class 5MT No45407 (in the guise of long-gone classmate No45157 *The Glasgow Highlander*) on the unfamiliar territory of the London, Tilbury & Southend line approaches Upminster with a 'special' working from London Fenchurch Street to Southend-on-Sea on 18 August 2000.

When construction ended, at Horwich Works in May 1951, there were 842 in traffic, making the 5P5F 4-6-0s the fourth-largest class of locomotives ever to work in Britain.

Right temperature

Though presenting nothing like the problems of the 'Jubilee', the boiler performance of the 5P5F 4-6-0 did need some fine-tuning. Stanier's first effort was pure Swindon: low-degree superheat, long lap and long travel valves, tapered and domeless, and attached to a Belpaire firebox. All perfectly sound except that, as with 'Princess Royal' Pacifics of 1933, a low superheat temperature did not suit LMSR conditions. Quite why this should have been has long been argued. The suggestion that the combustion characteristics of Welsh steam coal, as used by the GWR, made the difference is attractive but simplistic. It could have as easily been down to firing technique. All GWR crews came through the ranks learning how to get the best from the standard range of Swindon boilers. Conversely, LMSR men probably shared as many notions about firing and driving as there were constituent companies in that huge organisation.

Stanier responded immediately to the superheater's inadequacy, although it took four years to reach a permanent solution. The number of elements was increased, first to 21, then 24 and finally, beginning with No5452 in 1938, to 28. Simultaneously, the grate area was enlarged from 27.8 to 28.65 square feet and new boilers were fitted with domes to house the regulator (previously located, unsatisfactorily, in the smokebox). The effect of these modifications was to make the 'Black 5' responsive to most techniques of driving and firing.

Unlike the 'Jubilees', which were initially yoked to 3,500 gallon tenders, from the outset the Class 5s received new 4,000 gallon tenders to Stanier's design. There were other, less visible ways that Stanier put his individual stamp on the 'Black 5'. The valve settings were a great improvement on those of the GWR 'Hall', for example, and there was ample evidence that that the '5' was capable of higher speeds than its GW counterpart; 90mph was well within its compass. The cylinder casting benefited from extended valve chests that allowed the ports to be completely straight and therefore present no hindrance to steaming.

Gear changing

Stanier's successor, Charles Fairburn, left the design largely unaltered but his replacement, George Ivatt, had other ideas. Ivatt, who had been appointed Stanier's chief assistant in 1937, produced no fewer than 11 experimental variants of the Class 5. The modifications chiefly centred on assessing the value of roller bearings, both of Skefco and Timken origin, in improving reliability. However, the most far-reaching of Ivatt's attempts to refine the 'Black 5' concerned the valve gear. As with roller bearings, the aim was to reduce the cost of maintenance and the time spent on it. The Italian-designed Caprotti poppet-valve gear was not new to the LMSR: it had been fitted to ten 4-6-0s between 1926 and 1928. Twenty years on, however, it had been much improved and Ivatt's Caprotti-fitted 'Black 5' was redesigned

Its tender well-filled and displaying 'The Sherwood Forester' nameplates, 'Black 5' No45231 draws into Medstead & Four Marks with a Mid-Hants Railway service for Alton. After a couple of years based on the MHR, No45231 has migrated north to the East Lancashire Railway.

replacing veteran 4-4-0s, they transformed punctuality. October 1935 found 36 of the class working out of depots such as Perth and Inverness.

Its weight and length gave the 'Black 5' virtually unrestricted access to the LMSR system. They could grapple with loose-coupled goods and fitted (i.e. fully vacuum-braked) freights as competently as they handled semi-fast and even express passenger services. The free-steaming qualities of the design, allied to Stanier's careful attention to valve settings, comfortably accommodated speeds of around 90mph. Further orders for 5P5F 4-6-0s, as they were classified, followed and, in 1935, included the largest single locomotive-building contract placed by a British railway company – 227 from Armstrong Whitworth. The cost of £1,380,160 (£6,080 per engine) was covered by a low-interest government loan intended to stimulate the economy during the Great Depression. With a further contribution from Crewe, by the end of 1938 the LMSR could call upon the services of 472 'Black 5s'.

Wartime restrictions saw construction halted until April 1943, when a further 20 examples were built at Derby. Thereafter, the workshops at Crewe, Derby and Horwich turned out batches every year until 1951, three years after nationalisation.

Almost from the first the 'Black 5s' became associated with the West Highland line and several preserved examples have been rostered for the annual steam-hauled summer service between Fort William and Mallaig. On 25 June 1987, entrusted with the 11.05pm Mallaig train, No5305 crosses the famous concrete viaduct at Glenfinnan.

around the valve gear rather than the gear being adapted to suit an existing layout, which invariably resulted in an unsatisfactory compromise.

Results with the Caprotti engines were mixed. There was a notable increase in mileages between valve examinations – from 30,000 to 36,000 miles to between 40,000 and 48,000 miles – yet footplate crews noticed a falling-off in sheer 'pulling power' compared to the Walschaerts engines. Ironically, modifications to the camboxes on the last two engines to be built, Nos44686 and 44687, brought striking improvements and they became regarded as exceptionally strong machines. By now, though, construction was underway of the BR Standard

5MT 4-6-0 and the changes came to benefit its quota of Caprotti engines. In a further twist, one locomotive, the now-preserved No44767 *George Stephenson*, was equipped with outside Stephenson's link-motion valve gear.

From first to last

Taken overall the various tinkerings with the Stanier original brought only modest improvements. These later locomotives also incorporated devices that were to become obligatory on the BR Standard designs of the 1950s: self-cleaning smokeboxes, rocking grates and self-emptying ashpans. The Standard Class 5MT

IN PRESERVATION

The usefulness of the 'Black 5' continues. Of the 18 preserved examples, 13 have seen service at one time or another. Currently, five are in traffic, with at least three approved for main-line working.

No44767 *George Stephenson* Outshopped from Crewe on the eve of nationalisation, 31 December 1947, No44767 was unique among the 'Black 5s' in employing outside Stephenson link valve gear. It returned to steam during 1975 on the North Yorkshire Moors Railway and appeared at the Rail 150 celebrations at Shildon, where it was named *George Stephenson*. Withdrawn in 2001, its latest refurbishment is approaching completion.

No44806 Derby-built in 1944, No44806 came to the Llangollen Railway in 1993. Its

latest overhaul was completed in 2008.

No44871 Outshopped from Crewe in March 1945, No44871 has the dubious honour of being the last standard-gauge steam locomotive to be used by British Railways. In tandem with classmate No44781, it worked the farewell special of 11 August 1968. Now owned by engineer, Ian Riley, in 2006 No44871 moved to his works at Bury for overhaul.

No44932 The overhaul of No44932 is approaching its final stages at Midland Railway, Butterley.

No5000 Selected for preservation in 1967 as part of the National Collection, No5000 was stored at various locations before making a main-line return in 1979, working until the

late 1980s. It is now on static display at York.

No5025 Among the first 5P5F 4-6-0s to be delivered to the LMSR, by Vulcan Foundry in August 1934, No5025 enjoyed one of the longest working lives of any of the class. After overhaul at the Andrew Barclay locomotive works at Kilmarnock, No5025 arrived on Scotland's Strathspey Railway in 1975. It is now the subject of a £250,000 appeal to return it to working order.

No45110 It earned a place in railway history by heading British Railways' 'Farewell to Steam' railtour out of Liverpool Lime Street on the last day of steam traction, 11 August 1968. Soon after, No45110 was bought by the Stanier Black Five Preservation Society, and in 1970 found a home on the Severn Valley Railway. Though said to be in good condition

No45110 is waiting for an overhaul.

No45212 Twenty years in store ended when agreement was reached for an overhaul of the 'Black 5' that would see it shared between the Keighley & Worth Valley Railway and the North Yorkshire Moors Railway. No45212 steamed again in 2002.

No45231 Home to No45231 is now the East Lancashire Railway, one of four 'Black 5s' based at Bury.

No45305 Often judged the best turned-out of the preserved 'Black 5's, the 5305 Locomotive Association completed the latest overhaul to main-line condition in 2003.

No45337 After purchase in 1985, the locomotive was moved to the East Lancashire

4-6-0 of 1951 was no more than a modest reworking of the 'Black 5' design. This led the commentator, O.S. Nock, to observe that it might have been preferable for the ex-LMSR hierarchy of the Railway Executive to ignore accusations of bias and simply continue building the Stanier design. It had, after all, achieved a level of availability and reliability enjoyed by very few other British steam locomotive classes. For example, the average mileage between general repairs was between 150,000 and 160,000.

Along with another Stanier design, the 8F 2-8-0, the 'Black 5' served British Railways from its first day, 1 January 1948, to the final hours of standard-gauge steam on 11 August 1968. The last 'Black 5's were outshopped from Horwich in the spring of 1951 and the class remained intact until 1961 when No45401 became the first to be withdrawn, and then only because of collision damage. Only around 40 were scrapped up to the end of 1963, but then the cull began in earnest, with 151 withdrawals during 1968 alone. Nevertheless, that last month of steam still found 46 'Black 5's in traffic, all concentrated in the North West. On 3 August, the now-preserved No45212 had the melancholy duty of hauling the last timetabled steam-hauled passenger train on BR. One week later, No44781, 44871 and 45110 worked the excursions – the 'Fifteen Guinea Specials' – that were meant to bring down the curtain on main-line steam traction in Britain. However, two of that trio – Nos44871 and 45110 – defied the script and lived to tell a happier tale.

IN DETAIL (as built)

Class	'5P5F'
Built:	Crewe, Derby, Horwich works; Armstrong Whitworth, Scotswood-on-Tyne; Vulcan Foundry, Newton-le Willows, Lancashire
Designer:	Sir William Stanier
Number built:	842
Purpose:	Mixed traffic
Wheel arrangement:	4-6-0
Cylinders (x 2):	18.5 in diameter x 28 in stroke
Motion:	Walschaerts *
Valves:	10 in diameter piston valves
Wheels: Coupled:	6 ft 0 in diameter
Leading:	3 ft 3.5 in diameter
Tender:	4 ft 3 in
Boiler diagram:	EU44/3B
Boiler: Max. diameter:	5 ft 8.5 in
Pressure:	225 lb/psi
Heating surface:	2,009 sq ft §
Firebox:	171 sq ft
Tubes and flues:	1,479 sq ft
Superheater:	359 sq ft
Grate area:	28.65 sq ft ¶
Tractive effort:	25,455 lb (@ 85% boiler pressure)
Engine wheelbase:	27 ft 2 in
Total wheelbase:	53 ft 2.75 in
Engine weight:	72 tons 2 cwt to 75 tons 6 cwt ⊠
Coal capacity:	9 tons
Water capacity:	4,000 gallons
Max. axleloading:	17 tons 18 cwt
BR power class:	5MT

Certain engines fitted with Stephenson link motion or British Caprotti poppet–valve gear —see text.

§ Heating surface area given for the later series of locomotives with 28-element superheaters. Locomotives originally built with 14-element superheaters and subsequently modified with 21, 24 and finally 28 elements.

¶ Engines Nos5000-5224 had grates of 27.8 sq ft area.

⊠ Locomotive weights varied with various modifications.

Railway where its restoration was completed a decade later. Withdrawn in August 2005, an overhaul is underway.

No45407 Owned since 1997 by Ian Riley No45407 has since worked far-and-wide on the main line, including in the guise of long-gone classmate No45157 *The Glasgow Highlander*. On 13 November 2004, however, at a ceremony on the East Lancashire Railway, the engine gained a permanent name of its own – *The Lancashire Fusilier*.

No45428 After six years at the Birmingham Railway Museum, in 1973 No45428 came to the North Yorkshire Moors Railway and, by 1991, had completed around 45,000 miles working between Pickering and Grosmont. The engine's latest overhaul has included the fitting of the equipment necessary for

And the rest...

Always a Carlisle Kingmoor engine, Crewe-built 'Black 5' No44901 remains in scrapyard condition, stored in the former shed building at Barry, South Wales,. There are plans to restore it as a 'Super 5' incorporating ideas put forward by Michael Stanier, Sir William's grandson and a locomotive engineer. Locomotives Nos45163, 45293 also await restoration. That of No45163 is progressing well on the Colne Valley Railway, in Essex, where it was joined in 1996 by No45293 after many years rusting the North Woolwich Station Museum in London. Following its purchase by the Mid-Hants Railway in 2003, the rebuilding of 1937-built No45379 is well underway at its Ropley workshops.

main-line working, which will centre on the NYMR's Whitby shuttles.

The tender is complete and the boiler work (being undertaken at Crewe) is well advanced. Derby-built in 1943, No45491 was only ever based at two sheds, Corkerhill (Glasgow) and Carlisle Kingmoor. Withdrawn in 1965, it is now back in Derbyshire, at the Midland Railway Butterley and slowly, but steadily on the way to becoming a working 'Black 5' once more.

London Midland &
Scottish Railway

William Stanier

Class 5XP (6P)
'Jubilee' 4-6-0

(1934)

Celebrating the 'Jubilees'

Named to mark the Silver Jubilee of King George V in 1935, William Stanier's 'second-string' express engine – the 5XP – at first gave little cause for celebration. But they went from flawed design to firm favourite.

The swansong for the 'Jubilees' came on the Leeds–Carlisle–Glasgow expresses that were worked by Leeds Holbeck engines, including the now-preserved No45593 *Kolhapur*, here at the head of the 10.17 from Leeds on 29 July 1967. It is replenishing its tank south of Garsdale, at 1,100 feet above sea level, the highest water troughs in Britain.

Unlike the 'Princess Royal' Pacifics of 1933, Stanier was not entering unknown territory with his proposed three-cylinder secondary passenger locomotive. The fundamentals of the design were proven: the chassis of the two-cylinder 'Patriot' 4-6-0 was to be adapted for three cylinders and the boiler would be a development of that used successfully on his 'Black 5'. Even had Stanier wanted the safety net of prototype evaluation circumstances were against him. The LMSR fleet was short of modern, reliable second-tier passenger engines. New locomotives were needed quickly and, like the 'Royal Scots' of 1927, large numbers were ordered straight off the drawing board. Unlike the 'Scots', however, the gamble did not pay off.

In reworking the 'Patriot' chassis with three sets of long-travel Walschaerts valve gear, the drive was divided. The inside cylinder was located well forward and drove on to the front single-throw crank axle. The outside cylinders drove on to the crank pins of the centre pair of coupled wheels.

On to this chassis went a domeless taper boiler with Belpaire firebox developed from the Type 3B boiler employed on the 'Black 5' and using low-temperature superheat. It was a formula straight out of the Great Western handbook; Stanier had experienced its success first-hand while at Swindon. In contrast to the 'Patriots', where the superheater boasted 24 elements, the newcomer was limited to 14, leading to a temperature difference between the two devices of around 100

The Severn Valley Railway's autumn 1986 gala brought the superb sight of two maroon-liveried 'Jubilees' on shed at Bridgnorth. Being prepared for duty on the morning of 21 September are visiting No5593 *Kolhapur* and then SVR resident, No5690 *Leander*. Note the difference in tenders: No5690 riveted, No5593 welded.

Stanier had followed the Swindon credo too religiously. Churchward had optimised chimney and blastpipe dimensions around the draughting needed by his two- and four-cylinder engines, not the six beats per revolution of Stanier's three-cylinder design. The adoption of the 'jumper top' fitted to Swindon blastpipes had merely worsened the problem. This was a simple device intended to reduce wear on boiler components, particularly the firebox stays. It consisted of a flap that, in response to a fierce blast, temporarily lifted to increase the diameter of the blastpipe and lessen the force of the exhaust. However, three-cylinder locomotives exhausted less steam per beat and the draughting could not cancel out the jumper top's negative effect.

Righting the wrongs

Much experimentation with superheaters, boiler tubes and blastpipe dimensions was needed before the inadequacies of the 5XP were isolated and rectified. Credit for finding a solution goes to Stanier's Chief Draughtsman, Tom Coleman. However, no fewer than 113 were in service before No5665 emerged from Crewe with an improved boiler. It incorporated a 24-element superheater, reduced blastpipe diameter (from 5.125 to 4.75 inches), steam dome and separate top feed for the boiler feedwater. Later, in a further modification to the Type 3A boiler, a sloping firebox throatplate was fitted, instead of the usual vertical type. This enlarged the area available for combustion in the upper part of the firebox.

Additionally, at times during their careers, four engines were fitted with double blastpipes and chimneys. These included No45596 *Bahamas* which has retained the double exhaust it acquired in 1961 into preservation. The final, and arguably most telling modification, came in 1942 when – at the suggestion of Tom Coleman – engines Nos5735 and 5736 were fitted with the superb Type

degrees Fahrenheit. When this was wedded to a serious miscalculation in the draughting, Stanier found himself facing the first serious failure in his time with the LMSR.

Embarrassingly, when put to work on the Euston to Birmingham services, the new 4-6-0s proved inferior to the ex-London & North Western types they were replacing. The gases flowing through the tubes and into the smokebox failed to release much of their heat. Consequently the boiler could not produce steam at the rate needed. Not for the first or last time, the vagaries of thermodynamics had confounded a logical attempt at uniformity in boiler design.

Identifying the cause of the poor steaming proved far from easy. Nothing like the same problem had arisen with the 'Black 5' yet the boilers were virtually identical. The investigation took wrong turns (largely because facilities for scientific testing that would have pointed in the right direction did not exist on the LMSR). Modifications were made on pretty much a hit-or-miss basis but with no significant improvement. All the while, construction of the 5XP continued.

Predictably, footplate crews – especially ex-London & North Western men – formed unfavourable opinions about the Swindon-inspired newcomers. Notwithstanding their tendency to rough riding, many preferred the 'Patriots', while others insisted that the 5XPs could only be steamed satisfactorily at the price of an inordinately high coal consumption. While efforts to improve steaming continued a number of 5XPs were transferred from the Western to the Midland Division where Stanier and his assistant, Robert Riddles, hoped they would be received more favourably by crews still reliant on 30-year-old and more 4-4-0s. As the 5XPs struggled with loads that left the Johnson/Deeley 4P compounds untroubled, the verdict was similarly sceptical.

For the record

All 191 'Jubilees' entered British Railways service in 1948 and, three years later, their power classification was amended to 6P, although to most footplatemen they remained 5XPs. After painting three examples in light green and ten in lined black, BR applied its standard Brunswick green to the entire class.

Record cards show that on 1 January 1958, 74 'Jubilees' were allocated to the Western Division, 66 were on ex-Midland lines, 21 in the Central Division (essentially ex-Lancashire & Yorkshire territory) and 29 at Carlisle and in Scotland. They were allocated to depots ranging from Bristol (Barrow Road) and Kentish Town (London) to Holyhead, Leeds, Glasgow, Perth and Aberdeen.

The first 'Jubilee' to be withdrawn was No45637 *Windward Islands*, destroyed in the double collision at Harrow and Wealdstone in October 1952. Although withdrawals proper began in 1960 with No45609 *Gilbert and Ellice Islands*, the 'Jubilees' had the distinction of becoming the last Stanier-designed express passenger locomotives to remain in service. As late as 1965, they continued to be rostered for a Liverpool to Glasgow turn, Nos45627 *Sierra Leone* and 45698 *Mars* becoming the last 'Jubilees' to tackle the climb to Shap. However, with no fewer than 66 retirements during 1966, the following year saw their swansong on Leeds–Glasgow trains over the Settle and Carlisle line. No45562 *Alberta* was the last to be condemned, in November 1967.

2A boiler which, with its 250 lb working pressure, larger superheater and double exhaust, offered a tractive effort equivalent to the rebuilt 'Royal Scot' 4-6-0s. The results were so good that a plan was drawn up to replace all the 5XP boilers as they fell due for renewal but this never came to fruition.

In total, 191 5XPs were delivered over a two-and-half-year period from May 1934 to December 1936. Crewe delivered 131 while just ten were built at Derby (a 'rush order' for the 1934 Christmas services). The remaining 50 came from the North British Locomotive Company: Nos5557-5581 were constructed at its Hyde Park works in Springburn, Glasgow (distinguishable by their round worksplates) while Nos5582-5606 were the products of the Queen's Park plant at Polmadie and wore its trademark diamond plates. The first five Crewe-built engines were billed at £5,700, with the following 48 costing £6,600 apiece. After quoting a price of £5,720 per engine, North British suffered a loss on the order.

Cause for celebration

With the delivery of the last of the 5XPs, the problems of poor steaming and sluggish starting (another consequence of the low-degree superheat) were largely in the past. As if to celebrate, the class was selected by the LMSR to mark the Silver Jubilee of King George V and Queen Mary, which had fallen in 1935. A newer example, No5642, was chosen to exchange identities with the true doyen of the class, No5552, and be named *Silver Jubilee* – and with it, at least as far as enthusiasts were concerned – the 5XPs became the 'Jubilees' (usually abbreviated

to 'Jubs'!). No5552 looked the part, resplendent in gleaming black complete with chromium-plated fittings, lettering, cabside numerals and aluminium boiler bands. It was unveiled at Euston in April 1935 and over the following weeks toured the LMSR system.

The naming of the class enlarged on the 'Jubilee' theme with the dominions and territories of the British Empire and naval heroes, with associated battles and warships. For good measure, some famous locomotive names – *Sanspareil*, *Novelty* – were included while No5665 *Lord Rutherford of Nelson* honoured the distinguished scientist who had recently opened the LMSR's new research laboratory at Derby. Subsequent renamings reflected political changes: in 1958, No45610 – originally *Gold Coast* – was renamed in honour of the newly independent state of Ghana.

In 1937, test runs with No5660 *Rooke* saw the 'Jubilees' finally consign their indifferent start to history. The intention of the trials was to examine the feasibility of accelerating services over the Bristol to Leeds and Leeds to Glasgow routes. With loads of over 300 tons, *Rooke* proved the point, with a 55mph average on the former run and 56mph on the latter. Both runs included some fearsome climbs, notably the Lickey between Bristol and Birmingham and the Long Drag northwards from Settle to Ais Gill.

The cross-country run from York to Bristol and Leeds–Carlisle–Glasgow remained routes with which the 'Jubilees' were associated throughout their 30-year careers. They also became mainstays of the Midland main line between

IN PRESERVATION

No5593 *Kolhapur*

When withdrawn on 15 October 1967, *Kolhapur* had already been bought for preservation by 7029 Clun Castle Limited (also owners, as the name suggests, of the eponymous Great Western 'Castle' class engine). A popular performer during the 1980s and 1990s, it is currently housed, out of traffic, at the Barrow Hill Roundhouse Railway Centre in Derbyshire.

No45596 *Bahamas*

Final shed for this double chimney 'Jubilee' was Stockport Edgeley, from where it was withdrawn in July 1966. It was promptly bought by the Bahamas Locomotive Society and eventually moved to the Keighley & Worth Valley Railway where its last overhaul was completed in 1990. It is now stored awaiting a further refit. Like *Kolhapur* and *Leander*, *Bahamas* has been involved in working on the main line since preservation.

No5690 *Leander*

Withdrawn in March 1964, *Leander* joined over two hundred other engines in Woodham Brothers' scrapyard remaining there until May 1972 when it was bought privately and overhauled at Derby Works. Like classmate *Bahamas*, its most recent overhaul saw a return to steam on the East Lancashire Railway and *Leander* has again been approved for main line work.

No45699 *Galatea*

Rescued from Barry in April 1980, *Galatea*'s role was to provide a spare boiler for *Leander*. However, in 1995 a consortium of enthusiasts bought what was little more than a carcass and moved it to Tyseley Locomotive Works in Birmingham. Between 1996 and 1998 volunteers began *Galatea*'s restoration but in 2002 a dispute over ownership saw the engine move to Carnforth (base of the West Coast Railway Company). Here rebuilding – estimated cost £250,000, including casting two driving wheels – has resumed.

London St Pancras and Manchester, which included the fearsome climb to Peak Forest. Equally arduous, and seemingly unsuited to their 6 feet 9 inches driving wheels, was the hill-and-dale road through Ayrshire from Glasgow to Girvan and Stranraer. Yet they proved its masters and were liked by their Scottish crews.

Many crews came to prefer the three cylinders of the 'Jubilee' to the two of the 'Black 5', judging them better at 'keeping their feet', thanks to the additional torque delivered by the third cylinder. Others considered the 'Jubilees' more susceptible to indifferent handling than a 'Black 5' or similar, but they would not have been the first three-cylinder engines to draw such a comparison. They were agile engines with a fair turn of speed and, when necessary, could be 'hammered' without affecting the riding. At high speed, the exhaust beats combined into a single, furious roar with, at night, a spectacular firework display at the chimney. On the level, a 'Jubilee' in good condition maintained speeds in the eighties with little effort and was well capable of reaching the mid-nineties.

When it came to serviceability, the 'Jubilees' broadly met Stanier's targets for his new LMSR fleet and, in this respect, scored over the 'Patriots'. He anticipated an eight-day period between shed examinations; a mileage of 40,000 between piston and valve checks; 70,000 miles before wheels and axleboxes demanded attention; and 150,000 between boiler repairs and general overhauls. Daily preparation, though, was more time-consuming and arduous than, for example, with a 'Black 5' owing to the need to get to the inside set of valve gear.

IN DETAIL

Class	5XP 'Jubilee'
Built:	Crewe, Derby works; North British Locomotive Company, Glasgow; 1934-36
Designer:	Sir William Stanier
Number built:	191
Purpose:	Secondary and semi-fast passenger
Wheel arrangement:	4-6-0
Cylinders (x 3):	17 in diameter x 26 in stroke
Motion:	Walschaerts (three sets with divided drive)
Valves:	10.625 in diameter piston valves
Wheels: Coupled:	6 ft 9 in
Leading:	3 ft 3.5 in
Tender:	4 ft 3 in
Boiler diagram:	Type 3A§
Boiler: Max. diameter:	5 ft 8.375 in
Pressure:	225 lb/psi
Heating surface:	1,767 sq ft
Firebox:	181 sq ft
Tubes and flues:	1,279 sq ft
Superheater:	307 sq ft
Grate area:	31.00 sq ft ¶
Tractive effort:	26,610 lb (@ 85% boiler pressure)
Engine wheelbase:	27 ft 7 in
Total wheelbase:	54 ft 4.375 in
Engine weight:	79 tons 11 cwt
Coal capacity:	5 tons 10 cwt (Fowler tender)
	9 tons 0 cwt (Stanier tender)
Water capacity:	3,500 gallons (Fowler tender)
	4,000 gallons (Stanier tender)
Max. axleloading:	20 tons 5 cwt
BR power class:	6P

§ Two locomotives (No5735 Comet and No5736 Phoenix) rebuilt in 1942 with high-pressure Type 2A boilers.
¶ Engines Nos5552 to 5664 had grates of 29.5 sq ft area.
(Specification gives typical dimensions for locomotives fitted with domed boilers and 24-element superheaters.)

The Magnificent Mikados

The first (and only) British eight-coupled express passenger locomotive was the LNER's P2 2-8-2 – or Mikado – of 1934. It was all set to conquer Scotland, then…

The second of the P2s, *Earl Marischal*, appeared in October 1934 fitted with Gresley's standard conjugated Walschaerts valve gear. This arrangement was preferred for all subsequent construction.

The LNER's Nigel Gresley consistently attempted to find an exact solution to the problems presented by the operating department. In 1925, he built a pair of 2-8-2 freight engines (Class P1) expressly for the demanding Peterborough–London coal traffic. They took 100-wagon trains in their stride. Unfortunately, the project was self-defeating: most sidings and passing loops were too short to accommodate 100-wagon trains so nothing was gained. A decade on, history repeated itself.

For gradients, the toughest section of the East Coast main line is the 130 miles between Edinburgh and Aberdeen. Gresley's A1/A3 Pacifics were restricted to loads of around 450 tons on the Aberdeen run, which meant that sleeping car trains of 500 tons-plus had to be double-headed. Unlike the pre-Stanier LMSR, the LNER did not gladly tolerate double-heading (not for nothing did it have a

'big engine' policy), It was that policy that led to the building of a handful of mighty machines especially for the Edinburgh–Aberdeen line. With an eight-coupled wheelbase, they would have some 20 per cent more adhesion than the Pacifics and, to match the high adhesive weight, the tractive effort – at 43,462lb – would be the greatest of any British express passenger class.

Classified P2, Doncaster Works outshopped the prototype of these semi-streamlined three-cylinder 2-8-2s in 1934. The design of No2001 *Cock o' the North* revealed a significant French influence. It was fitted with the French-designed ACFI boiler feedwater heater (surprisingly, given the mixed results previously obtained with such gadgets) and the draughting arrangement was similar to that advocated by the Paris–Orleans Railway's André Chapelon. Exhaust was discharged through twin blastpipes and a double chimney, an idea first outlined by the Finnish engineer, Kyîsti Kylala, in 1919 but subsequently refined by Chapelon. (This adoption of the Kylala-Chapelon 'Kylchap' device was to play an important role in the later success of Gresley's Pacifics.) The use of poppet valves activated by a rotating camshaft was another unusual feature, and No2001 was the first engine to sport the trademark Gresley chime whistle.

On test, No2001 regularly attained 85mph – a previously unheard-of speed for an eight-coupled engine. The most remarkable of these trial runs took place on 19 June 1934, with No2001 in charge of a 650-ton train from King's Cross to Barkston, just south of Grantham. Northbound, the climb to Stoke summit is a lengthy one that peaks at 1 in 178. Nevertheless, it was only on the final approach that the heavily loaded 2-8-2 – developing more than 2,000 horsepower at the drawbar – dipped below 60mph.

French exam

In December 1934, this pride of the LNER visited France. The reasons were threefold. The first was to acknowledge the part played

by French engineers, such as Chapelon, in the design. Secondly, No2001 was to undergo static trials on the testing plant at Vitry-sur-Seine and, thirdly, Gresley wanted to demonstrate the case for building a similar plant in Britain. Test runs – using imported British coal – did take place between Tours and Orleans but proved little. Incompatibility between the LNER vacuum brake and the French Westinghouse air brake precluded No2001 from hauling passenger trains. It had to perform with nothing more than three dead engines in tow.

Meanwhile, a second 2-8-2, No2002 *Earl Marischal*, had been built. Instead of poppet valves it employed the conventional LNER arrangement of piston valves driven by two sets of Walschaerts valve gear, with derived motion to the inside cylinder. Gresley may have felt it useful to draw comparisons between the two types, although he must have been aware that the cam gear of No2001 was wearing with worrying rapidity. Additionally, No2002 was widely thought to be the better engine. For whatever reason, Walschaerts gear was preferred for the final four P2s, all built in 1936. These had a re-designed front end more akin to the streamlining of the A4 Pacifics, which had shown itself more effective in dealing with drifting smoke. In 1937, Nos2001 and 2002 were similarly restyled, with the former's rotary cam valve gear replaced by the Walschaerts variety.

Once in action between Edinburgh and Aberdeen, the P2s left no doubt about their ability to haul lengthy passenger trains, and were usefully employed on fish trains, too. Unfortunately, few platforms in Scotland could accommodate trains of more than 15 vehicles. Consequently, when a P2 was in charge of the kind of train length for which it was built, it invariably meant stopping twice at stations, disrupting schedules. There were maintenance drawbacks, too, with heavy wear on the motion and bearings. Inadequate guiding force in the leading pony truck allied to the sharp curves of the line placed stress on the long wheelbase of the engines.

It was saddening, if unsurprising, that Gresley's successor, Edward Thompson, ordered the rebuilding of the 2-8-2s. Between 1943 and 1944, they re-emerged from Doncaster as ungainly 4-6-2s, almost unrecognisable from the impressive machines built there only a decade earlier.

IN DETAIL *(as built)*

Class	P2
Built:	Doncaster Works 1934-36
Designer:	Sir Nigel Gresley
Number built:	6
Purpose:	Express passenger
Wheel arrangement:	2-8-2
Cylinders (x 3):	21 in diameter x 26 in stroke
Motion:	Rotary cam poppet-valve gear (No2001) ¶ Walschaerts with piston valves (Nos2001-06) (Gresley-Holcroft divided drive to the middle cylinder)
Wheels: Coupled:	6 ft 2 in
Leading:	3 ft 2 in
Trailing:	3 ft 8 in
Tender:	4 ft 2 in
Boiler diagram:	LNER Diagram 106
Boiler: Max. Diameter:	6 ft 1 in
Pressure:	220 lb/psi
Heating surface:	3,490.5 sq ft
Firebox:	237 sq ft
Tubes and flues:	2,477 sq ft
Superheater:	776.5 sq ft
Grate area:	50 sq ft
Tractive effort:	43,462 lb (@ 85% boiler pressure)
Engine wheelbase:	37 ft 11 in
Total wheelbase:	64 ft 0.875 in
Engine weight:	110 tons 5 cwt §
Coal capacity:	8 tons
Water capacity:	5,000 gallons
Max. axleloading:	20 tons 10 cwt

¶ *Subsequently replaced with Walschaerts gear.*
§ *The later streamlined P2s, Nos2002-06 weighed 107 tons 3 cwt.*

From Crewe to the Caspian

Intended to modernise the LMSR's freight locomotive fleet, the Stanier 8F proved its worth much further afield, in both peace and war. The 'eight freights' went on to serve British Railways until the last fire was put out in 1968.

Swindon-built (under Government order) in 1944, No48431 waits to back down on to its train at Keighley on the morning of 17 October 1992. The Old Oak Common (81A) shedplate reflects the fact that 8F 2-8-0s, including No48431, were based at the GWR's principal London shed for a time.

It handled more freight than any other of the 'big four' railways but the LMSR's investment in new motive power did little to reflect that. Instead it kept faith with the hundreds of six- and eight-coupled plodders inherited from its constituent companies. When new engines were needed it simply dusted off the Midland or London & North Western drawings and, with a few concessions to contemporary thinking, built some more.

When progress was made, as with the articulated Beyer-Garratt 2-6-6-2Ts of 1927, outdated and demonstrably flawed notions were allowed to compromise the design. This was the situation faced by William Stanier when he took over as CME in 1932. However, the requirement for a modern freight locomotive was but one of the items on his 'to do' list. Stanier chose to give priority to new passenger and mixed-traffic classes and reluctantly sanctioned the construction of yet more journeymen 0-6-0s.

One proposal for a heavy goods engine was a development of the successful three-cylinder 'Royal Scot' 4-6-0. However, it was agreed that employing three cylinders in a freight locomotive was a costly complication with most probably little benefit. Stanier knew of a better starting point: he had grown up with the Great Western's 2800 2-8-0 and seen it successfully imitated on a couple of occasions. The LMSR's new front-rank freight locomotive would similarly be a 2-cylinder 2-8-0 and the 1934 building programme included two engines, oddly described as 'experimental', to gain experience with the type.

While the inspiration may have been Great

Western, the design was firmly based on Stanier's proven 5P5F 4-6-0 of 1934 so there was very little by way of experiment. Stanier's ideas were broadly realised by his assistant, Ernest Cox, with the detail work undertaken by the Chief Draughtsman, Tom Coleman, and his team. They married a sound mechanical structure to a generously sized, free-steaming boiler. The Type 3C was a version of that used on the 'Black 5', shortened by 12 inches to suit the eight-coupled wheelbase, and the cylinders and valves were of identical dimensions to those of the 'Black 5'.

Naturally, the 8F reflected advances made since Churchward's time, not least in improving conditions for the crew. The cab showed a marked advance on that fitted to the 2800 thirty years earlier. With a maximum axleloading of only 16 tons, and the ability to negotiate curves of 297 feet radius, the 8Fs were intended to have the widest-possible route availability. Moreover, of an engine weight of 72 tons, 63 tons was available for adhesion.

The initial order was extended to 12 and these were delivered from Crewe during 1935. The newcomers were first based at Willesden, in London, and at two Midland line depots: Wellingborough, in Northamptonshire, and Toton, Nottinghamshire. They proved an immediate success, with the Toton engines entrusted with heavy coal hauls until then the preserve of the Beyer-Garratts. When combined with an increase in drawbar horsepower, the better riding of the 8Fs enabled them to work significantly heavier trains at higher speeds. The most demanding duties, such as the climb through the Peak District with 1,000 tons of limestone in tow, proved well within their capabilities. Though their principal role remained coal and mineral haulage, 8Fs worked all manner of services including passenger trains, where they proved capable 60mph and above.

Wartime role

The requirement for the 8Fs was judged less pressing than that for Class 5 4-6-0s so that, by 1939, just 126 were in traffic, numbered 8000-8125. Crewe had built 57 but, taking advantage of cheap government loans intended to help industry through the trade depression of the 1930s, the LMSR had contracted out the remaining 69, Nos8027-95, to Vulcan Foundry. Its plant at Newton-le-Willows delivered them between 1936 and 1937.

A dramatic change in the pace of construction followed the outbreak of a second war with Germany in September 1939. As in 1914, when the Great Central's 8K 2-8-0 was selected, Allied forces needed an eight-coupled 'engine of war'. Despite its comparative youth, the 8F had proved itself in service, was reliable and simple to maintain, had a wide route availability and had coped with difficult conditions. For the War Department and its Director of Transportation, Robert Riddles, there was no contest.

Beyer, Peacock and the North British Locomotive Company built 208 8Fs for the War Department, the first 58 in record time – just five months from the placing of the order. An additional 51 were requisitioned from the LMSR. Modifications were made to suit overseas operating conditions, such as the addition of Westinghouse air brakes to allow Continental passenger stock to be hauled. However, the addition of cab speedometers was surely unnecessary. The more practical changes involved substituting cheaper and more readily available materials. Instead of the high-tensile steel of the LMSR engines, mild steel was used for the main frames and adopted for the coupling and connecting rods. Solid pins and plain bushes replaced needle roller bearings in the motion.

Sun, sea and sand

With Europe under Nazi control, from the Russian frontier to the Atlantic, the Allies had to fight on other fronts, principally North Africa and the Middle East. As a result, many 8Fs – most converted for oil burning – were shipped round the Cape of Good Hope and through the Suez Canal for service with army units in Egypt, Iraq, Lebanon, Palestine, Persia (now Iran), Syria and Turkey. Some never reached their destination and went down with the ships carrying them.

Perhaps their most famous exploits came after the Germans launched their invasion of the former Soviet Union in 1941. Using the line between the Persian Gulf and the Caspian Sea, 8Fs conveyed vital supplies to the Russians. The detrimental effect of oil firing on the superheater elements meant that availability was not up to LMSR standards but the 8Fs performed remarkably well under difficult conditions, which included air attacks on their trains.

At home, given the 8F's versatility, the Railway Executive made it first choice to meet a wartime shortage of freight engines. Overriding local sensibilities, the government authorised across-the-board construction. Orders totalling 245 engines were shared among the Great Western (80 built at Swindon), the Southern Railway (105 outshopped from Ashford, Brighton and Eastleigh) and the LNER, with 60 built at its Doncaster and Darlington plants. Additionally, the LMSR workshops at Crewe, Derby and Horwich contributed a further 205.

By 1946, 852 8Fs had been built, making it the fourth-largest class of engines produced in Britain. There would have been more had the War Department not decided, in 1943, that an 8F took too long to construct and used too much of what had become scarce and costly materials, such as copper and brass. It was superseded by two more basic and cheaper alternatives, the 'Austerity' 2-8-0 and 2-10-0.

These new 8Fs were used by all four companies and were seen throughout Britain, even hauling express passenger services north of Perth on the Aberdeen and Inverness lines. Following nationalisation in 1948, all British-based 8Fs and 39 repatriated examples were taken into the stock of the London Midland Region. Five further WD engines came home from Egypt in 1952 for repair at Derby but instead of returning to Africa were sent to the

Currently the only 8F approved for main-line running, Crewe-built No48151 simmers under the ash tower at Carnforth on 9 March 1991.

IN PRESERVATION

No48151 Crewe-built No48151's restoration was completed in July 1987. Based at the Carnforth headquarters of the West Coast Railway Company it remains the only 8F approved for main-line operation.

No48173 Following 20 years languishing on the Avon Valley Railway, in late 2008 No48173 was bought by a director of Staffordshire's Churnet Valley Railway and has moved to its Cheddleton site. Restoration was expected to begin sometime during 2009.

No48305 Another Crewe product, No48305 entered service on the Great Central Railway in February 1995 and can usually be found working on either the Great Central Railway or the Churnet Valley Railway in Staffordshire.

No48431 One of 80 engines built under government directive at Swindon, No8431 entered traffic on the Great Western in 1944. Rescued in 1972, it first steamed on the Keighley & Worth Valley Railway in December 1975. Now housed in the K&WVR's Oxenhope museum, No48431 awaits an overhaul.

No48518 An unexpected consequence of wartime 8F construction at Swindon was that the boiler design was adapted by the GWR's Frederick Hawksworth for his 'County' class 4-6-0 of 1945. Sixty years on, this has sealed the fate of No48518, currently in store on the Vale of Glamorgan Railway. A project to build a 'County', none of which was preserved, will use the boiler off No48518. One day it will steam again as part of the resurrected No1014 *County of Glamorgan*.

No48624 If ever there was a 'cockney' 8F, it has to be Ashford-built No48624, which spent its entire working life allocated to Willesden. A 28-year project was completed in April 2009 when the 8F – in LMSR crimson-lake livery – steamed at Peak Rail's site at Rowsley, in Derbyshire.

No48773 NoWD307 became one of 42 8Fs sent to work on the Trans-Iranian Railway. Following transfer to Egypt in 1945, the engine returned to Britain in 1952, spending five years on the Longmoor Military Railway before being bought by British Railways for £3,500. Numbered 48773 (not the logical 48233), its BR career began at Polmadie (Glasgow) and ended at Rose Grove, Burnley on 4 August 1968. Five days later, No48773 became the property of the Stanier 8F Locomotive Society. Home since then has been the Severn Valley Railway and, in 1986, it was dedicated a 'memorial engine' by the Corps of Royal Engineers. This most famous of 8Fs now awaits overhaul.

No8274 This 8F, LMSR identity No8274, was requisitioned by the War Department and became WD348. It was shipped to Egypt and then became one of Turkish Railways' 'Churchills', TCDD No45160. Repatriated in 1989 by the Churchill (8F) Locomotive Co Ltd, a full overhaul, begun in 1990, is now being completed on the Gloucestershire Warwickshire Railway.

Longmoor Military Railway in Hampshire. Of this quintet, three became BR Nos48773-5, taking to 666 the number of 8Fs on British Railways' books by 1957.

Many, however, remained abroad and saw service with railways in Egypt, Iran, Iraq, Israel, Lebanon and Italy. Some Turkish-based 8Fs – appropriately nicknamed 'Churchills' – remained at work into the 1980s while Egyptian Railways fashioned a kind of hybrid 8F, using an identical chassis but employing a parallel boiler. Similarly, Iraq obtained a version from a German builder. A total of 186 were shipped overseas, the fates of some of which have never been resolved.

After eights

Throughout the BR years, at least up to 1966, the largest concentrations of 8Fs continued to be at those depots to which the first examples were posted. In November 1950, 63 were based at Toton, 43 at another Nottinghamshire shed, Kirkby-in-Ashfield and 50 at Wellingborough, all largely devoted to coal traffic. Even though maintenance standards declined, the 8Fs kept their reliability, with an average mileage of between 40,000 and 48,000 miles between valve and piston examinations – exceptional for a small-wheeled engine subject to fairly fast running. Even with the heaviest loads, an 8F could be driven for long periods on full regulator without any reduction in steaming or performance.

In 1960, after a derailment at Turvey, in Bedfordshire, No48616 became the first 8F to be condemned. Withdrawals proper began in 1962 with No48009 but, as late as April 1965, 632 remained in service, including 51 on the North Eastern Region and eleven on the Western Region. By January 1967, however, the total had been cut to 381, all on the London Midland. Of those, 252, were concentrated

in the north-west and it was in that area that the 138 survivors saw in the last year of steam operation, 1968. When the end came that August, they accounted for more than half of BR's remaining steam locomotives.

Lancashire-based 8Fs had the dubious distinction of soldiering on until the final day, 4 August. Twenty languished at Rose Grove shed, Burnley, and a further six at Lostock Hall, Preston; the former's Nos48318 and 48773 were officially the last to be retired.

Recreating a typical London Midland Region shed scene of the 1950s and 1960s at Haworth on the Keighley & Worth Valley Railway are Stanier 8F No48431 and Fowler 3F 0-6-0T No47279, with 'Jubilee' No45596 *Bahamas* to the rear.

IN DETAIL *(Engines numbered 8012 onwards)*	
Class:	**8F**
Built:	1935-46; Ashford, Brighton, Crewe, Darlington, Doncaster, Eastleigh, Horwich and Swindon works; Beyer Peacock, Manchester; North British Locomotive Company, Glasgow; Vulcan Foundry, Newton-le-Willows, Lancashire
Designer:	Sir William Stanier
Number built:	852
Purpose:	Heavy freight
Wheel arrangement:	2-8-0
Cylinders (x 2):	18.5 in diameter x 28 in stroke
Motion:	Walschaerts
Valves:	10 in piston valves
Wheels: Coupled:	4 ft 8.5 in
Leading:	3 ft 3.5 in
Tender:	4 ft 3 in
Boiler diagram:	Type 3C
Boiler: Max. diameter:	5 ft 8.375 in
Pressure:	225 lb/psi
Heating surface:	1,895 sq ft ¶
Firebox:	171 sq ft
Tubes and flues:	1,479 sq ft
Superheater:	245 sq ft
Grate area:	28.65sq ft ¶
Tractive effort:	32,438 lb (@ 85% boiler pressure)
Engine wheelbase:	26 ft 0 in
Total wheelbase:	52 ft 7.75 in
Engine weight:	72 tons 2 cwt
Coal capacity:	9 tons ⊠
Water capacity:	4,000 gallons ⊠
Max. axleloading:	16 tons 0 cwt
BR power class:	8F

¶ *Engines Nos8000-8011 had a grate area of 27.8 square feet and a total heating surface of 1,698 square feet.*

⊠ *Some engines subsequently exchanged tenders with 'Jubilee' class 4-6-0s, receiving ones holding 5 tons 10 cwt and 3,500 gallons.*

Gresley's Flying Machines

More than sixty years on, the record still stands: 126 miles per hour – over
two miles every minute. Sir Nigel Gresley's A4 Pacifics were engines that
took wing – in more than one respect.

Wearing British
Railways' first choice
for express passenger
locomotive livery
(subsequently deemed
insufficiently hard-
wearing), the one-
hundredth Gresley
Pacific No60007 poses
under the lights at
Buckley Wells, East
Lancashire Railway,
on 24 February 1996.
The A4 was visiting
for a 'Pacifics weekend'
that included No46229
Duchess of Hamilton
and No71000 *Duke of
Gloucester*.

In the late 1930s, at stations out of King's Cross, homebound north
Londoners might linger a while on the platform. They would check their
watches and, if it was around a quarter-to-six, listen out for a whistle. Not
just any whistle, but the deep chime that announced the approach of something
special. Under Nigel Gresley, the London & North Eastern Railway had recently
introduced three train services that, for its wealthier travellers, set new standards
for speed and luxury. Others, grappling with the economic depression of the time,
had to settle for the brief, but memorable, thrill of watching the 5.30pm from

King's Cross – the 'Silver Jubilee' – flash by, a blur of spiralling steam, silver-grey
coaches and ringing rails. At its head would have been a member of one of the
most celebrated classes of locomotive. To the LNER, they were simply the A4
Pacifics; generations of railway enthusiasts, however, had a more descriptive name:
they were the 'Streaks'.

Streamlining was in vogue during the 1930s. During a visit to Germany
in 1933, Gresley had been impressed by the Deutsches Reichsbahn's 'Flying
Hamburger', a streamlined diesel multiple unit. The LNER even considered

buying something similar for an accelerated service between London and Newcastle-upon-Tyne. Then, on 3 March 1935, one of Gresley's A3 Pacifics, No2750 *Papyrus*, proved that steam traction remained capable of matching, and even bettering, the diesel's performance. It demonstrated that the envisaged four-hour timing was achievable behind steam and, three weeks later, the LNER approved the building of streamlined train sets and the locomotives to haul them. On 6 September 1935, the first of the A4s, No2509 *Silver Link*, was outshopped from Doncaster. It had barely been run in when, three weeks later, on a press run to publicise the new 'Silver Jubilee' service, its maximum speed of 112.5mph broke the British record. Equally remarkably, it maintained 100mph for 43 miles.

On 30 September the inaugural 'Silver Jubilee' left Newcastle at 10.00am and, with just a stop at Darlington, arrived at King's Cross at 2pm. There was just time to clean and service the A4 before it took out the return service at 5.30pm. In its first two weeks of operation, the train was hauled exclusively by No2509, which covered 5,366 problem-free miles in the process. It was then joined at King's Cross depot by two more silver-liveried A4s, while a third – No2511 Silver King – was based on Tyneside, at Gateshead.

The success, both of the A4s and the 'Silver Jubilee', persuaded the LNER to introduce two other streamliners, the 'Coronation' and the 'West Riding Limited'. Garter blue was the livery chosen for these trains, and for the seven new A4s rostered to work them. Ironically, given what it did for his reputation, Gresley is said to have dismissed streamlining as a 'publicity stunt'. Nevertheless, he was looking to ways of of reducing air resistance and, therefore, getting more out of every ton of coal consumed.

The secret to the A4s' performance, however, was internal, not external. They benefited from experience with their predecessors, the three-cylinder A1s and A3s, and from the theories of, especially, French engineer, André Chapelon. He had demonstrated the value of allowing steam to flow freely, and the steam passages of the A4 were as unrestricted as possible, from the regulator valve to the chimney blastpipe. In March 1938, a new A4 became the first to be equipped with a device developed by Chapelon and a Finnish colleague, Kyîsti Kylala, the Kylchap double blastpipe and double chimney. That locomotive was No4468 *Mallard*.

A fitting honour

As Doncaster Works prepared to outshop the twenty-first of the A4s, which would also be the 100th Gresley Pacific, a railway enthusiast, K. Risdon Prentice, suggested naming it after the designer. The LNER board agreed.

On 23 November 1937, in garter-blue livery with wheels painted coronation red, No4498 entered traffic and, three days later, travelled to Marylebone Station in London for the naming ceremony. William Whitelaw, the Chairman of the LNER, unveiled the nameplates and presented Gresley with a miniature silver replica of the locomotive. The latter then drove the engine the length of the platform and back. It is not recorded whether or not he sounded the Crosby tri-tone chime whistle that, to LNER enthusiasts, remains one of the most thrilling sounds imaginable.

Construction of the A4s continued until July 1938 when No4903 *Peregrine* rolled out of Doncaster. Since they were now widely used on express services most of the later examples received the normal LNER passenger livery of apple green. Coincidentally with the appearance of *Peregrine*, on a test run on 3 July, *Mallard* set a new world speed record for steam traction of 126mph. The story of that day is recalled below.

By 1939, the A4s were entrusted with most of the LNER's east-coast expresses. They had proved remarkably trouble-free and the public loved travelling behind them, so much so that the LNER planned to introduce longer trains. This spurred Gresley who began working on a 'super A4' with a working pressure of 275 lb/psi and a tractive effort of 39,040 lb. Events later that year not only put an end to the scheme but to the A4s' high-speed exploits. Evidently not sharing Prime Minister Neville Chamberlain's hopes for peace, on 31 August the LNER suspended its

After turning on the Scarborough turntable, record-breaking A4 Pacific No4468 *Mallard* backs down to the station to take out a return 'Mallard 88' railtour for York on 9 July 1988, one of several trips organised to mark the 50th anniversary of the engine's world speed record.

three streamlined services, never to revive them as luxury trains. Three days later, Chamberlain informed the nation that Britain was at war with Germany.

Doing their bit

The LNER's first reaction was to place the 11 King's Cross-based A4s in store, along with their streamlined rolling stock, but it soon became clear that they could not have the luxury of seeing out the conflict in safety. The LNER would need every engine it could muster and the A4s demonstrated that speed was not their only asset. Like the A3 Pacifics and V2 2-6-2s, they hauled prodigious loads. On one occasion, No2509 *Silver Link* took 850 tons up the bank out of King's Cross and reached Newcastle within four minutes of schedule. During 1940, No4901 managed to average 76mph with a 730-ton train for more than 25 miles between York and Northallerton.

These feats were achieved as maintenance was cut to the minimum. The A4s received no special treatment and suffered the indignity of unlined black liveries along with every other member of the LNER fleet. Preparation time was further reduced by removing the valances covering the wheels and running gear. The chime whistles were also substituted, in case anyone mistook them for air-raid warning sirens! All but one of the A4s came through the war unscathed. The exception was No4469 *Sir Ralph Wedgwood*, destroyed in an air raid on York depot on 29 April 1942. The name was transferred to another member of the class, No4466 *Herring Gull*.

Under the LNER's 1946 renumbering scheme the A4s appropriately took over Nos1-34, but not in order of construction. Instead the first six were altered to those named after LNER directors, including the splendidly monickered *Andrew K. McCosh*. It says much about their egos that *Sir Nigel Gresley* was demoted to No7. It might have been expected that the arrival of two new classes of Pacific, Arthur Peppercorn's A1 and A2, would have displaced the A4s from their prestige duties. This was not to be the case. When the non-stop 'Flying Scotsman' was reintroduced on 21 May 1948, it was with A4 haulage.

One last hurrah

The number of A4s equipped with double chimneys and Kylchap blastpipes had remained at just four, including No60022 *Mallard*. When, during the 1950s, some steaming problems were experienced, tests were undertaken to find the cause. Poor-quality coal was one factor but it became evident that the same locomotive numbers were appearing in the reports, Conspicuously absent, however, were the four Kylchap-fitted examples. The penny dropped and, between May 1957 and November 1958, the apparatus was belatedly installed in the remaining 30 A4s. Steaming problems were eliminated but that November the first of the English Electric Type 4 diesels arrived on the East Coast Main Line.

They did little to undermine the A4s' supremacy. Another English Electric design, however, would prove their undoing. For some years both the East and West Coast Main Lines had reverberated to the sound of a bright-blue diesel-electric prototype. Generating 3,300bhp, *Deltic* was the most powerful of its breed in the country. After much debate, mainly centring on cost, British Railways placed an order for a production series of 22. Deliveries began in 1961 and, one by one, the principal east-coast expresses were turned over to 'Deltic' haulage. So

IN PRESERVATION

No4468 (60022) *Mallard* Retired from King's Cross in April 1963, *Mallard* was restored at Doncaster and returned to its original garter-blue livery. As one of its major attractions, *Mallard* has rarely left the National Railway Museum but, in the late 1980s, was returned to running order to mark the fiftieth anniversary of its world speed record in 1938. That done, *Mallard* returned to its York home.

No4496 (60008) *Dwight D. Eisenhower* In September 1945 No4496 *Golden Shuttle* had been renamed after the Supreme Commander of the wartime Allied forces (and, later, President of the United States). On 27 April 1964, No60008 was handed over to new American custodians and shipped to what would be its home to this day, the National Railroad Museum, Green Bay, Wisconsin.

No4488 (60009) *Union of South Africa* When retired from Aberdeen Ferryhill on 1 June 1966, No9 – as it would become known to all enthusiasts – was bought by John Cameron's Lochty Railway Society. A three-mile line near Anstruther was especially laid and *Union of South Africa* made its debut there on 14 June 1967. Subsequently approved for main-line work, No9 has now accumulated the highest mileage of all the A4 Pacifics. May 2007 brought a return to Scotland and a new home at Thornton.

No4489 (60010) *Dominion of Canada* In May 1965 Aberdeen Ferryhill's shedmaster sent No60010 to Darlington for repair. It did not return: the boiler was in such bad condition that the engine was condemned. No60010 was not broken up, however, but presented to the Canadian Railroad Historical Association, of Montreal.

No4464 (60019) *Bittern* Bought by enthusiast, Geoff Drury, in 1966, *Bittern* became the first privately preserved A4 to work a railtour on BR, beating *Sir Nigel Gresley* and *Union of South Africa* by some five months. Twice sold on, the engine is now owned by Jeremy Hosking and in 2007 was certified for main-line operation. Nominally based on the Mid-Hants Railway, *Bittern* has since performed regularly and reliably both on the main line and heritage railways.

No4498 (60007) *Sir Nigel Gresley* In March 1966 the A4 Preservation Society paid £4,500 to secure the future of No60007. It has since spent many times that sum keeping the Pacific in steam and on the main line. Its latest heavy overhaul, the third in preservation, occupied four-and-a-half years and cost £650,000, of which £320,000 came from a Heritage Lottery Grant. *Sir Nigel Gresley* returned to steam on the North Yorkshire Moors Railway on 5 August 2006, with an agreement to work on the railway during the summer seasons, and has since rejoined the main-line list.

One of the finest sights in preservation: an A4 Pacific at the head of Gresley-designed teak-bodied LNER stock. No60009 *Union of South Africa* heads away from Bewdley bound for Kidderminster with the Severn Valley Railway's teak set on 21 September 2002.

it was that on 9 September 1961, the 'Elizabethan' was steam-hauled for the final time, No60022 *Mallard* taking charge of the northbound service and No60009 *Union of South Africa* coming south.

On 29 October 1963, No60017 *Silver Fox* headed out of King's Cross with the 6.40pm to Leeds, the last appearance there of an A4 on a scheduled service. By the end of that year only 19 remained in service. A further seven had been despatched by December 1964 by which stage most of the survivors were congregating in Scotland, first at St Margaret's in Edinburgh then Aberdeen's Ferryhill depot. Here, rather than being reduced to secondary and goods workings, the A4s enjoyed something of an Indian summer, being entrusted with the Glasgow–Aberdeen three-hour expresses and trains over the Waverley route between Carlisle and Edinburgh.

An unbroken record

Along with his technical team, Gresley had been concerned about the braking capacity of the A4 and, in conjunction with the Westinghouse company, had undertaken some high-speed braking trials. Ostensibly, the runs with *Mallard* on 3 July 1938 were a continuation of those trials, but the rival LMS had recently snatched the British speed record with one of its new 'Princess Coronation' Pacifics and the LNER wanted to reclaim it. There was also the matter of the world record, then held by Germany: in May 1935, streamlined 4-6-4 No05.001 had touched 124.5mph on test between Berlin and Hamburg.

That July day, on the descent of Stoke bank, south of Grantham in Nottinghamshire, driver, Joe Duddington, and fireman, Tommy Bray, both of Doncaster depot, accelerated *Mallard* to 125mph – more than two miles a minute. For each of those minutes, the driving wheels went through over 500 revolutions and, at Milepost 90, the accompanying dynamometer car (a vehicle adapted to carry a range of locomotive measuring devices) recorded a world record of 126mph. The achievement made a legend of the A4, and instant celebrities of *Mallard*'s footplate crew.

IN DETAIL *(as built)*	
Class	**A4**
Built:	Doncaster Works; 1935-38
Designer:	Sir Nigel Gresley
Number built:	35
Purpose:	Express passenger
Wheel arrangement:	4-6-2
Cylinders (x 3):	18 in diameter x 26 in stroke
Motion:	Walschaerts (with Gresley-Holcroft derived motion to the inside cylinder)
Valves:	9 in diameter piston valves
Wheels: Coupled:	6 ft 8 in diameter
Leading:	3 ft 2 in
Trailing:	3 ft 8 in
Tender:	4 ft 2 in
Boiler diagram:	LNER No107
Boiler: Max. diameter:	6 ft 5 in
Pressure:	250 lb/psi
Heating surface:	3,325 sq ft
Firebox:	231.2 sq ft
Tubes and flues:	2,345.1 sq ft
Superheater:	748.9 sq ft
Grate area:	41.25 sq ft
Tractive effort:	35,455 lb (@ 85% boiler pressure)
Engine wheelbase:	35 ft 9 in
Total wheelbase:	60 ft 10.875 in
Engine weight:	102 tons 19 cwt
Coal capacity:	9 tons §
Water capacity:	5,000 gallons
Max. axleloading:	22 tons 0 cwt
BR power class:	8P

§ Corridor tenders originally held only 8 tons. The capacity was increased from 1937.

Gresley's Versatile V2

Many consider the mixed-traffic V2 to be Nigel Gresley's masterpiece.
It was certainly a willing workhorse, equally at home on express passenger
and goods duties. Its only drawback was a weight problem.

Visiting the Gloucestershire Warwickshire
Railway, the fine proportions of the V2
design are evident as No4771 *Green Arrow*
strides away from Winchcombe with an
afternoon train for Cheltenham Racecourse
on 26 Auust 2007.

One of the LNER's attempts to counter
the challenge from road transport was to
inaugurate a fast, overnight service between
London and Scotland that could convey anything
from parcels to bulk loads. The LNER's publicity
department bestowed the name 'Green Arrow' on
what was a forerunner of today's container train.
However, the combination of loads and schedules
called for something exceptional by way of motive
power. Gresley's A3 Pacifics would have been up to
the task but unfortunately they could not be spared
from passenger duties.

In 1935, the LNER set its Doncaster drawing
office the job of producing a new design for 'heavy
long-distance work'. The outcome was a 2-6-2, or
Prairie type. While such engines were popular in the
United States they were unusual in Britain. Here,
the 2-6-2 wheel arrangement had been confined
largely to tank locomotives. Essentially, the newcomer
was a development of the A3. Gresley's trademark
three-cylinder configuration was retained, along with
conjugated gear to the valves of the middle cylinder.
The boiler was a shortened version of that used on the
A3 and, at 6 ft 2 in diameter, the driving wheels were
six inches smaller.

Carrying works number 1837, the first of the V2s
left Doncaster on 13 June 1936. At first allotted the
running number of 637 (a photograph in that guise
had been taken on 1 June) it now bore No4771 on
the cabsides. It was also named *Green Arrow*, the
title by which the LNER was publicising its express
goods workings. The locomotive spent time 'running

in' around Doncaster, working on the Cleethorpes line and on stopping trains to Grantham and Peterborough, as well as taking over the afternoon Harrogate express from King's Cross.

Officially No4771 had been allocated to 'Top Shed' – King's Cross – on 22 June but did not make its first run to London until 3 July, at the head of the 2.35pm from Doncaster. Before long, King's Cross put *Green Arrow* to work in its express goods link – the role intended for it – and it was regularly entrusted with a key service, the afternoon fast freight from London to Glasgow, otherwise known as the 'Scotch Goods'. Relieved at Peterborough, No4771 usually returned on a Hull–

Following overhaul in the late 1990s, *Green Arrow* was returned to service in British Railways livery as No60800. Among many railtours, the 'Ocean Liner Limited' of 27 August 2001 from Taunton to Southampton brought the V2 along the Great Western main line. With the cooling towers of the power station looming in the background, and just a light exhaust at the chimney, *Green Arrow* drifts into Didcot.

King's Cross fish train. That summer also saw *Green Arrow* employed on passenger services, again to Peterborough and back.

It did not take the LNER's motive-power department long to realise it had an exceptional locomotive. On one run with the Glasgow goods, a 47-wagon train loaded to 610 tons, No4771 covered the 32.3 miles between Sandy and Peterborough in 38 minutes, with a top speed of 66mph. Christmas Eve 1936 saw *Green Arrow* display its full potential as a passenger locomotive. Rostered to take the 1.05pm relief 'Midday Scotsman' from King's Cross to Grantham, the V2 covered 60 miles at average of 70.9mph, with a maximum of 86mph at Arlesey.

Green Arrow was soon joined by four further V2s. As hoped, they proved capable of working vacuum-braked freights at up to 60mph. And there was a bonus: the V2s soon showed that they could ably deputise for the Gresley Pacifics on express passenger schedules. Indeed, in tip-top condition, a V2 could match an A3 for sustained high-speed running. One was timed at 93mph on the 'Yorkshire Pullman', while another attained 101mph on a test train.

However, these handsome thoroughbreds had one drawback. There were geographical limits to their versatility. With a 22 ton axleloading, the V2s were barred from around 60 out of every 100 of the LNER's route miles. All the ex-Great Eastern main lines, for example, were off-limits. What a difference a batch of V2s would have made to services there. However, any argument that the LNER would have been better advised to have produced a design around twenty per cent less powerful, but with a wider route availability, was about to be undermined. After 1939, the LNER would need all the 'big engines' it could muster to meet wartime requirements.

Wartime heroics

Whatever the V2s achieved in peacetime will always be eclipsed by their astonishing feats of haulage during World War II. As far as LNER enginemen were concerned, these were the engines that won the war, not the Stanier 8F or

Select few

Besides *Green Arrow* just a handful of V2s were named. In 1937, new No4780 became *The Snapper The East Yorkshire Regiment – The Duke of York's Own*. And if that were not enough of a mouthful, in 1938 No4806 was named *The Green Howard Alexandra, Princess of Wales's Own Regiment*. *The Snapper*, incidentally, was a nickname given the regiment during the American War of Independence. Three other V2s commemorated army regiments (No4843 *King's Own Yorkshire Light Infantry*, No4844 *Coldstreamer* and, in April 1958, No60964 *The Durham Light Infantry*). Two others celebrated public schools: No4818 *St Peter's School York AD627* and No4831 *Durham School*. Plans to adorn No4804 with the name of *The Royal Grammar School, Newcastle-upon-Tyne, A.D. 1545* were shelved at the outbreak of war in 1939 and never revived.

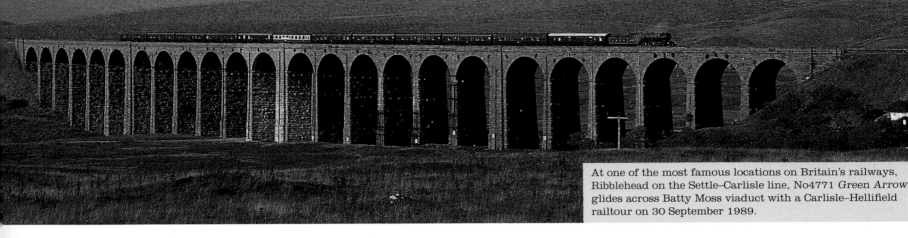

At one of the most famous locations on Britain's railways, Ribblehead on the Settle–Carlisle line, No4771 *Green Arrow* glides across Batty Moss viaduct with a Carlisle–Hellifield railtour on 30 September 1989.

American S160. The V2s were undaunted by the 20-coach-plus trains – loads of over 700 tons – that became commonplace on the East Coast Main Line. On at least one occasion, a single V2 hauled 26 packed coaches from Peterborough to London. Given this capability, it was not surprising that construction was permitted through the war years. They were the last Gresley-designed engines to be produced, the final examples – delivered in 1944 – bringing the total to 184.

The V2s performed equally competently for British Railways, making their mark on the 'Waverley' route between Carlisle and Edinburgh, and on the ex-Great Central main line between London Marylebone and Sheffield. However, as with most Gresley designs, they were susceptible to inadequate maintenance. Like any other locomotive, they could be 'flogged', but performances suffered as wear took its toll on the complex valve gear, or if the valve settings were allowed to drift out of alignment. Poor track conditions could lead to severe problems – some resulting in derailments – for the swing-link self-centring suspension of

IN PRESERVATION

During November 1941, *Green Arrow* had exchanged its lined apple-green livery for plain black. Like its classmates, the locomotive put in sterling work on the East Coast during World War II. Under the LNER's 1943 renumbering No4771 became No800 (although the change did not take place until November 1946) and, in February 1949, British Railways' No60800. It was also repainted in the BR standard mixed-traffic livery of lined black.

Up to nationalisation, *Green Arrow* had been a King's Cross locomotive, and would remain so until withdrawal, apart from a six-week period at Woodford Halse between mid-May and late June 1953. There was a pleasing surprise when, after overhaul at Doncaster, *Green Arrow* emerged from the Doncaster paintshop on 11 January 1958 in fully lined-out passenger engine green. It was the last change made to the engine, apart from the installation of Automatic Warning System apparatus (AWS), before withdrawal on 21 August 1962.

Two factors played a part in *Green Arrow*'s preservation. First, it represented Britain's premier class of high-powered, high-speed mixed-traffic engines and, second, the V2s were the only British 2-6-2 tender engines to go into series production. The monobloc cylinder casting of No4771 was intentionally not replaced so that the engine remained in as-built condition. It was a debatable decision, since cracks in the casting have probably ended *Green Arrow*'s time as a working engine.

However, the notion that *Green Arrow* might one day steam again would never have occurred to the British Transport Commission and its Curator of Historical Relics, the engine's

new custodians. *Green Arrow* first returned to Doncaster Works for a cosmetic restoration that included the fitting of a replacement boiler, one that had previously served on classmates Nos60825 and 60841. In April 1963, *Green Arrow* reappeared in its original LNER guise as No4771, and in fully lined apple-green livery. It remained in store at Doncaster until October 1964 when it joined a number of other preserved locomotives in the closed engine shed at Hellifield, in Lancashire.

The impetus to return *Green Arrow* to running order came from Norwich shedmaster, the late Bill Harvey. Offering assistance from members of the Norfolk Railway Society, his proposal was accepted and, on the night of 20 and 21 January 1972, the engine was towed from Sussex to Norfolk. Eight months later, on 12 August 1972, No4771 was steamed for the first time in almost ten years.

Steaming back

Winter elapsed before, on 28 March 1973, *Green Arrow* was allowed a trial run from Norwich to Ely and return. Based at Carnforth, in Lancashire, railtour work, chiefly along the Cumbrian coast and to Leeds occupied No4771 until 1975. On 31 August that year it appeared in the Shildon cavalcade, in County Durham, marking the 150th anniversary of the Stockton & Darlington Railway. *Green Arrow* then headed for York and was in steam for the opening of the National Railway Museum on 27 September.

A boiler retube sidelined the V2 until August 1977 but 1978 saw it involved in two landmarks for main-line steam: the first specials to be allowed to run over the Settle and Carlisle line and, on

the leading pony truck.

The demise of the V2s was not, initially, a result of the coming of diesels but the arrival on the Eastern and North Eastern Regions of the simpler, equally versatile 2-cylinder 9F 2-10-0. In February 1962, New England's No60850 became the first withdrawal. By the end of the year, more than a third of the class had been condemned. The V2s' swansong came on the Edinburgh–Aberdeen run, working alongside the last survivors from the A2 and A4 Pacifics. The final duty undertaken by the last V2 in traffic, Dundee's No60836, could not have presented a greater contrast with their earlier feats of haulage: the two-coach Alnwick branch train. No60836 was retired on 31 December 1966 leaving only the doyen of the class – No60800 *Green Arrow* – to be spared the torch.

LNER 'heavyweights' on Great Western territory: V2 No60800 *Green Arrow* and Peppercorn A2 Pacific No60532 *Blue Peter* were among the attractions at an Old Oak Common open day on 6 August 2000.

25 June, the inauguration of British Railways' 'Scarborough Spa Express'.

A further retube, this time undertaken in Hull by the Humberside Locomotive Preservation Group, kept *Green Arrow* out of service until August 1985. On 7 April 1986, the V2 made what was probably its first visit to Scotland. It was requested for a private charter from Edinburgh to Gleneagles, double-heading with BR Standard 9F 2-10-0 No92220 *Evening Star* – power to spare if ever there was! For five weeks during the summer of 1987, No4771 was in more familiar territory, based at Marylebone depot in London for a series of excursions to Stratford-upon-Avon.

By 1992, though, time had run out for *Green Arrow*. After undertaking its final railtour, from Carlisle to Bradford on 1 August, inspection at York revealed the boiler to need extensive repairs to the stays and copperwork. With the National Railway Museum unable to undertake the work, *Green Arrow* was consigned to static display. Indeed, it might have remained there without the beneficial intervention of a philanthropic industrial chemist (and railway enthusiast), Dr Michael Peagram, who financed an overhaul which was completed in 1998.

Since then, as well as main-line railtours, *Green Arrow* has visited several heritage railways and, in July 2003, returned to its birthplace of Doncaster. The V2 made its final run in the summer of 2008 after which the locomotive returned to the National Railway Museum, York.

IN DETAIL *(as built)*

Class	V2
Built:	Doncaster, Darlington works; 1936-44
Designer:	Sir Nigel Gresley
Number built:	184
Purpose:	Mixed traffic
Wheel arrangement:	2-6-2
Cylinders (x 3):	18.5 in diameter x 26 in stroke
Motion:	Walschaerts (with Gresley-Holcroft divided drive to inside cylinder)
Valves:	9 in diameter piston valves
Wheels: Coupled:	6 ft 2 in
Leading:	3 ft 2 in
Trailing:	3 ft 8 in
Tender:	3 ft 9 in
Boiler diagram:	LNER Diagram 109
Boiler Max. diameter::	6 ft 5 in
Pressure:	220 lb/psi
Heating surface:	3,110.74 sq ft
Firebox:	215 sq ft
Tubes and flues:	2,216.07
Superheater:	679.67 sq ft
Grate area:	41.25 sq ft
Tractive effort:	33,730 lb (@ 85% boiler pressure)
Engine wheelbase:	33 ft 8 in
Total wheelbase:	56 ft 2.125 in
Engine weight:	93 tons 2 cwt
Coal capacity:	7.5 tons
Water capacity:	4,200 gallons
Max. axle loading:	22 tons 0 cwt
BR power class:	6MT

London Midland &
Scottish Railway

Sir William Stanier

**'Princess
Coronation' class
8P 4-6-2 (1937)**

Crowning Moments for a 'Coronation'

'Coronation' Pacifics tackling Shap or Beattock banks at the head of Glasgow-bound expresses remain the most potent images of Stanier locomotives. Stanier's final design for the LMSR, they represented the zenith of four-cylinder locomotive development in Britain. For many, here was the ultimate British express locomotive.

No6233 *Duchess of Sutherland* in steam outside its home of the West Shed at Swanwick, on the Midland Railway, Butterley, on 20 May 2005.

During November 1936, the heroic efforts of one of the prototype 'Princess Royal' Pacifics, No6201 *Princess Elizabeth*, had demonstrated that the Euston to Glasgow run could be completed in under six hours. The downside was that the LMSR was under-equipped to capitalise on the achievement. In contrast to the 80-plus Gresley Pacifics then working on the rival LNER, it had but a dozen engines of equivalent ability. The situation was brought to a head when the LNER announced a new streamlined train for coronation year, 1937. With an A4 Pacific in charge, the 'Coronation' would bring Edinburgh within six hours of London. Prestige alone made this a challenge the LMSR could not ignore. All that was needed was a locomotive up to the job.

With Stanier on government business in India, examining the running of the state railway system, design work for the new locomotive passed to his Principal Assistant, Robert Riddles, and Chief Draughtsman, Tom Coleman. The 'Princess Royal' was their starting point and both were well aware of its strengths and weaknesses. It is said that Coleman had been responsible for persuading Stanier to pursue something more than an updated 'Princess'. However, it is unlikely that Coleman mentioned streamlining.

The LMSR had been evaluating streamlining since 1931 and had commissioned research from

Going undercover

It was beneath the 'upturned bathtub', as it was derided by some, that the crucial changes were made from the 'Princess Royal' of four years earlier. The 'Princess Coronation' Pacifics, as they were classified, benefited from a larger and much-improved boiler. To save weight, the boiler was fabricated from nickel steel and proved to be a first-rate steam-raiser. To this was added a huge grate area of 50 square feet and, with its 40 elements, the largest superheater of any British locomotive. From here, the steam circuit was arranged to allow steam unencumbered access to the cylinders and the complexity of four sets of valve gear was replaced by just two sets of outside Walschaerts motion, with the inside cylinder valves activated by rocking shafts working off the outside valve spindle crossheads.

At Robert Riddles' suggestion, a further change saw the driving-wheel diameter increased by three inches to 6 feet 9 inches. It was a move he subsequently regretted, claiming that smaller wheels would not have compromised performance but would have aided adhesion, especially when starting. Nevertheless, Riddles acknowledged that the 'Princess Coronation' represented 'a considerable advance over the first LMS 4-6-2s'.

the National Physical Laboratory. Unfortunately, what began as objective study had become a fashionable design trend. The streamlined casing produced for the new engines might have been evolved in a wind tunnel, but it was more about generating publicity than enhancing performance. Modest fuel savings were projected but the consensus was that only during long, continuous high-speed runs would the reduction in wind resistance justify the added weight of the casing.

Interestingly, where the wedge-shaped front of Gresley's streamliner, the A4 Pacific, was derived from railcars designed by the Italian motor engineer, Ettore Bugatti, the bathtub-like shroud of the LMSR engine owed most to German and American styling, in particular the New York Central Railroad's J3a and Deutsches Reichsbahn's O5 4-6-4s. The bulbous shape was a proven aerodynamic form and, according to some commentators, bettered the A4's 'wedge' shape in stimulating less atmospheric disturbance.

Beginning with No6220 *Coronation*, the first ten of the new Pacifics were streamlined. The livery of the initial five, a deep blue with four horizontal silver stripes converging in a chevron on the front of the locomotive, was that chosen for the LMSR's new high-speed service linking Euston and Glasgow, the 'Coronation

Scot'. As a response to the LNER's 'Coronation', however, it fell a little short. The rolling stock was refurbished rather than new and the anticipated six-hour timing turned out to be half-an-hour longer with a stop at Carlisle. However, the LMSR's caution was understandable. Punctuality was vital and it was preferable to have time in hand.

The first streamliners were outshopped from Crewe in June 1937 and, on 24 of the month No6220 was displayed at Euston. Simultaneously, No6221 *Queen Elizabeth* was unveiled at Glasgow Central. Five days later, No6220 left Euston bound for Crewe on a special run for LMSR dignitaries and the press. Clearly, from the preparations, something spectacular was planned. The choice of driver gave a clue: Tommy Clark of Crewe North had been in charge for the record-breaking runs of 'Princess Royal' No6201 *Princess Elizabeth* during November 1936.

Clark gave *Coronation* its head and the Pacific raced down Madeley bank, reaching – according to the LMSR's (but not everyone's) calculations – 114 miles per hour. It was a new British record, beating the one set by the LNER's A4 No2512 *Silver Fox* by just one mile per hour. On the approach to Crewe, however, exhilaration turned to alarm as the train approached at considerably more than the permitted speed. A fierce application of the brakes sent the crockery flying in the kitchen car, but that was the only

damage sustained and No6220 and its train remained upright. Stanier attributed this to the qualities of the front bogie, a variant of that designed by the French engineer, Alfred de Glehn, and familiar to Stanier from his time on to the Great Western. What speed Coronation might have attained without the intervention of the Crewe curves has since been a matter of speculation. Stanier and his team, it is believed, thought 120mph wholly attainable.

The return to Euston offered a much better example of what the 'Coronations' could accomplish, a sustained and controlled display of power output and high-speed running. The following month, on 5 July, the Pacifics began earning their keep on the 'Coronation Scot', but its modest loading of 297 tons and schedule of 4 hours 13 minutes for the 200-mile journey from Euston to Carlisle did not prove to be unduly taxing.

Right and proper

Stanier had been indifferent to the streamlining of the 'Coronations' but had gone along with the idea. Unsurprisingly he seized the opportunity to build some examples, Nos6230-6234, without streamlining for 'comparative purposes'.

According to Riddles, Stanier observed:

'I have decided it is better to please a fool than tease him; they can have their bloody streamliners but we will build five proper ones as well.'

Relieved of its casing, a powerful profile was revealed; just how powerful was soon shown by No6234 *Duchess of Abercorn*, the first locomotive of the class to be fitted with a double chimney.

On test between Glasgow and Crewe, the 'Coronation' confirmed its status as Britain's most powerful locomotive, developing 3,348 horsepower at the cylinders with a load of 610 tons. At the time it was climbing the 1 in 99 of Beattock bank at a steady 63 miles per hour. There was only one caveat – two firemen were needed to satisfy its appetite for coal.

It is at the cylinders and the drawbar that the work of a locomotive is done and, at the latter, No6234 was constantly generating between 1,750 and 2,000 horsepower. The recorded maximum was 2,511 hp. Importantly, this was no one-off achievement; the 'Coronations' were designed for haulage capacity as well as speed and such power outputs became the norm. Double chimneys became standard from No6235 onwards and were retrospectively fitted to all the existing

IN PRESERVATION

No46229 *Duchess of Hamilton* In 1938, the LMSR was invited to exhibit No6220 *Coronation* and a 'Coronation Scot' train at the following year's World's Fair in New York. However, No6220 was unavailable and No6229 *Duchess of Hamilton* was substituted. Renamed and renumbered, engine and train were shipped to the United States and went on to cover 3,121 miles and taking in 15 states and 38 cities.

Following the outbreak of war that September, the American authorities agreed to the LMSR's request that engine and train be stored. However, by 1943 so desperate was the need for motive power, the LMSR gambled on avoiding the U-boats and brought the *Duchess* home.

March 1961 saw No46229 make its final move, to Edge Hill, Liverpool. Withdrawn on 15 February 1964 having run 1,533,846 miles, it then found an unlikely rescuer. Both *Duchess of Hamilton* and No46233 *Duchess of Sutherland* were bought by the holiday camp operators, Butlin's.

When Butlin's decided to dispose of its

locomotives, agreement was reached for *Duchess of Hamilton* to be displayed at the National Railway Museum in York. It was 'adopted' by the Friends of the NRM through whose efforts the *Duchess* was returned to main-line running order. It steamed for the first time in preservation in April 1980. Five years and 13,223 miles of railtour work later No46229 required a second overhaul. On this occasion the Friends raised £225,000 to ensure that *Duchess of Hamilton* remained at work until 1998. Now returned to original maroon-and-gilt streamlined condition, No6229 is on display at York.

No6233 *Duchess of Sutherland* The only working 'Coronation' Pacific, No6233 *Duchess of Sutherland* was one of the non-streamlined examples outshopped from Crewe in July 1938. Withdrawn in February 1964, after seven years at Butlin's, Ayr, it arrived at Bressingham Steam Museum. Now in the care of the Princess Royal Locomotive Trust, No6233 took to the main line for the first time in 37 years in 2001. Its most celebrated

outing came on 11 June 2002 when it conveyed HM The Queen along the North Wales coast, the first steam-hauled royal train since 1967. *Duchess of Sutherland* bowed out of main-line work during 2009.

No46235 *City of Birmingham* On retirement in September 1964, No46235 had registered 1,566,677 miles. It was selected as

the only 'Coronation' to be publicly preserved and, wearing BR Brunswick-green livery, became the principal exhibit at Birmingham's Science Museum. Apparently, an entire building would have to be demolished if – as many enthusiasts earnestly wish – it is ever to be released from captivity and returned to working order.

engines. Inexplicably, though, No6235 *City of Birmingham* saw a return to streamlining which, for both performance and appearance, had clearly been shown to be an unnecessary feature.

Record-breaking, and high-speed luxury expresses such as the 'Coronation Scot', were discontinued during wartime. However, the prodigious haulage capacity of the 'Coronation' Pacifics guaranteed their continued usefulness and further construction was permitted. Streamlined Nos6235-6248 were delivered between 1939 and 1943, and a further nine non-streamlined examples were constructed up to 1948. To improve access and cut down maintenance time parts of the streamlined casing had been removed during World War II and, in 1945, came the predictable decision to remove it entirely.

The final two 'Coronation' class Pacifics, Nos6256 and 6257 were delivered in 1947-48, by which time George Ivatt had become the LMSR's Chief Mechanical Engineer. Ivatt introduced some significant innovations. Both engines had Timken roller bearings (with manganese steel liners) on all locomotive and tender axles, except the bogie. They had rocking grates, self-emptying ashpans and self-cleaning smokeboxes and the trailing truck was redesigned as a one-piece, delta-shaped casting. Some consider this, the final development of the Stanier Pacific, to have been Britain's finest express passenger design, surpassed only by the LNER A4 for speed and by no other design for power.

Colourful lives

Astonishingly, for a class of just 38, the 'Coronations' appeared in 12 liveries. Beginning with the blue-and-red streamliners, these also included LMSR lined crimson lake, wartime black, varieties of post-war black, British Railways experimental blue and BR standard lined green, this last the only colour to be carried by all members of the class. The final repainting came in the late 1950s when BR's London Midland Region turned out four 'Princess Royal' and sixteen 'Coronation' Pacifics in lined maroon.

Based at Camden (London), Crewe North, Edge Hill (Liverpool), Carlisle Upperby and Polmadie (Glasgow), the 'Coronations' continued serving the West Coast until the early 1960s. As well as Euston–Glasgow and Euston–Liverpool, they mainly worked between Crewe, Perth and Aberdeen and along the North Wales coast to Holyhead. The influx of English Electric Type 4 diesels and the spread of electrification north and south of Crewe spelled their end and all were withdrawn between 1962 and 1964, beginning with Polmadie's Nos46227 *Duchess of Devonshire*, 46231 *Duchess of Atholl* and 46232 *Duchess of Montrose* in December 1962. Last to be condemned, in October 1964, was Crewe North's No46256 *Sir William A. Stanier F.R.S.* An attempt to save it came agonisingly close to succeeding and, though three were saved, it should have been the fourth, joining LNER Pacific No60007 *Sir Nigel Gresley* as a lasting memorial to one of Britain's great locomotive engineers.

With power in reserve, No6233 *Duchess of Sutherland* eases the 'Royal Scot' out of Kidderminster (Bridgnorth-bound rather than Glasgow) on a Severn Valley Railway gala day, 23 September 2006.

IN DETAIL *(as built)*	
Class	**'Coronation'**
Built:	Crewe Works, 1937-48
Designer:	Sir William Stanier
Number built:	38
Purpose:	Express passenger
Wheel arrangement:	4-6-2
Cylinders (x4):	16.5 in diameter x 28 in stroke
Motion:	Walschaerts with rocking shafts to inside cylinders
Valves:	9 in diameter piston valves
Wheels: Coupled:	6 ft 9 in
Leading:	3 ft 0 in
Trailing:	3 ft 9in
Tender:	4 ft 3 in
Boiler type:	1
Boiler: Max. diameter:	6 ft 5.5 in
Pressure:	250 lb/psi
Heating surface:	3,663.5 sq ft (subsequently reduced to 3,637 sq ft)
Firebox:	230.5 sq ft
Tubes and flues:	2,577 sq ft
Superheater:	856 sq ft (subsequently reduced to 830 sq ft)
Grate area:	50.0 sq ft
Tractive effort:	40,000 lb (@ 85% boiler pressure)
Engine wheelbase:	37 ft 0 in
Total wheelbase:	62 ft 11 in
Engine Weight:	105 tons 5 cwt§ (108 tons 2 cwt streamlined)
Coal capacity:	10 tons
Water capacity:	4,000 gallons
Max. axleloading:	22 tons 9 cwt (22 tons 10 cwt streamlined)
BR power class:	8P

§Locomotives Nos46256 and 46257 weighed 106 tons 8 cwt.

The Benefit of Good 'Manors'

Intended to introduce modern motive power on secondary routes,
including those inherited at the 1923 grouping, the 'baby' in the Great Western's family
of 4-6-0s needed the attention of Swindon's 'test team' before giving of its best.

For the Great Western, the 1923 'grouping' when over 120 companies became a 'big four', was a fairly smooth transition. It simply absorbed its smaller neighbours, chiefly in South Wales. This extended family added some 900 locomotives to the GWR fleet, many of them six-coupled tanks working in the Welsh valleys and docks. In mid-Wales the Cambrian Railway contributed 99 engines (including five narrow gauge) and the Midland & South Western Junction, linking Cheltenham with the South Coast, a modest 29. The GWR now began evaluating its inheritance. Some locomotives were serviceable and others worthy of refurbishment (otherwise known as 'Swindonisation'). Certain engines performed specific roles and had to be kept as the GWR had nothing comparable. Many, however, were past their best and modern replacements were not always going to be found among Great Western ranks.

The tracks of the Cambrian and M&SWJR, for example, were of lighter construction than the GWR main lines and therefore out of bounds to its larger and heavier locomotive classes. This was fine as long as resident fleets worked, but eventually the need for new motive power could no longer be ignored.

The North Downs cross-country line linking Reading with Guildford, in Surrey, and Tonbridge, Kent, became a haunt of the 'Manors' during the 1960s. Reading-based (81D) No7813 *Freshford Manor* starts away from Shalford with the 12.16pm Redhill–Guildford on 20 November 1963.

Waste not

Collett had begun a process of 'cannibalising' redundant 4300 class Moguls in 1936, reusing the frames and motion for his 6800 'Grange' class 4-6-0s. He continued this policy with the newcomer, the smallest and lightest of the Great Western 4-6-0s and his last design before retirement.

The 7800 'Manor' class was designed to be economical in both construction and operation. Although a new type of boiler was produced for the class, the Swindon No14, together with new cylinders and mainframes, the driving wheels and motion were reclaimed from scrapped 4300s. However, a larger cab, with side windows, was deemed worthwhile. The tenders, too, were second-hand, mostly of the Churchward 3,500 gallon type built between 1905 and 1914

Among the routes earmarked for 'Manor' operation was the ex-Cambrian main line between Shrewsbury, Machynlleth and Aberystwyth. Others included Ruabon to Barmouth, via Bala Junction, and Aberystwyth to Carmarthen. Overall, the 'Manors' were allowed over several hundred more route miles than the 'Grange' 4-6-0s even though the latter were just 5 tons 2 cwt heavier.

The first of the 'Manors', No7800 *Torquay Manor*, entered traffic on 19 January 1938 and spent its first three months working out of Stafford Road depot, Wolverhampton. That March saw a move to Banbury and the engine would spend the next 14 years shuttling between that depot and Tyseley (Birmingham). By February the following year, 20 'Manors' were in service, all of them built at Swindon to Lot No316.

According to GWR publicity, the 'Manors' were expected to work to existing schedules and with existing loadings, but with an all-round increase in efficiency. Unfortunately, the parsimony prevalent at Swindon during the 1930s for once appears to have been misguided. Unlike the 'Granges' of 1936, where the employment of standard components and the re-use of redundant parts had produced a winning combination, the initial performance of the 'Manors' was disappointing. They gained a reputation as poor steamers and were unpopular with some footplate crews.

Minor changes, major improvement

Were it not for the outbreak of war and a consequent change in priorities, Swindon would have almost certainly recalled the engines for modification. That had to wait until 1952 when experiments undertaken at Swindon demonstrated the changes required. The improvement in steam-raising and all-round performance certainly made for better engines and endeared the 'Manors' to footplate crews. A briefing prepared on 13 March 1954 said of the modified engines: 'Reports have been received in respect of eight [engines] after service varying between two and eight months and these reports speak highly of the steaming qualities of the boiler.'

War had halted the proposed construction of a further 20 'Manors' but BR reinstated half the order and Nos7820-29 were outshopped during November and December 1950 (Lot No377). These post-war examples cost rather more than their predecessors, an average of £10,425 apiece, but no parts were re-used and they were paired with new rather than second-hand tenders.

IN PRESERVATION

No7802 *Bradley Manor* The locomotive was restored in 1993 and is available for service on the Severn Valley Railway.

No7808 *Cookham Manor* The first of the 'Manors' to be preserved, by August 1970 *Cookham Manor* had become resident at the Great Western Society's base at Didcot, Oxfordshire, and has been on static display for many years with no plans for a return to steam.

No7812 *Erlestoke Manor* First steamed in preservation on the Severn Valley Railway in 1979, No7812's latest, more protracted overhaul was completed in 2008 with owners, the Erlestoke Manor Fund, hoping to secure main-line certification.

No7819 *Hinton Manor* Long-time stalwart of the Severn Valley Railway fleet, *Hinton Manor* has been sidelined since 1992 awaiting a ten-year boiler overhaul. It is on display in a Swindon shopping centre!

No7820 *Dinmore Manor* After entering traffic on the West Somerset Railway in September 1995, ten years on No7820 was sidelined for its compulsory refit. This has yet to begin.

No7821 *Ditcheat Manor* Also requiring overhaul, No7821 has joined classmates Nos7820 and 7828 on the West Somerset Railway, which aims to buy the engine.

No7822 *Foxcote Manor* Bought from Woodhams' by the Foxcote Manor Society in 1975, No7822 returned to steam on the Llangollen Railway during April 1989. It remains a mainstay of the fleet there.

No7827 *Lydham Manor* Three years after departing Woodhams' in March 1973 *Lydham Manor* was ready to enter service on the Paignton & Dartmouth Railway – a remarkably swift restoration. Its most recent overhaul was completed in 2005.

No7828 *Odney Manor* Bought from Woodhams' in 1981, the much-travelled *Odney Manor* now awaits overhaul on the West Somerset Railway, which was sufficiently impressed to buy the 'Manor'!

Now one of a trio of 'Manors' based on the West Somerset Railway, No7828 *Odney Manor* makes a pleasing, if improbable, double-header with Stanier 'Jubilee' 4-6-0 No45596 *Bahamas* climbing through Burrs on the East Lancashire Railway with a Bury–Rawtenstall train on 15 October 1994.

By 1959, eighteen of the 'Manors' had congregated in mid- and South Wales. The largest contingent – eight – was based at the one-time Cambrian Railway headquarters of Oswestry, between Shrewsbury and Wrexham. Four were allocated to Machynlleth, east of Dovey Junction, four were kept at Carmarthen, while two of the class were stationed at Shrewsbury and frequently worked to Chester and Crewe. Of the remaining twelve, eight were in the West Country. Newton Abbot was responsible for three, Plymouth Laira for two and the Cornish sheds of St Blazey and Truro for a further three. Finally, there were single-engine allocations to Cardiff Canton, Croes Newydd, Gloucester and Tyseley.

Undoubtedly, throughout their careers, the most prestigious 'Manor' duty remained the 'Cambrian Coast Express', which they took over from one of the larger 4-6-0s (usually a 'Castle') at Shrewsbury and worked through to Aberystwyth. Inaugurated in 1927, the 'Cambrian Coast Express' ran for 40 years (with a gap during World War II) but a 'Manor' missed out on hauling the last working on 4 March 1967 because all had been withdrawn by then.

The 'Manors' had been the last class of GWR 4-6-0s to remain intact, the first withdrawal not coming until 1963. That April No7809 *Childrey Manor* of Shrewsbury was condemned and cut up at Swindon two months later. Half the class had been axed by May 1965 and, of the survivors, seven had gathered at Shrewsbury and three at Didcot. Four were divided between Cardiff East Dock and Wolverhampton Oxley, and there was a solitary example at Gloucester, No7808 *Cookham Manor*.

At some time in its working life each of the 30 'Manors' had worked on Cambrian metals but their swansong came on the Southern Region's North Downs line connecting Reading with Guildford and Redhill. Engine record cards put the average mileage for the first twenty, 1938-built examples at 806,000, but the ten 1950-built engines could muster only 419,000.

IN DETAIL *(as built)*

Class	7800 'Manor'
Built:	1938-50; Swindon Works
Designer:	Charles Collett
Number built:	30
Purpose:	Secondary passenger and goods
Wheel arrangement:	4-6-0
Cylinders (x2):	18 in diameter x 30 in stroke
Motion:	Stephenson
Valves:	10 in diameter piston valves
Wheels: Coupled:	5 ft 8 in diameter
Leading:	3 ft 0 in
Tender:	4 ft 1.5 in
Boiler diagram:	Swindon No14
Boiler: Max. diameter:	5 ft 3 in
Pressure:	225 lb/psi
Heating surface:	1,585 sq ft
Firebox:	140 sq ft
Tubes and flues:	1,285 sq ft
Superheater:	160 sq ft
Grate area:	22.1 sq ft
Tractive Effort:	27,340 lb (@ 85% boiler pressure)
Engine wheelbase:	27 ft 1 in
Total wheelbase:	52 ft 1.75 in
Engine weight:	68 tons 18 cwt
Coal capacity:	6 tons
Water capacity:	3,500 gallons
Max. axleloading:	17 tons 5 cwt
BR power class:	5MT

A Flawed Flagship

Southern Railway
Oliver Bulleid
MN 'Merchant Navy' class 8P
4-6-2 (1941)

Innovative, unorthodox, enigmatic – in many ways the Southern Railway's 'Merchant Navy' Pacific of 1941 mirrored the personality of its designer, Oliver Bulleid: they defied convention and divided opinion.

The restoration of 'Merchant Navy' Pacific No35027 *Port Line* was completed in 1987 and it spent several years working on the Bluebell Railway and making countless ascents of Freshfield bank, here hauling a five-coach train composed appropriately of Southern green stock. *Port Line* is presently undergoing overhaul at Southall, in west London.

Oliver Bulleid had been given the green light to produce what was outlined as a 'fast mixed-traffic locomotive'. However, the description failed to mention that it would be unlike any previous design in that category. The first proposals, for a 2-8-2 or 4-8-2, were dismissed on weight grounds, forcing Bulleid to revert to the more common 4-6-2 arrangement, although that was where convention ended.

The novelty started with the outer casing. It was portrayed as 'air-smoothed' rather than streamlined and supposedly allowed the engines to be cleaned in carriage-washing plants. Even the wheels were strikingly different. They compared with the American 'boxpok' pattern but Bulleid had developed – and patented – the design in conjunction with the Sheffield steelmakers, Firth Brown. Though lighter than the traditional spoked variety, the BFB wheel was stronger and gave greater all-round support to the outer tyre.

A further innovation was the use of electric lighting, not only for headcode lamps and tail lights, but to illuminate the injectors, front bogie, driving wheels, trailing truck and mechanical lubricators. The most controversial, however, was concealed beneath the outer shroud.

In theory, Bulleid's scheme for chain-driven valve gear operating within an enclosed oil bath was inspired. The apparatus should have been almost maintenance-free. In service, however, water had a habit of oozing into the oil bath. The resultant corrosion allowed oil to leak on to the track. Apart from inhibiting the operation of the valve gear, it created the perfect conditions for the driving wheels to slip wildly. More seriously, there were occasions when oil leaks set fire to the boiler lagging.

The redeeming feature of the design was the boiler. With a working pressure of 280 lb per square inch – higher than any other British locomotive at the time – and a superheat temperature of 400 degrees C, it was the finest steam-raiser ever developed in Britain. The firebox similarly broke new ground. Using all-welded steel rather than riveted copper brought savings in cost and weight. Additionally, steel overcame the expansion and contraction problems that would have arisen when a copper firebox was subjected to the levels of pressure and temperature Bulleid envisaged. Again, though, there was a gulf between the theory and the practice. The fabrication process pushed contemporary welding technology to its limit. Within seven years, the first ten boilers had to have their fireboxes replaced and X-ray inspections monitored the state of the welding in the others.

Highlighting the problems of the Bulleid Pacific, however, paints a misleading picture. Many of its features were outstanding: the smooth-riding trailing truck; the comfortable and well-protected cab; the excellent ashpan arrangement. Most importantly, in performance terms, it delivered everything Bulleid had promised.

Soon after the delivery of No21C1 (Bulleid preferred the European system of

An unlikely combination, but one to delight Bulleid enthusiasts, as rebuilt 'Merchant Navy' No35005 *Canadian Pacific* pilots rebuilt 'West Country' Pacific No34101 *Hartland* through Swithland, on the Great Central Railway, with the 1.01pm Loughborough to Leicester North dining train on 25 February 1995.

IN PRESERVATION

No fewer than 11 of the 30-strong 'Merchant Navies' escaped scrapping including No35029 *Ellerman Lines*, now a sectioned exhibit at the National Railway Museum. However, just three have been restored: Nos35027 *Port Line*, 35005 *Canadian Pacific* and 35028 *Clan Line*, the last two to main-line condition.

35005 *Canadian Pacific* Until recently, a main-line performer throughout southern England, *Canadian Pacific* currently awaits a boiler retube before resuming service on the Mid-Hants Railway, which now owns the locomotive.

35006 *Peninsular & Oriental S. N. Co* After a 22-year career based at one depot – Salisbury – No35006 was retired in August 1964. It has been housed at Toddington, on the Gloucestershire Warwickshire Railway, since 1983, and No35006 is now entering the final stages of its restoration.

35009 *Shaw Savill* Owner, Ian Riley, with much other locomotive work on his hands, has placed *Shaw Savill* – which has been dismantled – up for sale. It recently appeared on e-bay with a reserve of £100,000.

35010 *Blue Star* Housed at the East Anglian Railway Museum at Chappel & Wakes Colne in Essex, *Blue Star* remains unrestored.

It's on the cards

Although the Bulleid Pacifics excelled in BR's 1948 locomotive exchange trials, their record cards revealed less-flattering statistics. Since its introduction, the 'Merchant Navy' had undergone no less than 165 modifications. In spite of this, the engines averaged 62 days out of traffic each year for examination and repair. Although much of the blame could be attributed to the declining maintenance standards experienced after the war, the figures caused concern.

Once Oliver Bulleid had left for a post in Ireland, a proposal to rebuild the Pacifics gained support. The arithmetic was indisputable. The cost of rebuilding each engine (£5,615) would be offset by a projected annual saving of £11,770 in fuel and oil. Elimination of the most trouble-prone features would also increase availability. Since the class would be operating over the Weymouth and West of England main lines for the foreseeable future, there would be ample time to recoup the outlay (it took just four years).

The visible effects of rebuilding were the removal of the air-smoothed casing, replacement of the chain-driven valve gear by the Walschaerts variety, and the substitution of the stovepipe chimney for a more conventional casting. BR Standard-style smoke deflectors were fitted. Much else was replaced, but the supervising engineer, R.G. Jarvis, always maintained that the rebuilt Pacifics were 'still 90 per cent Bulleid'. Certainly the 'MNs' lost none of their capacity for fast running, exceeding the 100mph mark on occasion.

incorporating an engine's wheel arrangement within its number), it was decided to name the new Pacifics. The Southern Railway had commercial ties with many of the shipping lines then facing U-boat attack in the Atlantic. The 'Merchant Navy' class was an opportunity to honour the companies and those who served on their ships. Construction spanned seven years. Twenty were in service by 1945 but a final ten, beginning with No35021 *New Zealand Line*, did not appear until 1948.

The man who changed trains

Born in Invercargill, New Zealand, of British parents in 1882, Oliver Bulleid came to Britain on the death of his father in 1889. In 1901, he secured an apprenticeship with the Great Northern Railway at its Doncaster Works and, by 1907, had become assistant to the locomotive works manager. However, Bulleid wanted broader experience. In December of that year, he joined the French subsidiary of the American Westinghouse company, becoming assistant manager at its Freinville works near Paris (it was in France that he first encountered chain-driven valve gear). Four years later, Bulleid returned to the GNR as personal assistant to Nigel Gresley, who had taken over as Locomotive, Carriage & Wagon Superintendent. It was the beginning of an association that spanned more than 25 years.

Bulleid continued as Gresley's assistant when, in 1923, the latter became Chief Mechanical Engineer of the newly formed LNER. Gresley gave him a wide brief,

35011 *General Steam Navigation* Owned by Ace Locomotives, during 2008, No35011 was moved to the West Somerset Railway for its centre coupled wheelset to be removed and used to replace a cracked axle on 'West Country' Pacific No34046 *Braunton*. Despite this loss, a scheme to restore *General Steam Navigation* has been launched and it has been moved to a site at Sellindge, near Ashford in Kent.

35018 *British India Line* After 16 years languishing at Barry, salvation for No35018 came in March 1980 and it went to the Mid-Hants Railway. In May 2003, the locomotive moved to Portland, Dorset, for the completion of its restoration.

35022 *Holland America Line* Recently No35022 was sold to the owner of *Port Line* (below) essentially to supply parts for latter's rebuild to main-line condition.

35025 *Brocklebank Line* Rescued by the 35025 Brocklebank Line Association and estimated to be twenty per cent restored, No35025 is now based – along with No35011 *General Steam Navigation* – at Sellindge, Kent, where work is set to resume in earnest.

35027 *Port Line* Sold by owners, Southern Locomotives, along with No35022 (above) to enthusiast, Jeremy Hosking, ***Port Line*** is being restored to main-line condition at Southall, in west London. Since its existing boiler requires major repairs, that of No35022 will be substituted.

35028 *Clan Line* Bought by the Merchant Navy Locomotive Preservation Society in 1967, *Clan Line* first returned to steam in 1974. Three major overhauls later this most celebrated of the surviving 'Merchant Navy' locomotives continues to perform impeccably on railtours in southern England.

35029 *Ellerman Lines* Although disposed of as scrap in 1966, eight years later No35029 was secured by the National Railway Museum, York. In September 1979, it went on permanent display as a sectioned exhibit, the inner workings of boiler, firebox and cylinders there for all to see. At the press of a button, wheels and motion move effortlessly and silently.

ranging from rolling-stock design to locomotive testing and experimentation. The role suited Bulleid perfectly, giving him free rein to try out his ideas. He was also closely involved with Gresley's ground-breaking designs such as the P1 and P2 2-8-2s. The downside was that Bulleid was mostly isolated from the day-to-day practicalities of keeping locomotives running and this affected his later work.

It appears Bulleid was taken aback when, in 1937, he was offered the post of Chief Mechanical Engineer of the Southern Railway. The Southern had placed its faith in electrification and few significant additions had been made to its stock of steam locomotives during the 1930s. He promptly commissioned a report on the state of the entire steam fleet and, from its findings, was able to persuade the Southern's directors of the need to invest in new locomotives.

Although the climate of experiment that characterised his time on the LNER had changed to one of expediency, Bulleid was not to be deterred. He succeeded in gaining authority to produce what was summarised as a 'fast mixed-traffic locomotive' – the 'Merchant Navy'. He followed this with the equally radical Q1 0-6-0 of 1942 and, in 1945, a smaller version of the 'MN', the 'West Country'. Bulleid also undertook the mechanical design for the Southern's pioneering main-line d.c. electric and diesel-electric locomotives. His last design for the company was the ingenious, but flawed 'Leader' project, a steam locomotive intended to have the advantages of a diesel. It never went beyond prototype stage and was abandoned when Bulleid, a strong opponent of nationalisation, left Britain for a post with CIE (Coras Impair Eireann) in Ireland. He remained as Chief Mechanical Engineer until 1958, by which time he was aged 76! He died in 1970.

Hotly pursued by a Class 444 electric multiple unit on the down fast, 'Merchant Navy' No35028 *Clan Line* approaches Woking with one of the regular 'lunch circulars' from London Victoria on 14 February 2008. The train will return to London through Guildford, Redhill and Croydon.

IN DETAIL *(as built)*

Class	MN 'Merchant Navy'
Built:	Eastleigh Works; 1941-48
Designer:	Oliver Bulleid
Number built:	30
Purpose:	Express passenger
Wheel arrangement:	4-6-2
Cylinders (x3):	18 in diameter x 24 in stroke
Motion:	Bulleid chain-driven (Walschaerts)
Valves:	11 in diameter piston valves
Wheels: Leading:	3 ft 1 in
Coupled:	6 ft 2 in
Trailing:	3 ft 7 in
Tender:	3 ft 7 in
Boiler: Max. diameter:	6 ft 3.5 in
Pressure:	280 lb/psi (250 lb/psi)
Heating surface:	3,116 sq ft (3,063 sq ft)
Firebox:	275 sq ft
Superheater:	665 sq ft (612 sq ft)
Tubes:	1,242 sq ft
Flues:	934 sq ft
Grate area:	48.5 sq ft
Tractive effort:	37, 515 lb (33,495 lb) (@ 85 % boiler pressure)
Total wheelbase:	59 ft 6in (61 ft 6 in)
Engine wheelbase:	36 ft 9 in
Engine weight:	94 tons 15 cwt (97 tons 18 cwt)
Coal capacity:	5 tons
Water capacity:	5,000 gallons (6,000 gallons)
Max. axleloading:	21 tons 0 cwt (21 tons 19 cwt)
BR power class:	8P

Figures quoted based on first 10 examples after 1945, following earlier modifications. Changes through rebuilding post-1956 in brackets.

Artisan Among the Aristocrats

Designed by Edward Thompson and known to enthusiasts as 'Bongos', the B1 became the LNER's most numerous class. As such it was a more-than-useful complement to Gresley's 'big (sometimes too big) engines'. The B1's success, though, has done little for history's view of its creator's brief reign.

Nigel Gresley's policy of building often quite small classes of locomotives for specific tasks had left the LNER without a two-cylinder general-purpose design similar to the LMSR 'Black 5' or the Great Western 'Hall'. The V2 2-6-2 was an excellent mixed-traffic engine but too heavy for much of the LNER's system, including most ex-Great Eastern lines. Moreover, wartime had shown how the performance and reliability of Gresley's three-cylinder machines, with their conjugated valve gear to the middle cylinder, could decline if maintenance standards dropped (which, through lack of time, resources and staff, they inevitably did). The LNER needed its version of the 'Black 5' and in providing it Edward Thompson made his most significant contribution to the LNER fleet.

Nevertheless, in designing what was to become the B1 4-6-0, Thompson could not escape Gresley's shadow. True, it was the first main-line LNER class since 1923 to be built with only two cylinders but circumstances dictated most of the components be sourced 'from stock'. There was no time to design from scratch and, wherever possible, existing patterns, jigs and tools had to be used. With its 17 tons 15 cwt maximum axleloading, the B1 could operate over almost all the LNER's main lines while its tractive effort was inferior only to the Pacifics and V2s among passenger and mixed-traffic classes.

Fresh from overhaul, North British-built (1948) B1 class 4-6-0 No1306 *Mayflower* has Robinson 04 2-8-0 No63601 for company at Doncaster Works on 27 July 2003. Though strictly incorrect the LNER apple-green livery certainly suited this, Edward Thompson's finest design.

Home for No1306 *Mayflower* was for many years the Nene Valley Railway, where it is seen passing Castor crossing with a freight for Wansford on 8 September 2007. It has since transferred allegiance to the Churnet Valley Railway.

A large legacy

Originally designated Class B in Thompson's proposed standard locomotive scheme, the first of the new 4-6-0s, No8301, was built at Darlington Works and entered traffic on 12 December 1942. The second example, No 8302, did not appear until June 1943, by which time Thompson had reclassified the engines B1. Darlington was responsible for the first batch of ten, Nos8301-8310 being outshopped between 1942 and 1944. To assess their capabilities they were allocated to depots as diverse as Haymarket (Edinburgh), Gateshead, Neville Hill (Leeds), Gorton (Manchester), Stratford (London) and Norwich. When construction resumed in 1946, Thompson's renumbering scheme was being implemented and Nos8301-10 became Nos1000-1010.

By the time of Thompson's retirement in June 1946, just 24 B1s had been completed. However, the previous August he had taken the step of placing orders for a further 300 with two outside builders: Vulcan Foundry and the North British Locomotive Company. Interestingly, had these orders gone to LNER workshops subsequent cancellation would not have incurred any penalty. Vulcan Foundry and NBL, on the other hand, would have sought compensation. Was this Thompson's way of ensuring his best work – the largest class of locomotives to be built by the LNER – could not be undone by any successor? If so, he got his wish: the orders were fulfilled with NBL completing 100 engines by April 1947. Further orders meant that the last of 410 B1s was not delivered until June 1950. Overall, construction was split between the LNER plants at Darlington (60) and Gorton (10) with North British contributing 290 and Vulcan Foundry 50 engines apiece.

With their 6-feet 2-inches coupled wheels, as opposed to the 6-feet diameter of the LMSR 'Black 5', the B1s generally proved more at home on passenger and vacuum brake-fitted freights than general goods workings. They first made their mark on expresses in East Anglia, where they were a great success from the outset. B1s enjoyed similar success on the ex-Great Central main line between London Marylebone and Sheffield, with some crews preferring them to their Gresley A3 Pacifics (although it must be added that some of the A3s transferred to GC line sheds were not in the best of health). Gradually, the B1s went on to

IN PRESERVATION

No61264 Built by the North British Locomotive Company, works number 26165, and costing the LNER £14,985, No1264 entered traffic on 5 December 1947. It was sent to the Great Eastern section and spent 13 years working out of Parkeston shed, where its duties would have included the 'Hook Continental' and 'Day Continental' boat trains. On 27 November 1960, No61264 was reallocated to Colwick (Nottingham) remaining there until withdrawal on 21 November 1965. Renumbered departmental No29, it was retained at Colwick as a stationary boiler until 1967 when it had the dubious distinction of becoming the only ex-LNER locomotive to be despatched to Woodham Brothers' scrapyard at Barry, in South Wales.

Nine years rusting in the yard ended in July 1976 when No61264 – now the property of

the Thompson B1 Locomotive Trust – left for a new life at Loughborough, on the Great Central Railway. Here it was restored, not only to working order but, in 1999, to main-line running condition. No61264 has since made a nostalgic return to the Norwich and East Suffolk lines (touching 75 miles per hour at Manningtree) and worked in tandem with another LNER survivor, K1 2-6-0 No62005, on the West Highland. In November 2007 both surviving B1s were reunited at a LNER gala held at Barrow Hill Roundhouse in Derbyshire. No61264 is now undergoing overhaul.

No1306 *Mayflower* Another North British product, works number 26207, No61306 was a British Railways locomotive from the outset. It was to spend the bulk of its working life on Humberside, based at the two main depots in Hull, Dairycoates and Botanic Gardens. Its time in East Yorkshire ended on 25 June 1967 with a transfer to Low Moor, Bradford. Here it became one of the last B1s in service and, on 30 September took the last steam-hauled 'Yorkshire Pullman' out of Bradford.

Bought by Gerald Boden and renumbered and named No1306 *Mayflower*, this second of the surviving B1s has spent time at Steamtown Carnforth, on the Great Central Railway and back at Hull. For many years it was based on the Nene Valley Railway, Peterborough, a lengthy overhaul being completed in April 2003. The engine remains in the care of the 1306 Mayflower Group and is now based on the Battlefield Line at Market Bosworth in Leicestershire.

The down 'Scandinavian' from London Liverpool Street to Harwich Parkeston Quay passes Brentwood, Essex, on 14 June 1958 behind No61164. The B1s were successful on the ex-Great Eastern lines although, by this date, diesels had taken over most important duties.

displace a number of pre-grouping classes.

Inevitably the B1 became compared with Stanier's 'Black 5', with which it crossed paths in Scotland, the north and the Midlands. Any presumption that the B1 was inferior was emphatically disproved during the locomotive exchanges of 1948. Crews nevertheless came to regard the B1 as a 'sensitive' machine that needed attentive handling to deliver of its best. Those with self-cleaning smokeboxes demanded the greatest care and, in typical LNER fashion, the B1 responded to a thin fire with plenty of coal at the sides of the firebox. Crews had to become used to firing 'little and often' and to coping with the narrow LNER firebox door. In contrast the 'Black 5' seemed to tolerate any firing technique!

As well as being handsomely proportioned, the B1s were strong, competent engines. Sadly, they lasted, on average, just 20 years. Their working lives ranged from 10 years (No61395) to 23 years for No61002. First to be scrapped was No61057, in 1950. It was deemed beyond repair after a collision in fog at Witham in Essex. Its boiler, however, was recovered and remained in use until 1967. The first proper withdrawal came in November 1961 with No61085 and six years on, in September 1967, the last B1s – Nos61030, 61337 and the now-preserved No61306 – bowed out.

That legendary engineman, R.H.N. ('Dick') Hardy, knew the B1s from his times at Stratford, Norwich and Ipswich sheds. To the last, he and his team maintained No61059 in such immaculate condition that it became known as the 'Pride of Ipswich'. The last word in the B1 versus 'Black 5' debate can safely be left to him:

'A first-class B1 driven and fired as indicated would match a "5" in all classes of work. As a general utility engine subject to the worst excesses, a "5" was a tougher and more durable locomotive but this, and only this, was the only difference between the two types.'

IN DETAIL *(as built)*

Class	B1
Built:	1942-50; Darlington and Gorton works; North British Locomotive Company, Glasgow; Vulcan Foundry, Newton-le-Willows, Lancashire
Designer:	Edward Thompson
Number built:	410
Purpose:	Mixed traffic
Wheel arrangement:	4-6-0
Cylinders (x 2):	20 in diameter x 26 in stroke
Motion:	Walschaerts
Valves:	11 in diameter piston valves
Wheels: Coupled:	6 ft 2 in
Leading:	3 ft 2 in
Tender:	3 ft 9 in
Boiler diagram:	100A
Boiler: Max. diameter:	5 ft 6 in
Pressure:	225 lb/psi
Heating surface:	2,005 sq ft
Firebox:	168 sq ft
Tubes and flues:	1,493 sq ft
Superheater:	344 sq ft
Grate area:	27.5 sq ft
Tractive effort:	26,878 lb (@ 85% boiler pressure)
Engine wheelbase:	28 ft 0 in
Engine weight:	71 tons 3 cwt
Coal capacity:	7.5 tons
Water capacity:	4,200 gallons
Max. axleloading:	17 tons 15 cwt
BR power class:	5MT

The Strangest Thing

The six-wheel goods was the archetypal British locomotive, but the final development of the type could hardly have been less conventional. But to dismiss the Q1, as some have done, as the 'ugliest locomotive ever built' is to miss the point. As with those other wartime products, the WD 2-8-0s and 2-1-0s, appearance was down to circumstances, not aesthetics.

The unusual profile of the Q1 is evident as NoC1 emerges from Sharpthorne tunnel with a Bluebell Railway service for Kingscote. The boiler cladding could support no weight, while another economy saw the omission of running plates and wheel splashers.

The Southern had been investing heavily in electrification, inevitably to the detriment of its steam-locomotive stock. New construction was limited, especially on the freight side where its best engines were the S15 4-6-0s, but they numbered only 45. Its newest consisted of a class of 25 goods tank engines, the W 2-6-4T, and 20 lacklustre 0-6-0s of the Q class of 1938. Consequently, goods traffic remained largely entrusted to pre-grouping 0-6-0s, some – such as the S&ECR's C class still very capable – but others approaching, or even past retirement. The increase in freight working following the outbreak of war in 1939 emphasised the deficiency. It was to replace at least some of these veterans that the Southern's CME, Oliver Bulleid, set about designing a locomotive fit for its time. This last example of that most traditional of British locomotive types, the six-coupled goods, would arouse more controversy than any built over the previous 100 years.

In August 1940, the Southern's board accepted Bulleid's proposal to build 40 new freight locomotives. Starting more-or-less from scratch, the project would occupy almost two years. Bulleid's radical approach was dictated by circumstances. Much of the Southern's track had never been upgraded and weight restrictions were in place on many lines. They would be off-limits to a modern, conventional heavy freight locomotive such as the LMSR 8F 2-8-0. The Civil Engineer had confirmed that an engine with a working weight of under 54 tons (coupled to a tender that did not exceed 39.5 tons) would be allowed over 93 per cent of the Southern's route mileage, assuming it also met loading-gauge restrictions.

To generate the maximum-possible power, a locomotive of that size had to be designed around its boiler. Everything else had to be tailored to that and if it meant dispensing with the niceties so be it – not that Bulleid needed any excuse to be innovative. Additionally, wartime shortages dictated a need to save on materials as well as weight and this forced Bulleid into a radical re-thinking of the basics of locomotive design, but without any bold experiment.

Much of the Q1 was straightforward, with existing patterns used for many of the components. The cylinder dimensions and Stephenson valve gear were adapted more-or-less unchanged from the Q class. Elsewhere, though, Bulleid dispensed with almost every traditional embellishment – even wheel splashers and running boards. Weight savings were made by using wheels of the double-disc 'boxpok' pattern first used on the 'Merchant Navy' Pacific of 1941. They came in around ten per cent lighter than their spoked equivalents.

However, it was the boiler, or its appearance, that caused most comment. Bulleid employed a type of lightweight fibreglass, known as Idaglass, for the lagging but, since this could not bear any weight, the cladding was draped over the boiler rather than wrapped around it and carried on the frames. For convenience, the cladding was in two sections and the underside of the smokebox made flat so that it rested comfortably on the frame and cylinder casting. Additionally, the smokebox was shaped to give a greater volume than would have been obtained from an equivalent circular variety. It contained a five-nozzle multiple-jet blastpipe that led to a plain 'bucket' chimney.

The boiler barrel was in one piece, tapering from 5 feet 9 inches diameter to 5 feet, with the firebox backplates and throatplates fabricated using the same flanging blocks as the 'Lord Nelson' 4-6-0s. At 27 square feet, the firegrate was larger than that of any other British 0-6-0.

Throughout, to save weight and cost, fabrications were used instead of castings. The outcome was a locomotive developing over 30,000lb tractive effort but weighing only 51 tons 5 cwt – around 14 tons lighter than other classes of comparable power. The Q1 had the distinction of being not only the last, but the most powerful British 0-6-0.

Bare essentials

It is difficult now to appreciate the shock that must have been felt when, on 6 May, 1942, the first of the Q1s appeared at Charing Cross for inspection by the Southern's directors. At least one commentator described it as the ugliest locomotive ever built. That, however, was to miss the point. As with the War Department 2-8-0s and 2-10-0s delivered around the same time, appearance was not a consideration. Undeniably, though, the Q1 took the description 'austerity' to a new level.

NoC1 was soon demonstrating its capabilities on test freights between Norwood and Chichester. Three months later it was joined by classmate NoC3 in comparative trials with S15 4-6-0 No842 hauling 65-wagon trains between Woking and Basingstoke. On one occasion, NoC1 comfortably covered the 24 miles with around 1,000 tons in 58 minutes. The schedule for an 800 ton load was 66 minutes. There was, though, a price to pay for the 'bare essentials' approach that delivered the Q1's remarkable power-to-weight ratio.

With no protective running plates or splashers, at speed in the rain, fireman and driver leant out of the cab only when necessary! Ladders were needed to reach such items as the washout plugs and clack valves, and for cleaning. The omission of

IN PRESERVATION

NoC1 (33001) Unveiled at Brighton Works in March 1942, and after being shown to the Southern's hierarchy six weeks later, the first of the Q1s underwent trials before taking up the kind of routine duties that would occupy it for the ensuing two decades. Renumbered 33001 by British Railways in November 1950, it underwent its last general overhaul between 19 January and 14 February 1955 at Ashford Works. By June 1959, No33001 was on the books of Tonbridge shed, in Kent, but in February 1961 it was back on the Western Section at Feltham. A final move to Guildford came in September 1963.

By the time of its official withdrawal in May 1964, having covered 459,057 miles (most Q1s had final mileages between 400,000 and 500,000), No33001 had already been selected for preservation and stored at Nine Elms for five months. With the National Collection seeking a permanent home, it joined a number of other celebrity engines in, first, the paint shop at Stratford Works in London and then the former Pullman Company works at Preston Park outside Brighton.

On 15 May 1977, No33001 went on long-term loan to the Bluebell Railway where it received an 'intermediate' overhaul during 1980 and ran regularly until September 1983. A major overhaul was completed in 1992 and the Q1 – in its original guise as NoC1 – was recommissioned at Sheffield Park on 8 September. Now requiring a further 10-year refit, NoC1 has been reclaimed by the National Railway Museum, York.

Among a clutch of Bulleid Q1 class 0-6-0s gathered around the coaling stage at Guildford shed, in Surrey, on 17 April 1963 are Nos33018 and 33035. Guildford, like Feltham depot in south-west London, was always home to a number of the 40-strong class, while others saw out their working lives at Eastleigh, Nine Elms and Three Bridges.

In what could easily be a Southern scene from the 1940s, NoC1 climbs away from Horsted Keynes with a six-coach train of mixed vintage. This last of the 40 Q1s returned to steam on the Bluebell Railway on 9 September 1992. Now 'out-of-ticket' it has been reclaimed by the National Railway Museum.

steps and rails at the front end, however, was clearly an economy too far as it made smokebox clearance hazardous. Before long grab rails were bolted to the smokebox doors and either side of them.

The provision of steam heating was intended for when the Q1s hauled empty coaching stock but subsequently found greater use as the engines were increasingly rostered for passenger trains. Crews liked the ease with which the Q1 could be worked, the relative comfort of the cab and the accessibility of all the key components for maintenance. They were pleasantly surprised to find that, while officially limited to 55 miles per hour, Bulleid's 0-6-0 was capable of up to 75, even running tender-first, although there was a tendency to 'roll' at high speed.

The Q1s were expected to have a limited lifespan but instead served the Southern Railway and British Railways for two decades. Their haulage capacity was curbed only by a limited braking capability when hauling loose-coupled, non-vacuum-braked freights.

By the 1960s, all 40 had gathered at one of four depots: Eastleigh, Feltham, Guildford or Three Bridges. The first to be withdrawn was No33028 in February 1963. It had a defective cylinder judged not worth repairing. The final trio consisting of Nos33006, 33020 and 33027 departed Guildford in January 1966.

One lasting consequence of the Q1's strange appearance was the response of the 'spotters': seldom can one class of locomotive have had so many nicknames. They were variously known as 'Biscuit Tins', 'Biscuit Barrels', 'Charlies', 'Clockworks', 'Coffee Pots', 'Austerities' and, predictably, 'Ugly Ducklings'. Derogatory names aside, no one could deny that Bulleid's Q1s brought the 108-year history of the British 0-6-0 to a memorable and controversial conclusion.

IN DETAIL (as built)

Class:	Q1
Built:	1942
Designer:	Oliver Bulleid
Number built :	40
Purpose:	Freight
Wheel arrangement:	0-6-0
Cylinders (x 2):	19 in diameter x 26 in stroke
Motion:	Stephenson link
Valves:	10 in diameter piston valves
Wheels: Coupled:	5 ft 1 in
Tender:	3 ft 7 in
Boiler: Max. diameter:	5 ft 9 in
Pressure:	230 lb/psi
Heating surface:	1,860 sq ft
Firebox:	170 sq ft
Tubes and flues:	1,472 sq ft
Superheater:	218 sq ft
Grate area:	27 sq ft
Tractive effort:	30,080 lb (@ 85% boiler pressure)
Engine wheelbase:	16 ft 6 in
Total wheelbase:	40 ft 7.5 in
Engine weight:	51 tons 5 cwt
Coal capacity:	5 tons
Water capacity:	3,700 gallons
Max. axleloading:	18 tons 5 cwt
BR power class:	5F

The Hard-working Classes

Ministry of Supply/
War Department

Robert Riddles

**'Austerity' 2-8-0,
2-10-0 (1943)**

Unloved and uncared for, the 'Dub-Dees', as they were nicknamed, were never going to win a locomotive beauty contest. They were a product of wartime, and for wartime. No-one, least of all their designer, expected them to fulfil a peacetime role.

Steam leaking from every joint, cabside numbers barely legible under the grime, a rhythmic 'clank-clunk' from the connecting rods, a rasping bark from the chimney and, tailing into the distance, a rake of rattling coal wagons – this is the abiding image of the WD 2-8-0s in their British Railways days. That these 1940s workhorses were still around in the 1960s was in itself remarkable, since they started out as the world's first 'disposable' class of locomotives.

In the main, railways have had a beneficial influence on the world. Nevertheless, the lines that opened up continents, brought mobility and prosperity, and helped spread understanding, were equally capable of moving and supplying armies. Railways played vital roles on both sides during two world wars, chiefly as supply routes in Europe, North Africa, the Middle East and Asia.

The importance of railways saw administrations set up to organise the supply of locomotives and rolling stock. During World War I, the Allied forces borrowed large numbers of locomotives from railway companies. Similar requisitions took place at the outbreak of a second war with Germany. However, as planning got underway for the D-Day invasion, it became evident that only new construction would meet the need for locomotives and rolling stock. No reliance could be placed on the war-shattered European locomotive fleets. In both Britain and the United States work began on designs that would both meet military requirements and reflect wartime conditions. Speed and simplicity of construction,

In full Army 'exhibition finish', complete with white wheel rims, WD 2-10-0 No600 *Gordon* stands proud on shed at Bridgnorth, Severn Valley Railway. The 'LMR' on the tender refers to the now-defunct Longmoor Military Railway in Hampshire. *Gordon* is presently on display in the SVR's Engine Hall at Highley.

Basic equipment

The WD 2-8-0s were unsophisticated engines. For example, the tender water 'gauge' consisted of a device called a 'walking stick'. This was a metal pipe with holes drilled in it at regular intervals. When turned through 90 degrees, the level of water in the tender was indicated by which of the holes water poured out of!

On the footplate, the WD 2-8-0s had a curious shuffling gait and, at their worst, gave the crew a good shaking. But they were free-steaming, reliable workhorses and perfectly suited to trundling along at 30mph with heavy, loose-coupled freights. Even at the nadir of steam, crews could generally trust a WD 2-8-0, no matter how bad its condition, to do the job.

the use of low-cost components and materials, and the widest-possible route availability were paramount. The engines would also have to steam on low-grade fuel and tolerate minimal maintenance.

'Austerity' measures

In 1942, it needed a large degree of confidence, not to say optimism to start planning the defeat of the Nazi regime but with the United States now officially an ally the tide was turning. Planning began for all aspects of the Allied liberation, including transport. The Directorate of Transportation Equipment, a division of the Ministry of Supply, had been set up at the outbreak of war and charged with supplying the military's railway needs. It was headed by Robert Riddles, who had been seconded from his post as assistant to William Stanier on the LMSR.

The priority was for a utility locomotive similar to the Great Central 8K 2-8-0 that had served during World War I. For Riddles, the obvious candidate was the 8F 2-8-0 designed by his former chief, Stanier, but its downside was the cost of construction and the man-hours required. Nevertheless, orders were placed for 208 engines. It gave Riddles breathing space to produce a purpose-built design, one that reflected the prevailing conditions.

Riddles invited the North British Locomotive Company of Glasgow to become involved in the development, although there was no time for trial or experiment. Riddles took the 8F 2-8-0 as his starting point and adapted it for fast, low-cost construction. Most of the detail work was undertaken by one of the LMSR's finest draughtsmen, Frank Carrier. By summer 1942, the drawings were ready and 545 2-8-0s ordered from NBL. Paired with an eight-wheel 5,000 gallon tender holding nine tons of coal, the first 2-8-0, No7000, was delivered on 16 January 1943. Once all the components had been delivered, it had taken just ten days to assemble. It was essential that the locomotives should be able to operate in every theatre of war so they had steam brakes for the locomotive and the option of Westinghouse or vacuum braking for trains.

Deliveries continued at the rate of around five engines a week, twice the rate of the Stanier 8F, at times rising to seven. By now, additional orders had been placed with Vulcan Foundry of Newton-le-Willows, who produced 390 engines.

Ten wheels better

Although the 'Austerity' 2-8-0 met their requirements, the military authorities suggested to Riddles that a locomotive with an even lower axleloading and greater

Masquerading as what would have been the next locomotive in the sequence of British Railways WD 2-10-0s, No90775, NoWD601 starts away from the outer home signal at Medstead & Four Marks at its one-time home of the Mid-Hants Railway. The engine is now based on the North Norfolk Railway.

IN PRESERVATION

Three of the surviving WD 2-10-0s are based in Britain and a Swedish example of the WD 2-8-0 has been repatriated and been rebuilt to represent the class. It works on the Keighley & Worth Valley Railway which, interestingly, now has an almost complete fleet of World War II-built locomotives: WD 2-8-0; WD/Hunslet 0-6-0 saddletank; United States Army Transportation Corps S160 2-8-0 and 0-6-0 shunting tank; and a Stanier 8F 2-8-0. Five of the 2-10-0s are still extant in Greece, four of them based at the Thessaloniki locomotive depot.

War Department 8F 2-8-0
No90733 (WD No79257) Although none of British Railways' 733 WD 2-8-0s was spared the torch, in 1973 one of the Swedish examples, No1931, was repatriated and based on the Keighley & Worth Valley Railway. A 14-year project to return this surviving WD 2-8-0 to original condition was completed in 2007 when it made its debut as British Railways No90733.

War Department 8F 2-10-0
No600 *Gordon* (WD No73651) Named after General Gordon of Khartoum fame, No600 operated on the Longmoor Military Railway until closure in 1969. A new home was found on

flexibility would be of value in certain areas. Consideration was first given to a 2-8-2 but Riddles opted for the greater adhesion of a ten-coupled wheelbase. Although many of the components of the 2-10-0 – cylinders and valve gear, for example – mirrored the 2-8-0, there were significant differences between the two. The longer wheelbase allowed a larger boiler to be fitted and this was linked to a wide firebox, fabricated from steel rather than copper.

An order for 150 'Austerity' 2-10-0s, Nos3650-3749 (later 73650-73749), was placed with the North British Locomotive Company, which began deliveries in December 1943 and completed construction in 1945. Meanwhile, shipment of engines from Southampton to Dieppe to take up duties in France and Belgium had begun in August 1944.

On 9 May 1945, the day after Germany's surrender, 2-10-0 No73755 became the 1,000th 'war locomotive' shipped to Europe. By September 1945, a total of 1,085 engines had been delivered, 935 of the eight-coupled variety (only three of which did not go overseas) and 150 ten-coupled. Though the assumption was that the engines would be discarded once their task was completed, the 'Austerities' continued to perform useful work in peacetime. They were also employed in France, Belgium, Egypt, Greece, Syria, Sweden and in occupied Germany but by far the largest number congregated in The Netherlands where some continued working until the mid-1950s. Further afield, 12 2-8-0s were shipped to Hong Kong and used on the Kowloon–Canton Railway. At home, 733 2-8-0s became British Railways stock, some lasting until 1967.

There appears to have been less enthusiasm for repatriating the 'Austerity' 2-10-0s but British Railways did take 25 into stock. WD Nos73774-96/98-99 became

BR Nos90750-74. Based at Carlisle Kingmoor, Carstairs, Grangemouth and Motherwell, their lives were largely spent on freight traffic in southern Scotland. All were withdrawn between 1961 and 1962.

the Severn Valley Railway and No600 remained in service until the mid-1990s. It is now on display in the SVR's engine hall at Highley.

No90775 (WD No73652) One of two WD 2-10-0s repatriated from Greece No90775 is based on the North Norfolk Railway.

No3672 *Dame Vera Lynn* (WD No73672) Second of the 2-10-0s brought back from Greece, the North Yorkshire Moors Railway's No3672 is undergoing overhaul off-site, at Bury.

No73755 The 1,000th locomotive shipped to Europe after D-Day, 6 June 1944, No73755 worked in Holland for seven years before going on display in the Netherlands Transport Museum in Utrecht.

Class	War Department 2-8-0	War Department 2-10-0
Built:	1943-45	
Designer:	Robert Riddles	
Number built:	935	150
Purpose:	Heavy freight	
Wheel arrangement:	2-8-0	2-10-0
	Cylinders (x2):	19 in x 28 in
	(Diameter x Stroke)	
Motion:	Walschaerts	
Valves:	10 in piston valves	
Wheels: Coupled:	4 ft 8.5 in	
Leading:	3 ft 2 in	
Tender:	3 ft 2 in	
Boiler diagram:	——	BR11
Boiler: Max. Diameter:	5 ft 8.5 in	5 ft 9.875 in
Pressure:	225 lb/psi	
Heating surface:	1,991 sq ft	2,374 sq ft
Firebox:	168 sq ft	192 sq ft
Tubes and Flues:	1,512 sq ft	1,759 sq ft
Superheater:	311 sq ft ¶	423 q ft
Grate area:	28.6 sq ft	40 sq ft
Tractive effort:	34.215 lb	34,215 lb
	(@ 85% boiler pressure)	
Engine wheelbase:	16 ft 3 in	21 ft 0 in
Total wheelbase:	24 ft 10 in	29 ft 8 in
Engine weight:	70 tons 5 cwt	78 tons 6 cwt
Coal capacity:	9 tons	
Water capacity:	5,000 gallons	
Max. axleloading:	15 tons 12 cwt	13 tons 9 cwt
BR power class:	8F	8F

IN DETAIL *(as built)*

¶ *Superheating surface later increased to 338 sq ft.*

Southern Railway

Oliver Bulleid

**BB class
'Battle of Britain'/
WC class 'West
Country' class
7P5F 4-6-2 (1945)**

Travelling Light

From, in 1940, possessing not a single Pacific-type locomotive, a decade later the ex-Southern Railway area could call upon a fleet of 140. Whether a system where the longest run was from London to north Cornwall needed so many such engines remains open to question. Nevertheless, Oliver Bulleid's class of '45 grew to become Britain's largest group of express passenger 4-6-2s and, by some margin, remains so in preservation.

A chance to compare original and rebuilt light Pacifics at Waterloo on April 24 1966. Still in air-smoothed condition, No34064 *Fighter Command* stands on the left alongside rebuilt No34032 *Camelford*. Both are at the head of Weymouth-bound trains.

The line to Bude and Padstow along the north coast of Cornwall was a Southern outpost in Great Western territory. It was also one of the lines from which the first of Oliver Bulleid's Pacifics – the 'Merchant Navy' of 1941 – was barred. Its axleloading of 21 tons was too heavy for the bridges. Such restrictions, allied to a general requirement for a modern, general-purpose passenger engine, were the factors in the development of a scaled-down version of the 'MN', the so-called 'Light Pacific'. Modifications aimed at saving weight and so maximising the locomotives' route availability were very successful. With an axleloading of just over 18 tons, the 'Light Pacifics' were permitted over almost all the Southern system.

It can only be surmised that Bulleid, the Southern's Chief Mechanical Engineer since 1938, had great powers of persuasion. Perhaps, having gone to the lengths of tempting him from the LNER, the Southern's board felt duty-bound to go along with his ideas. From being a railway committed to electrification – it had not introduced a new express passenger engine since the 'Schools' of 1930 – the company had endorsed Bulleid's plan for 100 Pacific-type locomotives. Thirty would be 'Merchant Navies', the remainder 'Light Pacifics'. Astonishingly, given the snags with the first batch of 'MNs', the latter 70 were ordered straight off the drawing board.

Though smaller and lighter, these 'West Country' Pacifics – as the first batch became – shared many of the novel features of their bigger brethren, including the 'air-smoothed' casing, Bulleid-Firth-Brown wheels, clasp brakes, thermic siphons and chain-driven valve gear. As the 'Merchant Navy', they were three-cylinder machines – a formula that Bulleid had imported to Waterloo from his time at King's Cross, working as personal assistant to Nigel Gresley. The remainder of the design, however, was pure Bulleid, with all the flair and frustration that entailed. Consequently, the 'West Countries' inherited the idiosyncrasies associated with, in particular, Bulleid's valve gear.

Rebuilt 'West Country' No34027 *Taw Valley* approaches Didcot North Junction, where it will join the Didcot avoiding line, with the 'Cotswold Venturer' of 29 August 1993, bound for Oxford and Worcester.

The vital component shared by the two Pacifics was the Bulleid boiler. It may have had a prodigious appetite for coal but, as a steam-raiser, was unrivalled, at least on Britain's railways. As with the 'MN', welding was widely used in preference to riveting and contributed to weight savings that saw the design tip the scales at precisely 86 tons, compared to the 94.75 tons of its predecessor.

From Salisbury to Spitfire

In a drab, war-wearied Britain, the first of the new engines must have lifted the spirits as it emerged from the Brighton paintshop in May 1945. Its livery was a bright malachite green with sunshine yellow lining and the smokebox door sported a circular plate declaring 'SOUTHERN' with the date of construction below. As with the 'Merchant Navies', Bulleid used the Continental numbering system indicating the engine's wheel arrangement. The newcomer wore No21C101, the '2' indicating the number of leading axles, the '1' the trailing axle and 'C' the three coupled wheelsets. Initially, '101' looked an over-ambitious starting point for the series, but over the ensuing six years no fewer than 110 of these 'Light Pacifics' would be built, although only the original order for 70 would carry Southern Railway identities. The remaining 40 appeared under British Railways auspices.

As it had with the 'King Arthurs', 'Lord Nelsons' and 'Schools' classes, the Southern's publicity department came up trumps with names for the new Pacifics. They would celebrate cities, towns, villages, seaside resorts and tourist spots in south-west England that fell within Southern territory. The 'West Country' class, as it became, started with the cathedral city of Exeter. With due ceremony, No21C101 was named there on 10 July 1945.

By November 1946, the class numbered 48 and, with a few exceptions, was based in the West of England. However, they were soon working on the

A doctor's prescription

Before rebuilding, few attempts were made to modify the 'Light Pacifics'. One device, however, appears to have had an impact: the Giesl oblong ejector. This was the work of an Austrian inventor, Doctor Adolf Giesl-Gieslingen, and consisted of seven nozzles, with blower jets between them, which were arranged in line to exhaust upwards through a narrow chimney.

In place of Bulleid's favoured Lemaitre exhaust system a Giesl ejector was fitted to No21C164 *Fighter Command* (coincidentally the 1,000th locomotive to be built at Brighton when outshopped in June 1947). It not only improved the draughting but – thanks to Dr Giesl's 'Microspark Arrestor' – tempered the Bulleid Pacifics' inclination for spark throwing. Despite this, opinion of the Giesl ejector's effectiveness remained divided. Some commentators considered it brought a substantial improvement; others dismissed the experiment. It hardly mattered, since the benefits, if there were any, remained confined to *Fighter Command*. With the impending demise of steam, the cost of equipping others of the class could not be justified.

On Derby Day, in June 1947, the royal train was entrusted to No21C157, then only three months old. Later named *Biggin Hill*, the Pacific was withdrawn in May 1967.

Southern's Eastern and Central sections, too, and this prompted a change in the naming policy. With comparable inspiration, the publicity people chose names that were sure to have a resonance for those areas: the warplanes, airfields, Royal Air Force squadrons and personalities that had won the battle in the skies over Kent, Sussex, Surrey and Hampshire six years earlier. To the 'West Country' class was added the 'Battle of Britain'.

Top of the class

In 1948, the newly formed British Railways instigated a series of inter-regional locomotive trials. Along with the 'Merchant Navy', the Southern was represented by three carefully chosen 'West Countries', No34004 *Yeovil*, No34005 *Barnstaple* and No34006 *Bude*, and by three hand-picked crews from Nine Elms shed in London. It would be fair to say that these trios proved the stars of the show. Over both the Midland and Great Central routes, they put in scintillating performances working from London to Manchester,. The top performer, unquestionably, was *Yeovil*, which was despatched to Scotland to operate between Perth and Inverness.

Bulleid's aim was for his Pacifics to maintain their standard of performance from one general overhaul to the next, which anticipated 100,000 trouble-free miles. They were never to attain that level, with the principal culprit Bulleid's valve gear design. On paper it looks a sound idea. The radial gear, driven by endless chains, is fully enclosed – together with the inside connecting rod and crank – in a sealed oil bath.

However, far from requiring minimal maintenance as hoped for, this complex mechanism needed regular checks and attention, especially as high mileages accrued. It remains baffling that apparently no early attempt was made to rectify matters. After all, the 'Light Pacifics' were now the Southern's main express

passenger engines. Some of the worst failures came from the collapse of the middle big end. With no knocking audible and no smell of overheating to alert them, the first the crew knew of the problem was when the connecting rod pierced the floor of the oil bath!

It would be unjust, though, to dwell on the weaknesses of the design because this was a fleet of locomotives that offered an excellent power-to-weight ratio. The Bulleid boiler ensured they were seldom, if ever, short of steam and that was true even using the lowest grades of coal. Crews claimed they would steam on a tenderful of old boots!

Not his engines

Unsurprisingly British Railways' motive-power chiefs did not subscribe to the Bulleid fan club. Equally, Bulleid's opposition to the nationalised rail network did nothing for his cause. When it was suggested that modifications would improve

IN DETAIL *(as built)*

Class:	'West Country', 'Battle of Britain'
Built:	Brighton, Eastleigh 1945-51
Designer:	Oliver Bulleid
Number built:	110
Purpose:	Mixed traffic
Wheel arrangement:	4-6-2
Cylinders (x3):	16.375 in diameter x 24 in stroke
Motion:	Bulleid chain driven (* *Walschaerts*)
Valves:	10 in diameter piston valves
Wheels: Coupled:	6 ft 2 in
Leading:	3 ft 1 in
Trailing:	3 ft 1in
Tender:	3 ft 7 in
Boiler: Max. Diameter:	6 ft 3.5 in
Pressure:	280 lb/psi (* *250 lb/psi*)
Heating surface:	2,942 sq ft
Firebox:	275 sq ft
Tubes and flues:	2,122 sq ft
Superheater:	545 sq ft
Grate area:	38.25 sq ft
Tractive effort:	31,000 lb (* *27,715 lb*) (@ 85% boiler pressure)
Engine wheelbase:	35 ft 6 in
Total wheelbase:	57 ft 6 in
Engine weight:	86 tons 0 cwt (* *90 tons 1 cwt*)
Coal capacity:	5 tons
Water capacity:	4,500 gallons
Max. axleloading:	18 tons 15 cwt (* *19 tons 15 cwt*)
BR power class:	7P5F

* *Changes following rebuilding.*

the Pacifics' reliability and reduce maintenance costs, the BR hierarchy under Roland Bond seized the opportunity. A team at Brighton, headed by an ex-LMSR man, Ron Jarvis, was given the task of revamping both the 'Merchant Navies' and the 'Light Pacifics'. Eventually all 30 of the 'MNs' were modified but only 60 of their cousins, as the expected lifespan of the engines could not justify the cost.

Out went the chain-driven valve gear that now demanded a level of maintenance that was hard to justify or sustain. It was replaced by three sets of Walschaerts valve gear and mechanical lubricators. Working pressure was reduced from 280 to 250 lb/psi. Off came the air-smoothed casing, to be replaced by large, square smoke deflectors and the resemblance to the British Railways' Standard Pacifics was inescapable, and not at all coincidental. The Bulleid-Firth-Brown 'boxpok' wheels were retained along with the signature oval-shaped smokebox door but that would hardly have appeased Bulleid who not once was consulted about the rebuilding – or modification as it was officially termed. Ron Jarvis attested that the finished product was still '90 per cent Bulleid'. The designer disagreed: he was once played a recording of rebuilt Pacifics at work. 'Take it off,' Bulleid demanded, 'Those are not my engines!'

Twenty-one 'Light Pacifics' soldiered on until the last day of steam on the Southern, 9 July 1967. All but two were rebuilds, the exceptions being Nos34023 *Blackmoor Vale* and 34102 *Lapford*.

The sole Southern-liveried 'West Country', No21C123 *Blackmoor Vale*, awaits departure from Sheffield Park with the Bluebell Railway's Pullman dining train on 12 August 2007. *Blackmoor Vale* was withdrawn for overhaul in autumn 2008.

IN PRESERVATION

No34007 Wadebridge Restored on Cornwall's Bodmin & Wenford Railway but has since made a home on the Mid-Hants Railway.

No34010 Sidmouth Major boiler repairs are required and it is unlikely work will begin in earnest until 2010. Restoration could cost upwards of £500,000 and take three years.

No34016 Bodmin Saved from scrap in 1972, rebuilt *Bodmin* has been the flagship of the Mid-Hants Railway's fleet but now awaits overhaul.

No21C123 Blackmoor Vale Bought by the Bulleid Society upon withdrawal in 1967 and since resident on the Bluebell Railway. Withdrawn for overhaul in autum 2008.

No34027 Taw Valley Undergoing overhaul on the Severn Valley Railway.

No34028 Eddystone Rebuilt *Eddystone* returned to steam on the Swanage Railway in the spring of 2004.

No34039 Boscastle After several years in storage, an overhaul is underway on the Great Central Railway.

No34046 Braunton Equipped for, but not yet certified for main-line running, *Braunton* entered service on the West Somerset Railway during autumn 2008.

No34051 Winston Churchill Saved for the National Collection, home for *Winston Churchill* is the National Railway Museum, York.

No34053 Sir Keith Park Under restoration at the Swanage Railway's Herston Works. Finances permitting, No34053 could steam in 2010.

No34058 Sir Frederick Pile Withdrawn from Eastleigh in October 1964 and is being restored on the Avon Valley Railway.

No34059 Sir Archibald Sinclair Thirty years after being rescued from Barry scrapyard *Sir Archibald Sinclair* made its debut on the Bluebell Railway in spring 2009.

No34067 Tangmere *Tangmere* returned to the main line in 2003, at Old Oak Common, and has appeared regularly on railtours out of London to the south-east and West Country.

No34070 Manston Owned by Southern Locomotives Ltd and in original condition, *Manston* entered service on the Swanage Railway in September 2008.

No34072 257 Squadron *257 Squadron* was returned to working order in 1990. Currently awaiting an overhaul on the Swanage Railway.

No34073 249 Squadron No34073 donated components to classmate No34067 *Tangmere*. What remains is now stored on the East Lancashire Railway.

No34081 92 Squadron Restored by the Battle of Britain Locomotive Preservation Society in 1998, No34081 awaits overhaul on the North Norfolk Railway.

No34092 City of Wells No34092 is in the throes of a lengthy overhaul at the Keighley & Worth Valley Railway's workshops.

No34101 Hartland *Hartland* was restored in 1994 but is now out-of-traffic as a consequence of firebox cracks.

No34105 Swanage Its restoration completed in 1989, unrebuilt *Swanage* is currently awaiting overhaul at Ropley.

London & North Eastern
Railway

Arthur Peppercorn

**Class A1, A2
8P6F, 8P7F**

4-6-2 (1947/1948)

Mr Peppercorn's Pacifics

The last classes of 4-6-2s to be designed pre-nationalisation were the work
of the LNER's Arthur Peppercorn, and a fitting finale to the era
of the East Coast Pacific.

Some way away from its home shed, Aberdeen according
to the 61B shedplate, No60532 *Blue Peter* presents an
impressive profile on the demonstration line at Didcot
Railway Centre. In terms of tractive effort the Peppercorn A2
was the most powerful British express passenger designs.

With his retirement imminent in 1946 the LNER's Doncaster drawing office apparently did all it could to stall progress on Edward Thompson's plans for new locomotives. This was not solely down to the antipathy felt towards Thompson but an acknowledgement that, with one exception, his engines were an indifferent and ill-conceived bunch. Only the B1 4-6-0 of 1942 had merit and that was largely assembled out of existing components. Everyone, it seems, was waiting for 'Pepp', as Arthur Peppercorn was known to family, friends and colleagues. Peppercorn was in the mould of the late Sir Nigel Gresley and if anyone should be responsible for the next, and as it proved, last generation of LNER Pacific it was he.

On replacing Thompson in July 1946 one of Peppercorn's first actions was to revise and transform Thompson's final Pacific design. The first built to his design was outshopped from Doncaster in December 1947. Classified A2 and numbered 525, it represented a return to proven Gresley principles. However, the modernity of the design was also evident. A rocking grate, hopper ashpan and self-cleaning smokebox were incorporated and – following the example of Bulleid's Southern Railway Pacifics – electric lighting.

The class of 15 Peppercorn A2s, British Railways numbers 60525-39, was completed at Doncaster by August 1948. Unsurprisingly, with BR's motive-power policy heading in a different direction, a LNER order for 20 further engines was cancelled. They immediately displayed their qualities. They

Potted Peppercorn

Arthur Henry Peppercorn was born in 1889 and joined the Great Northern Railway in 1905, becoming Chief Mechanical Engineer of the LNER on 1 July 1946. By all accounts, Arthur Peppercorn was well liked by his colleagues. He was a modest and, in some ways, a shy man (the naming of A2 No525 after him was at the behest of LNER Chairman, Sir Ronald Matthews). For example, he was awarded the OBE in the 1945 Birthday Honours but twice refused it because he was anxious about attending the ceremony at Buckingham Palace. Eventually the medal was sent by post!

Reserved to the last, Peppercorn wanted his retirement party in 1949 to be a quiet affair. However, his associates were determined to show their appreciation and secretly arranged for the building of a superb model of A2 No525. After the toasts, a curtain was pulled aside to reveal the gift. Peppercorn was overwhelmed by the gesture and, in tears, told his wife, 'They got me, Pat!'.

were fast, free-steaming and immensely powerful. However, this did not preclude Doncaster from fitting five of the class – including the now-preserved No60532 *Blue Peter* – with double blastpipes and chimneys. The devices swiftly proved their worth with significant improvements in steaming capability and fuel economy. In a further modification, five locomotives were fitted for operations with multiple valve regulators.

The Kylchap effect

Peppercorn's Pacifics employed a new type of boiler that, having a two per cent nickel steel content, weighed 7 cwt less than the Thompson variety. It was topped by a Gresley-style 'banjo' dome, as opposed to the round-top type, containing a perforated steam collector. Surprisingly, given its dramatic impact when incorporated into Gresley's A4 Pacifics, the Peppercorn A2 was not equipped with the Kylchap double blastpipe and chimney arrangement – in retrospect, an opportunity missed. Instead, the first examples appeared with conventional single chimneys. One reason for this omission was that there was insufficient space in the smokebox to accommodate both the Kylchap apparatus and the self-cleaning screens.

However, at the last minute – May 1948 to be exact – it was decided to omit the latter from the last of the series, No60539 *Bronzino*, to make way for a Kylchap blastpipe. On test, the improvements were indisputable and five other A2s, including *Blue Peter*, had their existing chimneys replaced by Kylchap assemblies. They proved immensely strong engines and, in the questionable terms of tractive effort, Britain's most powerful express passenger locomotives.

Initially, the A2s were based at depots north and south of the border, ranging from King's Cross (London) to New England (Peterborough), York, Copley Hill (Leeds), Gateshead and Heaton (Tyneside), and Haymarket (Edinburgh). In the summer of 1949, examples were allocated to Dundee (two) and Aberdeen (three), primarily to replace unreliable Thompson Pacifics on the Edinburgh–Dundee–Aberdeen route and proved the ideal engines for its stiff gradients and sharp curvature. With their extra power when starting a load and rapid acceleration, they acquitted themselves so well on this run that five more were subsequently transferred to Haymarket.

During the early 1960s, the Edinburgh–Dundee–Aberdeen run supplied a fitting finale for the A2s with many memorable performances. However, it was on Stoke bank, in Lincolnshire, scene of *Mallard*'s 1938 world speed record, that No60526 *Sugar Palm* of York depot attained a record speed for an A2 of 101mph. The following year, in November 1962, *Sugar Palm* numbered among the first three withdrawals. The Aberdeen route still had work for them, though, and a final trio – Nos60528 *Tudor Minstrel*, No60530 *Sayajirao* and No60532 *Blue Peter* – remained at work there until June 1966.

In A1 condition

The starting point for Arthur Peppercorn's second Pacific design, the A1 of 1948, was Thompson's rebuild of No4470 *Great Northern*. While Thompson envisaged it as the prototype of a new class of big-wheeled 4-6-2s, his team at Doncaster saw it as a potential disaster. As with Thompson's A2, it has been alleged that detail design work was deliberately prolonged so scope for changes remained after his retirement.

Not all of Thompson's ideas were discarded. The steam circuit was first-class and the large firegrate was intended to counteract the poor-quality coal on offer in post-war Britain (even if it was the bane of firemen who were continually bending their backs to keep the firebed covered). In most other respects the A1 resembled its immediate predecessor, the A2. The principal difference was in driving-wheel diameter which, at six feet eight inches, was six inches greater and consequently made necessary a longer wheelbase. The arrangement of cylinders and valve gear was identical and the boilers

Britain's newest steam locomotive, Peppercorn A1 Pacific No60163 *Tornado*, made its first visit south of the Thames on 14 February 2008. Joining the south-west main line from the Addlestone loop at Byfleet & New Haw, *Tornado* heads for Andover with the 'Cathedrals Express'.

were interchangeable (although the smokeboxes and frames of the A1 were longer). Significantly, however, the Peppercorn A1s were equipped with Kylchap double chimneys and blastpipes from the outset.

The British Railways era was eight months old when the first of the A1s emerged from Doncaster in August 1948. Construction was shared with Darlington Works, which contributed 23 examples, and all 49 A1s were in traffic by the end of 1949.

The A1s were distributed the length of the east coast at King's Cross, Grantham, Doncaster, York, Copley Hill (Leeds), Gateshead, Heaton and Haymarket and became renowned for their reliability. By 1961, the class of 49 had run 48 million miles, equivalent to 202 miles each day and a figure unmatched by any other British Railways steam locomotive. Nevertheless, by January 1966 only No60124 *Kenilworth* and No60145 *Saint Mungo* remained on BR's books. The latter was the last to bow out, from York shed that June. In spite of a working life of only 17 years, it had covered around one million miles. There could be no disputing that, with the A1 and A2, Arthur Peppercorn had provided a fitting finale to three glorious decades of LNER express-passenger engine development.

IN PRESERVATION

A1 class 4-6-2 No60163 *Tornado* The *Tornado* story is one of revival rather than preservation. The absence of a Peppercorn A1 from the list of preserved locomotives has been rectified by building a fiftieth member of the class, a project that has taken somewhat longer – indeed, it was seventeen years – than its classmates and cost substantially more: around £2.35 million.

In 1990, the A1 Steam Locomotive Trust was formed to construct a new A1 Pacific. It would emphatically not be a replica but the first main-line steam locomotive built in Britain since *Evening Star* in 1960.

In the autumn of 2007, *Tornado* was rolled out of the workshop at Darlington and successfully steamed. It made a main-line debut with a return run between York and Newcastle and followed this with a trip from Darlington to King's Cross. Since then, the locomotive has been officially named by HRH The Prince of Wales at York.

A2 class 4-6-2 No60532 *Blue Peter*
Blue Peter was the last LNER Pacific to be withdrawn, from Aberdeen in December 1966. Bought from BR by the late Geoff Drury it has since been entrusted to the North Eastern Locomotive Preservation Group whose volunteers overhauled *Blue Peter* to main-line condition in 1990. An eventful decade ensued, taking *Blue Peter* back to Scotland and as far west as Plymouth. Its boiler 'ticket' having expired, *Blue Peter* is now on static display at Darlington Railway Centre.

IN DETAIL *(as built)*		
Class	**A1**	**A2**
Built:	1948-49; Doncaster, Darlington works	1947-48; Doncaster Works
Designer:	Arthur Peppercorn	
Number built:	49	15
Purpose:	Express passenger	Express passenger and goods
Wheel arrangement:	4-6-2	
Cylinders (x3):	19 in diameter x 26 in stroke	
Motion:	Walschaerts (divided drive)	
Valves:	10 in diameter piston valves	
Wheels: Coupled:	6 ft 8 in	6 ft 2 in
Leading:	3 ft 2 in	
Trailing:	3 ft 8 in	
Tender:	4 ft 2 in	
Boiler diagram:	LNER Diagram 118*	
Boiler: Max. Diameter:	6 ft 5 in	
Pressure:	250 lb/psi	
Heating surface:	3,141.04 sq ft	
Firebox:	245.3 sq ft	
Tubes and flues:	2,216.07 sq ft	
Superheater:	679.67 sq ft	
Grate area:	50.00 sq ft	
Tractive effort:	37,397 lb (@ 85% boiler pressure)	40,430 lb
Engine wheelbase:	36 ft 3 in	34 ft 4 in
Total wheelbase:	62 ft 5.25 in	60 ft 6.25 in
Engine weight:	104 tons 2 cwt	101 tons 6 cwt
Coal capacity:	9 tons	
Water capacity:	5,000 gallons	
Max. axleloading:	22 tons 0 cwt	
BR power class:	8P6F	8P7F

Some engines originally fitted with Thompson-designed Diagram 117 boilers.

The Brief Rule of 'Britannia'

British Railways
Robert Riddles
Class 7P6F
'Britannia'
4-6-2 (1950)

The 'Britannia' Pacific heralded a new era in British locomotive practice,
one intended to acknowledge the post-war realities of running a railway.
The 'Britannias' inaugurated the final phase of steam traction
in Britain but this last significant class of express locomotives
came to divide the nation. Loved in the east, they were loathed in the west!

The Standard Class 7 Pacifics succeeded in registering both a 'first' and a 'last'. They were the first of the British Railways Standard classes to enter service, and the last express-passenger steam locomotives to be built in Britain, at least in any quantity. Memories of the 'Britannias', as they quickly became known, are as diverse as opinions of their worth. Engine crews on the Eastern Region, accustomed to only underpowered 4-6-0s on East Anglian express services, welcomed their arrival. In contrast, their reception on the Western

Region bordered on the hostile. As the advance guard of the new generation of Standard classes, this 4-6-2 had to bridge long-standing cultural divides.

Designed at Derby and completed at Crewe during December 1950, the prototype, No70000 *Britannia*, entered traffic on 5 January 1951. However, perhaps the most celebrated member of the class was the fifth, No70004 *William Shakespeare*. It became an attraction at the Festival of Britain, a pageant held alongside the Thames in London during 1951. Resplendent in its 'exhibition finish'

Long before the train came into view, No70013 *Oliver Cromwell* could be heard thundering down the south-west main line after stopping at Woking with a 'Cathedrals Express' working. Proudly wearing its 32A (Norwich) shedplate, the 'Britannia' Pacific races along the down fast line at Brookwood.

it looked the model of engineering excellence. After the event No70004 remained in the capital and was allocated to the Southern Region depot at Stewarts Lane in Battersea. Here it was maintained in immaculate condition and assigned to the prestige 'Golden Arrow' boat train. There was no brighter, or more stirring image of the country's recently nationalised railway, and its new generation of locomotives, than *William Shakespeare*, a line of umber-and-cream Pullman cars in tow, storming Grosvenor bank at the start of the journey to Dover and Folkestone.

Uniform standards

In 1950, two years into the nationalised era, construction of designs from the old 'big four' companies continued. Some saw no reason to change this policy. The new regime, however, demurred. To progress, the unified system demanded uniformity in locomotives and rolling stock. The Railway Executive placed Robert Riddles in overall charge of producing a range of modern locomotives combining the best practice of the 'big four' companies but suitable to work on all six BR regions. The design work was entrusted to a committee headed by one of Riddles' ex-LMSR

colleagues, E.S. (Stewart) Cox. Locomotive exchange trials held in 1948 had been intended to help the design process, although it did not require much foresight to predict that certain cherished ideas, regardless of their effectiveness, would not be perpetuated under the new regime .

Riddles and his colleagues must have anticipated which among existing designs came closest to meeting the requirement for economy, versatility, simplicity and ease of maintenance. Riddles had been part of the Stanier revolution on the LMSR and had seen how George Ivatt had confronted post-war conditions. Each of the Standard designs, even the 9F 2-10-0, would owe much to LMSR practice and three were more-or-less continuations of Ivatt designs.

Two lessons to emerge from the 1948 trials did influence the design. It had become clear that large-diameter driving wheels were not necessary to maintain high speeds but that, as coal quality declined, wide fireboxes, with ample grate areas, were desirable if steaming was not to be compromised. The 'Britannia' was schemed with six 6 feet 2 inches coupled wheels, and with a trailing truck to support a large firebox. This allowed a boiler of a size that would not only work more efficiently at normal power outputs but could substantially increase steam production if circumstances demanded. The whole design of the 'Britannia' centred on fitting the largest boiler that the maximum axleloading – which was 20 tons 5 cwt – would allow.

Modern features included rocking grates and self-cleaning smokeboxes to reduce disposal times at running sheds. Longer-lasting manganese-steel axlebox liners were fitted and the first 35 engines were equipped with Timken roller bearings and self-aligning axleboxes on all axles. All were equipped with Melesco

The 'Fenman', here re-created on the Nene Valley Railway on 7 March 1992, was one of the prestige expresses on the Eastern Region's ex-Great Eastern lines and regularly rostered for 'Britannia' haulage, including as here by No70000 *Britannia* itself.

A problem or two

Their mixed reception on the Western Region was not solely responsible for taking some of the shine off the 'Britannias'. First, the cast-iron piston heads of No70000 broke. The cause was traced to the shallow steam dome where the level of steam intake was no more than 11.75 inches above the water level of the boiler. As a consequence water entered the cylinders and caused damage. The cure was relatively straightforward: the height of the intake (and therefore of the dome) was increased to 16.5 inches and new piston heads, of stronger cast steel, were substituted. Then, in July 1951, while working the 'Bournemouth Belle', the crew of No70014 *Iron Duke* experienced a new and unnerving phenomenon: the coupled wheels began shifting on their axles, which – to save weight – were of hollow section. The effect was noted on six other engines, and resulted in bent and – in the case of No70004 – broken coupling rods. In October, the order came to sideline all 25 engines built to date.

A partial cure was effected by plugging the axle ends but the root cause of the problem was in the fitting of the cannon-type roller-bearing axleboxes. It was a matter of fractions of an inch and remedied by changing the assembly procedure. The two cylinders of the 'Britannia' – unique among contemporary British Pacifics which otherwise had three or four cylinders – meant easier routine maintenance but the arrangement was responsible for a fore-and-aft movement, or 'shuttling', between engine and train. Modifying the tender drawbar spring considerably reduced the effect but the 'Britannias' never lost their reputation for rough riding.

Skirting the Severn estuary near Lydney, No70000 *Britannia* heads for Newport with a railtour from Gloucester to Hereford and Chester on 23 June 1994.

multiple-valve regulator headers, which had their valves on the saturated steam side, i.e. between the boiler and the superheater. This type of regulator offered finer control over steam admission to the cylinder and improved tightness when the valves were closed. Melesco steam dryers ejected water and impurities from the saturated steam entering the superheater, so keeping the superheater elements clean internally.

Doing Great Eastern

Stewart Cox, who was chiefly responsible for the design, had stated that they would run 'all day and all night'. On the Eastern Region they took him at his word. The timetable for the ex-Great Eastern main line between London's Liverpool Street and Norwich had not been significantly altered for some 40 years. For Locomotive Superintendent, Leslie Parker, the 'Britannias' were an opportunity for radical improvement. They were more powerful than the resident 4-6-0s but fell the right side of an axleloading limit that barred ex-LNER Pacifics. Two daily round trips to Norwich (460 miles) should present no problem. However, Parker had to fight for his new engines. On hearing that the Great Eastern line had asked for 'Britannia' Pacifics, one member of the Railway Executive is alleged to have exclaimed, 'What! Send our first batch of express locomotives to that tramway?'

During the first months of 1951 'Britannias' began to arrive at Stratford and Norwich depots. An exception was No70005 *John Milton*, which spent that April and May on the Rugby test plant undergoing performance and efficiency trials. By June, it had journeyed to Stratford to join twelve other 'Britannias' and play its part in transforming both the frequency and punctuality of the Norwich services. Over one four-week period, No70005 covered almost 11,000 miles and several Stratford 'Britannias' went on to register 100,000 miles a year. Briefly, the 'Broadsman' could claim the title of 'fastest train in Britain', something previously unimaginable on Great Eastern metals!

Their years on the Eastern Region, working to Cambridge, Cromer, Parkeston Quay, King's Lynn and Yarmouth as well as to Norwich, unquestionably represented the high-point in the 'Britannia' story. Nowhere were they so well received or appreciated, although the Southern Region enjoyed its brief flirtation with the class. No70014 I*ron Duke* for a time shared the 'Golden Arrow' duty with No70004 *William Shakespeare* while a third 'Britannia', No70009 *Alfred the Great*, was based at another London shed, Nine Elms. Here, too, it was given top billing and regularly hauled the 'Bournemouth Belle' Pullman.

This was in contrast to the welcome accorded the 'Britannias' on the Western Region. Around 15 spent time there but only one depot managed to get the best out of them, Cardiff Canton succeeding where Plymouth Laira and London's Old Oak Common failed. Blame for this has been attributed partly to drivers' difficulty in adapting to left-hand drive (all Great Western express engines placed the driver's controls to the right of the footplate). The Melesco multiple-valve regulator was judged insensitive compared to its Swindon counterpart and, accustomed to the greater adhesion of their 'Castle' 4-6-0s, drivers complained of excessive slipping. In their defence, wheelslip was not confined to the 'Britannias' but was a trait of all Pacific designs, controllable with careful handling.

Cardiff's 'Britannias' became star performers on the 'Red Dragon' and 'Capitals United' expresses and worked over the 'North and West' route through Newport to Shrewsbury and Chester. Nevertheless, yet even more could have been achieved by the Canton 'Britannias' had Paddington's planners shown the initiative of those at Liverpool Street and revised the South Wales timetable to suit them.

North-west frontier

By the summer of 1963 the majority of the 'Britannia' Pacifics had become concentrated on the London Midland Region. Ten were still based at March, in Cambridgeshire, and six were at Immingham but they eventually followed their classmates in migrating to north-west England. Their days as premier express engines over, the 'Britannias' were reduced to semi-fasts, freight and parcels workings. Some turns continued to take them into Scotland and over the Pennines to Leeds and Bradford. All but seven ended their days at Carlisle's Kingmoor depot (only five of the class were not based there at one time or another) and their twilight years saw the Class 7 Pacifics much in demand for enthusiast specials.

The first withdrawal came in June 1965, with No70007 *Coeur-de-Lion*. The shortest-lived was No70050 *Firth of Clyde*, delivered in August 1954 and retired just twelve years later. Nevertheless, as late as January 1967, 42 'Britannias'

remained in service but by the December of that year that figure had been reduced to 14. The impending closure of Carlisle Kingmoor in January 1968 spelled the end for all but one of those, No70013 *Oliver Cromwell*.

Design flaws aside, the 'Britannias' were reliable, free-steaming and hard-working engines. Regrettably, it was only for a brief period that they were maintained and utilised in a way that allowed them to display their capabilities, which included a fair turn of speed (the highest recorded by a 'Britannia' was 99 miles per hour). From the unveiling of No70000 *Britannia* in January 1951 to the retirement of No70013 *Oliver Cromwell* in August 1968, none of the class served British Railways for more than seventeen years. Nevertheless they managed to enjoy remarkably varied lives and succeeded in dividing opinion more than most locomotive designs.

IN PRESERVATION

No70000 *Britannia* The doyen of the class was in line for preservation following its early withdrawal from Newton Heath depot, Manchester, in May 1966. However, when classmate No70013 *Oliver Cromwell* was chosen for the National Collection, British Railways lost interest in *Britannia* and it was left to the East Anglian Locomotive Preservation Society. In 1971, *Britannia* was moved to the Severn Valley Railway, where its restoration occupied seven years. It then took up residency on the Nene Valley Railway but, in January 1987, left by road for Carnforth for the start of a four-year overhaul that would return *Britannia* to the main line, which is where it ran until 1997. Ownership of *Britannia* has since passed to millionaire enthusiast Jeremy Hosking, who is having the locomotive overhauled at Crewe.

No70013 *Oliver Cromwell* Following withdrawal in August 1968, No70013 spent some 36 years in the care of Bressingham Steam Museum, near Diss, in Norfolk. In 2004 the Museum's trustees agreed a move to the Loughborough workshops of the Great Central Railway where No70013 would be overhauled. Thanks to a public appeal and other contributions, *Oliver Cromwell* steamed again in 2008 – 40 years after its last main-line run. Though nominally based on the GCR, as well as working on the main line, it has since visited a number of heritage railways.

IN DETAIL *(as built)*	
Class	**7 'Britannia'**
Built:	Crewe Works, 1951-54
Designer:	Robert Riddles
Number built:	55
Purpose:	Express passenger
Wheel arrangement:	4-6-2
Cylinders (x2):	20 in diameter x 28 in stroke
Motion:	Walschaerts
Valves:	11 in diameter piston valves
Wheels: Coupled:	6 ft 2 in
Leading:	3 ft 0 in
Trailing:	3 ft 3.5 in
Tender:	3 ft 3.5 in
Boiler diagram:	BR1
Boiler: Max. diameter:	6 ft 5.5 in
Pressure:	250 lb/psi
Heating surface:	3,192 sq ft
Firebox:	210 sq ft
Tubes and flues:	2,264 sq ft
Superheater:	718 sq ft
Grate area:	42.0 sq ft
Tractive effort:	32,150 lb (@ 85% boiler pressure)
Engine wheelbase:	35 ft 9 in
Total wheelbase:	58 ft 3 in
Engine weight:	94 tons 0 cwt
Coal capacity:	7 tons (BR1, BR1A tenders) 9 tons (BR1D)
Water capacity:	4,250 gallons (BR1) 5,000 gallons (BR1A)
	4,725 gallons (BR1D)
Max. Axleloading:	20 tons 5 cwt
BR power class:	7P6F

The Crowd Pullers

In 1927 the LMSR's Henry Fowler began a locomotive family. With a few 'class differences', it would last four generations and, a quarter of a century later, evolve into one of the more successful of the British Railways Standard designs.

The years after World War I saw a growth in commuter traffic as increasing numbers chose to live outside cities. The Southern Railway met the challenge mainly through electrification; the three other post-grouping companies kept faith with steam. The Great Western added to its ranks of 2-6-2 tanks with the 6100 class, specifically designed for the Paddington–Slough–Reading–Oxford run. The LMSR also needed similar engines, not solely for the London area but for the Midlands, Manchester and West Yorkshire. They would be the precursors not only of other LMSR designs, but one of the most enduringly useful among the BR Standard designs.

George Hughes, the first Chief Mechanical Engineer of the LMSR, had considered building a 2-6-4 tank based on his successful mixed-traffic 2-6-0. No work was undertaken, however, until Hughes had passed the baton to Henry Fowler. With their free-steaming boilers, well-designed cylinders and motion and good draughting the first Fowler 2-6-4 tanks were an immediate success and were soon being timed at 80 or even 90 miles an hour on services out of Euston.

Further orders were delivered built between and 1929 and 1934 bringing the class total to 125. By now the engines were operating across the LMSR system, from the Central Wales line to assisting trains on Shap and Beattock banks. Clearly this was one of his predecessor's designs that William Stanier could develop further, and he had one particular application in mind.

Thanks to the Midland Railway's take-over of the London, Tilbury & Southend Railway in 1912, the LMSR found itself operating along the Thames Estuary from Fenchurch Street to Southend-on-Sea and Shoeburyness. Stanier made re-equipping the LT&SR a priority, but he had to contend with restrictions that had already ruled out the Fowler 2-6-4 tank. His solution was to rework the two-cylinder Fowler design as a three-cylinder machine that would deliver the necessary power within the limitations. Stanier also incorporated fresh ideas, notably replacing the Fowler parallel boiler with a tapered design.

Chiefly based at Plaistow, in east London, and Shoeburyness, the 37-

The inspiration for the Standard 4MT tank was the LMSR design of Charles Fairburn, numbers of which were built after nationalisation for the Southern Region. Both types can be compared as Standard No80014 goes smokebox-to-smokebox with Fairburn No42077 with a Tunbridge Wells to London Victoria train at Oxted in July 1959.

strong class was able to transform services, capably handling packed 12-coach trains on demanding schedules. They remained a mainstay of LT&SR services until electrification in June 1962.

Three into two

It had always been Stanier's intention to enlarge the class for wider use and eight further examples were outshopped from Derby in 1935 with two cylinders rather than three. He had concluded that, while the three-cylinder engines had a specific application on the LT&SR line, there was nothing in their performance that justified the extra construction and maintenance costs.

The Stanier two-cylinder 2-6-4 tank proved an extremely sound design and 206 were built up to 1943 to augment the 125 Fowler engines. Third, and last, of the LMSR's Chief Mechanical Engineers to add to the ranks of 2-6-4 tanks was Charles Fairburn. Modifications were made to the Stanier design and production restarted at Derby in 1945. Remarkably, except for 1944, between 1927 and 1950 not a year passed when Derby Works did not produce new tank locomotives.

However, neither Brighton or Derby had finished with the 2-6-4 tank. Originally, the intention was for both to continue building the Fairburn engine as one of the BR Standard classes. Closer investigation then revealed that the design would require extensive reworking if it was to satisfy BR's 'universal' L1 loading gauge. This laid down the limits for the height and width of all the Standard designs. The rakish curves of the fully welded cabsides, bunker and sidetanks of the Standard 4MT tank were a deft means of staying within the L1 proscriptions. It made for a handsome-looking locomotive.

After working shuttles between Exeter and Torbay as part of the Exeter Railfair, on 2 May 1994 Standard 4MT tanks Nos80079 and 80080 caught the last of the sun as they headed homewards in the Bristol direction.

Although Brighton took overall responsibility for the design, detail work – as with the majority of the Standard types – was farmed out to other BR workshops. Swindon, Doncaster and Derby all made contributions, with the last responsible for the design of bogies, pony trucks, wheels, tyres, axles and springing.

At 155-strong, the Class 4MT tank was the third-most numerous of the BR Standards after the 9F 2-10-0 and the 5MT 4-6-0 (251 and 172 respectively).

IN PRESERVATION

No80002 In traffic on the Keighley & Worth Valley Railway, West Yorkshire.

No80064 In store on the Bluebell Railway, East Sussex, awaiting overhaul.

No80072 Under restoration on the Llangollen Railway, North Wales. Expected to enter service in autumn 2009.

No80078 At work on the Swanage Railway in Dorset.

No80079 On display in the Engine Hall at Highley on the Severn Valley Railway in Shropshire.

No80080 One of two 2-6-4Ts in the care of

the Princess Royal Class Locomotive Trust. Awaiting overhaul at the Midland Railway, Butterley, Derbyshire

No80097 Under restoration at Bury, on the East Lancashire Railway.

No80098 Second of the class owned by the Princess Royal Class Locomotive Trust and normally based at the Midland Railway, Butterley, but often hired to other railways.

No80100 Awaiting restoration on the Bluebell Railway. A very long-term project!

No80104 Out-of-traffic, awaiting overhaul on the Swanage Railway.

No80105 First steamed in preservation in 1999 and normally based on Scotland's Bo'ness & Kinneil Railway.

No80135 In service on the North Yorkshire Moors Railway.

No80136 On loan to the West Somerset Railway from the Churnet Valley Railway but

it has now been withdrawn from service for an overhaul.

No80150 Stored on the Barry Island Railway in South Wales and in essentially scrapyard condition.

No80151 A working member of the Bluebell Railway fleet.

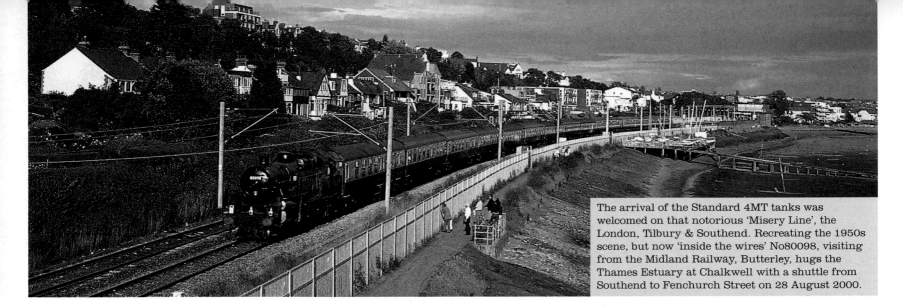

The arrival of the Standard 4MT tanks was welcomed on that notorious 'Misery Line', the London, Tilbury & Southend. Recreating the 1950s scene, but now 'inside the wires' No80098, visiting from the Midland Railway, Butterley, hugs the Thames Estuary at Chalkwell with a shuttle from Southend to Fenchurch Street on 28 August 2000.

Construction was undertaken at three workshops with Brighton bearing the brunt (130). It delivered the first, No80010, in July 1951, one of ten that went new to Tunbridge Wells West. Derby did not outshop No80000 until September 1952 and it, together with Nos80001-09 were sent to Scotland, as were all ten Doncaster-built engines (Nos80106-80115).

From Scotland to the south coast

The Standard 2-6-4 tanks were chiefly intended to update the motive power on increasingly heavy long-distance suburban and commuter trains. The Southern badly needed such engines, as did both the Glasgow area and the London, Tilbury & Southend line where the three-cylinder Stanier examples were being used to the full. Twenty-eight were despatched there and, based at Shoeburyness and Plaistow, they put in excellent work.

The Southern Region took both the first ten engines built (Nos80010-19) and the last (Nos80145-54) and retained them to the end. They worked services over the non-electrified outer-suburban lines such as that to Oxted and, in their later years, handled parcels and empty-stock workings out of Waterloo.

The first of the Standard 4MT 2-6-4 tanks (and the first of the 999 British Railways Standard locomotives) to be withdrawn was No80103 of Plaistow, London, in 1962. The final steam locomotive built at Brighton, No80154, enjoyed a working life of just ten years, being withdrawn from Nine Elms (London) in April 1967. The last of the class to be retired, coincidentally with the end of steam on the Southern that July, was Eastleigh's No80152.

Their versatility made the Class 4 tanks popular locomotives, something that has extended into preservation. With fifteen survivors, the class is numerically the largest of the preserved BR Standards. No fewer than ten have been, or are in service and, at various times, three have been approved for main-line working.

IN DETAIL *(as built)*	
Class	**'4'**
Built:	1951-57; Brighton, Derby and Doncaster works
Designer:	Robert Riddles
Number built:	155
Purpose:	Suburban and semi-fast passenger
Wheel arrangement:	2-6-4T
Cylinders (x2):	18 in diameter x 28 in stroke
Motion:	Walschaerts
Valves:	10 in diameter piston valves
Wheels: Coupled:	5 ft 8 in
Leading:	3 ft 0 in
Trailing:	3 ft 0 in
Boiler diagram:	BR5
Boiler: Max. diameter:	5 ft 3 in
Pressure:	225 lb/psi
Heating surface:	1,606 sq ft
Firebox:	143 sq ft
Tubes and flues:	1,223 sq ft
Superheater:	240 sq ft
Grate area:	26.7 sq ft
Tractive effort:	25,515 lb (@ 85% boiler pressure)
Engine wheelbase:	15 ft 4 in
Total wheelbase:	36 ft 10 in
Engine weight:	86 tons 13 cwt
Coal capacity:	3.5 tons
Water capacity:	2,000 gallons
Max. axleloading:	17 tons 19 cwt
BR power class:	4MT

A Solitary Aristocrat

In British Railways' service the *Duke* was an enigma: capable of outstanding performances but ultimately failing to fulfil its potential. Enginemen remained wary of this unique machine. Then the *Duke*'s dark secrets were uncovered.

After the most ambitious restoration yet attempted, it was a much-improved *Duke of Gloucester* that returned to its birthplace of Crewe on 22 July 1987 to mark 150 years since the Grand Junction Railway transformed a Cheshire hamlet into one of the world's great railway centres.

The *Duke* was born out of tragedy. Of the four locomotives involved in the Harrow disaster of October 1952, two were deemed past repairing: 'Jubilee' class 4-6-0 No45637 *Windward Islands* and 'Princess Royal' Pacific No46202 *Princess Anne*. The latter had only recently entered traffic, a rebuild of Stanier's experimental 'Turbomotive'. Its loss left a vacancy in the fleet of West Coast Pacifics that Robert Riddles, then heading locomotive matters on the Railway Executive, obtained authority to fill. Four years earlier, Riddles had lost the argument to include a Class 8 4-6-2 in the range of BR Standard classes. Now he could correct the omission, if only with a one-off.

Obtaining the desired power output called for three cylinders but this ran counter to the simplicity of construction and maintenance that were guiding principles for the BR Standard designs. Both Gresley on the LNER and Bulleid on the Southern had been devotees of three-cylinder propulsion but neither the former's divided-drive arrangement or the latter's chain-driven gear could be classed as 'simple'. Using three separate sets of Walschaerts gear also had its disadvantages from the maintenance viewpoint. It gave Riddles the opportunity to try a quite different system, one that had long interested him. It was the work of an Italian engineer, Arturo Caprotti.

Caprotti was an automotive engineer whose attention had been drawn to the inefficiencies of the steam locomotive. He had identified steam distribution as the key area and devised a form of locomotive valve gear that functioned in similar fashion to a motor engine. Instead of horizontal piston valves moving eccentric cranks, rods and levers, vertical poppet valves were operated by diagonal rotating camshafts. (Poppet valves are separate from each other with inlet and exhaust valves of different sizes.)

One end of each camshaft was driven from gearing mounted on the return crank on the centre driving wheel while the other was connected to the valve gearbox, mounted above the cylinder. Here the rotary motion of the shaft was redirected, using gears and cams, to actuate separate inlet and exhaust valves for each side of the cylinder. In Caprotti's original design the exhaust-valve timing was fixed, always opening and closing at the same points in the cycle. The inlet-valve timing, however, was adjustable, permitting different degrees of working.

Italian recipe

Compared to conventional arrangements, Caprotti's system – which he patented in 1919 – allowed greater control over the workings of the valves. It increased efficiency, gave excellent steam distribution and produced significant reductions in coal consumption. Although relatively costly to maintain, this was offset by deliverance from the wear-and-tear that plagued conventional motion parts.

The Caprotti arrangement was ingenious but not without drawbacks, as one eminent engineer observed. He was an Austrian, F.J. Kuretschka, and – with Arturo Caprotti's approval – put right many of the problems. Meanwhile, a British engineer, the Great Western Railway-trained, L.T. (Tom) Daniels, had come to develop a professional interest in poppet-valve applications in general and the Caprotti design in particular.

Daniels became Chief Engineer for Associated Locomotive Equipment, Caprotti's British subsidiary. He saw where further improvements could be made to the system, although it was not until after World War II that he could implement them. Daniels changed the camshaft design to include two exhaust cams instead of one. Additionally, he allowed them to be adjusted mechanically, like the inlet cams, so making all valve operations variable. It went on to make a worthwhile improvement on the fixed exhaust-valve events of the original Caprotti arrangement.

However, as with many refinements of the fundamental Stephenson principle, the Achilles heel of the Caprotti valve gear was its relative complexity. It consisted of small parts accommodated in compact housings and needed a careful touch. The placing of precision machinery in situations where it could be exposed to extremes of dirt and corrosion invariably brought problems.

Fundamentally flawed

Tom Daniels was co-opted to the *Duke of Gloucester* project and devised a version of the British Caprotti gear tailored to the design. Daniels recommended marrying the Caprotti gear to a Kylchap exhaust system, a suggestion endorsed by Riddles. This device had proved its capabilities on express locomotives on both sides of the English Channel, including a number of LNER Pacifics. Its superiority was beyond doubt so it was with dismay that both Daniels and Riddles discovered that an orthodox Swindon-type double chimney and blastpipe had already been fabricated for the *Duke*.

As an ex-GWR man, Daniels was sufficiently familiar with the Swindon pattern to judge its suitability or otherwise. While this exhaust system suited the draughting of the 'Castle' and 'King' 4-6-0s, Daniels contended that it would prove incapable of coping with the fierce exhaust generated by the Caprotti gear; the choke area was simply too small. His warning went unheeded and the fitting of the Swindon assembly was the first, and most damaging, of the miscalculations that would compromise the performance of the Class 8 Pacific. Others would only come to light years later, during rebuilding.

Little wonder the locomotive was criticised for its poor draughting and unhealthy appetite for coal and water. However, by now the date had been set for the end of steam and any incentive to right the errors in the *Duke*'s construction was removed. What, in theory, should have been a high-performance machine gained a reputation as temperamental, unpredictable and difficult to fire. It was no surprise that its working life was limited to eight years.

For Riddles and his colleagues, Ernest Cox and Roland Bond, *Duke of Gloucester* might have been the precursor of a class of 8P Pacifics. The first

Loaded to 12 vehicles, No71000 *Duke of Gloucester* departs Rugby with the down 'Midday Scot' (its sole regular turn) one day in September 1958.

published descriptions of *Duke of Gloucester* refer to it as a 'prototype', implying that it was intended as a testbed and a showcase for what could be achieved.

Built under order NoE486 at a cost of £44,655, No71000 left Crewe Works early in May 1954 and subsequently took up duties at Crewe North, whose engine crews quickly discovered the Pacific's unhealthy appetite for coal! Placed in the shed's No3 link, it stayed there for the rest of its working life, with the 'Midday Scot' becoming a regular turn. Upon withdrawal, on 24 November 1962, No71000 had covered some 280,000 miles, representing a yearly average of around 35,000. An indication of the inherent soundness of the design can be judged from the fact that the first heavy overhaul was not required until 135,717 miles.

Mission improbable

Initially, the *Duke* was set aside for the National Collection and placed in store at Crewe. However, in 1967, for reasons never revealed, that decision was reversed and only the cylinder assembly and valve gear were deemed of interest. The left-hand assembly was removed and subsequently placed on display, in sectioned form, in the Science Museum, London. The right-hand cylinder was also detached (presumably to stop the engine becoming unbalanced) and promptly vanished. The chimney, smoke deflectors and a number of other parts soon followed.

What remained – little more than a carcass consisting of a boiler, main frames, middle cylinder (minus cambox), cab frame and wheels – was sent to South Wales for scrap. No wonder the *Duke* earned the nickname of 'Project Impossible'. However, undeterred by the enormity of the task the 71000 Preservation Society raised Woodhams' price of £4,950 and, on 24 April 1974, No71000 left for the Great Central Railway.

Advance the *Duke*

Tom Daniels continued to play an active part in improving *Duke of Gloucester* in preservation. Most importantly, he recommended several changes to the valve gear and was able to produce the necessary drawings before his death in 1993. These covered the fitting of new exhaust cams, with a different profile giving later exhaust-valve release events. They would improve cylinder efficiency and reduce water consumption. There was just one problem: the Trust had nothing like the finance needed to produce these new components.

Then, in 1997, an application to the Heritage Lottery Fund proved successful with a grant of £233,380 towards a series of seven major modifications and a heavy overhaul. The improvements included the manufacture of a coal pusher for the tender, an increase in water capacity to 5,110 gallons, the installation of air-braking (essential if main-line running was to continue) and making Tom Daniels' new exhaust-cam design a reality. The total cost of the work was more than £338,000.

The result of the expenditure was evident when, on 3 September 2005 the locomotive snatched the record for a northbound climb to Shap summit between Carnforth and Carlisle. Hauling 13 coaches loaded to 510 tons and driven by the experienced Bill Andrews of the West Coast Railway Company, the engine was reported to have averaged 60 miles per hour over the five-and-three-quarter miles of 1 in 75 from milepost 31.5 to the summit. Taking 5 minutes 42 seconds for the climb, the *Duke* lopped 15 seconds off the record held by Stanier 'Coronation' Pacific No6233 *Duchess of Sutherland*.

Rebuilding No71000 occupied 12 years and the opportunity was taken to put right the errors that had blighted the locomotive during its British Railways days. The Kylchap exhaust was installed and a new ashpan was fitted of the dimensions originally specified. *Duke of Gloucester* steamed for the first time in 24 years in May 1986 and was officially commissioned on 11 November.

Further work was then undertaken to bring the locomotive up to the standard required for main-line running and, on 14 March 1990, the *Duke* undertook a loaded test run from Derby. The steaming rate – calculated at around 45,000 lb per hour – was phenomenal. Recalling the *Duke* from BR days some footplatemen were understandably apprehensive. Before long, they conceded this was a very different animal. One commented that it both 'felt and sounded totally different'.

Such authoritative judgements suggest that a full complement of Standard Class 8 Pacifics would have counted among the world's finest express passenger locomotives. Nominally based on the East Lancashire Railway, No71000 remains main-line certified.

IN DETAIL *(as built)*	
Class	**'8'**
Built:	Crewe Works, 1954
Designer:	Robert Riddles
Number built:	1
Purpose:	Express passenger
Wheel arrangement:	4-6-2
Cylinders (x3):	18 in diameter x 28 in stroke
Motion:	British Caprotti rotary-cam poppet-valve gear
Wheels: Coupled:	6 ft 2 in
Leading:	3 ft 0 in
Trailing:	3 ft 3.5 in
Tender:	3 ft 3.5 in
Boiler diagram:	BR13
Boiler: Max. diameter:	6 ft 5.5 in
Pressure:	250 lb/psi
Heating surface:	3,181 sq ft
Firebox:	226 sq ft
Tubes and flues:	2,264 sq ft
Superheater:	691 sq ft
Grate area:	48.6 sq ft
Tractive effort:	39,080 lb (@85% boiler pressure)
Engine wheelbase:	36 ft 9in
Total wheelbase:	59 ft 3 in
Engine weight:	101 tons 5 cwt
Coal capacity:	10 tons
Water capacity:	4,725 gallons ¶
Max. Axleloading:	22 tons 0 cwt
BR power class:	8P

¶*Later replaced by a 4,325 gallon tender fitted with a coal-pusher.*

A Heavy-freight Champion

Among the 12 Standard classes, the 9F heavy-freight locomotive was the most numerous and, operationally, had the greatest impact.
Sadly, it was denied the time to justify the investment. When completed in 1960, British Railways' No92220 was not just the last of the 9F freight locomotives, nor simply the conclusion of BR's nine-year 'Standard' construction programme. It marked the end of a 130-year railway journey.

The 9F was unique among the Standard classes. Where the other 11 designs fell into existing categories – express passenger 4-6-2, mixed traffic 4-6-0 and 2-6-0 and 2-6-4 and 2-6-2 passenger tank – the 9F broke fresh ground. For a start, the Class 9 power category was new to Britain. Second, the design shared very few components with its companions (elsewhere boilers, for example, were interchangeable). Third, and most significantly, those most closely involved with the 9Fs – footplate crews, running-shed foremen, regional operating officers – generally considered them the finest heavy-freight engines built in Britain.

A post-nationalisation assessment of the British Railways' fleet identified the most pressing need to be for mixed-traffic engines. Heavy freight appeared well catered for by the influx of more than 700 surplus War Department 2-8-0s. Moreover, every railway company – the Southern apart – had its quota of eight-coupled tender engines. In all, BR had more than 2,400 2-8-0s on its books.

There were those, however, who looked beyond the bare statistics. The motive-power officer of the Eastern Region, Leslie Parker, argued that a powerful, fast freight engine could work round trips, such as Peterborough to London and Annesley to Woodford Halse, within the footplate crew's eight-hour shift. Apart from higher average speeds, time would be saved on shed by fitting of rocker grates and hopper ashpans. The savings could be substantial. Unfortunately, he and his counterparts on BR's other regions had to wait until 1954 for the 9Fs to prove the point for them.

A heavy-freight engine had been included in the draft plan for the BR Standard types but there was disagreement over what form it should take. Some among Robert Riddles' design team, notably Ernest Cox, argued for a 2-8-2 configuration. Encouraged by the performance of his wartime ten-coupled 'Austerities', Riddles held out for a 2-10-0 wheel arrangement, and the additional

Doing the job for which it was built 9F 2-10-0 No92240 climbs Freshfield bank on the Bluebell Railway with a lengthy mixed goods, part of a driver-experience day. This Crewe-built (1958) 9F was first steamed in preservation 5 September 1990 but now languishes at Sheffield Park awaiting overhaul.

Following expiry of its main-line certification, No92220 *Evening Star* returned to its one-time haunt of the West Country and a stay on the West Somerset Railway. On 15 June 1989 it approaches Castle Hill, Williton, with an evening special from Minehead to Bishops Lydeard.

adhesive weight and traction that an extra set of coupled wheels would supply. Ten-coupled engines were commonplace elsewhere, in Germany, Russia and the United States, for example, but prior to 1943 only two ten-coupled engines had worked in Britain: the Great Eastern Railway's 'Decapod' of 1902 and the Midland Railway's 'Big Bertha' of 1919, whose sole task was to bank trains on the Lickey Incline between Bristol and Birmingham.

Cox's principal objection was that having to site the firebox above the rear wheelset would limit both its size and that of the boiler. As a consequence, steam production and power output would be compromised. However, this assumed a minimum driving-wheel diameter of 5 feet 3 inches. Riddles insisted that, given a well-designed 'front end' (cylinders, valves, steampipes and exhaust blastpipe) and free-flowing steam passages, a driving-wheel diameter of just 5 feet was adequate. The specification required a design that was capable of hauling 900 tons at an average of 35 miles per hour.

However, the ten-coupled wheelbase did present problems for the drawing office at Brighton Works. For example, in South Wales, the locomotives would be expected to negotiate the tight curves of the serpentine Ebbw Valley line. No sideplay could be allowed in the coupled axles so the ingenious solution was to omit the flanges from the centre pair of driving wheels, allowing the 9F to round curves of 400 feet radius (and as low as 300 feet at dead slow pace). This, added to a low axleloading of 15 tons 10 cwt, saw the class subject to few route restrictions.

New power in the land

The first 9Fs emerged from Crewe Works early in 1954 and were allocated to Ebbw Junction shed in Newport for steelworks traffic. Expectations were dampened, however, when the engines' regulators displayed an alarming tendency to remain stuck open and the steam brakes underperformed – an unnerving experience when travelling down a Welsh valley with 1,000 tons of coal empties swaying behind the tender! These matters resolved, the 9Fs began to garner the praise they deserved.

The coal, iron ore and steel traffic of South Wales was just one of the tasks earmarked for the 9Fs. On the North Eastern Region, they took over another tough job: conveying ore from the berths at Tyne Dock to the steelworks at Consett, only 23 miles away but 900 feet above sea level. Rakes of hoppers, loaded to around 800 tons, were hauled up gradients as steep as 1 in 49 by ten dedicated 9Fs – dedicated in every sense, since the engines were specially equipped with compressed-air pumps to operate the wagons' automatic discharge doors. Crews here, as elsewhere, relished working with the 9Fs: with 77 tons of adhesive weight on the coupled wheels, there was no danger of 'losing it' when starting heavy loads.

The 9Fs were equally at home on other demanding turns: the heavy anhydrite trains from Long Meg quarries in Cumbria to the ICI plant at Widnes, for example. On the Southern Region, six 9Fs were sent to Eastleigh shed to work 100,000 gallon oil trains, weighing 1,200 tons, from the Fawley refinery on Southampton Water to the distribution point at Bromford Bridge, near Birmingham. But these were the kind of duties they were built to do. Passenger

IN PRESERVATION

No92134 Built at Crewe in 1957, No92134 is back at its birthplace, with restoration being undertaken at The Railway Age. When completed, No92134 is earmarked for the Churnet Valley Railway in Staffordshire.

No92203 *Black Prince* * Almost as celebrated as the last of Lot 429, *Evening Star*, the first of that batch, No92203, entered traffic in April 1959. Retired in 1967, the 9F was bought by the artist and conservationist, David Shepherd, and spent many years on the East Somerset Railway. While there, *Black Prince* travelled to the nearby Foster Yeoman stone quarry and demonstrated the power of the 9F by moving a load of 2,162 tons, the heaviest ever hauled by steam traction in Britain. The demands are somewhat less on its present home of the Gloucestershire Warwickshire Railway.

No92207 Rescued from Barry in 1986, and since named *Morning Star*, although hampered by lack of funds, restoration of No92207 is underway at Shillingstone Station, on the North Dorset Railway.

No92212 Condemned in January 1968, the 9F languished at Barry until bought by 92212 Holdings in 1979. Restoration was completed on the Great Central Railway in September 1996. No92212 subsequently put down roots on the Mid-Hants Railway where it is presently under overhaul.

excursions to the seaside were quite another matter!

The Western Region was the first to discover that the 5-feet diameter wheels of the 9F were no obstacle to fast running and reports of speeds between 80 and 90 miles per hour became commonplace. It began to use them on summer passenger work (the absence of steam-heating precluded their use at other times) and the Eastern Region soon followed the lead. The London Midland then employed 9Fs on holiday trains to Blackpool and Llandudno. Some remarkable runs were logged as 9Fs replaced failed diesels on expresses. Before long, though, concerned about the impact on cylinders and running gear, operating departments literally put the brake on sustained high-speed running. The 9Fs' greatest impact on passenger services came on the Somerset & Dorset route. In taking 12-coach trains over the Mendip Hills unaided, they eliminated the uneconomic double-heading that beset the line. Sadly, it came too late to deter BR from closing it.

However, it was in revolutionising aspects of BR's freight operations that the 9Fs had their greatest impact. They proved exceptionally competent engines, in the process displaying a remarkable versatility. In every respect – steaming, riding, ease of operation, reliability, and the capacity to complete the tasks asked of them – they scored ten-out-of-ten.

By way of experiment

Four modifications were applied to the 9Fs but only one – the simplest and most obvious – proved successful. This was the fitting of double chimneys and blastpipes, from new with No92183 and retrospectively to a number of earlier examples. In contrast, the building of ten engines (Nos92020-29) with the Italian-designed Franco-Crosti boiler – a response to a government demand for BR to reduce its coal consumption by 10,000 tons per week – was ill-conceived. The Crosti boiler worked best with inefficient engines (which the 9F was not) and did not adapt to the constraints of the British L2 loading gauge. It created unpleasant working conditions for the crew and was soon discarded, although the engines retained their distinctive appearance.

For all they contributed to BR's freight business during the last 14 years of steam traction, the 9Fs could never repay an investment of around £7.5 million. That was inevitable once the timetable for disposing of steam had been accelerated. Engines with a good two decades of work left in them were scrapped after as little as five years' service. In hindsight, it can be asked why no attempt was made to sell them to developing countries where steam had a future.

Instead the class of 251 engines – 178 built at Crewe and 73 at Swindon – remained intact for just four years. The first withdrawals, of Nos92034, 92169, 92170, 92171, 92175, 92176 and 92177, were made on 31 May 1964, these last six from either Doncaster or New England (Peterborough) sheds. The last examples on BR's books were Nos92077, 92160 and 92167 that were retired from Carnforth depot, in Lancashire, in June 1968 and cut up at a Scottish scrapyard that same autumn.

Twilight star

By rights, the final main-line steam locomotive to be built for British Railways should have been No92250, numerically the last of the 251 9Fs and the 7,331st product of Crewe Works. It entered traffic in December 1958. However, the ex-Great Western works at Swindon subsequently fulfilled an earlier order for 18 engines that had been put on hold to accelerate the introduction of the 'Warship'

No92214 Banbury, Ebbw Junction and Severn Tunnel Junction were homes to No92214 during an all-too-short five-year working life. Following restoration by the 9F Locomotive Charitable Trust at the Midland Railway, Butterley, No92214 spent three-and-a-half years at Bury, on the East Lancashire Railway. It then returned to Butterley in August 2008.

No92219 After spending all but a month of its five-and-a-half year career based in Cardiff (first at Canton shed then East Dock), No92219 was condemned in August 1965. It was saved from scrap in 1984 and joined classmate No92214 at Butterley. No92219, however, awaits restoration.

No92220 *Evening Star* The story of this most-famous member of the class is told above. In recent times, *Evening Star* has been on display at the NRM's outpost at Shildon, County Durham. However, in September 2008, it returned to Swindon, taking the place of *King George V* at STEAM, The Museum of the Great Western Railway. The 'King' has moved to York.

No92240 This Crewe product spent most of its time based in London, first at Old Oak Common then, from September 1960 until withdrawal in August 1965 at Southall. Following acquisition it was located in the unlikely territory of the Bluebell Railway, where it returned to steam in 1990. After ten years' service, however, No92240 awaits overhaul.

No92245 Third of the surviving Crewe-built 9Fs, No92245 remains at Barry, not in the famous scrapyard, which has vanished, but in store on the Barry Island Railway. Intended as part of the defunct Wales Railway Museum project, it remains the property of the Vale of Glamorgan Council, who are open to offers!

* Name added following preservation. In BR days, Black Prince *was carried by BR Standard Pacific No70008.*

EVENING STAR

class diesel-hydraulics. Delivery of Lot No429, which had also been delayed by steel shortages, did not begin until April 1959 and occupied 11 months. The last of the batch, No92220, rolled out of the works in March 1960. It was also the last of some 60,000 steam locomotives built for Britain's railways over 150 years.

The choice of *Evening Star* could not have been more appropriate, and not solely for its associations with twilight. The precedent for the name went back to the Great Western's broad-gauge 'Star' class of 1837, and the very first *Evening Star* had served the GWR from 1839 until 1871.

At Swindon, on 18 March 1960, No92220's nameplates and commemmorative plaques were unveiled by Keith Grand, a member of the British Transport Commission. A week later *Evening Star* entered service with BR's Western Region at one of the principal South Wales depots, Cardiff Canton. Crews here liked the BR Standard engines – they had been the only ones on the WR wholeheartedly to take to the 'Britannia' Pacifics – and *Evening Star* became something of a prize possession. On 27 June 1960, they experienced the full potential of the 9F.

Replacing a failed 'Britannia' on the up 'Red Dragon' bound for Paddington, *Evening Star* took over a 13-coach train weighing 450 tons. This freight engine then put in a sensational performance, reaching 80 to 85 miles per hour on the falling grades on the approach to the Severn Tunnel. Over the next two days, and again on 1 and 15 July, No92220 was entrusted with the crack South Wales expresses, the 'Red Dragon' and the 'Capitals United', but the exhilaration of the Canton crews was not shared by their chiefs in the operating department. At express speeds, the 9F had a huge appetite for water and once had to make a stop at Reading to replenish its tank. Doubtless the sight of its coupled wheels spinning at over twice their stipulated speed also caused consternation.

Evening Star went on to spend time on the Somerset & Dorset and on

8 September 1962 was entrusted with the last through working of the 'Pines Express'. Returning to Cardiff (now at East Dock), *Evening Star* was retired in March 1965. At exactly five years, its revenue-earning life was shorter than any other member of the class.

Its historic status ensured *Evening Star* would be designated one of the National Collection's select band and it was subsequently returned to main-line condition, the work being undertaken at Didcot. However, since 1991 has been relegated to a museum piece.

IN DETAIL *(as built)*

Class	'9'
Built:	1954-60, Crewe and Swindon works
Designer:	Robert Riddles
Number built:	251
Purpose:	Heavy freight
Wheel arrangement:	2-10-0
Cylinders (x 2):	20 in diameter x 28 in stroke
Motion:	Walschaerts valve gear
Valves:	11 in diameter piston valves
Wheels: Leading:	3 ft 0 in
Coupled:	5 ft 0 in
Tender:	3 ft 3.5 in
Boiler diagram:	BR9 (BR12 Nos92020-29)
Boiler: Max. Diameter:	6 ft 1 in (5 ft 7.5 in Nos92020-29)
Pressure:	250 lb/psi
Heating surface:	2,550 sq ft (1,843 sq ft Nos92020-29)
Tubes and flues:	1,836 sq ft (1,274 sq ft Nos92020-29)
Firebox:	179 sq ft (158 sq ft Nos92020-29)
Superheater:	535 sq ft (411 sq ft Nos92020-29)
Grate area:	40.2 sq ft
Tractive effort:	39,667 lb (@ 85% boiler pressure)
Engine wheelbase:	30 ft 2 in
Total wheelbase:	55 ft 11 in
Engine weight:	86 tons 14 cwt†
Coal capacity:	7 tons (BR1B, BR1F, BR1G tenders) 9 tons (BR1C, BR1K)
Water capacity:	5,000 gallons (BR1G tender) 4,725 gallons (BR1B, BR1C) 5,625 gallons (BR1F) 4,300 gallons (BR1K) (Tenders of differing capacities were attached to various batches to suit operating needs. The exception was the BR1K, which was equipped with a mechanical stoker.)
Max. axleloading:	15 tons 10 cwt*
BR power class:	9F

†Engines Nos92020-29 originally weighed 90 tons 4 cwt; reduced to 83 tons 12 cwt after conversion to conventional draughting.

*Increased to 15 tons 19 cwt on engines Nos92020-92029 as built with Franco-Crosti boilers and to 16 tons 11 cwt on engines fitted with mechanical stokers, Nos92165-67.

Designers of an earlier era would never have tolerated the lacework of exposed copper piping serving the injectors and other equipment but when it came to the Standard classes, ease of maintenance was paramount. No92212 is in the capable hands of a Mid-Hants Railway crew.

Getting Shipshape, German-style

A bold example of European co-operation brought about the building of the Western Region's 'Warship' class diesel-hydraulics.

British Railways

BR/Maybach Type 4 'Warship' (Class 42,43) 2,200hp diesel-hydraulic (1958)

As the home (if not the birthplace, which was Paris) of Dr Rudolf Diesel, it was appropriate that Germany's railways led the way – at least in Europe – in developing diesel traction. It was to the Deutsches Bundesbahn that BR's Western Region turned when it came to establishing its diesel fleet. However, where their American counterparts had adopted electric transmission for diesel locomotives, DB's engineers had concentrated on developing the hydraulic system. This led the Western, alone among the BR regions, similarly to place its faith in hydraulic transmission and foster the notion that it was resurrecting the proud independence associated with the Great Western since broad-gauge days. The truth was somewhat different: British Railways wanted one of its regions to evaluate hydraulic transmission.

The experiment did not start well. The overall performance of the first five main-line hydraulics, a quintet of A1A-A1A locomotives built by the North British Locomotive Company in 1958, was disappointing. Nevertheless, the WR continued its quest and, looking to Germany, lighted upon the 2,100hp V200 class B-B diesel hydraulic. Built by Krauss-Maffei of Munich, the V200 was a standard design with – and this was the chief advantage of diesel hydraulics – an extremely impressive high power-to-weight ratio (26 horsepower per ton of engine weight).

On its exit from Bristol, the eastbound 'Bristolian' accelerates past Stapleton Road Junction and begins the climb to Filton Junction. From June 1959, with 'Warship' diesel-hydraulics in charge, the train was allowed just 100 minutes for the 118.3 miles to London.

The WR obtained a licence from Krauss-Maffei to build a variant of the V200 in Britain and the first of these locomotives, D800, was outshopped from Swindon in late 1958. By summer 1959, nine of the class were in service, concentrated at Plymouth Laira, the Western Region's first major diesel depot. Once predictable teething troubles had been overcome, the diesels recorded some impressive statistics. On average, they were covering 380 miles per day compared to the 153 miles of the 'Castle' class 4-6-0s they were lined up to replace. Some rosters required the diesels to cover 610-650 miles within 24 hours. Admittedly, they were being given intensive assignments that would fully exploit their continuous availability, but the comparison was nonetheless telling.

Construction continued until 1961, by which time the class totalled 71. Swindon Works constructed 38 while North British contributed the remainder. With two exceptions, the class was named after famous Royal Navy warships. While D812 became *Royal Naval Reserve 1859-1959*, the one landlubber was D800 *Sir Brian Robertson*, then chairman of the British Transport Commission.

The 'Warships' held on to the WR's prestige duties until the arrival of the more powerful 'Westerns' and then enjoyed an 'Indian summer' on the Southern Region where they proved ideal for the relatively lightly loaded Waterloo–Salisbury–Exeter services. However, they were not proving as durable as their German cousins and availability figures became a cause for concern. Demoted to secondary duties, British Railways' decision to standardise on electric transmission made the 'Warships' and other diesel-hydraulic classes clear targets for early withdrawal.

All had been retired by the end of 1972.

Diesel-hydraulics nose-to-nose: visiting the West Somerset Railway, 'Warship' NoD832 *Onslaught* encounters one of the locomotives that replaced it on front-rank expresses, Class 52 'Western' C-C NoD1010 *Western Campaigner*, in the yard at Williton.

Bristol fashion

One of the 'Warship' duties in the summer 1959 timetable was the 'Bristolian', which was accelerated to its fastest-ever schedule of 100 minutes between Bristol and Paddington, requiring average speeds of over 70mph. On the first day of diesel haulage NoD804 *Avenger* beat all previous records for the run, covering the 117.6 miles to Paddington in just under 93 minutes. The final 77.3 miles from Swindon took just 52.5 minutes, with the 100mph mark being exceeded on three occasions.

IN PRESERVATION

D821 *Greyhound* Swindon-built in 1960, *Greyhound* was withdrawn from Plymouth Laira in December 1972 to become the first main-line diesel to be preserved by a private group. After spells at Didcot, Reading and back at Swindon, in April 1981 the 'Warship' moved to the North Yorkshire Moors Railway where it ran 153,171 miles in ten years. For a time, it masqueraded as a fictional German cousin, V200 No021/220 021 *Windhund!* After appearing at open days at Laira and Old Oak Common, D821 moved to the Severn Valley Railway. It subsequently visited several preserved railways, including the East Lancashire, where it worked in tandem with the other surviving 'Warship', D832 *Onslaught*.

At a ceremony at Falmouth, D821 was temporarily renamed *Cornwall* and twinned with the present-day Royal Navy Type 22 frigate of the same name. Withdrawn in 2002 to have 'A' end Maybach engines replaced, *Greyhound* re-entered SVR service the following year. Recently it has been sidelined at Kidderminster for the 'B' engine to be overhauled.

D832 *Onslaught* A 1961 Swindon product, *Onslaught* was also retired in December 1972 and transferred to British Railways' Departmental Stock. It became a 'dead load' vehicle based at Derby Research Centre. Acquired for preservation the 'Warship' was based on the East Lancashire Railway and came under the umbrella of the Bury Hydraulic Group. Here its restoration to working order was only achieved by using a large number of components off scrapped classmate D818 *Glory*. It has also been fitted with a Mekydro transmission sourced from a withdrawn German V200. Of late, *Onslaught* has been on an extended visit to the West Somerset Railway.

IN DETAIL *(as built)*

Class	42/43 'Warship'
Built:	1958-61; Swindon Works; North British Locomotive Company, Glasgow
Designed:	Krauss-Maffei, Munich, German Federal Republic; Swindon Works
Number built:	71 (D800-70)
Purpose:	Express passenger
Engines:	Two Bristol-Siddeley Maybach MD650 12-Cylinder V-type of 821kw (1,135hp) at 1,530rpm §
Power output:	2,270hp
Transmission:	Hydraulic. Two Mekydro-Maybach type K104 hydraulic transmissions containing a permanently filled torque converter and four-speed automatic gearbox.
Wheel arrangement:	B-B
Wheel diameter:	3 ft 3.5 in
Weight:	78 tons 0 cwt §
Maximum tractive effort:	52.400lb (223kn)
Continuous tractive effort:	46,900lb (209kn) at 11.5mph §
Maximum speed:	90mph
BR power rating:	Type 4

§ Locomotives D833-D870 employed two North British Locomotive Company/MAN (Maschinenfabrik Augsburg, Nurnburg) L12V 1821 BS each of 1,100hp. Locomotive weight was increased to 79 tons 10 cwt and maximum tractive effort to 53,400 lb.

Whistle While You Work

British Railways

BR/English Electric Type 4 (Class 40) 2,000hp 1 Co-Co1 diesel-electric

(1958)

It was only a trill emanating from the engine, but it was a sound peculiar to English Electric diesel-electrics. Whatever officialdom chose to call the class – Type 4, Class 40 – to enthusiasts they have always been 'Whistlers'.

The pioneer English Electric Type 4, NoD200 (40.122), now part of the National Collection, bursts into life at Stratford Major Depot on 26 March 1991 during an event marking the closure of the ex-Great Eastern facility. Another East Anglian diesel stalwart, Class 31 NoD5583 (31.165) stands alongside. In 1958, NoD200 inaugurated the accelerated London Liverpool Street to Norwich service.

The English Electric Type 4 hit the headlines on 18 April 1958 when the class leader, D200, left London's Liverpool Street with the first diesel-hauled express to Norwich. A large headboard on the front of the locomotive proclaimed the significance of the event. Schedules on the ex-Great Eastern main line were to be accelerated in much the same way as the introduction of the 'Britannia' Pacifics had allowed seven years earlier.

Following that debut, the ten pilot engines, NosD200-209, costing £100,000 apiece, performed well enough in Eastern Region service to merit further orders. NosD200-05 were based at Stratford and D206-09 across London at Hornsey. With a top speed of 90mph, the 2,000hp Type 4 became British Railways' first express passenger diesel to go into production. The soundness of the design meant that few changes were needed and 200 were delivered up to 1962.

Appropriately hauling a rake of carmine-and-cream Mark Ones, NoD306 (40.106) rumbles through Wansford at its home on the Nene Valley Railway, just a few miles from the East Coast Main Line where the Class 40s put in much good work.

It was, though, a design with antecedents, all based around English Electric's 16SVT Mark II engine. This power plant – then rated at 1,600hp – had been used in the LMSR's two 1947 Derby-built prototype diesels, Nos10000 and 10001. Uprated to 1,750hp, it then powered two 1Co-Co1 locomotives, Nos10201 and 10202, built at BR's Ashford Works in 1951. They were to a blueprint drawn up by the Southern Railway, its Chief Mechanical Engineer, Oliver Bulleid, being responsible for the mechanical side and the external appearance, but nationalisation had intervened before construction got underway. A third example of the Southern design, No10203, was delivered in 1954 with the English Electric engine further uprated to 2,000hp. Both engine, and No10203's 1Co-Co1 wheelbase and bogies (the outer guiding axles were unpowered), were adopted for the Type 4. It came in at nearly 70 feet long and weighing 133 tons.

A feature of the Type 4 was its nose compartment, which performed two functions. First, it housed the traction motor 'blower' for the adjacent bogie. Second, it was a way of overcoming the trance-like effect of 'sleeper flicker' that could distract drivers of flat-fronted diesel and electric locomotives. The nose led the driver's line-of-sight forward of the track. (Experience later showed that the problem could be overcome equally successfully with careful cab design.)

As most coaching stock was still steam-heated, the EE Type 4 was equipped with a steam-heating boiler. It could replenish its boiler water supply from the water troughs that remained in place on some main lines even though the steam locomotives for which they had been installed were fast disappearing.

Initially, some questioned the power offered by the EE Type 4. They argued that 2,000hp was on the low side compared to what, for example, a Stanier 'Coronation' Pacific could produce. However, as with all diesels, that power was constantly available (which was not always the case with steam traction, especially in its sunset years). Consideration was given to uprating the engine to 2,400hp but the idea was rejected.

The second batch of Type 4s was drafted on to the West Coast Main Line but only as an interim replacement for steam before electrification. On the east coast the diesels were not equivalent to the Gresley A4 and Peppercorn A1, A2 Pacifics and were pushed to keep time. Before long the Eastern, North Eastern and Scottish Regions were seeking for something more

IN PRESERVATION

D200 (40122) Retired in 1985, D200 was saved for the National Collection and briefly returned to traffic for enthusiasts' specials. In later BR days, NoD200 was renumbered out-of-sequence as No40122, taking a number made vacant by the scrapping of NoD322 after an accident in 1967. It is normally displayed at York.

D212 (40012) *Aureol* Saved by the Class 40 Appeal, *Aureol* moved to the Midland Railway Centre (now Midland Railway Butterley) where NoD212 made its debut in July 1993. Now sidelined by that bane of Class 40s, bogie fractures, an appeal has been started to raise £100,000 for repairs.

D213 (40013) *Andania* One of the 1959-built Class 40s, NoD213 became part of the West Coast fleet hauling services between Euston, the Midlands, the north-west and Glasgow. It is now kept at the Barrow Hill Roundhouse, Staveley, Derbyshire.

D306 (40106) *Atlantic Conveyor* With Vulcan Foundry occupied building the production series 'Deltics', during 1960 English Electric's other plant, Robert Stephenson & Hawthorn at Darlington, was tasked with building a batch of twenty Type 4s. NoD306 (works number RSH8136) was completed there in October 1960 and spent most of its working life on the London Midland Region.

Renumbered No40106, the locomotive was unique among the 40s in never exchanging its green livery for BR corporate blue, making it popular for railtour duties. Based at Longsight (Manchester) when withdrawn in 1983, the locomotive was bought by an enthusiast and moved to the Great Central Railway. Since February 1990, NoD306 has been based on the Nene Valley Railway.

D318 (40118) Another Darlington-built Type 4, NoD318 (40118) escaped scrapping by becoming one of the quartet of Class 40s recruited to haul engineers' trains. Condemned following the failure of a traction motor, it was bought by the 16SVT Society (that being English Electric's classification

for the 16-cylinder Type 4 engine). A victim of frost damage and vandalism, No40118 has been moved to Tyseley Locomotive Works, Birmingham, for restoration.

D335 (40135) D345 (40145) The Class 40 Preservation Society has been responsible for saving both these 1961-built (Vulcan Foundry) Class 40s. No40135 was bought from British Railways in February 1984, No40145 in May. Both are based on the East Lancashire Railway, with the former in BR green livery and the latter in blue. Along with working on the ELR, No40145 is approved for main-line running.

powerful. On the west coast, however, electrification work had seen schedules relaxed with generous recovery times and the locomotives were seldom taxed. Acknowledging the London Midland Region's links with the port of Liverpool, Type 4s NosD210-35 were named after famous ocean liners.

Side-by-side with steam

With a twenty tons axleloading conferring a fairly wide route availability, later batches were allocated to the North Eastern and Scottish Regions. Here, as elsewhere, the Type 4s gave excellent service. They were robust and reliable, with consistently high availability. This was especially commendable as, before the building of dedicated maintenance depots, diesels had to co-exist in steam running sheds. Such conditions were alien to keeping complex items such as traction motors in good order and some diesel classes suffered as a consequence.

The introduction of higher-powered diesels such as the 'Deltics', Brush Type 4 and Class 50 – another English Electric product – together with the completion of electrification from Euston to Glasgow, saw the 'Whistlers' downgraded from top-link duties. (The nickname came from the distinctive sound made by the turbocharger.) They found fresh employment on Manchester–Crewe–Holyhead, York–Newcastle and Glasgow–Aberdeen services. Appearances on freight also increased greatly.

Under BR's Total Operations Processing System (TOPS) the EE Type 4s became Class 40. The first withdrawals came in 1976, with Nos40005, 40023 and 40102. At over 130 tons, they now looked underpowered compared with newer designs. As a product of the late steam age they also lacked airbraking and electrical train heating; additionally some were suffering from fractures of the plate frame bogies. By 1981 all 130 survivors had been concentrated on the London Midland Region and, three years on, that number was down to thirteen. The last passenger turn came on 27 January 1985 with the now-preserved No40012 working from Birmingham to York. All were retired the following day, although four were briefly reinstated to Departmental Stock for use on engineers' trains.

Another angle on D306, crossing the River Nene, its waters producing a perfect reflection, on the way to Peterborough. Following the tradition of naming the EE Type 4s after famous merchant vessels, NoD306 commemorates *Atlantic Conveyor*, a ship sunk during the 1982 Falklands conflict.

IN DETAIL *(as built)*	
Class	**40**
Built:	1958-62; English Electric at Vulcan Foundry, Newton-le-Willows, Lancashire and Robert Stephenson & Hawthorn, Darlington, County Durham
Designed:	English Electric
Number built:	200 (D200-399)
Purpose:	Mixed traffic, chiefly passenger
Engine:	English Electric 16-cylinder 16SVT MkII
Power output:	2,000hp (1,480kw) (1550hp/1156kw at rail) at 850rpm
Transmission:	Electric. Six English Electric 526/5D axle-hung traction motors
Wheel diameters:	3 ft 9in (powered); 3 ft 0 in (guiding)
Wheel arrangement:	1Co-Co1
Weight:	133 tons
Brake force:	51 tons
Maximum tractive effort:	52,000lb (231kn)
Continuous tractive effort:	30,900lb (137kn) at 18.8mph
Maximum speed:	90mph
Route availability:	6
BR power rating:	Type 4

Peak Performers

The honour of becoming number 'D1' in the stocklist went to a British Railways-built locomotive and this lofty status reflected in a name that was itself 3,206 feet high!

D uring the late 1950s, British Railways' major main-line diesel-engine suppliers – Bristol-Siddeley, English Electric and Sulzer – refined their designs to deliver higher outputs without a proportionate increase in size and weight. One class of diesel to benefit from this work was the 'Peak' class, a Type 4 1Co-Co1 diesel-electric built in British Railways' workshops at Crewe and Derby (and the only one of the Type 4 classes to be schemed in a BR drawing office). The name 'Peak' derived from the first ten locomotives, which were named after the highest mountains of England and Wales. The sequence began with Scafell Pike in the Lake District, at 3,206 feet England's highest. Subsequently many in the class carried regimental names from withdrawn 'Royal Scot' 4-6-0s.

The single 12-cylinder Sulzer engine in these first ten examples produced 2,300hp but was uprated to 2,500hp for all subsequent construction. (Later the output was increased still further to 2,750hp, when the engine became the heart of the 'Brush 4' Co-Co.) This apparently small increase in output boosted performance

Built at Derby in 1961 and originally numbered D32, 'Peak' No45.132 comes to a halt at Medstead & Four Marks with a Mid-Hants Railway service from Alton to Alresford.

IN PRESERVATION

NoD4 (44004) *Great Gable* Under repair at Midland Railway Butterley, in Derbyshire.

NoD8 (44008) *Penyghent* In service at Peak Rail, between Darley Dale and Matlock, Derbyshire.

NoD14 (45015) Stored at Shackerstone, on Leicestershire's Battlefield Line, awaiting extensive rebuilding.

NoD22 (45132) Part of the Mid-Hants Railway fleet but currently under repair, with the generator set being attended to off-site.

NoD40 (45133) Retired May 1987, No45133 has become one of a group

of 'Peaks' kept at the Midland Railway Butterley. It is under repair.

NoD53 (45041) *Royal Tank Regiment* Also based at Butterley, No45041 was acquired by the Peak Locomotive Company in 1996 and has been returned to working order.

NoD61 (45112) *The Royal Army Ordnance Corps* Maintained at Barrow Hill Roundhouse, Staveley, Derbyshire, No45112 is to be fitted with On Train Monitoring to permit its main-line career to resume.

NoD67 (45118) *The Royal Artilleryman* The theft of much of its copper cabling has forced the storage of No45118 on the Northampton &

Lamport Railway while insurance issues are resolved.

NoD86 (45105) Retired in May 1987 and preserved six years later, No45105 is undergoing refurbishment at Barrow Hill.

NoD99 (45135) *3rd Carabinier* The overhaul of NoD45135 is progressing well in the workshops of the East Lancashire Railway.

NoD100 (45060) *Sherwood Forester* Another occupant of Barrow Hill Roundhouse, NoD100, now numbered 45060, resumed operations in 2009. It has since visited the Swanage Railway and appeared at the Eastleigh 150 event.

significantly, particularly as the Sulzer engine had to move a hefty 138 tons of locomotive as well as its train. In a further variation, the final 56 examples employed Brush traction equipment instead of Crompton Parkinson, all of which changes merited three separate classes in the TOPS list: 44, 45 and 46.

The first ten 'Peaks' were briefly allocated to Camden, in London, for use on the West Coast Main Line but swiftly transferred to the Midland Main Line out of St Pancras. They worked through to Derby, Nottingham, Sheffield and Leeds, and to Manchester before the closure of the line through the Peak District. Other duties took them over the Settle–Carlisle route from Leeds to Edinburgh. Their extra power was welcomed on the revitalised Newcastle–Leeds–Manchester–Liverpool expresses where the new schedules demanded such locomotives.

One key advantage of diesel locomotives is their ability to run much greater mileages than steam locomotives between servicing stops. They are limited only by the capacity of their fuel-storage tanks. In the early years of British Railways dieselisation, however, this capability was woefully under-used. Opportunities for inter-regional working were limited by the lack of standardisation in the locomotive fleet and, as a consequence, crews' inexperience.

However, by the end of 1961, classes such as the 'Peaks' had reached sufficient numbers (193 in their case) to allow enginemen of all regions to become acquainted with them. This allowed some interesting examples of inter-regional collaboration. The route from Bristol to Newcastle by way of Birmingham, Derby, Sheffield and Leeds was one. A 'Peak' would travel through the night at the head of the 7.25pm sleeping-car express from Bristol, arriving at Newcastle at 4.33am. It then began its southbound journey on the 6.25am goods from Newcastle's Heaton yard to York, returning to Bristol on the 12.52pm express from York. The later series locomotives (Classes 45 and 46) could be seen as far apart as Cornwall and central Scotland.

The prodigious tractive effort of the 'Peaks' (up to 70,000lb in later versions) made them first-rate heavy-freight haulers and this increasingly became their role as they were displaced from passenger work by the newer Brush Type 4s. Class 45s and 46s remained on cross-country and other passenger and goods services into the 1980s. The 46s were judged 'non-standard' and had vanished by 1984 but the final Class 45s soldiered on until 1988.

One of the first series of 'Peaks, the ten Class 44s, NoD4 *Great Gable* (44.004) accelerates away from Rothley with a Great Central Railway service for Leicester North. These locomotives were rated at 2,300bhp; the later Classes 45 and 46 were uprated to 2,500bhp.

NoD120 (45108) Midland Railway Butterley is home to NoD120 which was withdrawn in August 1987 and bought by the Peak Locomotive Company in 2008.

NoD123 (45125) Retired in January 1987, NoD123 is at work on the Great Central Railway in Leicestershire.

NoD135 (45149) *Leicestershire and Derbyshire Yeomanry* Condemned in September 1987, No45149 was preserved and moved to the Gloucestershire Warwickshire Railway where its repair is currently underway.

NoD147 (46010) Derby-built in 1961, No46010 was included when the Llangollen Railway decided to dispose of part of its diesel fleet. No offers forthcoming, the locomotive remains in North Wales while the owners consider their options.

NoD172 (46035) *Ixion* Though withdrawn in 1984, D172 was spared for use at Derby Research Centre, becoming No97403. Named after a character from Greek mythology, *Ixion* arrived at Crewe Heritage Centre in June 2006 for completion of its latest overhaul.

NoD182 (46045) Another of the Peak Locomotive Company's stable (bought in 1992), NoD182 returned to traffic in 1995 and remains a working locomotive at Midland Railway Butterley.

IN DETAIL *(as built)*

Class	44, 45, 46 'Peak'
Built:	1959-1963
Designed:	British Railways, Derby
Number built:	10 (Class 44) 127 (45) 56 (46) D1-D193
Purpose:	Express passenger, mixed traffic
Engine:	Sulzer 12-cylinder 12LDA28A twin-bank pressure-charged (Class 44) 12LDA28B (45, 46)
Power output:	1720kw/ 2,300hp (Class 44) 1865kw/2,500hp (45, 46) at 750rpm
Transmission:	Electric: Six Crompton Parkinson CP17181 axle-hung traction motors (Class 44); C172A1 (45); six Brush TM73-68 Mk3 traction motors (46)
Wheel arrangement:	1Co-Co1
Wheel diameter:	3 ft 9 in (powered); 3 ft 0 in (guiding)
Weight:	135 tons (Class 44) 138 tons (45, 46)
Brake force:	63 tonnes
Maximum tractive effort:	50,000 lb (Class 44) 55,000 lb (245kn) (45, 46)
Continuous tractive effort:	30,000 lb (133kn) (Class 44) 31,600lb (141kn) 45, 46) at 22.3mph.
Maximum speed:	90mph
Route availability:	7
BR power rating:	Type 4

British Railways

**BR/Maybach
Type 4 (Class 52)
'Western' 2,700hp
C-C diesel-
hydraulic**

(1961)

A Diesel by Design

The 'box-on-wheels' notion of the diesel was challenged by the 'Westerns', locomotives that combined style with substance.

In one significant respect, the last of the Western Region's diesel-hydraulic designs was also a 'first'. The British Transport Commission's Design Panel had been set up too late to have any great influence on the earlier diesel designs. In addition, some manufacturers were reluctant to acknowledge that an outside agency might contribute to scheming an appropriate look for their products. However, the 'Westerns', as they were named, benefited greatly from the expertise of a consultant industrial designer. The happy outcome was that the 'Western' was one of the first main-line diesels where, subject to technical constraints, the fullest attention was paid to the styling. The striking, almost rakish machine that emerged from Swindon Works was a refreshing antidote to the blandness of many of its forebears.

The 'Westerns' were conceived after it became apparent that the 'Warship' diesel-hydraulics, which had entered traffic in 1958, were under-powered for a number of duties. Design work began in 1959 and, like their predecessors, the 'Westerns' were almost entirely enclosed in a 'skirt' down to rail level. It was, though, cut away to expose the six-wheel bogies. Thanks in part to this outer shell of stressed skin, all-welded construction, the weight was kept down to 108 tons in full working order.

Power was derived from two Bristol-Siddeley-Maybach MD655 engines, an uprated version of that used in the Swindon-built 'Warships'. Each of these power plants produced 1,350hp at 1,500rpm from its twelve cylinders, which were arranged in a 'V' formation. The engines were pressure-charged by single exhaust-gas turbo-chargers and intercooled. Voith-North British transmissions transferred that power to the bogies, where the six axles gave a high tractive effort for the comparatively low axleloading. Each transmission contained three torque converters, each optimised for a particular speed range. A filling pump

A starry line-up of diesel hydraulics around the turntable at Old Oak Common, London, on 6 August 2000. Two preserved Class 52 'Westerns', NoD1015 *Western Champion* and D1023 *Western Fusilier*, from the National Collection, flank 'Warship' NoD821 *Greyhound*. On the right, D7076, one of four survivors from the 101 Class 35 1,700bhp 'Hymek' B-Bs built by Beyer, Peacock in Manchester between 1961 and 1964.

IN PRESERVATION

NoD1010 *Western Campaigner* Acquired from the Foster Yeoman quarrying company in 1975, D1010 came to the West Somerset Railway in January 1991. In the care of the Williton-based Diesel & Electric Preservation Group, it returned after overhaul in 2007 but it now needs still further extensive attention.

NoD1013 *Western Ranger* Retired after 1,320,000 miles, NoD1013 came under the care of the Western Locomotive Association and arrived at its current home of the Severn Valley Railway in 1978. It worked regularly from then and, after engine refurbishment, is again available for traffic.

NoD1015 *Western Champion* The only one from among the surviving 'Westerns' currently approved for main-line running, the Diesel Traction Group's *Western Champion* is usually to be found at the English Welsh and Scottish Railway's traction maintenance depot at Old Oak Common in west London.

NoD1023 *Western Fusilier* Built at Swindon in 1962, *Western Fusilier* was chosen to represent the 'Westerns' in the National Collection. Nominally based at York, it is in working order and occasionally loaned out to heritage railways and centres.

Towards a brighter future

Alongside their external styling, the first two 'Westerns' drew attention with their liveries. NoD1000 was painted in a shade described as 'desert sand' while NoD1001 wore a rich maroon. Both were a refreshing change from the monotony of BR standard green that had been applied to all other diesel classes. The argument that lighter colours would not wear well and would show the dirt was losing ground as steam traction was eliminated. Operating conditions were now relatively clean and the new diesel depots included locomotive-washing facilities. However, the fitting of cast number- and nameplates with raised numerals and letters harked back to a Great Western tradition. As the name suggests, all these names had a 'Western' prefix, such as *Western Glory*, *Western Champion* and *Western Envoy*.

circulated oil first through the converter in use then through a heat exchanger where the heat was transferred to the engine-cooling water. Cardan shafts took the drive to an intermediate gearbox that was mounted on the bogie and then to the final drive gearboxes on the axles.

The late delivery of some parts, including the German-made transmissions, delayed the locomotives' entry into service. It was not until January 1962 that the prototypes, NoD1000 *Western Enterprise* and NoD1001 (later named *Western Pathfinder*) began trials. The production run was set at 74, with construction shared between two BR workshops, Swindon and Crewe, the first – and last – diesel-hydraulics to be built there.

Birmingham–Wolverhampton–Shrewsbury run. They initially performed up to expectation but then reliability dramatically declined. A problem arose with the bogies at speeds more than 80mph as the transmission-shaft roller bearings had a habit of seizing. All the locomotives were withdrawn temporarily for checks to be made and, for a time, the 'Westerns' had something of a bad name in the WR's running department.

These question marks against the 'Westerns' simply emphasised an already-evident drawback of the diesel-hydraulics: maintenance costs were noticeably higher compared to the equivalent diesel-electric classes. True, the two small engines employed in the hydraulic designs were lighter and easier to remove for servicing but that hardly compensated for the day-to-day problems faced by maintenance staffs. However, in top condition, they made light work of hauling heavy passenger and freight trains over the testing grades of South Devon and on the undulating main line through Cornwall. Though the specified maximum was 90mph, they frequently topped the 100mph mark.

The 'Westerns' remained in service into the 1970s. However, as they could not be used with the newer air-conditioned or electrically heated rolling stock, they were displaced, first by Class 47 and 50 diesel-electrics, and then by High-Speed Trains. Many ended their days working stone trains originating from quarries in the Westbury area. Their high starting tractive effort of 72,600lb was invaluable in starting these heavy loads.

The high cost of care

When first delivered the 'Westerns' – as expected – were rostered for the principal West of England expresses but additionally appeared on the Paddington–

NoD1041 *Western Prince* Part of the extensive diesel fleet on the East Lancashire Railway, *Western Prince* unfortunately requires a good deal of work before running again. Repairs to the transmissions and reversers are needed along with attention to the gearboxes and cooling system.

NoD1048 *Western Lady* Retired in February 1977 and privately preserved,

Western Lady is being restored at the Midland Railway, Butterley, in Derbyshire.

NoD1052 *Western Courier* Second of the Severn Valley Railway-based 'Westerns', like *Western Ranger*, *Western Courier* is in the stewardship of the Western Locomotive Association. The locomotive is presently undergoing an overhaul that will include the immense task of complete rewiring.

IN DETAIL *(as built)*	
Class	**52 'Western'**
Built:	1961-64; Crewe and Swindon works
Designed:	British Railways/BTC Design Panel
Number built:	74
Purpose:	Express passenger
Engines:	Two 12-cylinder, V-configuration Maybach MD650 of 1,350hp (1007kw) at 1,500rpm
Power output:	2,700hp
Transmission:	Hydraulic: Two Voith-North British L630rV hydraulic transmissions each containing three torque converters
Wheel arrangement:	C-C
Wheel diameter:	3 ft 7 in
Weight:	108 tons
Brake force:	50 tonnes
Maximum tractive effort:	72,600lb
Continuous tractive effort:	45,200lb (201.2kn) at 14.5mph
Maximum speed:	90mph
Route availability:	6
BR power rating:	Type 4

Emperors of the East Coast

It was the sound – the ground-shaking rhythm of 36 pistons working in harmony – as much as the sight that excited the senses. The 'Deltics' proved that diesels didn't have to be dull!

Tackling the 1 in 35 climb towards Goathland on the North Yorkshire Moors Railway, 'Deltic' No55.019 *Royal Highland Fusilier* roars out of Grosmont tunnel with a train for Pickering, passing Peppercorn K1 2-6-0 No2005 awaiting its next duty. No55.019 now operates out of Barrow Hill Roundhouse, Derbyshire.

I magine standing on a station somewhere on the West Coast Main Line in the mid-1950s. An express hastens through with a Stanier Pacific or 'Royal Scot' at its head; a freight rumbles by behind an antique 0-8-0 or Fowler 0-6-0. It's all very familiar. Then, from a distance, comes a throbbing sound belonging to no steam-powered machine. In a blur of blue, yellow and silver-grey, the locomotive roars by, trailing a rake of maroon coaches. You just make out the carriage indicator boards: 'The Red Rose: Euston–Liverpool'. All that lingers is a pungent haze from the exhausts of two Napier 'Deltic' diesel engines.

The engine manufacturers, Napier & Sons, were part of the English Electric group. In 1947, they designed a high-power diesel engine for the Admiralty. Intended for Royal Navy patrol boats, each cylinder contained two opposed pistons with the 18 cylinders arranged in a triangular formation. A camshaft was positioned at each corner of the triangle. The distinctive shape, corresponding to the Greek letter 'delta', gave rise to the name 'Deltic'. It was a powerful item: with the engine speed continuously variable between 600 and 1,500rpm, maximum output was 1,650hp.

The main generators supplying electrical power to the traction motors were mounted directly on the engines, one on each. Their armatures were connected in series and either could be bypassed if, as sometimes occurred, only one engine was in use. Six traction motors, one on each axle, drove their associated axles through a pinion on the motor armature shaft and a gear wheel on the axle.

English Electric visualised a further application for the Napier engine and in 1951 began construction of a prototype main-line diesel locomotive. It took four years, and cost £250,000, but in 1955 the 'Deltic' was ready to begin trials on British Railways. Delivering 3,300 horsepower from its twin 18-cylinder two-stroke, water-cooled engines, this Co-Co diesel-electric had the accolade of being the most powerful single-unit diesel locomotive in the world.

'Deltic' was based on the London Midland Region and mainly used on heavy London–Liverpool expresses. At the time, not only were diesels still a rarity, but the livery – blue with yellow chevron stripes – was a striking departure from the BR standard colours of green and black. The performances of the prototype were as striking as its looks and, after successful trials on the heavy grades of the Settle to Carlisle line, it passed to the Eastern Region.

Power and glory

In planning its diesel programme British Railways had not anticipated the need for something in the 'Deltic' power class. High-performance, twin-engined machines were costly to build and maintain. However, the prototype had made its mark with the Eastern Region management. It saw the 'Deltic', with its capacity for sustained fast running, as a way of accelerating services on the East Coast Main Line. It probably concluded, too, that no other diesels could satisfactorily replace its fleet of ex-LNER Pacifics, particularly the Gresley A4s.

An order was placed with English Electric for 22 production 'Deltics' at £200,000 each and delivery took place over a 12-month period from March 1961. There were some changes to the design. An already relatively low weight – made possible by the compactness of the power plants – was further reduced by seven tons and the length over buffers increased by 5 feet 6 inches to 69 feet 6 inches.

The bogie wheelbase was reduced by ten inches to 13 feet 6 inches and there were alterations to the bodyshape to avoid clearance problems. The stress-bearing bodysides were of Corten-steel and the roof panels of thick-gauge aluminium alloy. Fuel capacity was set at 900 gallons.

A new timetable based on 'Deltic' haulage was introduced in the summer of 1962. Three prestige services – 'The Elizabethan', 'The Talisman' and 'The Flying Scotsman' – were given six-hour timings between King's Cross and Edinburgh while other trains to Yorkshire and the north-east were accelerated. Subsequent upgrading of the ECML permanent way allowed the 'Deltics' to realise fully their potential. Happily running flat out for long periods, they maintained speeds in the high nineties and frequently exceeded 100mph for long periods. It allowed more time to be clipped from the schedules: one train, for example, was allowed just 91 minutes for the 138.5 miles from Retford to King's Cross, requiring an average speed of 91.32mph.

By now, with around 400,000 miles to its credit, the prototype 'Deltic' had been retired. Still the property of English Electric, in 1963 it went on display at the

IN PRESERVATION

NoD9000 (55022) *Royal Scots Grey*

The doyen of the production 'Deltics' was in running order when bought by the Deltic 9000 Fund (later Deltic 9000 Locomotive Ltd) and first based on the Nene Valley Railway. A York-based concern bought *Royal Scots Grey* in 2004 and set about an overhaul that was completed in August 2006. Before long NoD9000 suffered a major power-unit failure and was forced to operate on one engine. A Napier marine engine was located and installed in August 2007. However, during 2008, concerns were raised about this replacement and NoD9000 was withdrawn. Repairs were undertaken and D9000 (as 55022) has resumed service on the East Lancashire Railway.

NoD9002 (55002) *The King's Own Yorkshire Light Infantry* NoD9002

joined the stud of Gateshead 'Deltics' on 9 March 1961 and remained based there until transferred to York in May 1979. Rededicated there on 12 December 1980, it was retired on 2 January 1982 and handed over to the National Railway Museum.

NoD9009 (55009) *Alycidon* Named at

Doncaster 21 July 1961, NoD9009 joined the 'racehorses' at Finsbury Park until reallocated to York in May 1981. Bought by the Deltic Preservation Society it was based on the North Yorkshire Moors Railway, performing regularly until 1990. In conjunction with its latest repair, NoD9009 became the first 'Deltic' be fitted with the Train Protection and Warning System (TPWS) necessary for main-line operation. Following running-in on the NYMR during 2007, the locomotive is now working out of Barrow Hill.

NoD9015 (55015) *Tulyar* Another of the

Finsbury Park 'Deltics', *Tulyar* entered service on 13 October 1961. It hauled expresses out of King's Cross for almost twenty years before retirement in January 1982. First acquired by an enthusiast and moved to the Midland Railway Centre, in 1986 *Tulyar* was sold on to the Deltic Preservation Society for £12,000. The locomotive ran for some years, visiting several preserved railways until, in December 1992, becoming an unlikely lot in an auction at Christie's in London.

It did not meet its reserve but was subsequently sold. *Tulyar* is now based at Midland Railway, Butterley, where its latest overhaul is in its final stages.

NoD9016 (55016) *Gordon Highlander*

Withdrawn 30 December 1981, No55016 was bought by the Deltic 9000 Fund for £7,500 with the long-term aim of restoration but with the interim role of a – quote – 'twelve-wheeled mobile source of spares'. However, with finance provided by Porterbrook Leasing, No55016 was restored to main-line condition, albeit at the price of wearing Porterbrook's ghastly purple livery!

In July 2008 D9016 was sold to the Harry Needle Railroad Company who put the locomotive up for sale again and, when a bid from Direct Rail Services was accepted, fears were raised that *Gordon Highlander* might be broken up. However, DRS have said the locomotive will be returned to working order – a task that includes replacing the bogies – and to that end have moved the 'Deltic' to Barrow Hill near Chesterfield.

NoD9019 (55019) *Royal Highland Fusilier* NoD9019 entered service at

Haymarket in December 1961 and, twenty years on, worked British Railways' last scheduled Deltic-hauled service, the 3.30pm from Aberdeen to York on 31 December 1981. It then became the first of the class to haul a train in preservation, on the North Yorkshire Moors Railway on 22 August 1982. By spring 1999, NoD9019 had been approved for main-line work and on 22 May rekindled memories of the 'Deltic' heyday by covering the 188 miles from King's Cross to York in 2 hours 4 minutes.

An intermediate body repair presented the chance to install TPWS and, in 2005, NoD9019 became the first 'Deltic' to appear on the main line for two years. It remains in working order, operating out of Barrow Hill depot in Derbyshire.

In the original two-tone green that so suited the design, the doyen of the 'Deltics', No D9000 *Royal Scots Grey* is in unusual territory at Waterloo, London, one of the exhibits at 'Network Day' on 1 October 1988. The locomotive sports the 'winged thistle' 'Flying Scotsman' headboard.

Science Museum, London, but was later moved to the National Railway Museum in York. The production 'Deltics' went on to record even greater mileages, most passing the two-million mark over twenty-year careers. In that respect they gave an excellent return on their high capital cost.

A two-tone green livery suited them well and they quickly gained names. Famous regiments shared the honours with the LNER's evergreen source of inspiration, champion racehorses. The former were based at Haymarket (Edinburgh) and Gateshead while the latter were maintained at the new diesel depot at Finsbury Park in north London.

Like the best racehorses, they garnered something of a cult following, especially as their retirement approached. Displaced from top-link duties after 1978 by High Speed Trains, most were based at York and used on secondary work, including some trans-Pennine services. They took part in a large number of railtours, culminating in the 'Scotsman Farewell' of January 2 1982 with No55015 *Tulyar* hauling the train from King's Cross to Edinburgh and No55022 *Royal Scots Grey* on the return. Most ended their days based at York, relegated to working secondary services. Six have been preserved and, between 1997 and 2003, four of those saw use on main-line charters. As of 2009, the prototype was on display at Locomotion, the NRM's offshoot at Shildon, County Durham.

IN DETAIL *(as built)*

Class	55 'Deltic'
Built:	1961-62; Vulcan Foundry, Newton-le-Willows. Lancashire
Designed:	English Electric
Number built:	22
Purpose:	High-speed express passenger
Engines:	Two Napier 'Deltic' D18-25 eighteen cylinder (piston-opposed) two-stroke engines each of 1,650hp (1,230kw)
Power output:	3,300hp (2,462kw)
Transmission:	Electric: Six English Electric EE538/A traction motors
Wheel arrangement:	Co-Co
Wheel diameter:	3 ft 7 in
Weight:	103 tons
Brake force:	51 tonnes
Maximum tractive effort:	50,000 lb (222kn)
Continuous tractive effort:	30,500 lb (136kn) at 32.5mph
Maximum speed:	105mph
Route availability:	5
BR power rating:	Type 5

A Brush with Success

British Railways
Brush Type 4 (Class 47) 2,750hp Co-Co diesel electric
(1962)

If Britain's railways had a diesel equivalent to the mixed-traffic steam locomotive, it has been the 'Brush 4'. Equally at home on passenger and freight, this 'maid-of-all-work' has served every rail region since its introduction in 1962.

These were the locomotives that should have been built at the very outset of British Railways' dieselisation programme in the mid-1950s. That way, some expensive and embarrassing flops may have been avoided. The 'Brush 4', as it has always been known, was the most modern of the early BR diesel classes, a radical design compared to its predecessors. It had its origins in a successful prototype produced by Brush Traction: NoD0280 *Falcon* was one of three produced by British manufacturers to meet BR's requirement for a design towards the top end of the Type 4 power range. Those built by the Birmingham, Carriage & Wagon Company (NoD0260 *Lion*) and English Electric (NoDP2) acquitted themselves well but it was *Falcon* that received the vote, albeit with a change of engine.

The engine and ancillary equipment were housed in a lightweight, stressed-skin body shell that spread the locomotive weight throughout the superstructure. That way, the heavy underframes and chassis that were needed to carry other diesel

One of no fewer than 512 'Brush 4s' to see service with British Railways, a work-stained Class 47/0, No47.008, rumbles through Southall, west London, at the head of a rake of bogie petroleum tankers. This example began life as D1530 and was withdrawn in October 1989.

designs could be exchanged for two swing-bolster three-axle bogies. All six axles were powered and the weight kept down to 114 tons, giving the 'Brush 4' a much wider route availability than some of its lower-powered predecessors.

The 2,750hp power plant originated with the Swiss Sulzer company, an uprated version of the LD engine already employed in the 1Co-Co1 'Peak' diesel-electrics introduced in 1959. Loughborough's Brush Traction supplied the electrical gear, such as the traction motors, and undertook the assembly of what became one of the most enduring and reliable classes of diesel locomotives. The advance over the 'Peaks' was marked, primarily because the improvement in power output was wholly available for haulage. A 2,750hp locomotive has no more of its weight to shift than a 2,000hp one.

The first twenty 'Brush 4s' went to the Eastern Region where they quickly showed their worth, proving capable substitutes for failed 'Deltics' on east-coast expresses. Further large orders followed with construction shared by Brush (310) and BR's works at Crewe (202). By 1968, 512 examples were in service – the largest number of any British diesel class, apart from the Class 08 shunter. Over the years, the 'Brush 4' was allocated to every region except the Southern, although they regularly appeared on SR metals.

Following their success on the Eastern, batches of 'Brush 4s' were allocated to the Western and London Midland Regions where they displayed the power to handle most types of passenger and freight services. After trials on the WR demonstrated that the class was capable of sustained speeds of over 100mph, the original stipulated maximum speed of 90mph was raised to 95mph.

In the 47 years the 'Brush 4' (Class 47) has been in service, it has undergone several modifications to successfully extend its working life. These included downrating the output to 2,580hp, reducing stresses on engine components but with no significant reduction in performance. This proved especially beneficial in overcoming minor problems that arose when working the heaviest (around 1,500 tons) freight trains.

Examples were also modified for specific duties, such as those equipped for

Fresh from a repaint to two-tone green, Brush 'Type 4' No D1524 poses at Old Oak Common on 6 August 2000. Owned by the Manchester-based Newton Heath Diesel Traction group, this example from the 35-or-so preserved Class 47s is based on the Embsay & Bolton Abbey Steam Railway near Skipton, in North Yorkshire.

push-pull operation on express services between Glasgow and Edinburgh and Glasgow–Aberdeen (an application that caused disquiet in some engineering quarters). Others were allocated to 'merry-go-round' pit-to-power station coal trains and had to be fitted with an automatic slow-speed 'creep' control. This allowed the locomotives to haul their coal trains through unloading plants at power stations, discharging their hopper wagons while travelling at a speed of just half-a-mile an hour.

Still serving

Displaced from passenger work, the Class 47s found fresh employment on freight services and a large numbers congregated at depots such as Tinsley (Sheffield). The first to be withdrawn was NoD1734, then only eight months old, which was wrecked in an accident at Shrewsbury in 1965. In December that year NoD1681 was condemned after being derailed at Bridgend, in South Wales. In an extraordinary incident, on 13 March 1971, NoD1562 was destroyed when its power plant – which had been experimentally uprated – exploded at Haughley Junction, on the main line between Norwich and London.

One locomotive became the testbed for two later diesel-electric classes. Following derailment at Peterborough in 1974, No47046 was repaired using a 16-cylinder Ruston-Paxman engine developing 3,250hp. Renumbered No47601, it effectively became the prototype for the heavy-freight Class 56. Later, as No47901, it became the proving ground for the 3,300hp Ruston power plant incorporated in the Class 58 Co-Co of 1983.

Later modifications to the Class 47s included equipping a batch with extra fuel tanks (47/8) and these were mainly used by Virgin Trains on its cross-country services. Beginning in 1997, 34 'Brush 4s' were selected to be re-engined with a 2,500hp General Motors (Electro-Motive Division) power plant. Reclassified Class 57, 12 – with a maximum speed of 75mph – joined the Freightliner fleet while 16 – rated for 95mph – were adopted by Virgin Trains, becoming its 'Thunderbirds': all took names from the eponymous television puppet series!

Porterbrook leased five to First Great Western, while prototype, No57601, joined the West Coast Railway Company at Crewe. Two Class 47s, Nos47798 *Prince William* and 47799 *Prince Henry*, were for a time set aside to work the royal train, a duty now largely entrusted to Class 67 Co-Cos.

Up to 1986, withdrawals had been limited to accident casualties (five) but by the end of 1992, 61 had been retired, with a further 86 going by the end of 1995. Rail privatisation then halted the decline; redundant Class 47s were a clear choice for newly formed Train Operating Companies requiring motive power, As of February 2009, the extant Class 47s numbered 103, with more than 30 still at work on the main line on behalf of companies such as Direct Rail Services and the West Coast Railway Company.

IN PRESERVATION

With some 35 'Brush 4s' preserved, space precludes printing the full list here. Most are based, as might be expected, on heritage railways but a number are stored at private locations. The list includes the first two built, NoD1500 *North Eastern* (47401) and NoD1501 *Gateshead* (47402), which are based at the Midland Railway, Butterley, and East Lancashire Railway respectively. Among other notable survivors are NoD1656 (47798) *Fire Fly* at the National Railway Museum, NoD1661 (47840) *North Star* on the West Somerset Railway. NoD1662 (47484) *Isambard Kingdom Brunel*, last recorded in store in Wishaw, Scotland, and NoD1943 (47770) *Great Western* at Tyseley Locomotive Works, Birmingham.

IN DETAIL *(as built)*	
Class	**47** (Original condition)
Built:	1962-67; Crewe Works; Brush Traction, Falcon Works, Loughborough, Leicestershire
Designed:	Brush Traction
Number built:	512 (D1500-1999, D1100-11)
Purpose:	Mixed traffic
Engine:	Sulzer 12-cylinder pressure-charged 12LD-A28-C
Power output:	2,750hp (1920kw) at 800rpm
Transmission:	Electric: Six Brush TM64-68 Mk1 or Mk1a axle-hung traction motors
Wheel arrangement:	Co-Co
Wheel diameter:	3 ft 9 in
Weight:	109-123 tons
Brake force:	60 tonnes
Maximum tractive effort:	55,000 lb (267kn)
Continuous tractive effort:	30,000 lb (133kn) at 27mph
Maximum speed:	95mph
Route availability:	6
BR power rating:	Type 4

Acknowledgments

My thanks are due the editorial team at David & Charles – James Brooks, Martin Smith and Jane Trollope – for their enthusiasm and expertise (and tolerance of my attachment to last-century technology!).

Thanks, too, to the members and affiliates of what might be termed the 'Walton and Weybridge Railway Circle': Barry and Houda Alaoui-Cheyne; Nick Blyth; Richard Derry (whose locomotive surveys, published by Irwell Press, have proved a useful reference); Simon Devitt; Mike Hall; Vince Hathway; Keith Lawrence (without whose intrepid driving and knowledge of the railway landscape my photographic archive would be much the poorer); Gus and Linny Romero; Dave Sackett; Brian Seddon, Chairman of the Bulleid Pacific Locomotive Owners' Association; David Smith and Ian Woollatt. Their encouragement and interest have been generously given and warmly welcomed.

Peter Herring
Walton-on-Thames
Surrey
July 2009

About the Author

Peter Herring has been a railway enthusiast for longer than he cares to remember and as a professional writer he has combined his career with his love of trains. He was editor of the magazine *Steam Classic* for more than six years, writing hundreds of articles and making use of his considerable photographic archive. He has also written numerous articles for other publications and is the author of three previous books on trains and locomotives, including *Yesterday's Railways* for David & Charles.

Picture Credits

Unless otherwise specified, all photographs are from the author's or publisher's collections.
l = left; r = right; m = middle; b = bottom; t = top

23, 161 © T.E. Williams; 32, 139 © Stanley Creer; 34 © G.W. Household; 49, 83 © Rev Arthur C. Cawson/National Railway Museum/Science & Society Picture Library; 53 © Kenneth Field; 63 © D.H. Ballantyne; 74 © S.D. Wainwright; 2, 95tl © G.A. Richardson; 108 © D.A. Anderson; 130, 177, 180 © John Goss; 157 © Derek Cross.

Back cover: all Peter Herring, except (top-left) © G.A. Richardson; (top-middle right) © D.A. Anderson; (top-right) © E.R. Wethersett; (bottom-left) © G.W. Household.

A3 No4472 *Flying Scotsman* leads A2 No60532 *Blue Peter* out of Loughborough, Great Central Railway.

Index

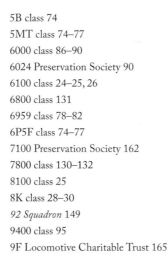

A line up of Bulleid Pacifics at the Eastleigh Works 100 event, 24 May 2009, including rebuilt 'Merchant Navy' class 4-6-2 No35005 *Canadian Pacific*; newly restored 'Battle of Britain' 4-6-2 No34070 *Manston*; and rebuilt 'West Country' 4-6-2 No34028 *Eddystone*.

Index

Two of LNER's finest mixed traffic designs departing Wansford on the Nene Valley Railway – B1 4-6-0 No1306 pilots V2 2-6-2 No4771 *Green Arrow*.

Index

Index

An evening scene at Ropley, Mid-Hants Railway, where A4 Pacific No60009 Union of South Africa and BR Standard 4MT 2-6-4T No80104 cross with up and down trains. In the background are 'Battle of Britain' Pacific No34081 *92 Squadron* and 'West Country' Pacific No34016 *Bodmin*.